The Wrong Messiah

Dedicated to my good friend
Martin
with thanks for deep conversations,
wise counsel and excellent beer.

The Wrong Messiah

Nick Page

HODDER &
STOUGHTON

First published in Great Britain in 2011 by Hodder & Stoughton
An Hachette UK company

1

A CIP catalogue record for this title is available from the British Library

ISBN 978 0 340 99627 0
Printed and bound in the UK by CPI Mackays, Chatham ME5 8TD

Hodder & Stoughton policy is to use papers that are natural, renewable and
recyclable products and made from wood grown in sustainable forests. The
logging and manufacturing processes are expected to conform to the
environmental regulations of the country of origin.

Hodder & Stoughton
An Hachette UK company
338 Euston Road
London NW1 3BH

www.hodderfaith.com

CONTENTS

Introduction: The Right Messiah

On my desk is a Jesus action figure.

It is five inches tall, made of plastic and possesses 'poseable arms to reach toward the heavens, and wheels in his base for smooth gliding action'. I keep him there for two reasons: (1) his poseable arms give me a very good place to hold my pencil, and (2) he is a constant reminder of what I'm up against.

For many of us, our mental image of Jesus is a bit strange, a bit artificial. We have grown accustomed to the Sunday School Jesus: 'gentle Jesus, meek and mild' who wandered around Galilee wearing a nightie and being nice to people. Many elements of his story – Christmas, the miracles, his death and resurrection – have become part of the iconography of our culture. We wear crosses around our necks. Our children are baptised in an imitation (albeit not a particularly good one) of the activities of Jesus' mentor, John the Baptist. Words from the story infiltrate our language: football fans scream 'Judas!' at a player who has chosen to transfer to an opposing team (usually for a great deal more than thirty pieces of silver); 'we're going to be crucified' say politicians expecting a disaster at the next election; and the name of the founder of Christianity has become a common swearword. Nearly two thousand years after his death, Jesus is everywhere.

And yet so much of what we think we know is wrong. The Jesus who appears in the paintings, the stained-glass windows and even the TV shows is a white, long-haired, pale-skinned individual, not a short, dark-skinned first-century Palestinian. The golden crosses hanging round the necks of rap stars are a bizarre parody of the two chunks of splintered, rough timber on which Jesus was crucified, their timber bloodstained and splintered from frequent re-use. Even the name we use – Jesus – is a name he could never have been called in his lifetime.

The real Jesus was passionate, angry, intense, deliberately provocative. He wasn't an aristocrat or a warrior; he wasn't orthodox in the observance of his faith; he wasn't a priest, he was a builder from 'up north'. He was a healer, a trouble-maker, a boat-rocker. He told stories so pointed that they moved people to violence. He welcomed the outcast, touched the untouchables, did apparently impossible things and then told everyone to have a go.

'Who do people say that I am?' Jesus once asked his disciples (Mark 8:27).

Good question.

'Let the reader understand'

A few things before we start.

This is a sequel – or perhaps a prequel – to my book *The Longest Week*, a careful historical survey of the last week of Jesus' life. So readers who think that chapter 9 is not detailed enough will find that *The Longest Week* fills the gaps.

In *The Longest Week* I make a claim for dating the crucifixion to Friday 3 April, AD 33.[1] All the Gospels agree that Jesus was killed on a Sabbath, and that it was Passover. Since Passover is timed by the full moon, we can work out the possible candidates. And it comes down to two: AD 30 and AD 33. I have chosen AD 33, since that makes much more sense in the light of Pilate's situation. Before that date he had no real need to make any concessions to the Jews, but in AD 33, as we shall see, he was politically vulnerable. This date also works well with Luke's description of John the Baptist's work starting in the fifteenth year of Tiberius.

In order to explore Jesus' life, I've had to suggest a chronological harmony of the Gospels. This is a notoriously difficult task, since the Gospels are not histories as we would understand them: they are, primarily, expressions of faith, designed to explain and pass on the stories of Jesus and leading to a climax with his resurrection. Which is not to say that they don't contain historical information, it's just that it tends to be arranged in different ways. All the Gospels arrange things. Sometimes they put stories and sayings together thematically. At other times, if they don't know exactly when an event happened, they place it where it fits best.

Matthew, Mark and Luke are known as the Synoptic Gospels, from *syn*, meaning 'together', and optic, meaning 'seen'. Broadly speaking, they all see things one way. So when I talk of the Synoptics, I'm talking about those three. John, however, is a bit different. John sees Jesus' work mainly from a Jerusalem perspective.

Combining these four Gospels into one coherent narrative is not easy. There are some clues, some triangulation points, where all four Gospels contain the same event. There is also a mass of historical data: dates, places, people, events. But the task inevitably involves some supposition and compromise. I'm certainly not claiming to have solved all the problems, but I have had a stab, because I don't believe the Synoptic version and John's version of Jesus' life to be inherently contradictory. There are differences in the accounts, but ultimately I believe that the Gospels are historically reliable documents – at least as historically reliable as any of the other documents which are often put up against them. And what I hope to show in this book is that they paint a coherent, believable picture of Jesus of Nazareth.

Reliable is not the same as objective. Objectivity is a very recent idea in historical writing, and an illusory one at that. The Gospels are not unbiased. They were written to show that Jesus was the Messiah. But then again, all books are biased. That's what makes them interesting. You want an unbiased book? Go and read the telephone directory.

In any case, the Gospels are not our only sources for exploring the life of Jesus. There is archaeology, early Jewish writings such as the Mishnah, and, especially, the works of Josephus, the first-century historian. And, when it comes to the idea of Jesus as the Messiah, Josephus is not a bad place to start.

Jesus-who-is-called-Messiah

Flavius Josephus was a soldier who fought against Rome during the great Jewish revolt of AD 66–70, before changing sides and, eventually, moving to Rome. He was born around AD 37/38 and lived to a ripe old age, dying sometime after AD 100. His Jewish name is Joseph ben Matthias, but he's known as 'Flavius' after the Flavians, the emperors Vespasian and his sons Titus and Domitian, who were Josephus' patrons and supporters. It's a bit like calling Samuel Pepys, Carolignian Samuel. Or Jacobean William, for Shakespeare.

His first book was the *Jewish War*, written c. AD 79, an account of the rebellion from the viewpoint of someone who got out while he could. (Josephus was initially captured, but after prophesying that the general who captured him – Vespasian – would become emperor, he was allowed to live and used as a go-between. When Vespasian did indeed become emperor, Josephus had it made.)

Some twenty years later he wrote *Jewish Antiquities,* a twenty-volume history of the Jewish people, and in that book we find two significant references to Jesus.

The first comes in Book 18 where Josephus writes:

> Now there was about this time Jesus, a wise man, *[if it be lawful to call him a man,]* for he was a doer of wonderful works, a teacher of such men as receive the truth with pleasure. He drew over to him both many of the Jews, and many of the Gentiles. *[He was the Christ;]* and when Pilate, at the suggestion of the principal men amongst us, had condemned him to the cross, those that loved him at the first did not forsake him, *[for he appeared to them alive again the third day, as the divine prophets had foretold these and ten thousand other wonderful things concerning him;]* and the tribe of Christians, so named from him, are not extinct to this day.[2]

There is a lot of debate about this passage. Clearly a later Christian editor has got at this text and added some bits in – which I have marked with the brackets. But if you take them out, you get a perfectly reasonable account of Jesus from the perspective of someone who was not one of his followers. And it confirms the basic outline of the story as we have it in early Christian creeds and in the Gospels: Jesus was a wise man and miracle worker, he drew both Jews and Gentiles to him, he was executed by Pilate at the suggestion of the Jewish aristocracy. And even though he was crucified, his followers are still around.[3]

Why were they still around? Well, that is explained by a second reference to Jesus. In Book 20, Josephus describes the death of a minor religious figure in the run-up to the revolt. During a power vacuum in the city, Ananus, the high priest, has a man called James executed:

> Being therefore this kind of person [i.e. a Sadducee] Ananus, thinking he had a favourable opportunity because Festus had died and Albinus was still on his way, called a meeting of judges and brought into it the brother of Jesus-who-is-called-Messiah, James by name, and some others. He made the accusation that they had transgressed the law and he handed them over to be stoned.[4]

James is such an insignificant figure that he has to be identified by his brother. And that's the point. His brother was *not* an insignificant figure. By Josephus' time, many people believed that James' brother Jesus was the 'so-called Messiah'. The word 'messiah' originates with the Hebrew *masiah* (2 Sam. 22:51; 23:1), which means one who is 'anointed' or 'smeared' with oil. The Greek version, Christos, comes from the Greek verb *chriein*, meaning 'to anoint'. This is where Christians got their name from.

Josephus himself is not a big fan of the concept of the Messiah. He distances himself from it, calling it, at one point, an 'ambiguous oracle ... found in their sacred scriptures to the effect that at that time one from their country would become ruler of the world'.[5] Clearly to Josephus, as the Christians continued to spread, that was the significant thing about Jesus: his followers thought he was the Messiah.

Equally clearly, Josephus thought that they were wrong.

'Look! Here is the Messiah!'

If Jesus was the wrong messiah, the question is, 'What did the right Messiah look like? What kind of Messiah were they expecting?' That depends on who 'they' were. Because there was no monolithic, orthodox Judaism in the first century. There were, instead, a number of different Judaisms.

Josephus, for example, talks about four types: the Sadducees, Pharisees, Essenes and one he rather vaguely calls the fourth way. But even within those groupings there were different flavours. There were different 'schools' of Pharisaical thought, for example. (The New Testament contains both extreme and what you might call moderate Pharisees. Clearly someone like Nicodemus, whom Jesus meets in Jerusalem, is not the same kind of Pharisee as those who wanted to have Jesus stopped or even killed.)

What's more, Josephus is rather simplifying things for a Roman audience. There were Jews spread throughout the Roman Empire and they had differing ideas and theologies. And there were also all sorts of apocalyptic Jewish sects knocking around. Not to mention the many Jews, who, when faced with the categories mentioned here, would tick the box marked 'none of the above'.

There was, of course, some common ground. No matter which brand of Judaism you espoused, the Torah (the first five books of the Bible – aka the Law, the books of Moses, the Pentateuch, etc.) was the bedrock, the basis. There were groups which said that Judaism was more than the Torah, but there were no groups which said Judaism was less than the Torah. And they did share common ideas, such as the uniqueness of Israel and the idea of there being one God, even if they differed in their interpretation. They also shared many practices, such as Sabbath observance, dietary laws and following the Jewish festival calendar. And, of course, all male Jews were circumcised, even those who converted to Judaism in later life.

But beyond that, there was a wide variety of views and beliefs. Some Jews believed in life after death, others didn't; some said that all images of living things were profane, others had pictures of animals and plants on their walls (but no humans). Most believed in ritual immersion, but some argued that it had to be in running water, while others said that standing water was OK. Some believed in mythical demons, in the evil eye, in the zodiac. There were many, many Jews and many different Judaisms. In that sense, Jesus' disciples, all the people who listened to him and followed him, did not think that they were becoming 'Christians' – that term was not to be invented for another twenty years or so. They thought they were encountering a new kind of Judaism.

And one of the things on which these different Judaisms disagreed was the nature of the Messiah. The idea that all Jews were waiting for the Messiah is not true. Some were. Perhaps, in Roman-occupied Palestine, many were. But elsewhere the Messiah didn't figure so much. Philo, a first-century Jewish writer and philosopher from Egypt, makes no mention of the Messiah.

And even among those who were expecting the Messiah, different groups were all expecting different kinds of Messiah. For example, the Qumran community, from whom we have the Dead Sea Scrolls, apparently believed that the messianic task would be accomplished by two figures: a Davidic kingly Messiah, and a high priest. Other Jewish literature from around the time portrays him as a warrior, or an anointed priest, or a king or even a wise man.[6] We can see this in the Gospels. In John chapter 7 the crowd argue over whether Jesus is the Messiah. Some say it's impossible, because he comes from Galilee and everyone knows that the Messiah must come from Bethlehem. Others disagree, saying that 'when the Messiah comes, no one will know where he is from' (John 7:27).

So what were their expectations? What did they think the Messiah would be like? Well, we can say some things.

The Messiah was human. He might be doing God's work, but he was not God. There are times in the Hebrew scriptures when the boundaries blur slightly (e.g. Psalm 45:7, Ezekiel 34), but he was still expected to be a man. When Peter says to Jesus, 'you are the Christ,' he is not saying that he is God. That interpretation came later.

The Messiah was a king. Quite what this meant was a matter of interpretation, but Messiah certainly meant 'King of the Jews'. The assumption was that the Messiah, the true God-given king, would replace the earthly royal dynasties of the Herods or the Hasmonaeans.

The Messiah would usher in the age to come. The Messiah would be the person through whom God would bring a new age of peace and prosperity. A return from exile, a new Exodus.

The Messiah would renew the temple. The temple was associated with David, the first great king. The book of Zechariah, itself a dense cloud of messianic prophecies, is also intimately concerned with those who rebuilt the temple after the exile.

The Messiah would defeat Israel's enemies. A messianic psalm, quoted by Jesus, says 'The Lord says to my lord, "Sit at my right hand until I make your enemies your footstool"' (Ps. 110:1; Luke 20:43). The *Psalms of Solomon*, a Jewish text written sometime after 63 BC and before AD 70, says that the Messiah will 'purge

Jerusalem from Gentiles ... drive out the sinners from the inheritance', 'smash the arrogance of sinners like a potter's jar', and 'shatter all their substance with an iron rod'.[7] Victory in battle was a non-negotiable for the Messiah.[8]

The Messiah will be successful. A failed Messiah is an oxymoron. Any Messiah who got beaten was not the Messiah, but a deceiver. As N.T. Wright puts it, 'The category of failed but still revered Messiah ... did not exist.' [9]

And this is where we have to start. Because Jesus barely fits into any of these categories. He died a failed revolutionary leader. He was a peasant, not a king, and when people tried to make him a king, he ran away. Far from smashing Israel's enemies to pieces, he said we should love them and not even call them rude names. After his death not much changed, except that the fishermen who followed him started a cult. There was no new age. Looked at dispassionately, Jesus was a complete failure by any measure. (Except for being human. And according to the Christians he only scored 50 per cent at that.)

To his opponents, Jesus had none of the qualifications that a Messiah should have. To them, he was a wino who kept bad company, had no respect for tradition and who ended up dying the most shameful death possible. Just how wrong can a Messiah be?

And yet, despite that, those who followed him, those who, some fifteen years after his death got nicknamed Christians, came to see Jesus as the Messiah. They believed that the person who just didn't fit – the cornerstone which the builders rejected – turned out to be the Christ, the Messiah, the anointed of God. They were convinced that he was right all along.

And this book is an attempt to find out why.

1. Bethlehem, 5–4 BC

The old king was dying.

He had done well: survived to nearly seventy – remarkable for someone of his time. Especially remarkable given all the scheming against him. But he had seen them all off, executed all those who plotted against him, even his own sons. Even his own wife.

Mariamne. That was her name. Yes, he regretted that. Some days he was confused, forgot that he'd had her executed. Some days, they told him, he wandered the palace just calling out her name.

His mind was failing. And his body, this carcass which had created a kingdom from nothing, was falling apart. He was flushed with a fever, his skin itched uncontrollably. There were pains in his bowels, inflammation in his abdomen. His feet were swollen, rotting, like fruit too long on the tree. He had difficulty breathing, had convulsions. Most horrifyingly of all, his groin was putrefying, eaten up by worms.

The people probably thought it a fitting punishment for all his monstrous deeds. The old monster, dying in a suitably monstrous way. The people had always hated him, despite the magnificent buildings and the status he had given to the nation. They had never forgiven him for being half-Jewish, for making friends with Rome. But that was the Jews for you. In thrall to the past; in Jerusalem, especially, obsessed with their temple, their purity. They never understood, in their religious zeal, just what kind of deals you had to make with the Romans in order to survive.

Even now they were causing trouble.

News of his illness spread through the capital as quick as

the plague. Two zealous young idiots infected by some ultra-fundamentalist rabbis. Hoisted themselves down from a rooftop using thick ropes and cut down the golden eagle that stood over the western gate. Their mistake was simple: he wasn't dead yet.

Rage and anger worked where all the oils and balms could not. It energised the king: he had forty of the ringleaders arrested and raised himself from his sickbed to interrogate them. The two men and their rabbis were burned alive, and the forty men who were captured were also executed. He was even able to recover enough to go out and address the people, who were now terrified that his rage would engulf them all.

But now the end was inevitable. The stench of putrefaction and decay was too overwhelming to be ignored. And now, too, there were men here, from the east. Mystics. Stargazers. Men who believed – horror of horrors – that a new prince was about to be born.

Mariamne. That was her name …

'The birth of Jesus, the Messiah'

Few stories have exercised such a grip on the collective imagination of the Western world as the story of Jesus' birth. In thousands of churches, schools and playgroups hard-hearted innkeepers turn away cherubic Marys and their usually embarrassed boy-husbands. Surprisingly clean shepherds tend flocks of cotton-wool sheep, angelic choirs sing, and a pink and plastic baby Jesus is carefully laid in the manger of yellow straw. The event has become a foundation myth of the cult of consumerism, legitimising three days of overspending and overindulgence.

But the real story is harsher. More dangerous. It begins with shame and scandal, and ends with a massacre. Not much cause for celebration there, one would think.

The story only features in two out of the four Gospels – Luke and Matthew – and they agree on very few details. Luke begins in Nazareth, Matthew in Bethlehem. Matthew has no angelic visit to Mary, Luke none to Joseph. Matthew sends them off to Egypt, Luke has them simply return to Nazareth. Matthew has his mysterious Magi, Luke his grubby shepherds. After the birth, Luke's Jesus goes to the temple; Matthew's goes into exile in Egypt. Luke has faithful Jews singing hymns over the baby; Matthew a maniacal king ordering a massacre. They agree on only a few items: Jesus' parents were called Mary and Joseph, he was born in Bethlehem during the reign of Herod I (aka Herod the Great), after the birth he ended up in Nazareth. Oh, and his mother was a virgin.

Where are we to start with this? The miraculous stories of Jesus' birth have been the subject of speculation, argument and even vitriol. Many scholars simply reject the story *in toto*. It is a piece of early church propaganda, they say: dodgy historical details combined with a desire to emphasise the deity of Jesus and fit in with biblical prophecies. The Scriptures say that the Messiah must be born in Bethlehem, so the early church invents a census to take his parents there for the birth. The Greek translation of the Hebrew Scriptures says that a virgin will give birth, so Matthew and Luke fly in an angel.

Certainly, the historicity is problematic. There is no way to prove the virgin birth. No medical records exist and no similar event has ever been recorded. But the idea of complete invention has some difficulties as well. It assumes a one-way process: that the early church scoured the Scriptures for prophecies and then invented stories to make the details fit, but they could just as easily have had the stories in front of them, and then found echoes or prophecies in the Scriptures. One of the most important activities of the early church was studying the Hebrew Scriptures to see if they had anything to say about Jesus. This was an activity which they believed had been inaugurated by Christ himself on the road to Emmaus. They worked from Christ backwards, as it were.

Also the idea of stories being inventions to 'fulfil' Scripture might work with Matthew, but runs into a buffer with Luke, who mentions Mary's virgin birth and the visit to Bethlehem, but makes no attempt to link them with ancient prophecies. One would have thought that, if Luke had gone to all the trouble of inventing the journey and the census, he would at least have taken the opportunity to point out that it fulfilled a prophecy, but he doesn't even mention it.

Another reason to question the 'invention' theory is that quite often the invention seems a little strained. Matthew, for example, in his tale of the massacre of the innocents, cites a verse from Jeremiah about Rachel weeping for her children. The problem is that this is based in Ramah, which is eleven miles north of Bethlehem and on the other side of Jerusalem. Rachel was, admittedly, buried in Bethlehem, but even so, it is a bit of a stretch to imply that Matthew invented the entire massacre just so that he could include one tenuous line of prophecy set in the wrong location. It is more likely that he was recording a genuine church tradition, and then found a prophecy which he thought fitted. In fact, the early church tradition about it was strong. As early as the second century there were people in Bethlehem who claimed to know the exact place where Jesus had been born.[1]

But whether we're dealing with authorial invention or early church tradition, we are still left staring down the barrel of the miraculous. Virgin births are not biologically possible, unless Mary was an amoeba. Stars do not hover over towns.

It has been popular in certain circles to demythologise Jesus, to remove the miraculous entirely, in the hope that it will reveal the historical Jesus. It does not. What it reveals is the forgettable Jesus. Without the miraculous there is no reason why Jesus should have been remembered by his followers, no reason why they should have braved sickness, hardship, persecution, ostracism and even death to tell their stories.

Jesus – the *historical* Jesus – performed, or was believed to have performed, miracles. That is *why* people talked about him, *why* he was remembered. Whether we're talking about the beginning of his life, the end of his life, or loads of the bits in between, we cannot ignore the miracles. Tidy them away, and they keep bursting out. Turn your back on them, and they bite your behind.

I am not going to ignore them in this book. But nor am I going to try to prove them or disprove them. What tools would I use? There are no first-century medical reports; no psychiatric tests to show that a demon-possessed boy was really schizophrenic; no DNA tests to show who Jesus' father really was. There are only the accounts in the Gospels. The testimonies of people who said, 'This is what I saw.'[2]

Rather than trying to prove or disprove the events described in the Gospels, what I am going to do is to explore them. Look at their setting, their purpose and intent, the people involved and the messages of the miracles, the message they sent out to the people who encountered them and the audience who first heard the tales. The miracles are messages: so what are they saying?

'During the time of King Herod'

Although in the West we celebrate his birthday on 25 December, the exact date, even the exact year, is unknown. There are some clues in the Gospels, however. The birth took place during the reign of Augustus (Luke 2:1) and Jesus was 'about thirty' when he began his public campaign (Luke 3:23). And it took place while that old monster Herod was still alive.

The date of Herod's death is generally agreed to be 4 BC. According to Josephus, Herod's death took place before Passover and after an eclipse of the moon.[3] There was certainly a partial lunar eclipse on the night of 13 March 4 BC. Passover in 4 BC was on 11 April. So it is usually concluded that Herod died between these two dates, somewhere around the end of March/beginning of April in 4 BC.

Other dates have been suggested. Clement of Alexandria suggests a date in November 3 BC.[4] And some scholars have suggested that Herod died not in 4 BC, but a couple of years later in 2 BC.[5] However, the weight of historical opinion is firmly on the side of the spring of 4 BC for the date of Herod's death.

It is likely that Jesus was born a few months or even weeks before Herod died – not least because the type of paranoid, malevolent behaviour described by Matthew fits perfectly into the fevered atmosphere of the Jewish court in the last, diseased months of the old king's life. Although Matthew says that Herod ordered all boys under the age of two to be killed, that does not mean, as some have taken it, that Jesus was two years old. Herod was simply taking no chances. If Jesus was born in 7/6 BC it would be impossible for him to be described as 'around thirty' in AD 29, when his main work began.

So it makes sense to assume that Jesus was born in late 5/early 4 BC. We can go further. We can make a rough stab at guessing Jesus' birth by using a detail in the story about his relative. Before Jesus was conceived and born, there was the birth of his relative John.

'The priestly division of Abijah'

The story of the birth of John the Baptist tells us that his family came not from Galilee, but from the hill country of Judea. His father Zechariah was a rural priest, part of the priestly order of Abijah. In theory a priest was allowed to marry any pure-born Israelite, but many chose only to marry within the tribe, among priestly stock. This is the case with Zechariah, who married Elizabeth, a descendant of Aaron (Luke 1:5).

Rural priests were supposed to assist at the temple twice a year. Priests were divided into twenty-four divisions, each of which went to the temple twice a year for one week, to help out with the services. A tradition recorded in the Mishnah, however, makes it possible to guess the date on which Zechariah was officiating. (The Mishnah was compiled around AD 200. It's a collection of Jewish rabbinic law, which had previously only existed in oral form.) It states that at the destruction of the temple, the division of Jehoiarab was on duty, the first of the twenty-four priestly orders, or courses. The order of Abijah is the eighth of the courses. Since the temple was destroyed by the Romans on 4/5 August AD 70, some historians have suggested that, in 6 BC, the division of Abijah was on duty twice that year, during February and July.[6]

Supposition, of course, and based on the assumption that the Mishnah is correct. But it does allow us to reconstruct the events as described in the Gospels. Zechariah is on duty in the temple at the end of July/beginning of August 6 BC, where he has some kind of visionary encounter and is struck dumb. Luke tells us that his wife became pregnant 'after those days' (Luke 1:24), say in the next couple of weeks. (This is no virgin birth: Zechariah has to be present – talking or not.) Then Elizabeth goes into seclusion for five months (Luke 1:24) and in February – the sixth month – Mary conceives. Three months later John is born, and six months after that, some time around November, Jesus.[7]

All of this is pure speculation, but there is some corroboration elsewhere. The date of 25 December for Jesus' birthday was not agreed until the fourth century AD. Before that, in AD 194, Clement of Alexandria, in a work called *Stromateis*, plumped for 18 November. It is certainly possible that the time of year of Jesus' birth was handed down from generation to generation, if not the actual year itself. In the absence of any published records, recording years was trickier than identifying the season in which someone was born.[8] So maybe our reconstruction is not so very far out.

Let's take things forward again. If we go for a date of November/December 5 BC for the birth of Jesus, how well does that tie in with Luke's statement that Jesus was 'about thirty' at the time of his baptism? Well, first we must remember that there is no year 0. In other words, Jesus would have been four years old in November/December 1 BC and five in November/December AD 1. Second, it is likely that Jesus' baptism took place in the autumn of AD 29. Jesus would have been thirty-two then, turning thirty-three in the November/December of that year. This fits well with John's 'about thirty' description.

A birth date for Jesus of 2/1 BC would not change things significantly. Under that dating, Jesus would be twenty-eight or twenty-nine when he was baptised – again pretty much 'about thirty'. With such ancient accounts, all suggested dates come with a health warning, but this is the chronological framework I am going to adopt in this book.[9] (See page 16 for a chronological chart.)

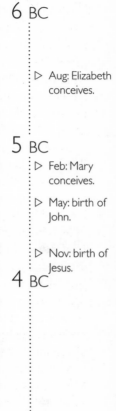

6 BC

▷ Aug: Elizabeth conceives.

5 BC

▷ Feb: Mary conceives.

▷ May: birth of John.

▷ Nov: birth of Jesus.

4 BC

'His name is John'

Six months before Jesus arrived, Mary's relatives Elizabeth and Zechariah had a baby boy whom they called John. John is a baby in the tradition of the Old Testament miraculous births like Isaac, Samson and Samuel. Like some of those Old Testament mothers, Elizabeth is getting on in years. Like Samson, John must never drink 'wine or strong drink' (Luke 1:15). Samson was a Nazirite, a special group of people who abstained from alcohol, cutting his hair and any contact with impurity (Num. 6:1–8). It is not stated anywhere that John is a Nazirite, but the echoes are there.[10] His life was to be dedicated to the Lord, and he and his disciples were noted for 'eating no bread and drinking no wine' (Luke 7:33).

THE WRONG MESSIAH

Chronological Background

5 BC
Nov/Dec Jesus Born
Massacre in Bethlehem; escape to Egypt;
Herod dies; family return to Nazareth

1 AD
Nov: Jesus' 4th birthday
Nov: Jesus' 5th birthday

15th year of Tiberius (Aug AD 28 – Aug AD 29)

29
John the Baptist's work begins. Jesus 'about thirty' (Luke 3:23)

5
Archelaus deposed. Judea becomes Roman province

10
Passover: Jesus 'lost' in Jerusalem

30
Jesus' baptism and temptation (Mark 1:9–12)

Jesus in Jerusalem for Passover (John 3:1–21)

Jesus in Judea; John near Salim (John 3:22–24)

15

31
Arrest of John the Baptist; Jesus moves to Capernaum (Mark 1:14)

20

Jesus in Jerusalem for 'festival' (John 5)

32
Feeding of 5000 (John 6:1–15)
Jesus in Tyre, Sidon and Caesarea Philippi (Mark 7:24–9:32)

25
Jesus in Galilee/Samaria (Luke 17:11)
Jesus in Jerusalem for Tabernacles (John 7:10–10)
Jesus in Jerusalem for Dedication (John 10:22–39)

28
29 15th year of Tiberius
Nov: Jesus' 32nd birthday
30 Nov: Jesus' 33rd birthday
See detail - - - - - - ->
31
32
33

33
Jesus in Judea (John 10:40)
Raising of Lazarus (John 10:40)
Jesus in Ephraim (John 11:54)

Jesus in Jerusalem for Passover (Mark 11; John 1)
Death and resurrection

Elizabeth, Zechariah and John lived in the hill country of Judea (Luke 1:39). The region covers the high ground, not only of Judea but of Ephraim as well, stretching some forty miles or so from Beersheba in the south to Jerusalem in the north, with its centre at Hebron. Bethlehem would also be in this region.[11] The exact location is not known. The traditional 'tourist' site is Ain Karim, five miles from Jerusalem, but that identification only dates from the sixth century onwards. Another suggestion has been the town of Juttah, about five miles south of Hebron.

According to Luke, it was into these hills that, in perhaps late February 5 BC, Mary came to visit Elizabeth, who was her relative. In John's Gospel, John the Baptist claims not to have known Jesus: 'I myself did not know him, but the one who sent me to baptise with water said to me, "He on whom you see the Spirit descend and remain is the one who baptises with the Holy Spirit"' (John 1:33). So the best we are talking about here is a fairly distant cousin. Whatever the nature of the relationship, her name was Mary and she had news. She was pregnant.

'The virgin's name was Mary'

Mary was poor. Although the social status of Jesus' parents has been a subject of much discussion, the general impression is that both Mary and Joseph came from a simple, peasant background.[12] The word 'peasant' is not a pejorative term: it simply describes those who lived a simple rural working-class lifestyle.

Certainly Luke believed Mary was poor. He attributes a song to her – known now as the Magnificat – which is a hymn of triumph for the lowly and humble over the wealthy and puffed-up. 'He [God] has brought down the powerful from their thrones,' she sings, 'and lifted up the lowly; he has filled the hungry with good things, and sent the rich away empty' (Luke 1:52–53). This song makes no sense at all unless Mary – and the man she was to marry – were 'lowly', poor and even hungry. She would hardly sing about the rich being sent away empty if she came from a moneyed background. The fact that Mary and Joseph were poor is backed up by the sacrifice they later give at the temple. Luke records that they sacrificed 'a pair of turtledoves or two young pigeons' (Luke 2:24), which was the sacrifice you gave if you were too poor to sacrifice a sheep.[13]

Poor, then, and young as well. Although older marriages did occur, the usual age for a Jewish girl to be married was between thirteen and sixteen. Marriage itself was usually arranged through an intermediary. Although the betrothed couple did not live together or, naturally, consummate the marriage, they were viewed as having already entered a binding relationship. If the would-be husband died before the wedding, his fiancée was technically a widow.[14] A betrothal, like a marriage, could only be dissolved through death or divorce. It was a legally binding contract, hence Joseph's reluctance to do something as drastic as break off the engagement.[15]

Jewish couples probably married around a year after their betrothal during which time the details of the marriage contract would be hammered out between the two families.[16] The bride's family would provide a dowry, a payment to the groom for marrying the daughter. It might come as cash, or in the form of land, goods, possessions, animals. (It sometimes even came as slaves.) The aim was to give the couple some capital to start their marriage. They could use it to buy furniture, animals, land, a house.

Did Joseph and Mary even make it as far as the wedding feast? The text does not say. Usually the marriage itself was celebrated with a feast at the house of the father of the groom. First the bride would be prepared at her family home, then she would leave her home and be taken in procession through the town or village to the home of the groom's family. There she would be formally introduced into her husband's home. After that there would be blessings and festivities and then the marriage would be consummated. Following this the new bride would live with her husband's family.[17] It was less like Western marriage and more like a football transfer.

All this, one imagines, Mary sacrificed. No public procession for her. No seven days of festivities following the wedding day. Jewish weddings usually lasted a week, with a lot of feasting among one's friends. The well off were known to invite large numbers of guests – sometimes the entire village – to the wedding. Joseph and Mary may have done this. There might have been hurried arrangements, the dowry hastily organised in order to hush up the scandal. But there would have been talk, gossip. In a village as small as Nazareth, people would have *known*.

'Joseph her husband was a righteous man'

What of her husband? In the Gospel accounts, Joseph is a rather strange, silent figure. Not a word is spoken by him. He is described as an 'upright' or 'righteous' man (Matt. 1:19), a devout Jew who in later years made it a habit to travel to Jerusalem each year to observe the Passover (Luke 2:41). Perhaps he was proud of his descent from the royal line of King David. When it came to naming his sons – and, as we shall see, he had several – he called them good Jewish names: two named after Bible heroes (Joshua and Jacob) and two after the heroes of the Maccabean revolt, when Israel gained independence (Judas and Simeon).[18] Joseph may well have been a relative. Many cousins married each other: you kept things in the family.

Although he is frequently depicted in art as a decrepit old figure, that idea comes from a later, fictional account of Jesus' nativity written around AD 200. Known as the *Protevangelium of James,* the work is an infancy gospel, containing fabricated stories of Jesus' childhood. It is one of the first works to promote the doctrine of the perpetual virginity of Mary – the idea that not only was Mary a virgin at Jesus' birth, but she remained so for ever more. In order to do this, the book has to explain away the fact that Jesus had brothers and sisters, so the writer of the *Protevangelium* came up with a solution: make them Joseph's children from a previous marriage. Thus it claims that Joseph was an elderly widower when he married Mary.

The *Protevangelium* is pure fiction. It dresses Joseph up as an old man in order to justify a point of doctrine. As one writer puts it, 'Nearly everything claimed for Mary over the past two thousand years is simply not to be found in the New Testament.'[19] Luke and Matthew say nothing about perpetual virginity, immaculate conception or the assumption of Mary. They don't say that Joseph was old or that he had previously been married.

And they don't tell us when he died. He was alive when Jesus was twelve (Luke 2:41–43), but even if he was dead by the time Jesus was baptised, that doesn't mean he was old. The normal age of marrying for Palestinian Jews in New Testament times would have been about sixteen for a man and about fourteen for a woman. Joseph was a peasant worker in a hard manual profession. He came from

19

a background of poverty, rather than wealth. He lived in what we today would consider unsanitary conditions. Some experts believe that very few people, maybe as low as 3 per cent, survived to the age of sixty and that 90 per cent were dead by their mid-forties.[20] If he married Mary at sixteen and lived to a normal life span for that time, he would have been dead around AD 20, ten years before Jesus began appearing in public.

Joseph was young. He was courageous, and generous. Matthew says Joseph 'planned to dismiss her quietly' (Matt. 1:19). This might have cost Joseph financially. Legally, Joseph had the right to impound the dowry of a fiancée who was guilty of adultery, but that would have meant hauling her before a public tribunal. It may well be that by keeping the whole thing quiet, Joseph was forfeiting the right to any money.[21]

So what we have in this story is not an elderly man and a demure young woman. We have two young people – teenagers, in our terms – caught up in a whirlwind of dreams and visions and shocking, scandalous pregnancy. Whispers of illegitimacy and scandal must have hung around Jesus all the time he was in Nazareth. Poor parents from a nowhere town. It is an inauspicious start for a would-be Messiah.

Joseph, of course, did not divorce Mary. When the truth was revealed to him in a dream he married her. And not long after, he took her away. South. To Bethlehem.

'This was the first census'

The census is also a problem historically, although for different reasons. This time it is not a question of biology, but of history. 'In those days a decree went out from Emperor Augustus that all the world should be registered. This was the first registration and was taken while Quirinius was governor of Syria' (Luke 2:1–2).

Luke tells us a number of things about it.

▷ It was an imperial decree, and it covered 'all the world' (i.e. the Roman Empire).
▷ It was the 'first registration'.
▷ It occurred during the governorship of Quirinius.
▷ People had to return to their home towns.

There are many difficulties in this. According to Josephus, Quirinius, or P. Sulpicius Quirinius, to give him his full name, came to Syria in AD 6, when Coponius was appointed prefect of Judea. We know that he instituted a policy of taxation which was heavily resisted by the Jews and which even resulted in armed resistance under a local leader called Judas the Gaulonite. What is more, we know that Quirinius had instituted other censuses: an inscription on a gravestone in Venice records that he instituted a census of Apamea in Syria, but gives no date for it.[22] But all of that is a decade too late.

It may be that Luke has his governors mixed up: Tertullian, the early church apologist, claimed that the enrolment was taken 'in Judea by Sentius Saturninus', which would be earlier. Perhaps Tertullian was issuing a correction, but Luke is generally very accurate with regard to chronology. When he knows a detail, he supplies it. And Luke, in fact, is careful to distinguish this census from that of AD 6/7. He says that this is the 'first' census (Luke 2:1). And later on, in Acts, he refers to the uprising of Judas the Galilean in the days of the second census (Acts 5:37). This shows that he did know his recent history. It is inconceivable that he would have got the two censuses mixed up. And it is hardly likely that he would have described Jesus as 'about thirty' in AD 29/30 if the census that he actually meant was one which took place in AD 6/7. Jesus would have been closer to twenty.

It is certainly possible that Quirinius was governor twice: once during the reign of Herod and again in AD 6–7. Quirinius was in the east at the time, fighting a tribe in the Taurus Mountains in Asia. This would have meant drawing on the military headquarters at Antioch, described as 'the Pentagon of the East'.[23]

Whatever the case, Luke must be overstating the extent of the enrolment – if a census really had covered the whole empire there would surely have been some other record of it. So maybe it wasn't a census at all. The Romans would not try to assess the citizens of a client-kingdom like Judea: that was Herod's job. He was their tax-gatherer. In fact the word translated as 'census' does not mean quite that. The word itself is *apographe*, which mean 'registering' or 'enrolling'. Josephus, talking of the census of AD 6–7, uses a different word for the assessment – *apotimesin*.[24] What we are talking about is a written-down list. A census would normally be associated with taxation, a registration with some other legal or imperial matter.

So what was this list? One plausible suggestion is that it was an oath of allegiance. Certainly there was one of those held in Rome in the thirteenth year of the consulship of Augustus – 2 BC. According to Josephus, some years before that, around 7 BC, relations between Herod and Augustus became strained. To prove his loyalty, Herod decided that an oath would be taken by all the people. This was an occasion 'when all the people of the Jews gave assurance of their good will to Caesar, and to the king's government'.[25] Some machinery for ensuring that it had been done would have had to be used, which may well have required people to return to their home towns.

In the event, there was widespread reluctance to swear any loyalty to Caesar among the Jews and some six thousand Pharisees refused to take the oath. Why they took such exception to it, we do not know. Perhaps the oath was similar to that imposed on the inhabitants of Paphlagonia at Gangra in 3 BC, which included a promise to inform on anyone who was planning action against the Romans.[26] So it is possible that this was a registration not for tax purposes, but for the purposes of loyalty. Even so, 7 BC is still too early for our purposes.

At the end of the day we simply do not have enough information to be entirely certain. We do not know enough about Roman government of the provinces at this time. Since the Romans left the day-to-day government in the hands of local leaders and client-kings, it is perfectly possible that a registration in Judea would use as its starting point the strong historical attachment which the Jews felt for their tribal and ancestral relationships.[27] Perhaps the situation is best surmised by Sherwin-White, who called the whole debate an 'agnostic stalemate'.[28]

What Luke does say is that Joseph and Mary returned to Bethlehem. Joseph might have been required by the terms of the oath-taking to return to his ancestral home. He might, being a 'righteous' man, have realised that the Messiah had to be born in Bethlehem. Or he might just have been looking for an excuse to get out of town.

'There was no place for them in the inn'

For two thousand years, innkeepers have had some of the worst PR imaginable. Every year, in pre-schools and playgroups, schools and churches, Mary and Joseph are turned away by an innkeeper, before finding shelter in a stable. But if we read the story carefully a different picture emerges, one in which there is no inn and no stable.

Here is what Luke says: 'While they were there [Bethlehem], the time came for her to deliver her child. And she gave birth to her firstborn son and wrapped him in bands of cloth, and laid him in a manger, because there was no place for them in the inn' (Luke 2:6–7). The Greek word Luke uses for 'inn' is *kataluma*. This can mean 'inn', but more often means 'guest room', 'spare room', or anywhere you might put visitors. In fact, Luke uses it in this way elsewhere in his Gospel: in the account of the Last Supper, where two disciples are told to go and ask, 'Where is the guest room [*kataluma*], where I may eat the Passover with my disciples?' (Luke 22:11). The Last Supper did not take place in an inn. It took place in an upper room, a space for guests. This argument is further reinforced when we look at the only place in Luke's Gospel where he does specifically mention an inn: in the story of the Good Samaritan (Luke 10:34). In that instance, the word he uses is a different Greek word, *pandocheion*. So, if he had meant an inn in Bethlehem, why did he not use *pandocheion*?

Because there was no inn. Mary and Joseph were going to Joseph's family home. They would not need an inn; they would stay with relatives. But the relatives were poor and their home was crowded, there was no more room in the *kataluma*. So they laid the baby elsewhere in the house: in a manger, an animal's feeding trough.

No inn, then, but what about the stable? Surely the presence of a manger indicates that? No, not really. In peasant homes of that time, the manger was not in another building, but inside the house. These homes were simple, two-level structures: there was the lower level where the everyday living took place, and an upper mezzanine level where the family slept. Or, if they were caves (and many people did live in caves at the time), the family slept in the central parts and towards the back, with the animals kept at the entrance. At night their animals would be brought into the lower level of the house, both for security reasons and to keep the house warm – their body heat acted as a kind of primitive central heating. There would have been mangers set into the slope to the upper level, and it was there that Jesus was laid.

So, no inn. And no stable either. In Luke's version of the tale, Jesus was just put downstairs with the animals, because the rest of the house was full.[29]

The story of Jesus' birth, therefore, is not one of exclusion but of inclusion. No one in that peasant community turned Joseph and Mary away. They made room for them. This was, for the Gospel writers and their first audiences, the most important fact: this was a story about the Son of God coming into the world of simple peasants. Joseph's relatives made a place for Jesus in the heart of their household. They did not shun Mary, even though her status would have been suspect and even shameful: they brought her inside. They made room for Jesus in the heart of a peasant's house.

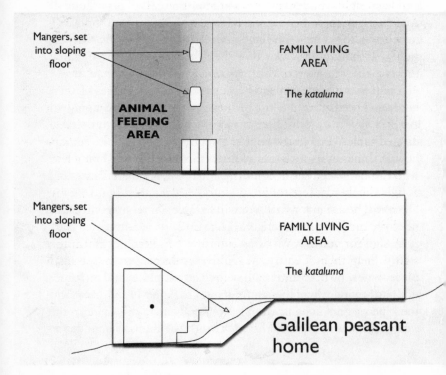

Mangers, set into sloping floor

FAMILY LIVING AREA

The *kataluma*

ANIMAL FEEDING AREA

Mangers, set into sloping floor

FAMILY LIVING AREA

The *kataluma*

Galilean peasant home

'There were shepherds living in the fields'

'Do not teach your son to be a shepherd.' That is what it says in the Mishnah: 'Abba Gurion of Sidon says in the name of Abba Gurya, "A man should not teach his son to be an ass driver, a camel driver, a barber, a sailor, a herdsman, or a shopkeeper. For their trade is the trade of thieves."' [30]

Herdsmen did not enjoy good reputations. Another rabbinical list includes them alongside other disreputable low-lifes such as dice-players, usurers and tax-collectors.[31] The assumption was that they were cheats. The Mishnah says it was forbidden for orthodox Jews to buy wool, milk or kids directly from the herdsman, who was assumed to have stolen them: 'It fell off the back of a flock, guv.' Shepherds, then, were widely suspect and discredited. 'For herdsmen, tax collectors and publicans, is repentance hard,' it was said.[32]

Most trades involving herding or driving animals were seen – by certain sections of the Jewish community at least – as inherently degrading and disreputable. These people were deprived of civil and legal rights; under law they could not be called as witnesses.[33] And yet it is these people, according to Luke, whom God calls to witness this birth. The outcast, despised shepherds, without rights, without even a roof over their heads, inadmissible in law: they are the witnesses to the birth.

Throughout his teaching, Jesus used favourable images of shepherds and herdsmen. The use of these metaphors is an anomaly in rabbinic literature, which tends to view them as shifty, unreliable, discreditable.[34] But Jesus thought they were good people. Perhaps he was thinking back to the stories of his birth, to the first guests who came through the door of the house where he was born.

The shepherds were told to go into Bethlehem and find a baby: 'This will be a sign for you: you will find a child wrapped in bands of cloth and lying in a manger' (Luke 2:12).

'A sign for you ...' We often interpret this verse as meaning a sign to help them identify the child. But Bethlehem was a small place: a new birth would not be hard to find and a newborn baby not hard to identify. The sign refers not to who the child is, but to the kind of person he is. The sign is *for them*, for their benefit. It tells them that he is one of them. This is not about them identifying the baby, it is about the baby identifying with them. This is what the manger signifies to the shepherds: he is one of us.

Thus right at the start of the story we are made aware that, in some senses, everything is wrong. The Messiah, the Son of David, should not be born in a peasant's household. Those who welcome him into the world should not be the outcasts and the impure. But that is exactly what happened.

Too often, the story of Jesus' birth is depicted as a story of exclusion and rejection. That is not the case, however. Jesus was welcomed by the people of Bethlehem. They brought him into the heart of their homes. The ordinary Jewish peasants and the oppressed Jewish herdsmen saw that he was one of them.

The people of Bethlehem – innkeepers included – did not reject Jesus. They made room for him. And they were to pay a heavy price for their welcome.

'He was called Jesus'

After the birth, Mary and Joseph stayed with their family in Bethlehem. And eight days after his birth, Jesus was circumcised. Luke says that it was on the day of his circumcision that he was named: a practice which is attested in other rabbinical literature.[35]

The name they gave him was Jesus.

Or not. Because Jesus is derived from Ιεσους (*Iesous*) – the Greek version of his name and the language in which the New Testament is written. His actual Hebrew name was Yeshua, which in turn is a short version of Joshua (in Hebrew, Yehoshua), the great hero of the entry into the Promised Land. His parents would have called him Yeshu – the shortened, Galilean version of Yeshua. Certainly that is the name by which he is referred to in the ancient Jewish literature, and it probably reflects the local Galilean pronunciation.[36]

In Jesus' day the Jews, out of respect, did not name their children after the most important figures in their history – no Moseses, Solomons, Davids or Aarons. But Joshua, he was division two, as it were. Yeshua was one of the most common names of the day – the sixth most popular name among Palestinian Jews of the time. In Josephus' works there are twenty or so Jesuses, half of whom belong to the same time as Jesus of Nazareth.[37]

According to the British Office of National Statistics, the sixth most common boy's name in 2008 was Alfie (Joshua was number five).[39] In British terms, the Messiah was called Alf.

That Jesus is the Greek version of the Hebrew name Yeshua is a fact which most Christians know, but few really process. The name Jesus is so ingrained into our Western consciousness that it is almost impossible to erase it, to go back to a time when he was not Jesus of Nazareth, but Yeshu, the son of Yehosef and Miriam.

It is salutary that the only physical characteristic we know for sure about

Top Ten Boys' Names among Palestinian Jews, 330 BC – AD 200[38]	
1	Simon/Simeon
2	Joseph/Joses
3	Lazarus/Eleazar
4	Judas/Judah
5	John/Yohanan
6	Jesus/Joshua
7	Ananias/Hananiah
8	Jonathan
9	Matthew/Matthias/Mattathias
10	Manaen/Menahem

Jesus is that he was circumcised. Circumcision on the eighth day was demanded by the Torah, the Law.[40] It signified membership of the nation and an obligation to live under the Law. Jesus was Jewish. He was born as a Jew, he lived as a Jew, he died as a Jew. The translation of his name into Greek was necessary for his message to be heard throughout the world, but in a way it started a process which has been going on ever since: the 'de-Jewification' of Jesus. In many cases it is not a deliberate process, but when people forget that Jesus was Yeshu, it not only affects their understanding of his actions and message as portrayed in the Gospels, it can also lead to suspicion, fear, hatred and violence.

His Jewishness is certainly apparent in the next little part of the tale. Forty days after the birth, his parents took Jesus to the temple, the most 'Jewish' place in the entire world.

> When the time came for their purification according to the law of Moses, they brought him up to Jerusalem to present him to the Lord (as it is written in the law of the Lord, 'Every firstborn male shall be designated as holy to the Lord'), and they offered a sacrifice according to what is stated in the law of the Lord, 'a pair of turtle-doves or two young pigeons'. (Luke 2:22–24)

27

The main purpose of the visit was to complete the purification of Mary.[41] After giving birth a woman was considered unclean for forty days – or eighty if she had given birth to a daughter. During this period she was not allowed to enter the temple or touch any sacred object (Lev. 12:1–8). The sacrifice they make is significant: the use of pigeons as an alternative to lambs or goats was a concession to the poor.[42]

Along with this event, Luke inserts stories he has received of Simeon and Anna, two prophet-like figures who attest to the uniqueness of Jesus. Simeon is something of a vague figure, but Anna – the name is short for Hannah – is a credibly detailed presentation. A devout worshipper who spent all her days in the temple, she was the daughter of Phanuel, from the tribe of Asher; she was eighty-four, and had been widowed many years earlier, after just seven years of marriage. She is given no direct speech – unlike Simeon and his famous *Nunc dimittis* – but she speaks to everyone 'looking for the redemption of Jerusalem' (Luke 2:38).

The curious feature is her attribution to the tribe of Asher. She is the only Jewish figure in the New Testament who comes from one of the northern tribes – all the others come from Benjamin, Judah or Levi. She is, in fact, an outsider.[43]

Asher's territory was in the western hills of Galilee. When the Assyrians conquered the northern kingdom of Israel in 733 BC, most of the inhabitants were taken into slavery and deported. Some remnants presumably remained, but the area was predominantly Gentile until it was conquered by the Hasmoneans. Anna, then, may be a remnant, one of the few who got away, who escaped exile and destruction in Assyria and clung to the land, tenaciously holding on to their tribal ancestry. Or, more likely, she may have been descended from the thousands of Jews who survived beyond the Euphrates, in Jewish communities such as those at Nisibis and Adiabene. Jewish leaders in Jerusalem maintained contact with these eastern Diaspora communities through letters; of especial importance were communications giving the dates of the major Jewish festivals. The rabbis, too, maintained contact. There are letters from Gamaliel to Pharisaic Jews in the Diaspora, and Rabbi Akiba is said to have visited the region on his travels.[44] There was a rabbi known as Rabbi Nahum the Mede active in Jerusalem during the last days of the second temple. This implies that either he or his parents moved from Medea to Jerusalem.

Luke's details about Anna indicate a real historical figure. This is someone who would be well known and well remembered in Jerusalem. Those little details indicate that Anna came from the east, perhaps with her father Phanuel, many years earlier.

She is, of course, not the only traveller from the east who is associated with the birth of Jesus.

'Wise men from the East'

Let's kick one thing into touch straight away: there were not three of them, and they were not kings: 'In the time of King Herod, after Jesus was born in Bethlehem of Judea, wise men from the East came to Jerusalem, asking, "Where is the child who has been born king of the Jews? For we observed his star at its rising, and have come to pay him homage"' (Matt. 2:1–2).

The word translated 'wise men' is *magoi*, singular *magos*, from which we get our word 'magus'. The root of the word is *mageia*, the Greek word for 'magic'. By the early Christian era the word had come to be associated with astrologers from Chaldea (the ancient name for the marshy lands in the far south of Mesopotamia), many of whom travelled west to share their expertise. Astrology and astronomy were not really separate arts in ancient times. The Magi believed that earthly events were signified by heavenly signs and that the accurate observation of celestial phenomena would help them predict and interpret real, earthly events. Belief in astrology was common in ancient times. Roman emperors routinely consulted their official astrologers. In Acts, the proconsul of Cyprus, Sergius Paulus, has a Magi called Elymas Bar-Jesus as an advisor (Acts 13:7–12). It was not a profession without risks, especially if the prophecies proved unwelcome. The *Magi* and *Chaldaei* were frequently expelled from Rome throughout the first century and Augustus, although a believer in astrology, passed a law which made it a criminal offence to consult an astrologer about the fate of the emperor. Kings and emperors were prone to kill those who brought them bad news – another possible reason why the Magi decided not to return to Herod on their way home.[45]

The star has been taken as an example of Matthew's 'find-a-prophecy-and-make-a-story-to-fit' technique. In Numbers 24:17 Balaam son of Beor says, 'I see him, but not now; I behold him, but not near – a star shall come out of Jacob, and a sceptre shall rise out of Israel' (Num. 24:17).

In Jesus' day this had become a popular messianic prophecy. Several mentions occur in the Dead Sea Scrolls and it was also applied to Bar Kokhba, who led the revolt against the Romans in AD 135. But the curious thing is that Matthew does not actually quote the verse. Elsewhere you just cannot stop him quoting the Old Testament, so why on earth would he not do that now? Perhaps he did not invent it. Perhaps he was recording a historical event, albeit one with some rather perplexing details.

Another thing: for the early church, magic was a Bad Thing. In Acts we read of a magician from Samaria who 'amazed them with his magic' (Acts 8:11). He became known as Simon Magus and was a popular villain in early Christian fiction. In an apocryphal book called *The Acts of Peter*, he engages the apostle in a series of magical battles, including flying through the air. He is eventually defeated by Peter's prayer that he fall to the ground. The book is the *Harry Potter* of its day (or *Harry Peter*, perhaps). Magic, in the book of Acts, is frowned upon. Elymas Bar-Jesus is defeated by Paul and converts in Ephesus burned all their magic books (Acts 13:9–10; 19:19). Early Christian writers almost always use *magos* in a pejorative sense. So to invent a story where the Magi are actually the heroes would be a very odd thing for Matthew to do.

Celestial phenomena were commonly accepted as accompanying significant events. We have already seen how the eclipse of the moon portended the demise of Herod (of which more later), so it is hardly surprising that the early church should have remembered a tradition of a star accompanying the birth of Jesus. The big question, and one which has filled many books and far too many web pages, is what kind of celestial phenomenon was it?

Let's be quite clear: stars do not move in the way described in Matthew 2:9. They do not settle over a place. The most popular and perhaps most credible explanation is that it was not a star at all. Matthew's account seems to confirm this. The Magi themselves come literally 'from the rising', i.e. the direction of the rising stars in the east, but they observed the star 'at its rising' (Matt. 2:2), indicating the appearance of the star in the evening.[46] Herod asks them 'the exact time when the star had appeared' (Matt. 2:7) and the answer gives him what he believed to be the specific birth date of the threat to his throne.

All this rising and falling indicates that it was not a star but a planet. Babylonian astronomers of the time kept careful records of planetary movements, especially Jupiter, which they associated with Marduk, the supreme male Babylonian deity, comparable to the Western god Zeus or Jupiter. These records show us that the planets of Jupiter and Saturn appeared together in the constellation of Pisces settling at their apogee on the Babylonian Arahsamna 20/21 – in our terms 12/13 November, 7 BC.[47] This is an extremely rare conjunction, not to be repeated for another 854 years.[48] And some scholars believe that to Babylonian astrologers Pisces represented Palestine and the Levant.

This may be another reason why Herod had his soldiers kill all the boys under two. Two years back from November 7 BC brings us to November 5 BC, exactly the time that, in our reconstruction, Jesus was born. 7 BC is too early for Jesus' birth – too old for Luke's 'about thirty' reference, but it could certainly have taken the astrologers a long time to make the journey. It was a long and arduous trek from Medea to Palestine.

And proper arrangements had to be made. This was both a scientific and a diplomatic expedition. Magi often held prominent political roles in Persia.[49] There was to be a new king in Judea and, as to the nature of this king, they would have had a source for information about the Messiah: the huge number of Diaspora Jews in Persia. It is quite possible, therefore, that they filled out the background information to their astrological observations by talking to the same groups of Diaspora Jews from whom Anna came.

The gifts they bring with them certainly fit in with the idea of an embassy from the east. Babylonian priests burned frankincense on altars made of silver. More widely, they are luxurious, expensive gifts associated with royal courts. Frankincense was grown in Syria, but most supplies of this and myrrh came from the area which is now Saudi Arabia and Somaliland.[50] So, although they are seen as separate symbols – gold for a king, frankincense for a priest, myrrh for embalming – they are quite probably just the normal, luxury gifts which a diplomatic mission would bring. At its roots, the journey of the Magi may well originate in a real diplomatic mission and a real conjunction of planets.

None of this explains why the star was still there when they arrived, nor the idea of movement and settling over the stable – details which give this part of the story a fairy-tale kind of air.

This fairy-tale quality, however, does not extend to a happy ending. Because the mission of the magi led to a massacre.

'He sent and killed all the children'

The massacre of the children is the forgotten story of Christmas. It is carefully hidden away, in the dog days after the big celebrations. Yet it is a crucial element of Jesus' early years. The death of Herod was to play a huge role in defining the atmosphere in which Jesus was to grow up.

There is no record of this event anywhere in contemporary history. But why should there be? This was not some high-class assassination. No aristocratic family, no one who *mattered*, was involved. The killing of a few peasant babies would hardly make a blip on the seismograph of Herod's crimes.

Some scholars claim that Matthew has merely invented it to fulfil the prophecy from Jeremiah 21:15. But, as we have seen, signs of invention are a little lacking. Ramah is eleven miles away from Bethlehem, on the opposite side of Jerusalem. Nor is the quotation in any way a messianic prophecy. Certainly Matthew intends us to see an Old Testament parallel – it is the Exodus story starring Jesus as Moses and Herod as Pharaoh, killing the newborns. But again it is hard to see why Matthew, or anyone else in the early church, should invent such a story just to present Jesus as the new Moses.

More likely is that the tradition of the slaughter of the children was already current in the early church. The early church believed that Herod had massacred the children of Bethlehem and that Jesus had only escaped through divine intervention.

In fact, the event fits perfectly with the fevered paranoia of the king's final days. He was certainly dying at the time, and the manner of his death was driving him insane.

'Those who were seeking the child's life are dead'

Josephus describes the death of Herod I in full, gory detail:

> After this, the distemper seized upon his whole body, and greatly disordered all its parts with various symptoms; for there was a gentle fever upon him, and an intolerable itching over all the surface of his body, and continual pains in his colon, and dropsical tumours about his feet and an inflammation of the abdomen, – and a putrefaction of his privy member, that produced worms. Besides which he had a difficulty of breathing upon him, and could not breathe but when he sat upright, and had a convulsion of all his members; insomuch that the diviners said those diseases were a punishment upon him for what he had done to the rabbis.[51]

It's a gory description: mild fever, intolerable itching, continuous pains in the colon, tumours in the feet like dropsy, inflammation of the abdomen, putrefaction of genitals, shortening of breath and convulsions (but apart from that he was fine). Many suggestions have been made as to the disease, including diabetes, cerebral arteriosclerosis, cardiac failure, hepatic cirrhosis and amoebic dysentery. A doctor I consulted suggested venereal disease or even a sandfly bite. The worms are a particularly gruesome detail, but these were frequently cited in the deaths of notorious people. In Herodotus, after Pheretime of Cyrene takes excessive and brutal vengeance on the Barcaeans for the murder of her son, she falls ill and dies 'a horrible death, her body seething with worms while she was still alive'. In 2 Maccabees, Antiochus Epiphanes leads an expedition against Jerusalem, during which he is injured, and at the end worms swarm within his body and his entire army is revolted by the stench. In the book of Acts, Herod's grandson Agrippa is devoured by worms. Later Christian legends of Judas Iscariot describe him wandering the streets, worm-eaten.[52]

Whatever the modern diagnosis, to the Jew who had suffered under Herod the cause of his death was not diabetes or syphilis, or even the sandfly, but retribution. He was being punished for his sins – and what sins they were.

Herod ruled Jewish Palestine from 37 BC to 4 BC.[53] He had been born nearly seventy years earlier into an Idumean family, from the region south of Judea, and his grandfather had converted to Judaism during the reign of John Hyrcanus I (134–104 BC). Herod's father, Antipater, was advisor to Hyrcanus II and was later made *epitropos* (overseer) of Judea in 47 BC. At the age of twenty-five Herod was appointed governor of Galilee and made a name for himself by his aggressive campaign against the various brigands and local warlords.

It was the start of a career which was marked by two things: strategic brilliance and brutal aggression. Herod was a monster, but he was a brilliant monster. When Pompey conquered Judea in 63 BC, Herod knew that he would only succeed through unswerving loyalty to Rome.

Even through the dark days, when his father was murdered and he was forced to flee the country, his loyalty to Rome and the value of his own personal abilities were recognised. When the Hasmonean king Mattathias Antigonus allied himself with the Parthians against the Romans, Herod made his way to Rome, where he was crowned king of Judea. He returned to Judea in 39 BC, and in the summer of 37, aided by the Romans, he finally drove Antigonus out of Judea. The kingdom was his.

After a ten-year period of consolidation, he embarked on a massive building and regeneration programme. He rebuilt Samaria and named it Sebaste, in honour of Augustus. He developed a showpiece Greco-Roman city at Caesarea, together with a huge man-made harbour – the largest in the Mediterranean and home to the Judean navy.[54] He built a chain of mountain-top palace-fortresses. In Jerusalem he created the biggest temple complex in the ancient world. Indeed, his additions to the temple turned it into a pilgrim city to a degree that it had never been before. It was Herod who introduced innovations such as the Court of Women and the Court of Gentiles.[55] Jews throughout the Greco-Roman area of influence supported the temple through their temple tax – itself a recent innovation, arising probably in the reign of Salome Alexander (from 76/5 through to 67 BC), or even later.[56] The pilgrims brought with them money to spend on accommodation, food and offerings. More than anyone else, apart from maybe Solomon, Herod was responsible for the establishment of the Jewish temple as the centre of Jewish religious life.

Yet despite this, there were hesitations about his Jewishness.

Josephus calls him a half-Jew.[57] Why? Probably because he was privately supportive of some very un-Jewish customs. He sponsored temples to pagan gods in other parts of the Roman world. His coins contained images with pagan associations. And while he built the temple in Jerusalem, he also built a theatre, hippodrome and amphitheatre.[58] Also, as we shall see, the rise of the temple was not welcomed by all Jews, some of whom felt it was symbolic of the bankrupt faith of their leaders.

Strategically, then, he was successful, but domestically his life was marred by a terrible paranoia and distrust. Despite the passionate love he felt for his wife, Mariamne, in 29 BC he had her executed because he believed her to be plotting against him. He was never the same after that. Josephus records him calling her name, wandering through the palace in search of her, absent-mindedly telling the servants to summon her.[59] The sons he had by her – Alexander and Aristobulus – never forgave him and the last decade of his life was corrupted by intrigue and lies. Despite the political and economic success of his reign, despite the fact that he was given the title 'friend of the Romans' and 'friend of Caesar', he was never short of enemies elsewhere. When a plot to assassinate him was revealed by an informer, it was the informer who was torn to pieces by the mob.[60] His network of spies and informers were everywhere. He is said to have slipped out of the palace in disguise to listen to the 'off-the-record' opinions of his subjects. And according to Josephus, the network of fortresses, starting with the Antonia overlooking Temple Mount in Jerusalem and encompassing Masada, the Herodium and the Machaerus, were designed to protect Herod not against invaders, but against an uprising of his own people.[61]

His behaviour is even described in a Jewish work called *The Testament of Moses*, written early in the first century AD: 'An insolent king will succeed them … He will slay the old and the young and he will not spare. And he will execute judgments on them, just as the Egyptians did.'[62]

His last years were particularly violent. He killed his three eldest sons – the last of them just five days before his own death. Around 7 BC he killed three hundred of his own officers, whom he accused of plotting with his sons against him: 'He also brought out three hundred of the officers that were under an accusation, as also Tero and his son, and the barber that accused them, before an assembly, and brought an accusation against them all.'[63]

Around the same time he killed the leaders of those six thousand Pharisees who had refused to take the oath of allegiance. It was not their refusal that earned his wrath, so much as their prophecy that 'God had decreed that Herod's government should cease, and his posterity should be deprived of it; but that the kingdom should come to her and Pheroras, and to their children'.[64] He also killed all those within the court who agreed – or were suspected of having agreed – with this prophecy. It was not only Magi who suffered for unpopular prophecies.

On the day of the lunar eclipse he is recorded as having executed Matthias, a former high priest. A little while later he executed the ringleaders of those who had pulled down the golden eagle over the temple and the rabbis whose incendiary teaching had inspired them. They believed that the eagle – a graven image – defiled the temple, even though it was probably on one of the outer gates, the 'royal entrance' as it were, over the walkway that led from the upper city. They also believed that Herod was too close to death to care. They were wrong.[65]

In this context the massacre of the children fits perfectly. We do not have to imagine that many children were involved. If the population of Bethlehem was around a thousand strong, then perhaps twenty boys would have been born in a two-year period. Infant mortality was high, so not all of these would have survived. This is not a large-scale massacre.[66] It is a government cull – an intervention to stop the spread of disease.

Even so, for such a cunning political manipulator, his handling of the Magi's visit and the subsequent events seems rather clumsy. Why let the Magi go and then send someone after them later? Why not send an armed guard to accompany them?

The answer may be in his illness. He was not in any state to make rational decisions. He was suicidal: at one point he had attempted to stab himself with a fruit knife. He issued orders that, even by his standards, were more egomaniacal than ever. Aware that his people would not mourn his loss, he had 'the eminent men of every village in the whole of Judea' locked up in the hippodrome at Jericho, with instructions that on his death they should be executed. This, he believed, would ensure that every family in Judea would weep – if not for Herod, then for the men they had lost. (His sister, who was charged with this task, refused to go through with it. After Herod's death the men were released.) It is like reading about the last days of a dictator, a Kim Jong-il, a Ceaușescu. Given this background, it is perfectly understandable that what appears just an irrelevance one day would be perceived as a real threat the next. One suspects that, were this story related anywhere other than in the Gospels, it would be accepted without question. It is entirely characteristic of this mad, dangerous, dying king.

The story of Jesus' birth is the story of a small village society welcoming a newborn into their midst – and paying the price. In some ways, the people of Bethlehem were the very first persecuted church; they were the first people to welcome Jesus, and the first people to be punished for it.

As it happened, that massacre was futile – because Jesus and his family had already gone.

'Flee to Egypt, and remain there until I tell you'

According to Matthew, Jesus escaped into Egypt, his father having been warned in a dream. Bethlehem is only some thirty-five or forty miles from the border and the quickest and safest route would have been across to the free city of Ashkelon and then down the coast via Gaza. Maps of the journey often have Jesus and his family travelling deep into Egypt, but there is no reason to assume they ventured that far. Since it was safe for them to visit Jerusalem forty days after the birth, the visit of the Magi and the massacre must have occurred sometime in the first few months of 4 BC. Probably, in fact, after the eclipse of the moon on 11 March 4 BC, which heralded the onset of Herod's final illness. Since Herod died in early April, the family only needed to be in Egypt for a few weeks. It's possible they were there longer, of course. But not necessary. (See table on page 38.)

So probably around seven weeks after his birth, Jesus and his family were in Egypt. The Gospel simply states that Jesus went into Egypt and returned when Herod had died. Since Herod died around the beginning of April 4 BC, a matter of weeks would

37

be enough, sheltering just across the border, out of reach. This may be a reason why Luke does not mention it. It was not, in fact, that big a deal. Jesus was not raised in Egypt. He simply went there for a short time.

Eventually, Herod died and was buried, in the Herodium, a palace-fortress about twelve kilometres south of Jerusalem. His tomb was lost for centuries until, in 2007, an archaeological team under Professor Ehud Netzer discovered an ornately decorated sarcophagus, roughly halfway up the hillside and in the precise spot given by Josephus. The body was long gone and of the tomb only fragments remain.

Joseph hears the news in

NOV
5 BC
▷ Jesus' birth.
▷ Jesus circumcised.

DEC

▲
40 days
▼

JAN
4 BC
▷ Family visit temple.

FEB

MAR
▷ 11 Mar: lunar eclipse.
▷ Visit of Magi. Family escape. Massacre in Bethlehem.
APR
▷ Death of Herod.

Herod's final illness ▲▼
Family in Egypt ▲▼

another dream and so they tentatively return across the border. And there they have a surprise: Archelaus has replaced Herod as king of Judea. Up until a few days before Herod's death, Antipas had been named king. Now the kingdom was to be shared by three of Herod's remaining sons: Archelaus, Antipas and Philip. (They were all young men: Archelaus was nineteen, Antipas seventeen and Philip only sixteen.)[67] This sudden change explains why Joseph appears surprised to find that Archelaus is king – and when we look at Archelaus's actions following the announcement, we can see why Joseph had no desire to stay in Bethlehem, in Judea.

Archelaus spent the statutory week mourning his father before ascending a golden throne at the temple. Initially he was greeted

with acclaim. Aware of his own lack of popularity, he agreed immediately to the demands of the crowd for the lightening of direct
taxation, the lowering of customs duties and the release of some
prisoners. He agreed, in fact, to whatever they wanted. Soon,
however, things began to change. A number of Jews began loudly
to mourn the men whom Herod had killed over the affair of the
golden eagle. There were demands for the deposition of the high
priest. When Archelaus sent officers to talk to the mob, they were
pelted with stones. He sent a cohort of soldiers to try to quell the
unrest, but the Jews in the temple stoned them and killed most of
them. It was Passover time and Josephus gives a vivid picture of the
bizarre atmosphere of the feast: after the cohort had been pelted
with stones and most of the men killed, the tribune barely escaped
with his life. 'Then,' writes Josephus, 'as if nothing strange had
happened, they [the mob] turned to sacrifice.'[68] Archelaus in the
end did what his family did best: he sent in more troops who killed
three thousand people and closed down the festivities. Passover was
cancelled. It was not a good start to his reign.

Imagine Joseph, then, returning to this kind of news. It is the late
spring of 4 BC, perhaps. He crosses the border and returns to Bethlehem, only to hear stories of bloodshed in the temple and arguments over the claimants to the throne. Not the time to keep this
mysterious child-king near Jerusalem. Time to make tracks again.
Time to head north, to Galilee and the obscurity of Nazareth.

But obscurity is not what they found.

Instead they found a war zone.

2. Nazareth, 4 BC – AD 28

Galilee was theirs. When they knew for sure, when they were *certain* that the old boy was dead, he acted. Lightning fast. He'd been waiting for this. Biding his time, circling like a desert lion waiting to pounce. Waiting for forty years, since the old king was governor of Galilee, since the day he executed his father.

So Judas called his men from the caves and the hills and the hidden places. They came together: men with grudges, men with ambition, men with scores to settle. And they headed for Sepphoris. This was payback. Jubilee. The payment of the debts.

A good moment, too. The Romans were dithering. Herod's sons, those beardless boy-kings, had run to Rome, to ask Augustus to make them king. Let them go, there would be no kingdom when they returned.

Sepphoris was easy. The city was soft. Full of Greeks and pagans, their skins smooth from the baths, their minds weakened by luxury. Good at collecting taxes from people who couldn't fight back, but when it came to a fight …

So they took it. Him and his men, like a proper army, marching into Sepphoris. Herod's centre in Galilee. They took the city – and with it, all those weapons. All that money.

Lots of fights now. Scores to settle, not just with the Romans, but with all those others who had the same idea. Well, let them try. This was his moment to be king. He'd beat them all. Tear them into pieces. Scare them into submission.

The Romans would come, of course they would. But he'd be ready. Him and his men.

Galilee was his. Jubilee. The payment of debts.

'He returned, having received royal power'

Rumours of Herod's death were enough to spark protests in Jerusalem; his actual, confirmed death set the kingdom ablaze.

His two sons, Archelaus and Antipas, had gone to Rome, to stand in front of Augustus and argue over the will. Archelaus wanted his father's latest will confirmed, the one made just before the old king died. Antipas wanted it overruled in favour of one made only a few months earlier, which made him sole king of Judea.[1] While they were away, haggling and arguing, revolts broke out throughout Judea.

The legate in Syria, Varus sent a legion of troops to Jerusalem, but his precautions were undermined by his subordinate, Sabinus, procurator of Syria, who tried to use these soldiers to grab Herod's fortresses and 'search for the king's money'. It was Pentecost and tens of thousands of Jews – Galileans, Idumeans, men from Jericho and the Perea – marched to the capital, not just as pilgrims this time, but furious at the cupidity and greed of Sabinus. They joined with those in Jerusalem in seizing the city, closing in on the Romans from all sides.

Hand-to-hand fighting broke out in the temple and just when it looked like the Romans might be overwhelmed, they set fire to the colonnades. The roof collapsed, and those rebels who survived the fire were slaughtered. The Romans, stupidly, took the opportunity to grab some loot, taking four hundred talents from the 'unguarded treasury of God'.[2] Furious, the Jews redoubled their efforts, besieging Sabinus in the palace.

Meanwhile the unrest had spread. There were 'ten thousand disorders in Judea', while in the country districts 'many seized the opportunity to claim the throne'.[3] In Idumea there was a revolt of two thousand of Herod's veteran troops. In the plains near Jerusalem, a former shepherd called Athrongeus, 'whose hopes were based on his physical strength and contempt of death', tried to claim the throne, aided by his four brothers.[4] He was to remain at large for several months. Others were more swiftly dispatched. In the Perea, Simon, a royal slave renowned for his glamorous looks, led a band of robbers on a tour of plunder, burning the palace at Jericho and other magnificent houses, until he was trapped and executed in a ravine by Gratus, commander of the royal infantry.

Then there was Galilee.

In 46 BC, during his rise to power, Herod had captured and killed a bandit called Hezekiah, who had been terrorising the area next to Syria. Although Josephus uses the word 'bandit', these were not simple highwaymen or robbers, but politically motivated groups of guerilla fighters. Like the Taliban in Afghanistan, or the jungle guerillas in South America, their robbery and murder had a political edge.

When Herod died, Hezekiah's son Judas saw his chance for a long-awaited revenge. He gathered a large number of men and attacked the palace at Sepphoris, the largest city in Galilee and the administrative centre of the region. Sepphoris contained the treasury for the area, as well as a store of weapons for local troops. Judas 'seized upon all the weapons that were laid up in it, and with them armed every one of those that were with him, and carried away what money was left there'. His aim, apparently, was to set himself up as the local king of Galilee.[5]

But by now the Romans were mobilising. Varus, legate of Syria, collected two legions from Antioch and marched south to the aid of the legion in Jerusalem. In retaliation for the situation in Galilee, Varus ordered an attack on the region:

> When [Varus] had now collected all his forces together, he committed part of them to his sons, and to a friend of his, and sent them upon an expedition into Galilee, which lies in the neighbourhood of Ptolemais; who made an attack upon the enemy, and put them to flight, and took Sepphoris, and made its inhabitants slaves and burnt the city.[6]

How much of Sepphoris was destroyed is unknown, but if they followed the usual Roman tactics, the devastation to the local area would have been significant. Fields destroyed, houses burned, families decimated. A wound which would never heal.

And crucifixions. We know from Josephus that in pacifying Judea, Varus brought in great numbers of prisoners. Most of these he would have exported as slaves. But 'the ringleaders were crucified – about two thousand'.[7]

Crucifixion was not used on citizens, it was reserved for the groups which Rome most wanted to keep afraid. The primary target group for this kind of death were slaves, but it was also widely used on foreign rebels. Especially, it was used on the Jews.

It is a cruel irony that for so many years the Jews have been held somehow responsible for the cross, when it was so often a punishment inflicted on them. In the days preceding the Jewish revolt, the Roman procurator Florus used crucifixion as a punishment for those who mocked him. He had a large number of Jewish citizens and members of the Jewish aristocracy picked at random, put in chains and then crucified.[8] We do not know that crucifixion was used in suppressing the revolt in Galilee, but if not, it would be the exception rather than the norm.

Whatever the case, Jesus and his family returned to a region in shock, traumatised by the aftermath of the uprisings. And Nazareth was only three miles south of Sepphoris: the very epicentre of the revolt. Jesus, of course, was a baby at the time, but he must have grown up suffused with the folk-memory of the district: tales of atrocities, stories of relatives and friends sold into slavery, and a deep distrust of their rulers and those who wanted to rule.

And, like every other ordinary Jew, he grew up in an atmosphere of fear.

We think of the Roman Empire as being 'civilised' largely because they had a highly developed legal system and they knew how to build roads. What we forget is that the Roman Empire was, above all, a military dictatorship. The emperor ruled through fear. Few statements illustrate Roman power more forcefully than the advice of Plutarch to the rulers of an occupied province – rulers like Archelaus and Antipas: 'You who hold office are a subject, ruling a state controlled by proconsuls and by the procurators of the emperor ... Do not have great pride or confidence in your crown, for you see soldiers' boots just above your head ...'[9]

If that was true for client-kings, then how much more was it true for the ordinary peasant. Any stepping out of line and the Romans would descend with crushing force. Even criticism was likely to get you into trouble:

> For once Rabbi Judah and Rabbi Jose and Rabbi Simeon were sitting, and Judah son of proselytes was sitting with them. Rabbi Judah began and said: 'How excellent are the deeds of this nation. They have instituted market places, they have instituted bridges, they have instituted baths.' Rabbi Jose was silent. Rabbi Simeon ben Yohai answered and said: 'All that they have instituted they have instituted only for their

own needs. They have instituted market places to place harlots in them; baths for their own pleasure; bridges, to collect toll.' Judah, son of proselytes went and reported their words and they were heard by the government. They said: 'Judah who exalted shall be exalted; Jose who remained silent shall be banished to Sepphoris; Simeon who reproached shall be put to death.'[10]

Simeon, reputedly, escaped death, but only by fleeing into hiding and spending the next fourteen years in a cave. Admittedly this story comes from around AD 135, in the wake of two Jewish uprisings, so Rome was not in the mood to be lenient. Nonetheless, it reflects a common understanding: anti-Roman behaviour will be punished.

This is another often-forgotten aspect of Jesus' Jewishness: he grew up with the background hum of fear. Occupied people are always afraid at some level. There is always the knowledge that those in charge can do what they like with you, and you will not be able to do anything about it. This, indeed, was the lot of the majority of Jews in the Roman Empire, who were viewed with suspicion and mistrust. In Galilee, a known area of sedition and rebellion, it would have been worse.

Fear of the Romans, fear of tax-collectors, of harvest failure, of arbitrary punishment. Fear of death. Fear that someone will step out of line and that many people will suffer for it. It was in this region, resentful, fierce, grieving for its lost, that Jesus lived and learned and played and worked. In Nazareth, where, in the words of Luke, 'The child grew and became strong' (Luke 2:40).

'A town called Nazareth'

Many Christian biographies of Jesus pay little or no attention to the years at Nazareth. They were not 'ministry', not his *real* work. But Nazareth was crucial. Before he was Jesus Christ, he was Jesus of Nazareth. Nazareth made him the man he was. It was where he was raised and educated. At Nazareth he attended synagogue, learned Hebrew, read the Torah. Nazareth gave him the images to fill his stories, the vocabulary for his later work. The problem is, of course, that the Gospels tell us very little about this time. So can we find anything at all about it? In the words of Nathanael, 'Can anything good come out of Nazareth?' (John 1:46).

First, the village itself. Nazareth was just one of these hundreds of villages, small and insignificant, perched on a ridge above the surrounding countryside. Estimates of the population vary, but it was probably not more than 400 people. According to Josephus there were 204 cities and villages in Galilee, so Nazareth was just one among many.[11] We know of only two real Galilean cities: Sepphoris and Tiberias. By far the majority of the communities were small, averaging around 300 people, occupying perhaps two to five acres of land.[12]

There was little in these villages of what we would recognise as a market economy. No shops as such. Instead, most of the Galilean population were peasant farmers; producer-consumers, to use the social-scientific term. They ate what they grew. They lived together in family groups, sharing an oven, a millstone for grinding wheat and a cistern for storing water. The village would provide a communal wine press and olive press. What you did not have, you bartered for.

Galilee had a majority of small landowners and the culture and soil allowed for a diversity of farming. Families could be self-sufficient owning a field, some sheep and goats, chickens, a donkey and perhaps a cow. They would have olive and fruit trees: figs, pomegranates. A vegetable garden for leeks, lentils, beans, peas, cucumbers, onions, garlic. Prosperity was owning your own vine.

'Are not his sisters here with us?'

The text indicates that Jesus was the eldest of at least seven children. 'Is not this the carpenter, the son of Mary and brother of James and Joses and Judas and Simon, and are not his sisters here with us?' (Mark 6:3). We have already seen that Jesus was not his real name: he was Yeshua. A similar 'Westernisation' has happened to at least one of his brothers. The character in the New Testament known as James, brother of Jesus, is actually Jacob – *Iakob* in the Greek. It is at least possible that Jesus could have been called 'Iesous' in his lifetime – by the Greek-speaking Jews he met in Jerusalem, for example (John 12:20). But it is completely impossible for anyone in the New Testament ever to have been called James. The name was not invented until 1,300 years later. Curiously, even though Jacob is a popular boy's name today, translators still insist on calling Jacob 'James': just one more way in which the Jewishness of Jesus' background is subtly forgotten.

Let's examine these brothers, though: Jacob, Joses, Judah and Simon (Mark 6:3). Good solid Jewish names: the patriarch Jacob and three of his sons. Or perhaps the latter two had a political edge, commemorating two of the Maccabean leaders who had led Israel to independence before the Romans came along. The names of Jesus' sisters have not been preserved. Later Christian tradition identified them as either Assia and Lydia, or Mary and Salome.[13] There is no evidence in the text, but the latter pairing sound more likely in the light of the list of popular names given below.[14]

Over the years, the status of these 'brothers' has been challenged – more due to dogma than anything else. Catholic theology, to support the doctrine of Mary's perpetual virginity, argues that they were his cousins; the Eastern Orthodox Church teaches that they were step-brothers, children of Joseph from a previous marriage.[15] As we've seen, there is no indication in the Gospel texts that this is Joseph's second marriage: the text assumes that this is the first time for both of them. (And if these were children from an earlier marriage, why are they not with Joseph and Mary on the trip into Bethlehem and Egypt?)

However, the Greek word for cousins, *anepsios*, is never used of James and the others, either by the Gospel writers or the early Christians. Paul speaks unequivocally of James, 'the Lord's brother' (Gal. 1:19), and then of the global 'brothers of the Lord' (1 Cor. 9:5). The word that the New Testament uses for Jesus' brothers is *adelphoi* – and at no point in the New Testament does the word *adelphoi* mean 'step-brothers'. Nor did Josephus think Jacob/James was a cousin. He considered him the brother of Jesus.

The view is further reinforced by the early church. Hegesippus, writing around AD 170, does not just call Jacob/James a brother, he goes on to

Top ten girls' names among Palestinian Jews, 330 BC – AD 200	
1	Mary/Miriam
2	Salome
3	Shelamzion
4	Martha
5=	Joanna
5=	Sapphira
7	Berenice
8=	Imma
8=	Mara
10=	Cyprus
10=	Sarah
10=	Alexandra

clarify that he was only a brother 'in the flesh'. For Hegesippus, of course, Jesus was the Son of God, so Jacob/James could not be his full brother. The idea that he might have been a cousin would have been a neat get-out for Hegesippus, but he does not go there. Tertullian (c. AD 160–220) also talks about Jesus' brothers, and since Tertullian had a high view of virginity you would have thought he would have been a fan of the perpetual virginity thing.[16]

Since Matthew specifically states that Mary did not have sex with Joseph 'until she had borne a son' (Matt. 1:25), it is reasonable to assume that, after the admittedly unusual events of Jesus' birth, they lived as a perfectly normal man and wife. Jewish culture assumed that a married couple would have children; it was an obligation, not an option.[17] The simplest explanation is that which we find in the Gospels. After Jesus was born, Mary and Joseph had other children. Jesus was the eldest of five sons born to the couple.

We do not know how many of Jesus' extended family lived in the clan dwelling in Nazareth, but there clearly was an extended family in the village. Mary's parents must have lived there, and later in life Jesus had at least one sister-in-law. In 1 Corinthians 9:5 Paul talks about those apostles who take their wives around with them on their travels and includes the brothers of the Lord in the list. Assuming that those brothers reached marriageable age before Jesus left Nazareth, their wives would have come to live in the family home.

There were aunts and uncles and cousins as well. We can find those by triangulating the different descriptions of the women standing around the cross:

▷ Mark has Mary Magdalene, and Mary the mother of James the younger and of Joses, and Salome (Mark 15:40).

▷ Matthew has Mary Magdalene, and Mary the mother of James and Joseph, and the mother of the sons of Zebedee (Matt. 27:56).

▷ John has Jesus' mother, and his mother's sister, Mary the wife of Clopas, and Mary Magdalene (John 19:25).

Some of these may be the same person, but named according to different relationships. In particular, Matthew lists 'the mother of the sons of Zebedee', whereas Mark has 'Salome'. This was probably the same person: Matthew, aware that his readers did not know who Salome was, explains her significance. But she could also be the same person whom John terms 'his mother's sister'. If this is so, it would make the apostles John and James Jesus' cousins on his mother's side. Admittedly the women referred to may be different women – all three Gospel writers say that these women were 'among' the women who were there; but this identification would make sense of the mother's request that her sons be given special precedence in heaven (Matt. 20:20–23). They were family.

Finally, there is another story which might shed light on Jesus' extended family. According to the early church historian Hegesippus, the successor to James as leader of the Jerusalem church was a man called Symeon, the son of Clopas. Eusebius, who gives us this anecdote, wrote that 'He [Symeon] was a cousin – at any rate so it is said – of the Saviour; for indeed Hegesippus relates that Clopas was Joseph's brother.'

Anecdotal, admittedly, but again it does make some sense. Having had one family member of Jesus in charge, it is natural that the early church continued the tradition. So they selected Symeon, Jesus' cousin on his father's side. Go back to the women around the cross, and we find 'Mary of Clopas', i.e. Mary, wife of Clopas (John 19:25). Put all that together, and you get Joseph's brother Clopas, his wife Mary, and their son Symeon who succeeds his cousin James to the leadership of the Jerusalem church. (We shall meet Clopas again.)

After all that, we can draw a family tree like that opposite. How many of these lived in Nazareth during Jesus' formative years? Maybe Aunt Salome, before she married and went with her husband Zebedee to Capernaum. What it does show is that Jesus grew up in a normal extended Jewish family, with all its joys, trials and tensions.

'How does this man have such learning?'

In the ancient world, formal education was rare, and literacy rates were very low. The presence of scribes in many Jewish villages attests to widespread illiteracy; the word 'school' never occurs in the Gospels and only once in the entire New Testament – and

The Family of Jesus

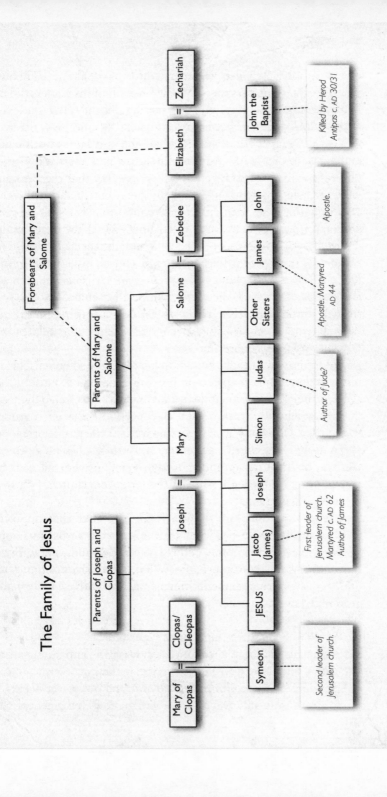

that is in Ephesus. Having said that, it is likely that Jewish boys received a better education than their contemporaries among the Gentiles. After all, theirs was a religion, if not of the book, then of the scroll. The Torah, the great written law code, was the bedrock of their faith. To be able to read and discuss this work was something to aspire to, and something to be admired in everyone who could. Josephus states that children were taught to read and learn the laws of their forebears.[18]

In everyday life, Jews spoke Aramaic. Certainly this was the language which Jesus used in his teaching and telling of stories, in his discussions with his disciples and while growing up in Nazareth. Some sayings of Jesus contain puns which only work in Aramaic. A few events preserve his actual words: '*Talitha cum*' in Mark 5:41; the *Abba* prayer; '*ephphatha*' ('be opened'), spoken to the deaf man in Mark 7:34. Even on the cross, he cried out in Aramaic. Jeremias has identified twenty-six Aramaic words spoken by Jesus and preserved in the Greek text of the Gospels, including *gehinnam*, *rabbi*, *reqa*, *mamona* (mammon) and *satana*.[19] Not to mention many Aramaic place names and personal names.

The other 'common' language was Greek. Ever since the time of Alexander the Great, Greek had been the shared language of the Mediterranean world. Greek was, like English today, the international language of commerce and trade. (The language of tourism, also: in the temple in Jerusalem there was an inscription warning Gentiles not to enter the inner courts. It was written in Greek.) It is estimated that of the 80–100,000 people living in the region of Jerusalem, 8,000–16,000 would have spoken Greek. That is about 10–15 per cent of the community.[20] But Greek would also have been useful and spoken elsewhere, particularly in districts where there was contact with the trading communities on the coast. Caesarea, the Roman capital of Judea, had as many Greeks as Jews living there.

So Jesus probably picked up some Greek later in life. After all, he lived close to Sepphoris, the biggest Hellenistic town in the region and a place where many Gentiles lived. He also visited Jerusalem, where he would have heard Greek being spoken.

According to Luke, Jesus could read Hebrew (Luke 4:16–17) but by Jesus' day Hebrew was the language of religion, of the faithful.[21] It was used in the temple liturgy and in debates among pious Jews and also, of course, in reading the Torah, the Law. 'What is the father's duty towards his son?' asks one rabbinic document, answering itself, 'He shall teach him the law.'[22] Although there were different sects and movements in the second temple period, all of them accepted the Torah as fundamental to Jewish life. The Law of Moses was the base note, the common denominator, the basic rule book for life.

Education meant to a great extent studying and discussing the Torah, the Law, the 'Books of Moses'. In the later rabbinic period, children began with the passages from Leviticus, and only moved on to Genesis later. A rabbinical saying answers the question 'Why do children begin with the book of Leviticus and not with Genesis?' by suggesting that it was because 'children are pure and the sacrifices are pure, so the pure deal with the pure'.[23] (Anyone who has had anything to do with children knows that this cannot possibly be true.)

Religion dominated life. Boys would learn how to read the books of the Torah, to recite the *shema* – the prayers before meals – and the graces for after the meals, the family and community prayers which helped them to be part of their community. To be part of the community was to be a worshipper. That was what the community did.

Boys, you will notice. No teaching for girls. Rabbi Eliezer maintained that 'there is no wisdom for a woman except at a spindle'.[24] Women had to have a basic knowledge of the Torah, since they had to deal with the clean and unclean food and with the preparations for the festivals and Sabbath – but they were there to resource the men. There were some women who through listening in synagogue and personal application gained further knowledge, but women who could *argue* Torah were very much the exception.

Education – and, indeed, childhood – ended at the age of twelve or thirteen, after which the boy was expected to take up his father's trade. Gifted children, from well-off families, might be allowed to take their studies further and go to a *bet midrash*, a rabbinical school, to sit at the feet of the teachers of the law. This is what Paul, a contemporary of Jesus, appears to have done, becoming a disciple of one of the leading rabbis, Rabbi Gamaliel.

Certainly in later life Jesus' learning earned him respect. He was called 'rabbi', 'teacher', even though it was clear that he had no formal learning. 'How does this man have such learning, when he has never been taught?' ask the Jerusalem Jews rather patronisingly (John 7:15). This hillbilly from a nondescript village in Galilee had been educated! Their surprise indicates that Jesus and his brothers were something of an exception. And for that we probably have to thank Joseph. Given what he knew of his son's origins, no doubt he had him educated to some degree. And one thing we know about Joseph is that he was a devout Jew. As well as making sure that his boy could read the Torah, as well as sending them to school, Joseph took his family to Jerusalem to celebrate Passover, each year.

And when Jesus was twelve, they lost him.

'They went up as usual for the festival'

Life in first-century Palestine was dominated by two things: farming and festivals. And the two were closely linked, because most festivals were, in fact, harvest festivals. Pentecost or Weeks celebrated the wheat harvest – the single most important crop in the ancient world, sown in late October or early November and harvested in May or June. Before that, Passover was linked to the second most important crop, barley, which grew best in the dry areas of southern Samaria and Judea. In the autumn there was the festival of Booths – Sukkoth or ingathering – the end of the agricultural year. These were the three major festivals and it was expected that pious Jews would travel up to Jerusalem for the celebrations.

> Three times a year all your males shall appear before the LORD your God at the place that he will choose: at the festival of unleavened bread, at the festival of weeks, and at the festival of booths. They shall not appear before the LORD empty-handed; all shall give as they are able, according to the blessing of the LORD your God that he has given you. (Deut. 16:16–17; also Exod. 23:14–17)

One wonders how many hard-pressed Galilean peasants could afford the time to go even once a year: it took around a week to get to Jerusalem from Galilee. But clearly many people made the journey. Although only men were obliged to go, women accompanied their families, as is the case here. Some people were exempt: the Mishnah gives a list of those who were excused attendance, including deaf-mutes, babies, women, slaves, hermaphrodites, the blind, the sick, the old and the lame. From an early age, boys were expected to accompany their fathers to the temple. Only a son who 'cannot hold his father's hand to go up from Jerusalem to the Temple mount' was considered exempt.[25]

Luke's story of the boy Jesus debating in the temple (Luke 2:41–51) is the only episode in the Gospels from Jesus' childhood. Given what happened in the episode, Joseph and his family were obviously part of a large pilgrimage group. Most travellers in those days travelled in groups, if they could. Groups offered protection and reduced the demands on the individual for planning and executing such a trip. In this case the group would have contained Jesus' extended family of course: Mary, Joseph and some of the children – but also perhaps family from other areas in Galilee. Later Jesus attended some kind of family wedding in Cana, so it is possible that members of the party joined them from there. They made these trips regularly, according to Luke. After their father died, Jesus' brothers continued their habit of going up for the festivals (John 7:10).

Pilgrims made their way to Jerusalem all year round, but at three times of the year, the city was especially overcrowded: at the great festivals of Passover, Sukkoth or Tabernacles, and the feast of Weeks or Pentecost. There were normally about 45,000 people in Jerusalem, but at these times as many as 150–200,000 pilgrims may have tried to cram into the city. Some of them would have found rooms in the city itself, but most of them would have had to sleep wherever they could: in tents or makeshift shelters, doorways, shacks.

It was vital for Jerusalem itself that people made the journey. 'No one shall come to the LORD empty-handed,' said Deuteronomy, and by Jesus' day there was a clear minimum spend. Every male had to give an offering to be burned on the altar worth at least two pieces of silver, and a peace offering worth a *maah* of silver – one sixth of a shekel and the smallest silver coin.[26] At Passover, Jews were expected to pay the temple tax, and people gave other money offerings to the temple all year round.

The Jewish Calendar

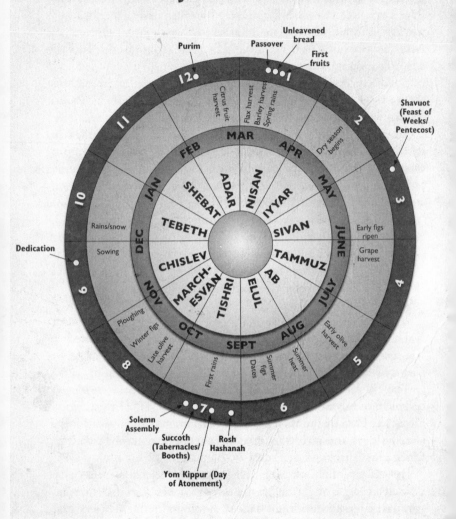

Jerusalem was a temple economy. It relied on temple tourism, on pilgrim groups coming to the city and spending their money. Herod had made Jerusalem into a five-star religious attraction: Jews came from around the empire to see the Holy City and to worship at the festivals. The account of the feast of Pentecost in Acts shows us just how far away these Jews came from: 'Parthians, Medes, Elamites, and residents of Mesopotamia, Judea and Cappadocia, Pontus and Asia, Phrygia and Pamphylia, Egypt and the parts of Libya belonging to Cyrene, and visitors from Rome, both Jews and proselytes, Cretans and Arabs' (Acts 2:9–11a).

All these pilgrims needed services and help. They needed to buy food and lodging. Perhaps a pilgrim group like Jesus' would have relatives or family in the city. Perhaps they would camp outside. Some pilgrims found accommodation in hostels attached to a synagogue. An inscription discovered in Jerusalem in 1914 reads:

> Theodotus, son of Vettenus, priest and synagogue chief, son of a synagogue chief, grandson of a synagogue chief, had the synagogue built for the reading of the law and for the teaching of the commandments, as well as the hospice and the accommodations and the water-works as lodging to those who need it from abroad, [the synagogue] whose foundations had been put down by the fathers and the elders and Simonides.[27]

This synagogue, which was a place for teaching and discussion, was also a hostel, a guest house for Jews from the Greco-Roman world who came to visit the city.

They would also need food to eat: the streets leading to the temple mount were lined with shops and stalls. There were shops along the base of the mount itself. All around the pilgrims were stall-holders and street-vendors selling food, religious trinkets, fancy glassware, jars of cheap wine, mounds of bread.[28]

For many inhabitants of Jerusalem, the festivals must have offered a chance of earning some income. Elsewhere I have drawn comparison with the city of Mecca, home to the Hajj, the largest annual pilgrimage in the world. The Hajj is an ancient festival, a survivor from the days of the great festivals. For centuries, the inhabitants of Mecca have made the bulk of their income from providing places to stay and food to eat for these millions of pilgrims. As one traveller noted in 1888, nearly all the inhabitants of

Mecca were engaged in the 'business' of Hajj:

> Mecca has no hotels ... every Meccan becomes an hotel keeper
> whether he has a whole house, or only one storey or half a storey
> ... all Meccans therefore are interested in getting on good terms
> with several sheikhs [i.e. *mutawwifin* – local guides] as on the other
> hand the latter set great store on extensive connections among the
> public.[29]

Jerusalem has no port, no river, no agricultural land nearby.
These harvest festivals were a harvest for Jerusalem as well. Religion was the only crop which Jerusalem grew. As we shall see,
Jesus' attitude to the money-making operation of the temple was
to be the cause of considerable conflict later on.

He and his family went to the temple mount. This vast space
was different from the rest of Jerusalem. It was spacious – the
only real public open space in the city. And unlike the rest of the
city – especially the crowded and squallid lower city, the temple
plaza was kept in a state of exceptional purity and cleanliness.[30]
For this reason, the Court of Gentiles, which was open to all,
foreigners included, was a place where people came to meet, to
discuss, to talk, even to do business. This is certainly the location
where, in later years, Jesus taught and mocked and argued and
told stories. And it was probably where, aged twelve, he sat down
to ask questions.

The precociously gifted child is a staple of ancient biography.
Josephus described how, as a boy of fourteen, he won 'universal
applause for my love of letters'. But in another way this is not really a childhood story at all. Although we would regard a twelve-
year-old as a child, in first-century Judea a boy of twelve could be
considered a man.[31] Certainly at thirteen he was expected to take
up adult responsibilities. At that point he could be called as a witness, he could marry, and serve as a leader in prayer. At twelve he
was in transition. Some rabbis considered twelve to be the age at
which vows were binding and at which a boy could be expected to
fast for a whole day. (Parental punishment was also more severe at
twelve.)[32] This, then, is a boy on the cusp of being a man. Grown
up but not yet an adult. This is an in-between story, a coming-of-
age story, a threshold story. He is on the edge here, standing in the
doorway between childhood and adulthood, and standing between

two fathers. And this boy-man demonstrates wisdom, understanding, a sharp wit and a high degree of independence. Also, it has to be said, a certain amount of insubordination.

Passover was an eight-day celebration. Mary and Joseph probably stayed there for the duration, before packing up and heading back north with their caravan of travellers from Galilee. It is only at the end of the day, when they come to bivouac for the night, that they realise the boy is not with them; not, as they assumed, travelling in some other part of the caravan. The boy is missing. One can picture Mary and Joseph returning, panic-stricken, along the route. Retracing their steps. When they eventually find him in the temple courts, asking and answering questions, apparently ignorant of all their anxiety, they exhibit all the expected traits of hurt, bewildered parents: 'Why have you treated us like this? Don't you know we've been worried sick about you?'

Jesus' response has often been presented as 'correcting' them, putting them in their place: 'Why were you searching for me? Did you not know that I must be in my Father's house?' (Luke 2:49). Jesus is not contrite, not even respectful. But as so often with Jesus' sayings, everything depends on the tone. It can easily be read as more innocent than that. He is genuinely surprised that they were worried and concerned: isn't it obvious – given what they know about him – where he would be? It's a sign of things to come. Often, in the future, Jesus' actions – obvious to him – will be painfully bewildering to his family.

Later, fictionalised portraits have Jesus taking the lead role. *The Infancy Story of Thomas* has Jesus silencing the teachers with his brilliance, while in the *Arabic Gospel of Infancy* he proceeds to teach them medicine and astronomy![33] Like those rennaissance pictures of the infant Jesus, in which he is not a child, but a yoda-like little old man, Jesus is assumed to be fully formed, the adult sage in the child's body. But there is nothing inherently supernatural about this story and no indication that Jesus is actually teaching the scholars. What he is doing is asking them questions and answering the counter-questions they put to him.[34] This is not to say it is not extraordinary. The event introduces one of Luke's favourite words, *existanai*, a verb which he uses twice as much as the rest of the New Testament writers put together. In

57

classical Greek it meant 'out of one's mind', but Luke uses it more to indicate amazement and astonishment: you might say it was all a bit mind-blowing.[35]

The story is certainly evidence of Jesus' wisdom, but it is also evidence that he was hungry to learn. For a boy from Nazareth – Nowheresville, Galilee – the atmosphere of Jerusalem must have been a heady brew. There is a sense of excitement, of eyes being opened. This is what Torah discussion could be like. It's the kind of teaching he had back in Nazareth, but on steroids. And here no one puts him in his place, because there is no place to put him in. He is free from all the background. Here he is not Yeshu, the boy with the dodgy background, the builder's son. For the first time, on the eve of manhood, he is listened to because of what he has to say, rather than who he is, or is not.

It is surely this sense of excitement that caused him to disobey his parents. And he was disobeying. He must have known what he was doing. Three days' separation from his parents is not like nipping down the road to the shops when you are expected to stay in. Every evening of those three days, the temple closed down. Where did he go? What did he do?

There is a sense here of breakage, of Jesus slipping the bonds of the parental home and looking for a new role in life. This, in fact, is the real point of the story. Luke closes his account with Jesus returning to Nazareth and choosing the path of obeying his parents: 'Then he went down with them and came to Nazareth, and was obedient to them. His mother treasured all these things in her heart' (Luke 2:51). The point is not the insubordination to his parents, but the subordination of his real desire. That is what gives this story its strange intensity. It is a sacrifice story.

He could have had a future in Jerusalem, surely. A noted scholar, debating and discussing with the rabbis and the sages. But instead he opts for obedience, for submission. He returns with his parents to Nazareth. To spend the next fifteen years of his life on a building site.

'Isn't this the carpenter?'

And Jesus increased in wisdom and in years, and in divine and human favour (Luke 2:52)

He may have increased in wisdom, but in our terms he didn't increase much in height. The usual Hollywood image of Jesus as a six-foot-tall willowy blond hippy is completely wrong. From an analysis of skeletal remains, it has been estimated that the normal height for a man of Jesus' time was between 5 feet 1 inch and 5 feet 4 inches.[36] If Jesus was representative of the people of his time, he would have been not far over five feet tall, with dark skin, short-cropped black hair and deep brown eyes. Like the normal peasant workers of the time he would have worn a tunic and an outer cloak, which doubled up as his bedding.[37]

He followed his father into the family trade. Relatives usually worked together. Jesus probably worked alongside his father and brothers in the workshop, just as the 'fishermen' disciples are depicted as working alongside their brothers and fathers. The family was the most powerful defining force in ancient society. Broadly speaking, your family set the default values for your life. Your kin affected what job you did, who you married (and where you lived after marriage, if you were female), what network of friends you had, who your patrons were. It also, to a huge extent, defined your religion and your politics.[38]

The word the Gospels use for the family trade is *tekton* (Mark 6:3). Despite the traditional translation as 'carpenter', *tekton* was actually the Greek word for a general builder, a construction worker, with a wide range of skills, including stonemasonry and metalwork.[39] Wood was a scarce commodity in Israel generally, but especially so in the parts of Galilee where Jesus lived; that is why people built houses out of stone, or simply dug caves into the sides of hills. Of course he worked in wood: doors, tables, chairs, small pieces of furniture. (A later writer, Justin Martyr, claimed that Jesus made ploughs and yokes. Probably true. Someone had to make such things, after all.) The vocabulary of the workshop is found in his teaching: green wood and seasoned wood, of workmen concerned about the speck of sawdust in someone else's eye when there is a huge great beam of wood in theirs. But he also worked in other materials. A *tekton* had to be able to turn his hands to a number of different crafts, including stonemasonry and basic metalwork.[40]

Joseph & Sons, Builders and Carpenters: active not only in

Nazareth but also, probably, in the surrounding area. If it was sometimes hard in a small village like Nazareth to find regular work, they could always go just over the hill to Sepphoris. Because there, Herod Antipas was creating a fine new city.

The Roman emperor Augustus had ratified that controversial final will of Herod. Archelaus was given the title Ethnarch and allotted Idumea, Judea and Samaria; Philip got Trachonitis and Batea; Antipas was called Tetrarch – literally 'ruler of one quarter of a kingdom' – and given the Perea and Galilee.

Antipas was a sophisticated Roman client-ruler. Raised and educated in Rome, once he gained possession of Galilee, he decided that what it needed was modern, cosmopolitan cities. He started with Sepphoris and made it, according to Josephus, 'the ornament of Galilee'.[41] It was Herod Antipas's place of residence in Galilee from around 2 BC up to the point where he started work on Tiberias some twenty years later.[42]

Did Jesus and his family work on the building sites of Sepphoris? It has been the subject of frequent speculation. And Jesus' stories contain references to building – more, indeed, than to woodworking – and big buildings at that. Houses with foundations. Cornerstones. People underestimating the cost of building a tower. There is, of course, no proof – the city is not mentioned in the New Testament at all. But it seems hard to believe he never went near the place: a rider on horseback could have done the journey in fifteen minutes, and for Jesus it would have been less than an hour's walk.[43] Although there was no direct route between the village and the city, the main road to the city went past Nazareth to the east, through the nearby – and much larger – village of Japha.[44]

It is reasonable to imagine Jesus and his father making trips to a city where there was labour needed and money to be earned. There was plenty of work to be done. Herod built an elaborate water supply, along Roman lines.[45] One of the most important building projects in Sepphoris was the theatre, built to contain more than five thousand people. Archaeologists argue about whether the theatre was built in the late first century, or during the time of Jesus, but there are a number of reasons for thinking that a theatre would have been among Antipas's constructions. His father, we know, was a great theatre-builder.[46] There was a

A reconstruction of a first-century *tekton's* workshop in Nazareth.

theatre at Caesarea Maritime, where the Roman administration was based. There was one in Jericho and even one in Jerusalem, built by Herod in 28 BC to house games held in celebration of Octavius's victory over Antony and Cleopatra. There were theatres in Sebaste/Samaria, in Sidon, and in the cities of the Decapolis, the ten Greek cities east of Galilee.

At the very least, Jesus must have observed these building operations. Interestingly, images from theatres can be found in his stories and sayings as well. He calls people 'hypocrites' – the word occurs some seventeen times in the Gospels and it comes from the Greek word *hypokrites*, meaning 'actor' (e.g. Matt. 6:2, 5, 16). Actors on the Greek stage frequently performed in large masks, designed to reflect the kind of characters they were playing. Behind the masks, of course, was the ordinary person, playing a role. Jesus took this concept and applied it to the religious leaders of the day, all dressed up in their religious costume and wearing their 'masks' of piety. Also, when he had to talk to a huge number of people on the shores of Lake Galilee, he turned a boat into a stage, and a hillside into an amphitheatre. He understood the technology of building and theatres. He understood how the things worked.

What did the people of Galilee think of these cities? The people in the cities were not like them. Sepphoris had at least some of the features of a Roman-Hellenistic city, with its theatre, its colonnaded streets, and probably bathhouses and suchlike.[47] There were Greek-speaking Jews and Gentiles there: Greek was the administrative language and Sepphoris was the administrative hub. Antipas' administration was largely Gentile. Hellenisers, modernisers, their names in Josephus are in Latin – Justus son of Pistus, Compsus son of Compsus, and Cripsus.[48] Antipas and his followers – the Herodians – were an urban elite in the middle of a rural Galilee. Around AD 20, when Jesus was twenty-three, Antipas began the construction of a sister city named Tiberias, after the new Roman emperor, with whom Antipas had a close friendship.[49]

Both Sepphoris and Tiberias were Greek-style cities in the midst of a Jewish Galilee. Rome-lite. 'I can't believe it's not Caesarea.' The bling of Roman culture must have been a bit glaring, amidst the homespun clothing of rural Galilee. The inhabitants of the ancient Roman cities trusted in those cities to provide them with security, law enforcement and jurisprudence, entertainment, hygiene and places of worship. People in rural Galilee took, perhaps, a more jaundiced view of things. What justice you received in the courts of the Roman Empire depended on your social status, wealth and usefulness to the state. Villages used their own synagogue-based courts to decide local disputes. In the 'higher courts' a peasant had little chance of seeing justice.

That the Galilean villagers were antagonistic towards Sepphoris and the urban elite can be seen by their actions during the great revolt of 66–70. Sepphoris took a pro-Roman stance and refused to get involved. Early in the revolt, rebels from Galilee pillaged the city. In a later attack many inhabitants fled to the fortress in an attempt to avoid slaughter. They eventually employed the services of a band of mercenaries to protect themselves.

Throughout Roman Palestine there was a gulf between town and countryside: the towns consumed, the countryside produced. The urban world had, to varying degrees, Greek culture; the cities had their names rooted in Greek and Latin: Sebaste, Caesarea,

Junias, Tiberias, Paneas, Apollonia, Neapolis. They were places with their foundations rooted in the cult of emperor worship and the triumphalism of the Roman Empire. They were, in the words of one scholar, 'in your face' cities: built in an overtly 'foreign' style with the tax revenue from the peasants of the region, and appointed lavishly for the elite.

The fact that Jesus was a *tekton*, a builder, would not have been seen at odds with his later role as teacher and 'rabbi'. The rabbis and sages of the time were not academic theologians – it was not until after Jesus' time that the term 'rabbi' became attached to any formalised academic training. Indeed, it was expected that rabbis would also have a trade and that Torah learning did not happen on its own: 'Rabban Gamaliel, son of R. Judah the Patriarch, says, "Fitting is learning in Torah along with a craft, for the labour put into the two of them makes one forget sin. And all learning of Torah which is not joined with labour is destined to be null and cause sin."'[50]

Labour gave them independence and some degree of freedom. Shemaiah, a scribe from the generation before Jesus, said, 'Love labour and hate mastery and seek not acquaintance with the ruling power.' Or, in Neusner's pithy, pointed translation: '(1) Love work. (2) Hate authority. (3) Don't get friendly with the government.'[51]

'Do not worry about tomorrow'

The hallmark of a peasant existence has been characterised as 'political powerlessness and straitened economic circumstances'.[52] Peasants in Roman Palestine laboured under a heavy tax burden. How heavy is a matter of some argument, but historians reckon that anything between 30 and 60 per cent of their production was claimed in taxes, not only taxes to the Romans, but also the tithes to the temple, which Jews saw as an obligation to God.[53]

Josephus records the annual revenues of the different parts of Palestine. Antipas's annual revenue from Galilee was 200 talents, equivalent to 1.2 million denarii.[54] Archelaus, initially in charge of Idumea, Judea and Samaria, grossed three times as much, at 600 talents. Taxes were often paid in kind, however, rather than in money. You might have to pay in figs, wine, olive oil, or grain. Or you might have to work for the tetrarch, on one of his many building projects.

Thus any peasant family – and Joseph and Mary were not much different – started each year with three main priorities:

▷ to grow enough food to feed the family, the animals and provide seed for next year's crop;

▷ to grow surplus food to barter for other services such as metal objects, pottery and, maybe, the services of a *tekton*;

▷ to grow more surplus to pay your tithes and taxes.

The taxation system was designed almost exclusively for the benefit of the elite. To put it bluntly, wealth flowed upwards – to the ruling families, and then to the occupying power. Throughout the Roman Empire, the wealth and power were in the hands of an aristocratic elite – perhaps no more than 2–5 per cent of the population – ruling huge areas of territory.[55] Although client-kings such as Antipas and Philip were responsible for maintaining infrastructure such as roads, aqueducts and harbours, the dominating factor was what benefited the ruling class, not what was for the good of the peasants. To be fair, not all the income went to Antipas. He would have to pass on a significant amount to the Romans in tribute. The tribute might be in the form of an annual payment, or it might come in the form of gifts to honour their imperial patron, such as a temple or a gift of money to endow a favourite city of the emperor.[56]

Whoever ended up with it, this was taxation entirely without any form of representation. Peasants had no say in their government, and no influence over the level of taxation. Between one third and one quarter of the peasant harvest went in the form of land tax payable to the Romans or to the Herodian kings. In hard years – years of famine – the tax burden might be relaxed, but for the most part it was onerous. In the face of this powerlessness, all peasants developed alternative strategies: lying, deceit, hiding or finding someone lower down the scale to exploit. And, occasionally, armed rebellion.

That covers the money for Antipas. But for the Jewish peasant in Galilee, there was the temple as well. Every peasant was supposed to pay a tithe for the upkeep of the temple in Jerusalem. According to the later rabbinic tradition these tithes were:

▷ a tenth of the harvest for the priests;
▷ a tenth of the remainder for the Levites;
▷ a tenth of what remained after that for a second tithe. This was payable in the first, second, fourth and fifth year, with a 'poor man's tithe' in the third and sixth year of the Sabbath cycle.

In addition, if you had enough food to be worth transporting over roads and bridges to take to the city, you would be hit by tolls and border tariffs.[57] If we look at the diagram below, we can see that the peasant might be left with only 39–48 per cent of their harvest. All the rest went in taxes.

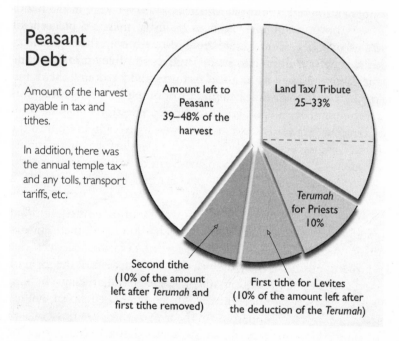

Peasant Debt

Amount of the harvest payable in tax and tithes.

In addition, there was the annual temple tax and any tolls, transport tariffs, etc.

Amount left to Peasant 39–48% of the harvest

Land Tax/ Tribute 25–33%

Terumah for Priests 10%

Second tithe (10% of the amount left after *Terumah* and first tithe removed)

First tithe for Levites (10% of the amount left after the deduction of the *Terumah*)

The effects of this were manifold. There was no real incentive to improve efficiency or try different ways of doing things. Why improve the yield if any surplus in time, produce or money was just grabbed by the aristocracy? Rabbi Gamaliel is reputed to have said, 'This empire gnaws at our substance through four things: its tolls, its bath buildings, its theatres and its taxes in kind.'[58] So there was resentment – of the Romans certainly, but also of the temple, which took its own slice of the cake.

Then there was debt. One bad harvest and you could be tipped over the edge. To make up the shortfall you would have to borrow, and then hope for a bumper harvest the next year to pay back what you owed. If that did not happen... The result for many families must have been a spiralling descent into poverty. Indeed, as we shall see, the issue of debt provides the background to many of Jesus' parables.

Above all there was worry, a constant gnawing anxiety. Worry about whether the rains would come in the wet season, or whether the hot sirocco wind would kill the crop. Worry about what you would eat. Worry about the future.

It is obvious, in this light, why Jesus' message focused so strongly on liberation, on freedom. Not freedom from Rome, as such: armed rebellion just led to another set of rulers taking control. What he grew up to proclaim was a much deeper freedom. Freedom from the whole inhumane, oppressive structure.

Freedom from money. Freedom from possessions.

Freedom from fear.

3. Wilderness, AD 28–30

Even in autumn it was hot. Shimmering, unearthly. A barren, hostile landscape, devoid of life, save only for the River Jordan, sinuous, serpentine, coiling through the rocky terrain, heading inexorably down to expire in the great Salt Sea.

As they neared their destination, the noise levels increased. Crowds were gathering. As if for a festival. But there was no temple here, save the landscape that God had made. No ritual baths, except the muddy river. No priests or Levites to make the sacrifices.

Well, one. One priest. Sort of. Dressed in a camel-hair robe, like the desert dwellers. Thick leather belt. Rough clothes. People said he was Elijah returned in his fiery chariot. The language was fiery enough: challenging people to change their lives. Telling them how their ways must be mended. And talking, in dark, apocalyptic tones, of the one who was soon to come. The last prophet, on his final mission.

He stood there, waist-deep in the Jordan, the reeds which fringed the banks trampled down by those who went to have him wash them. They splashed their way towards him. Jumped feet first into a river of repentance, drank deeply of a forgiveness they thought they could never taste. It was ritual purification, for the incontrovertibly impure.

It was autumn AD 28. And the Baptiser was at work.

'More than a prophet'

Luke is specific about the date:

> In the fifteenth year of the reign of Emperor Tiberius, when Pontius Pilate was governor of Judea, and Herod was ruler of Galilee, and his brother Philip ruler of the region of Ituraea and Trachonitis, and Lysanias ruler of Abilene, during the high-priesthood of Annas and Caiaphas, the word of God came to John son of Zechariah in the wilderness. (Luke 3:1–3)

It is the first precise time marker for the events of the Gospels. Tiberius succeeded Augustus as emperor on 19 August AD 14. If we date the regnal years from the death of Augustus, then the fifteenth year of Tiberius' reign would start on 19 August AD 28 and end on 18 August AD 29.[1]

This also fits in with the others Luke mentions in his list:

▷ Pilate was procurator of Judea from AD 26 to 36.

▷ Herod Antipas reigned in Galilee from 4 BC to AD 39.

▷ Philip was tetrarch of these northern Transjordanian territories from 4 BC to AD 34.

▷ Annas was high priest from AD 6 to 15 and his son-in-law Caiaphas from AD 18 to 36.

The only mystery here is Lysanias of Abilene, since little is known about him. Abilene was west of Damascus and an earlier Lysanias ruled the area before 36 BC. But this later model is only known from odd references in Josephus and from an inscription found at Abila which cannot be earlier than the reign of Tiberius.[2]

The Gospels describe the area of John's operation: 'the wilderness ... all the region around the Jordan' (Luke 3:2–3; Matt. 3:1). The term 'wilderness', as used in the Bible, covers a wide-ranging area, but in relation to John the Baptist the Gospels imply the northern end, 'all the region around the Jordan' where the river wound down to the Dead Sea.[3]

'He was in the wilderness', writes Luke, 'until the day he appeared publicly to Israel' (Luke 1:80). This was his home. His parents lived in a town in the hill country of Judea. The wilderness was always on his doorstep.

The wilderness held a strong symbolism for Jews. It was a place of temptation and threat. It was unsettling, unnerving, spiritually wild; it was where weird things happened. The wilderness demon Azazel lived there (Lev. 16:8–10). Demonic seducers haunted the empty places (4 Macc. 18:8).

It was a place of physical danger as well. There were bandits and rebels hiding out in the ravines. Revolutionary, apocalyptic groups habitually gathered there. In Paul's time an Egyptian leader led four thousand assassins into the wilderness (Acts 21:38).[4] Fake Messiahs and apocalyptic prophets would gather their followers in the wilderness, luring them there with promises of deliverance. Later Jesus was to warn against such people: 'If they say to you, "Look! He is in the wilderness", do not go out' (Matt. 24:26).

The wilderness was linked with the return of the Messiah. Isaiah predicted that 'the LORD will comfort Zion; he will comfort all her waste places, and will make her wilderness like Eden, her desert like the garden of the LORD' (Isa. 51:3; see also Isa. 35:6–7; 41:18–20). Rocky pathways would be made smooth and straight, the ground made level. 'In the wilderness prepare the way of the LORD, make straight in the desert a highway for our God' (Isa. 40:3). The Messiah would be on his way.

Other splinter groups took inspiration from these passages of Scripture. The Essene community at Qumran applied Isaiah's words to themselves: 'They are to be segregated from within the dwelling of the men of sin to walk to the desert in order to open there His path. As it is written "In the desert prepare the way of [YHWH] straighten in the steppe a roadway for our God."'[5] Indeed, since the discovery of the Dead Sea Scrolls in 1947, the possibility of relationship between John the Baptist and the wilderness-based Qumran community has been the subject of heated discussion. There are problems, however, not least the fact that no one can be entirely sure who the owners of the Dead Sea Scrolls actually were, or, indeed, whether those who hid the scrolls were in fact part of the nearby community at Qumran Khirbet.[6] The general consensus is that the Qumran community were Essenes. An external reference – a text believed to have originated with Dio Chrysostom (c. AD 40–112) – states that the Essenes lived by the Dead Sea.

Was John a member of their community? After all, they were both in the Judean wilderness; they both advocated a separation from the Jerusalem temple; they both went very big on ritual immersion.[7] But these similarities do not make John a card-carrying Essene. All they show is that there were other people with similar outlooks, drawn into the desert to seek purity and holiness, expecting the imminent arrival of the kingdom of God, and saying rude things about those in charge in Jerusalem.

So, it was a wild place. A place of messianic expectation. A richly symbolic place. But not inaccessible. John's Gospel supplies us with two locations where John the Baptist is encountered: Bethany beyond the Jordan (John 1:28; 10:40) and Aenon near Salim (John 3:23). As we shall see, arguments rage about where these were, but neither were far from 'civilisation'. Both were near important highways. John the Baptist was not a solitary monk-like hermit, eking out an existence in a cave or cell. He operated in places where it was easy for people to come and see him, to listen to him. He *wanted* people to come.

And come they did. From Jerusalem, from Galilee, from Judea, all the region along the Jordan, hundreds; thousands, perhaps, came to see him (Matt. 3:5–6). What did they see? Well, talking of symbolism, John's clothing was a dead giveaway: 'Now John was clothed with camel's hair, with a leather belt around his waist, and he ate locusts and wild honey' (Mark 1:6).

The echoes of Elijah are unmistakable. Elijah is described as a 'hairy man, with a leather belt around his waist' (2 Kgs 1:8). Elijah was a man of the wilderness. According to the Hebrew Scriptures, he had been carried off to heaven in a fiery chariot: he had never really died, and therefore was expected to return some day. John sounded like Elijah, he looked like Elijah; maybe he actually was Elijah.

John, however, denied the exact identification. But, like Elijah, he was a rigorously uncompromising critic of power, particularly of royalty. 'What did you go out into the wilderness to look at?' asked Jesus, 'A reed shaken by the wind? ... Someone dressed in soft robes? Look, those who wear soft robes are in royal palaces. What then did you go out to see? A prophet? Yes, I tell you, and more than a prophet' (Matt. 11:8–9).

The reeds refer to the Jordan, fringed as it was with the tall reeds. But they also refer to someone else: Herod Antipas, whose coins bore the image of reeds and whose clothing was definitely the soft robes of royalty.[8] It is the first-century equivalent of a t-shirt slogan. Everyone knew that royalty did not wear camel hair. Indeed, the shame of such clothing lay behind an event at the court of Herod I. Josephus talks about a time when the sons of Herod's wife Mariamne protest against the fact that Herod gave away their mother's finest robes to his later wives. They threaten to replace these royal robes with haircloth.[9]

John is dressed to oppose. And opposition is the key to understanding the Baptist – because the really interesting thing about John is not so much what he was, but what he was not.

He was not a priest. And he should have been.

'He was serving as priest before God'

John's father, Zechariah, was a priest and his mother came from the priestly tribe of Aaron (Luke 1:5). John, by rights, should have followed in his father's footsteps. But he turned his back on his family tradition and went, not to the temple, but to the wilderness; not to serve the elite of Jerusalem, but to the people of the Perea and Judea and even Samaria; he was a priest not to temple pilgrims, but to tax-collectors and prostitutes. John was a significant enough figure to merit a reference in Josephus:

> John, that was called the Baptist … was a good man, and commanded the Jews to exercise virtue, both as to righteousness towards one another, and piety towards God, and so to come to baptism; for that the washing [with water] would be acceptable to him, if they made use of it, not in order to the putting away [or the remission] of some sins [only], but for the purification of the body; supposing still that the soul was thoroughly purified beforehand by righteousness … [many] others came in crowds about him, for they were greatly moved [or pleased] by hearing his words.[10]

Baptism is John's USP, his most distinctive practice. John's job description is given in two forms in the New Testament: 'the baptist' and 'the baptiser'. Scholars think that the latter was the more historical form. The fact that the nickname for him stuck shows how crucial an element it was of his overall practice.

The first century saw an increasing emphasis on purity among Jews in Judea. As one rabbi wrote, 'Purity broke out among Israel.'[11] One of the key ways in which Jews demonstrated this purity was through ritual bathing. Jerusalem was full of *miqvaot*, ritual baths in which worshippers were supposed to immerse themselves before coming to sacrifice or for a festival. They are found in the Herodian palace of Masada.[12] The Qumran complex also contains numerous stepped bathing pools and the community endorsed total immersion: 'No man should bathe in water which is dirty or which is less than the amount which covers a man.'[13]

The Essenes, though, believed that the penitent sinner had to deal first with his own sin, before going into the water.[14] Repentance and righteous living purify the soul: the water only cleanses the outside. In John's washing, too, it was the repentance which made you clean; the 'soul was thoroughly purified beforehand by righteousness'. What the washing did was demonstrate the seriousness of purpose. John was offering people a form of ritual purification, but one which started with the inside. What really distinguished John from other people promoting ritual bathing was the place where he was doing it and the people to whom it was offered.

To the Qumran community, those outside the community were considered impure.[15] But John offered purity to anyone. The people who came to John included tax-collectors, soldiers and prostitutes – people excluded from the temple worship (Matt. 21:32; Luke 3:12–14). John was, if you like, an anti-priest. A high priest in camel hair, waist deep in the Jordan *miqvaot*. His actions are priestly actions: ritual cleansing, fasting and prayer (Luke 5:33; 11:1). But he did them in the wrong place and he offered them to impure people.

Of the crowds which went to receive baptism at John's hands, three social groups are mentioned specifically: tax-collectors, soldiers and prostitutes.

Prostitutes – well, their impurity goes without saying. But tax-collectors were just as bad. In the Mishnah it says, 'If a tax-gatherer enter a house, [all that is within] the house becomes unclean.' Tax-collectors were cheats, frauds, *collaborators*. The local face of occupation.

Soldiers as well – now that is interesting. Because many of them would have been Gentiles. Herod's army had been composed of both Jews and non-Jews, but the elite troops – those trusted as his bodyguards – appear to have been Gentiles, drawn from the region around Sebaste and Caesarea. During Herod's reign, however, Jews were granted exemption from military service in the Roman army. This was partly a reward for Herod's loyalty, and partly a recognition that their strict observance of the Sabbath made them pretty useless if you wanted to fight any time on a Saturday. It follows, then, that the army became predominantly Gentile. In Herod's funeral cortège, for example, the procession was led by his Gentile elite corps, then Thracians, Germans and Gauls, and then the rest of the army.[16] When the Romans took direct control of Judea, and Samaria, they recruited troops from Sebaste and Caesarea: Samaritans and Greeks – both, by their very nature, impure.

So the three types of people specifically mentioned as being baptised by John were viewed by the majority of their fellow Jews as being outcasts, collaborators. John's baptism offered an ecstatic experience of hope for those who believed that they were permanently excluded.

Which is not to say that he did not make demands of them. Luke lists some specifics about John's preaching: he told tax-collectors not to take more than they were owed, and he instructed the soldiers not to 'extort money from anyone by threats or false accusation, and be satisfied with your wages' (Luke 3:13–14).

Tax-collectors habitually added whatever they liked to the amount they charged – that was how they made their profit. As for the soldiers, John was asking them to change the main way that they made ends meet. No soldier earned a great deal in the Roman army; extortion and bribery were one of the ways in which you made it work. John demands more: not even a request for a raise. This might have had serious consequences for a squaddie asked by his commander to grab some money from the local victims.

John's activities were in direct opposition to the temple and its ideals of purity and impurity. In the wilderness, in the valley, he was offering a radical alternative to the temple, high on its hill in Jerusalem. John's message, then, is hardline. Anti-establishment. Everything that John said, everything he was, was a calculated challenge to the leadership in Jerusalem. He was not *hiding* in the wilderness. He was commenting. Criticising.

He was offering people a new start. There was one other time when ritual immersion was used, and that was in the conversion process, when a Gentile became a Jew. For proselytes – Gentiles who had decided to embrace Judaism – their immersion in a *miqvaot* marked a clear line between the Gentile past and the Jewish future. It was, in the words of Craig Keener, 'Judaism's most widespread once-for-all immersion ritual'.[17] For the Gentiles who immersed themselves in the Jordan there must have been the sense of joining a new faith, a new community. But what about the Jews who accepted his message? Was he really telling *them* to 'convert'? To become properly, *intentionally* Jewish?

'You brood of vipers'

To the orthodox official Jews from the temple, John's behaviour must have appeared outrageous. And when representatives of Jewish orthodoxy did come out of the city to see what was going on, he let them have it between the eyes:

> But when he saw many Pharisees and Sadducees coming for baptism, he said to them, 'You brood of vipers! Who warned you to flee from the wrath to come? Bear fruit worthy of repentance. Do not presume to say to yourselves, "We have Abraham as our ancestor"; for I tell you, God is able from these stones to raise up children to Abraham. Even now the axe is lying at the root of the trees; every tree therefore that does not bear good fruit is cut down and thrown into the fire.' (Matt. 3:7–10)[18]

This is Grievous Bodily Preaching. Why did John feel the need to attack the temple establishment? Why did he set himself up in opposition? By the time John was speaking, the temple apparatus had become inextricably bound up with the exercise and pursuit of power. As we have seen, the appointment of the high priest was political, exercised first by Herod and then by his son Archelaus.

Archelaus had proved to be a disaster as a ruler. He had his father's brutality, but none of his cunning. When he and Antipas had gone to Rome to argue over who should govern, they had been followed by a Jewish delegation who issued a long catalogue of the crimes of Herod I, argued that Archelaus was merely more of the same and pleaded for their freedom:

> Now, the main thing they desired was this: That they might be delivered from kingly and the like forms of government, and might be added to Syria, and be put under the authority of such presidents

[i.e. Roman governors, prefects, etc.] of theirs as should be sent to them; for that it would thereby be made evident, whether they be really a seditious people, and generally fond of innovations, or whether they would live in an orderly manner, if they might have governors of any sort of moderation set over them.[19]

In the end Augustus confirmed Archelaus as ethnarch, on condition that he 'governed his part virtuously'. But the Jewish delegation's prophecy proved correct. On his return, Archelaus immediately replaced the high priest with one of his own choosing. He rebuilt the palace at Jericho, diverting half the water supply from the village nearby to water his gardens. He broke Jewish law by marrying his brother's wife. And he 'behaved savagely not only towards the Jews but also towards the Samaritans'.[20]

After ten years the citizens had had enough. In AD 6 another delegation went to Rome, this time made up, according to Josephus, of the 'principal men of Judea and Samaria'. Clearly the Jews and Samaritans had overcome their mutual hatred to defeat a common enemy. Archelaus was summoned to Rome, his wealth was confiscated and he was banished to Vienne in Gaul.

After that, the Romans took direct charge. Samaria, Idumea and Judea became the province of Judea and the Romans installed a prefect to govern it. The prefect, however, had no intention of living in Jerusalem: he made Caesarea his capital and delegated authority to the next layer down in the imperial organisational chart: to the high priest and the aristocratic families of Jerusalem. Under Roman rule, the high priest became a direct Roman appointment. The Romans had a policy of rotating the position among three or four families. And they were not appointed in order to run services in the temple, in which the Romans had little or no interest. They were appointed to collect taxes and maintain law and order. The high priest and his deputies were Roman retainers, reliant on the prefect for their position.

Far from being respected, most of the evidence shows that the official leaders of the Jewish people at the time of Jesus were almost universally hated.[21] The detestable Herodian dynasty had simply been replaced by its lackeys. Even centuries later the fear and hatred of these families was still remembered. In the Babylonian Talmud, Abba Saul ben Batnit says:

Woe is me because of the house of Boethus;
  Woe is me because of their staves!
Woe is me because of the house of Hanin [i.e. Hanan or Ananus];
  Woe is me because of their whisperings!
Woe is me because of the house of Kathros;
  Woe is me because of their pens!
Woe is me because of the house of Ishmael the son of Phabi;
  Woe is me because of their fists!
for they are High Priests and their sons are [temple] treasurers and
their sons-in-law are trustees and their servants beat the people with
staves.[22]

All the main high-priestly families are represented in this lament
– the houses of Boethus, Kathros, Phabi and the family to which
Caiaphas belonged, the house of Hanin (Hanan or Ananus). What
is remembered is their behaviour: the nepotism, the physical force,
the beatings and the fists; the financial power, the secret, political
machinations. The fact is that after the demise of the temple in AD
70, not a single Jewish source expresses any kind of regret for the
disappearance of the temple aristocracy. They missed the temple,
but never the people who ran it.[23]

The first of the high priests following direct Roman rule was
so unpopular that he was removed from the post. The Roman
leadership replaced him with a man plucked from obscurity –
Ananus, son of Seth. Ananus – or Annas, as he is called in the
Gospels – proved a much more canny operator, and his family
was to dominate the post of high priest for the next sixty years.
Annas was high priest from AD 6 to 15 and five of his sons were
to hold the same office.[24] Caiaphas, who was appointed in AD 18,
was his son-in-law. He too was from the house of Hanin, albeit
through marriage.

This was more like a feudal monarchy than a religious appointment. It not only led to great wealth and power for the high priest
and his clique, it also drove a wedge between the upper echelons of
the priesthood and the rural priests like John's father Zechariah –
the 'grunts' who did the day-to-day work in the temple. The rural
priests were part of the peasantry. They were from a different social
class from those who occupied the more privileged positions. These
poorer, rural priests became argumentative, even rebellious.

Later on, during the Jewish revolt, the hatred between the 'temple priests' and the 'popular priests' came out into the open, with the two factions abusing each other and even pelting each other with stones. Josephus records how some of the poorer priests starved to death in the days immediately before the Jewish rebellion, because the high priests had seized the tithes which were their only form of sustenance.[25]

Whether John had seen such antagonism for himself, we do not know. There is no indication in the Gospels that he ever went to Jerusalem. But he was clearly convinced that the temple in Jerusalem could never provide what people really needed.

'The axe is lying at the root of the trees'

John's message was one of apocalyptic doom: the day of judgement was coming, the day when the tree would be chopped down. Only if people repented would they be saved.

First-century Judea was alive with apocalyptic movements. For hard-pressed peasants, steeped as they were in the great tales of Israel's past, revolution was often linked with the inauguration of a new age, an age of justice, hope, peace and plenty. The day of the Lord, when the powerful, the rich and those foreign Gentile invaders would get their comeuppance.

Perhaps the best known of these wilderness, apocalyptic communities – the Essenes at Qumran – thought of themselves as 'the congregation in the wilderness' holding fast to the faith in the end times.[26] Like John, they were rooted in opposition to the temple, which they saw as hopelessly corrupt. They attacked their opponents in similar ways to John, calling their enemies – presumably the temple aristocracy – the men of falsehood, sons of darkness, serpents 'which creep in the dust'.[27]

As well as the Qumran community, Josephus describes various impostors and revolutionary leaders who led groups out into the wilderness, assuring these desperate followers that they would witness miraculous signs of deliverance. Later in Pilate's reign, an anonymous Samaritan leader led a movement to restore the temple on Mount Gerizim. (Pilate ruthlessly crushed them.)[28] Around AD 45 a rebel called Theudas led a band of followers across the Jordan. (He and his followers were also crushed, by the Judean governor Fadus.)[29] The biblical iconography was unmistakable: uprising dressed as exodus. The pattern is similar: a popular preacher captures the imagination of the ordinary, oppressed peasant. They march to a biblical location in expectation of a miraculous event. The Romans mash them to pieces.

John was no violent revolutionary, and Josephus is keen to make that clear. But he was an apocalyptic preacher. He warned of a coming judgement: 'His winnowing-fork is in his hand, and he will clear his threshing-floor and will gather his wheat into the granary; but the chaff he will burn with unquenchable fire' (Matt. 3:12; Luke 3:17).

John was preaching forgiveness and repentance in preparation for an apocalyptic event, an event which would bring judgement on the powers and authorities. He baptised people, but he also made it clear that the baptism he provided was only the first: 'The one who is more powerful than I is coming after me; I am not worthy to stoop down and untie the thong of his sandals. I have baptised you with water; but he will baptise you with the Holy Spirit' (Mark 1:7–8).[30]

The later rabbis were used to being served by their disciples, but there was one thing those disciples did not do: untie or carry the master's sandals.[31] Jesus was to use the same imagery – to act it out, in fact – in his radical reshaping of the power structures among his followers. But first it was John who claimed that he was not worthy even to act as the slave of the one who was coming.

Soon he was attracting significant numbers of followers: Josephus records that the size of the crowds was so great that Antipas began to get alarmed.[32] It was into this intense atmosphere that Jesus came, probably in the autumn of AD 29. The 'one who was more powerful' arrived.

And the first thing he did was to get baptised.

'I need to be baptised by you'

Using the time data in John's Gospel Jesus' baptism has to be before his visit to Jerusalem in AD 30. Some time towards the end of AD 29, probably. Christians in the second century AD commemorated Jesus' baptism on 6 January. Could be. It is pretty likely that John's campaigns took place in the autumn and spring. The summer heat would have been too intense for John and his follow-ers to gather in the wilderness. By autumn, however, the intense heat would be abating.[33] One autumn festival in particular fits perfectly with John's message as the Gospels record it: the Day of Atonement, on the tenth day of Tishri – our September/October. Jews would have been preparing for the great fast, with its theme of repentance. At the festival, one goat would be sacrificed to the Lord, while the other – the scapegoat – would be driven out into the wilderness, bearing the people's sins to be consumed by the demon Azazel.[34]

We don't know the exact time. Nor the place. Theodosius, a fifth- or sixth-century pilgrim, was shown a site which was near the Jordan, and opposite it, the place where the prophet Elijah was believed to have ascended to heaven – but this is a late tradi-tion.[35] John's Gospel links it to Bethany; across, or opposite, or beyond the Jordan, of which more in a moment.

Jesus' baptism by John is one of the irrefutably historical facts of the Gospels. The reason is simple: embarrassment. For a church which believed Jesus to be sinless, the idea that he needed John's baptism was inconvenient to say the least. (It is called the criterion of embarrassment – i.e. any story which is potentially embarrassing for the church has a strong argument for authentic-ity.) Why would he need to be baptised if he was perfect? Of what sin could he need to repent?

But baptised Jesus was – and, although the accounts in the Gospels differ slightly, in each case the Spirit of God descends on Jesus like a dove. In the Synoptics a heavenly voice is heard: 'You are my Son, the Beloved; with you I am well pleased' (Mark 1:11; Luke 3:22).[36]

The Spirit descends on Jesus, confirming his identity, either to the crowd or to John. Or to both. The Spirit speaks, appropriately, in the words of Isaiah: 'Here is my servant, whom I uphold, my chosen, in whom my soul delights; I have put my spirit upon him; he will bring forth justice to the nations' (Isa. 42:1).

So why did Jesus do it? The most obvious solution is that Jesus considered himself in need of forgiveness. That was why every-one else did it. But this does not sit very neatly with ideas of the perfect sinlessness of Jesus. Early theologians suggested a range of possibilities: that he was baptised in order to purify the waters of baptism (Ignatius of Antioch, c. AD 35–107); that he was an example for all humanity (Justin Martyr, c. AD 100–65); even that he did so at the urging of his family (the *Gospel of the Hebrews*, c. AD 80–150).[37] It could have been an act of solidarity, a collective alignment with the aims and methods of John. To be baptised by John, after all, was an act of rebellion, of opposition to the temple. Or maybe Jesus was thinking ahead, looking to establish it as the norm for his future followers.

All these are possibilities. But I think a strong reason why he did it, and why he then immediately went off into the wilderness on his own, was to prove something, not only to John and the other people watching, but also to himself. In John's Gospel, John the Baptist says:

'I saw the Spirit descending from heaven like a dove, and it remained on him. I myself did not know him, but the one who sent me to baptise with water said to me, "He on whom you see the Spirit descend and remain is the one who baptises with the Holy Spirit." And I myself have seen and have testified that this is the Son of God.' (John 1:32–34)

It was the baptism which opened John's eyes to who Jesus was. So perhaps recognition is the key issue here: recognition and confirmation. Truths previously intuited suddenly become clear, relationships which were only dimly sensed are made close and complete.

In that sense it was not the symbolic meaning of baptism which was important to Jesus, but the experience itself. Jesus' work was founded on the belief that he was the Son of God, empowered and anointed by the Holy Spirit. As James Dunn writes, 'It is certain that Jesus believed himself to be empowered by the Spirit and thought of himself as God's son.'[38] But *when* was he sure of this? *When* did he finally know?

Although the accounts of the baptism differ, all agree that Jesus was hailed as God's Son. The various accounts seem to show the event solidifying as it goes on: so Mark's 'You are my Son' (Mark 1:11) becomes Matthew's more objective 'This is my Son' (Matt. 3:17). Luke is keen to stress that the Holy Spirit came in bodily form as a dove (Luke 3:22).

In that sense, what happened to Jesus in the waters was the starting point, the proof that he was who he thought he was. This was why he needed to be baptised, because it confirmed to him what he had, perhaps, previously intuited – that he was who he thought he was. During baptism, Jesus experienced God in a way which he had not previously done before.

Christians are fond of presenting a fully formed Jesus, a man-shaped God, who knew, from birth, what he had to do and how he was to do it, who wandered around in a divine certainty complete with halo. Like those icons: the baby with the halo, the piercing eyes and the imperial upraised hand. Of course, before this he must have had some awareness: the stories of his mother, the events of his birth, his experience in the temple would have shown that he was marked out. But that is not the same as saying he understood right from the start how it would go. Jesus was not working to a script; he was coming to a realisation.[39]

At his baptism Jesus understood, as he had not done before, who he was and what he was here to do. It is the baptism which gives birth to his teaching and campaigning, and the descent of the dove which empowers him to the next stage of his career: the performing of miracles.

From here, Jesus headed into the wilderness on his own. Something had happened. He had heard the voice of God. He had experienced the Spirit.

Now he needed to put it to the test.

'He was in the wilderness for forty days'

According to the Synoptic Gospels his baptism was followed by forty days of temptation in the wilderness. Mark simply has the bare bones: 'And the Spirit immediately drove him out into the wilderness. He was in the wilderness for forty days, tempted by Satan; and he was with the wild beasts; and the angels waited on him' (Mark 1:12–13).

It is Luke and Matthew who give more specifics about the nature of that temptation, three temptations in particular:

> If you are the Son of God, command this stone to become a loaf of bread. (Luke 4:3)

> To you I will give their glory and all this authority; for it has been given over to me, and I give it to anyone I please. If you, then, will worship me, it will all be yours. (Luke 4:6–7)

> If you are the Son of God, throw yourself down from here, for it is written, 'He will command his angels concerning you, to protect you', and 'On their hands they will bear you up, so that you will not dash your foot against a stone.' (Luke 4:9–11)

The event is mysterious, miraculous. It's a test, of course. The desert was a place of proving, a place which exposed weakness. Its harsh light revealed any human frailty. And the Old Testament allusions are obvious: Jesus is Elijah in the wilderness (he too was fed by angels). He is Noah in the boat for forty days and forty nights. He is Moses in the desert.

The first temptation is obvious: you're hungry, so make some bread. But there is another symbolism here. It has been suggested that the provision of bread, the feeding of the hungry, was also a sign of the Messiah. One of the things that the Messiah would do was provide a banquet for the poor.[40] It is noticeable that, later, when Jesus did provide bread for people, they tried to make him king. So maybe there is a more subtle political statement here. I think, however, the core of it is straightforward. Use your power to satisfy yourself, says the tempter.

There is certainly a political element to the second temptation: the vision of all the kingdoms of the world. 'You can have them

all,' says Satan. 'Just worship me.' What is interesting here is the assumption that the kingdoms are Satan's to give away. The glory and authority of the worldly kingdoms 'has been given over to me', he says (Luke 4:6). The assumption is that the Roman Empire and all worldly kingdoms are in the grip of an evil power, with their godless idols of wealth, power and nationalism. But political, temporal power was a route which Jesus continually rejected. Jesus knows that peace cannot come about through coercion.[41] Both of these visions, moreover, took place in the wilderness. The first is easy enough: Jesus would only have had to look out of whatever cave he was sheltering in to see a field of stones. The second must by its nature be visionary, although the devil leads Jesus to a 'high place'. The traditional site, the so-called Mount of Temptation, might be a candidate: it is about three kilometres north-west of Jericho and overlooks the Jordan valley. Some type of mountain-top experience, then.

But the third temptation takes place in a very specific location. For that temptation, Jesus went to Jerusalem. According to Luke and Matthew, the devil took him there, by which we imagine Jesus was led to the pinnacle of the temple. The usual Christian assumption is that Jesus was somehow carried through the air in some Harry Potteresque moment, to land on the roof of the temple. But the general conclusion among scholars is that the pinnacle of the temple does not refer to the temple building itself, the

The wilderness of Judea. Looking north from the Jerusalem – Jericho Roman road.

83

sanctuary, but to the highest point of the temple complex. This would be the south-east corner, where Herod's temple mount rises over the Kidron valley below.

This area, in Jesus' time, was covered by a colonnaded walkway known as Solomon's Portico. Here is the description in Josephus:

> This cloister deserves to be mentioned better than any other under the sun; for while the valley was very deep, and its bottom could not be seen, if you looked from above into the depth, this farther vastly high elevation of the cloister stood upon that height, insomuch that if anyone looked down from the top of the battlements, or down both those altitudes, he would be giddy, while his sight could not reach to such an immense depth.[42]

Despite the mystical nature of these events, there is no reason why Jesus could not simply have walked there, out of the wilderness, up to Jerusalem, over the Mount of Olives and into the temple itself. Depending on where Jesus was in the wilderness, the journey would have taken one or two days. (Again, just as an illustration, the Mount of Temptation is only some thirteen miles from Jerusalem.)

Either way, Jesus arrives at the temple. Looks around. Contemplates the power and the wealth that could be his. He crosses the temple plaza. Enters Solomon's Portico. It is a journey that takes him literally and metaphorically right to the very edge.

But why the pinnacle? And why does the devil ask him to throw himself off? It is an odd challenge. The traditional interpretation concentrates on the angelic rescue as a sign of divine power and authority. But there would have been plenty of ways to do that which didn't involve a suicidal plunge. I believe that a fragment of early church tradition holds a clue. It is the only other place where the pinnacle of the temple is mentioned.[43]

The passage comes from Eusebius' *Ecclesiastical History*, a book written in the fourth century AD, but which preserves facts (and legends, traditions and sheer fiction) from earlier centuries. At one point Eusebius relates the death of James, the brother of Jesus. From Josephus we know that James was stoned to death – illegally – by order of the high priest Ananus. The event took place in AD 62, during a power vacuum between the death of one Roman procurator and the arrival of his replacement.

The pinnacle of the temple from the east. The circle marks the high point.

Eusebius records more details, including a rather overembel-lished version from a writer called Hegesippus, who says that James spent so much time kneeling in prayer that his knees 'became hard, like a camel's'.[44] But before wandering off into Hegesippus's fantasy world, Eusebius quotes a much simpler ver-sion: 'Now the manner of James' death has already been shown by the words of Clement we have quoted, who has placed it on record that he was cast down from the pinnacle and beaten to death with a club.'[45] The quote comes from a lost work attributed to Clement of Alexandria.[46]

It shows that the early church, at least, preserved the idea that those who were convicted of blasphemy, those who were stoned, were cast down from the pinnacle. The practice of stoning people is misnamed, really, since the usual procedure was to throw them down from a high point first. This is certainly reflected in the Gos-pels, where Jesus is rushed to a 'cliff' near Nazareth (Luke 4:29). Significantly, in John's Gospel, Jesus is twice threatened with ston-ing, both times in the temple and the second time in Solomon's Portico (John 8:59; 10:22, 31–32). There is also a possible reference in Josephus: when the Zealots took charge of the temple they killed one of their opponents, a man called Zecharias, and 'threw him down out of the temple immediately into the valley beneath it'.[47]

The inference is clear: people thrown down from the pinnacle of the temple were blasphemers, they were to be stoned. So perhaps that explains the real nature of the temptation. The temptation is for Jesus to change the ending, to change his fate. 'You know how this is going to end,' says the devil. 'They're going to kill you. Because that's what happens to people like you. But you can save yourself.' On the cross that temptation was to be echoed in the mouths of the jeering crowd: 'Come down and save yourself' (Matt. 27:40; Mark 15:30; Luke 23:37).

'Save yourself.' This is the one temptation which recurs again and again in his work. When Peter tries to persuade Jesus not to go to Jerusalem, the rebuke – 'Get behind me Satan!' – seems completely over the top. It seems, in fact, to be cruel and unkind. But when we see it in this context, as a continuation of the most severe temptation that Jesus faced and was to face, it is much more understandable.

This is the temptation which Satan will dangle before Jesus time and time again: 'You can change things. You don't have to do this. You can escape.'

He tempts Jesus to change the ending of the story, an ending which, even then, they both seem to know.

'This took place in Bethany'

The Synoptic Gospels have Jesus returning to Galilee after the temptation, but the fourth Gospel has a different picture entirely. John does not include the temptation in the wilderness at all. Instead, he depicts a 'week' during which John the Baptist testifies to the status of Jesus, Jesus meets his first disciples, and finally Jesus returns to Galilee, to attend a wedding at Cana.

Assuming the authenticity of the desert experience, and that John 1:32–34 refers to events at Jesus' baptism, then this 'week' must come after the temptation but before Jesus' Galilean campaign. In fact, in this model, the whole of John 1:19–4:54 takes place between Luke 4:13 and 4:14.

The 'First Week' in John's Gospel		
Day 1.	John the Baptist's witness concerning Jesus.	1:19–28
Day 2.	John the Baptist's encounter with Jesus.	1:29–34
Day 3.	John the Baptist's referral of disciples to Jesus.	1:35–39
Day 4.	Andrew's introduction of his brother Peter to Jesus.	1:40–42
Day 5.	Returns to Galilee. The recruitment of Philip and Nathanael.	1:43–51
Day 6.		
Day 7.	The wedding at Cana.	2:1–11

In John's Gospel the events of this 'week' take place in 'Bethany across the Jordan where John was baptizing' (John 1:28). 'Bethany beyond the Jordan', as it is most often translated, is not found in any writing outside John's Gospel. Origen, writing around AD 200, suggested that the real place was a place called Bethabara, a village on the west bank of the Jordan, just north of the Dead Sea. This tradition was adopted by Eusebius and the later church, and it is illustrated in the Madeba Map – a sixth-century mosaic map of the region.[48] But Origen appears to have chosen the site purely because of its name: Bethabara means 'House of Preparation', which he thought appropriate for Jesus' baptismal site. There is no evidence that this is the place John meant.[49]

Others have suggested that it took place at the other end of the Jordan, in the region of Batanea, in the Transjordan and north-east of Lake Galilee.[50] This location would fit in well with the presence of Galileans among John's disciples, as the region is close to Bethsaida and Capernaum. But it works less well with other traditions: that Jesus went immediately into the wilderness after his baptism, that the region of John's influence was the wilderness of Judea, and that crowds came to John from Jerusalem and Judea (Mark 1:5; John 1:19). Luke notes that John went 'into all the region around the Jordan' (Luke 3:3) so it is possible that he did come north. On the whole, though, it seems far more likely that John the Baptist was still in the southern part of the Jordan valley.

There is, however, another intriguing possibility. Here is what we know of this 'Bethany'.

▷ It is close enough so that a delegation from Jerusalem could be sent out there (John 1:19, 24).

▷ Jesus had lodgings nearby (John 1:39).

▷ There were fig trees there (John 1:48–49).

It is entirely possible that the Bethany John describes is the Bethany mentioned in the other Gospels and later in John – the village of Martha, Mary and Lazarus, and Jesus' base for his last week in Jerusalem. The Greek literally reads, 'These things in Bethany happened beyond the Jordan where was [the one] John baptising.' The assumption is that John is describing it in this way to distinguish it from the Bethany near Jerusalem. But John has not actually mentioned that Bethany yet. The distinction could be between Bethany (where these dialogues are occurring) and the place across the Jordan where John was previously baptising. It is perfectly possible to read this sentence another way: 'This took place in Bethany across the Jordan [from] where John was baptising.'

Bethany is south of the Judean wilderness, where Jesus has been fasting. Admittedly it is not that near the Jordan river itself – from Bethany, near Jerusalem, the river is about eighteen miles away, down through the valley. But nowhere in this passage does John say that John the Baptist was actually baptising at the time. He was conversing, talking with his disciples. This would also explain another curious detail: the fact that on the third day of that week, two disciples go to see where Jesus lives.

> They said to him, 'Rabbi' (which translated means Teacher), 'where are you staying?' He said to them, 'Come and see.' They came and saw where he was staying, and they remained with him that day. It was about four o'clock in the afternoon. (John 1:38–39)

This does not sound like a tent pitched in the desert, or a rough mat laid out in a cave. It sounds like lodgings in a house. We know that Jesus stayed in Bethany when he went to Jerusalem. We know that Bethany was the home of Lazarus, Mary and Martha – some of Jesus' most dedicated supporters. Was this the time when he met them? Was this the start of his association with the village?

Later on, Jesus makes reference to seeing Nathanael under a fig tree. Perhaps this was a miraculous vision; or perhaps this was an actual fig tree. You do not find fig trees in the wilderness, but you do get them in Bethany: later in the Gospels, Jesus will use one as an illustration.[51]

'We have found the Messiah'

Wherever this Bethany was, it was here that Jesus first meets some of those who will become his key disciples, Galileans who had come down from the north to be a part of what was going on. At Bethany he first encounters Andrew, Simon Peter, Philip and Nathanael as well as an unnamed disciple who may be the Beloved Disciple, the author of John's Gospel (John 1:39–51).[52] These were followers of John – to some extent – before they became followers of Jesus. In John's Gospel they pass, as it were, from John the Baptist to Jesus.

In fact, they literally 'follow' Jesus. When he notices them, they ask to spend time with him. What Andrew and the other disciple want to know is where this 'rabbi' is staying. In both Jewish and Greek culture, students or disciples sometimes stayed with their teacher. Certainly they spent time with them and it is likely that such rabbis taught from their homes. Here, Jesus takes them back to where he is staying and they spend the day with him, until the tenth hour – 4 p.m. (John 1:37–39).

Andrew is sufficiently impressed by this experience to go and get his brother Simon, and it is here that John has Jesus renaming Simon: 'You are Simon son of John. You are to be called Cephas (which is translated Peter)' (John 1:42). *Kepha* is the Aramaic word for rock; Peter – *petros* – is the Greek translation. Simon was to be Jesus' rock; sturdy, supporting, although at times prone to crumble alarmingly.[53]

The next day – day five of John's week – Jesus decides to go home and calls Philip to accompany him. Philip, Andrew and Simon Peter were from Bethsaida, according to John. Bethsaida was not in Galilee but in Gaulanitis, part of Herod Philip's territory. Jews were actually the minority in Bethsaida and they had settled the area, a little akin to modern Israeli settlers on the West Bank.[54] Perhaps the Gentile surroundings of the tetrarchy of Philip served to increase the zeal of these young Jews for their faith.

Philip then goes and finds Nathanael. Nathanael, in fact, is only mentioned in John's Gospel. This absence has led many to identify him with Bartholomew, of the Twelve, but that is not necessary. Not all of Jesus' disciples were part of the inner Twelve. Nathanael may well be the source for John's material about Galilee, since he came from Cana (John 21:2).[55] Their meeting is a curious little cameo, reflecting a common challenge to Jesus' messianic claims: 'Can anything good come out of Nazareth?' (John 1:46).

It is the first recorded instance of the Wrong Messiah syndrome. In a culture which valued historical parallels, Jesus' origins were inadequate qualifications for the Messiah. Nazareth is obscure, unremarkable, unremarked. It is never mentioned in the Old Testament (nor, come to that, in the Midrash, the Talmud or, indeed, in any contemporary writings). For Nathanael it just does not compute. Perhaps, given Nathanael's home town of Cana, there is also a sense of local rivalry. Jesus convinces Nathanael of his credibility by telling him, 'I saw you under the fig tree before Philip called you' (John 1:48).

Christians tend to assume this is a miraculous vision – Jesus seeing something which he could not possibly have seen, although quite what Nathanael was up to under the tree then becomes an intriguing and perplexing question. John, however, does not file it under 'miraculous': for him Jesus' first miraculous sign is still some days away at the wedding in Cana. Possibly it relates to the image of the fig tree, and its identification as a metaphor for Israel. Rabbinic teaching said that the place to read and study Torah was under a fig tree, because the fig tree was a symbol of Israel.[56] So it may be that Jesus is recognising Nathanael's passion, his desire, his study of the Torah.

Nathanael is a person who rests in the shade of Israel's heritage and past. But too much study of the past makes you blind to the possibilities of the present. Nathanael's rejection of Nazareth is based on historical precedent. Jesus did not seem to care much for history. The only thing he ever wanted to do with history was change it.

'There was a wedding in Cana of Galilee'

According to John's Gospel, after the 'week' spent in Bethany, Jesus returned to Galilee, to Cana. The occasion – which presumably took place sometime over the winter of AD 29/30 – was a wedding; a family wedding, it seems, to which Jesus' mother was also invited and which Jesus attended along with his 'disciples' (John 2:2).

Now standing there were six stone water-jars for the Jewish rites of purification, each holding twenty or thirty gallons. Jesus said to them, 'Fill the jars with water.' And they filled them up to the brim. He said to them, 'Now draw some out, and take it to the chief steward.' So they took it. When the steward tasted the water that had become wine, and did not know where it came from (though the servants who had drawn the water knew), the steward called the bridegroom and said to him, 'Everyone serves the good wine first, and then the inferior wine after the guests have become drunk. But you have kept the good wine until now.' (John 2:6–10)

As we have seen, wedding feasts could last for a week, or maybe two. It was expected, at a wedding, that guests would contribute to the marriage feast, and as their leader Jesus would be expected to be responsible for the contributions of his group. To Mary, therefore, this is a perfect opportunity to fulfil his duties as a guest. Initially, in fact, she is not after a miracle, she is asking for Jesus to do what is expected of guests: to contribute something to avoid the embarrassing situation.[57]

Jesus, of course, does the unexpected. Initially he seems distant from his mother, dismissive even. 'Woman,' he says of her worries about the wine, 'it's somebody else's problem.' His mother, as mothers have across the centuries, pays no attention to her son's objections and just tells the servants to do as he says. And Jesus orders that six stone jars should be filled with water, which he then turns into wine.

As we have seen, ritual bathing and washing was important in Jesus' day. It is this kind of water which the stone jars – each holding the equivalent of twenty or thirty gallons – were intended to hold. Not drinking water, but the water used in ritual purification.[58]

Everything in the Jewish world was either pure or impure. No in-betweens. And impurity could be caught, contracted like a disease. You became impure by touching something that was impure: a corpse, a menstruating woman, a Gentile. Hypothetical discussions of how water itself might become impure fill the writings of the rabbis: if pure water was poured into an impure vessel, would the impurity travel back up the stream and thus pollute the pure water? And what about the vessel itself? Could that become impure?

The rabbis ruled that ceramic and glass vessels could become impure, thereby contaminating the water within them. But stone was OK. Stone vessels, it was ruled, could not become impure. That made them perfect for storing purifying water, and many stone vessels like those in this story have been unearthed by archaeologists.

It is not, therefore, ordinary water which Jesus turns into wine in this story. It is the water used for ritual bathing. It is the first example of Jesus' significant transformation of the Jewish purity laws. He had seen, through John's work, how ritual bathing could happen anywhere and for anybody. Now he was taking the subversion to an even deeper level.

This, for John, is the first of Jesus' 'signs'. The water has been transformed – turned not just into cheap plonk, but into really good wine. Unlike John the Baptist, Jesus was not to be known for his asceticism, for fasting and abstinence. What characterised Jesus' mission more than anything else was the concept of feasting, of celebration. John the Baptist announced the imminent arrival of the kingdom of God; Jesus gave it a 'welcome home' banquet. Water into wine; religious ritual into celebration. The message is clear: forget washing, let's party.

Following the miraculous events at the wedding, John states that he 'went down to Capernaum with his mother, his brothers, and his disciples; and they remained there a few days' (John 2:12). Joseph, we note, is missing from the list. At this time, Jesus and his family seem still to be together. Perhaps they wintered at Capernaum; perhaps, as John states, they were there just for a little while. Whatever the case, the next time we hear of Jesus he is not in Capernaum, but in Jerusalem.

'He was in Jerusalem during the Passover festival'

According to John's Gospel, Jesus returned to Jerusalem for Passover. This would be spring, AD 30, the first time he had been in the city since his temptation at the pinnacle perhaps six months earlier. John's account places two events here: the cleansing of the temple (John 2:13–22) and the night-time visit of Nicodemus (John 3:1–21).

The Synoptics place the temple protest much later in Jesus' career, at the beginning of the last week of his life. Perhaps John was in possession of a tradition which placed the story earlier, perhaps he placed it here in his Gospel for theological reasons. It is perfectly possible that there were in fact two protests – whenever Jesus visited Jerusalem he seems to have caused a bit of an uproar. But the similarity of John's story to the words in Mark is so close that it is probable this is the same event; placing this event right at the beginning of Jesus' work emphasises its oppositional nature. Whatever the case, those in charge demand to know by what authority Jesus is doing things:

> The Jews then said to him, 'What sign can you show us for doing this?' Jesus answered them, 'Destroy this temple, and in three days I will raise it up.' The Jews then said, 'This temple has been under construction for forty-six years, and will you raise it up in three days?' (John 2:18–20)

The date helps us to fix this visit. The forty-six years refers specifically to the temple building, the *naos*, in Greek, which Herod began to rebuild or expand in 19 BC. We best understand this passage as referring to the idea that the temple building has been standing for forty-six years. If the work was completed in 18/17 BC, forty-six years brings us to AD 29/30. So we are talking about Passover, AD 30.[59]

And one evening, during his week's stay, he had a visitor: a man called Nicodemus.

'There was a Pharisee named Nicodemus'

Nicodemus was a Pharisee (John 3:1). The Pharisees have been frequently characterised as holier-than-thou people who spent their time loading rules and regulations onto other people. Call someone 'a Pharisee', and we cast them as a sanctimonious hypocrite: pompous, self-satisfied, smug. Of course, such a caricature owes its origins to Jesus' stinging criticism of the Pharisees as recorded in the Gospels. They were 'whitewashed tombs' (Matt. 23:27), looking pious but full of evil.

No doubt there were some Pharisees like that – as there are in any religious movement – but what is interesting about the Pharisees is that they were, at heart, a kind of grass-roots holiness movement. They were popular in the rural areas and the poorer parts of the cities, precisely because they were attempting to redefine Judaism in a way which the ordinary Jew could follow. They did create a mass of rules and regulations which, judging by Jesus' criticisms, caused difficulty and confusion, but they did so because they wanted to help people observe the Jewish faith. Their rules and regulations, complex though they are, were an attempt to deal with the complexities of Torah law in everyday life. Their rulings reflect life in the villages and hamlets of Palestine, with all its myriad conflicts and difficulties.[60]

If they were trying to help, though, to solve the problems of observing Torah law in everyday life, why did Jesus lay into them so much? The answer seems to lie in the nature of that solution. The Pharisees solved the problem of obeying the laws by weaving a web of even more intricate laws and decisions. Reading the Mishnah – the code which was developed from this tradition – one is struck by the sheer complexity of everything.

Jesus' solution was simpler: don't do it. Cut through the religious red tape. It is popular among scholars to argue that Jesus was not really opposed to the rules and regulations at all, and that the passages saying this in the Gospels are later Christian inventions, created by anti-Jewish factions within the young church. But there are simply too many instances where Jesus butts up against Jewish purity laws of one kind or another to see them all as inventions. The church may have emphasised these criticisms, but the constant refrain of the Gospels is that Jesus had no time for the minutiae of religious observance if it got in the way of real repentance and real relationship. He ate with the wrong people, he did not wash properly (Mark 7:15), he did not see the need for fasting (Mark 2:19), his Sabbath observance was questionable (Matt. 12:1–8). He did not even acknowledge the priority of Moses' instructions (Mark 10:2–9).

Both the Pharisees and Jesus wanted to democratise holiness, but they went about it in different ways. Jesus' approach was to shatter the taboos:

> Listen to me, all of you, and understand: there is nothing outside a person that by going in can defile, but the things that come out are what defile. (Mark 7:14–15)

> The sabbath was made for humankind, and not humankind for the sabbath; so the Son of Man is lord even of the sabbath. (Mark 2:27–28)

Jesus was not throwing out the Torah, nor was he abandoning Judaism. What he was doing, it seems, was redefining the relationship of a Jew to the Torah. For Jesus the Torah was no longer the ultimate standard.[61]

This, then, is the root of Jesus' complaint against the Pharisees. It was not their aims but their solutions which were wrong. Where the Pharisees believed that they were helping people to worship, Jesus charged them with burdening people with more regulations. And, frequently, they weren't living up to their own rules. Jesus pointed out, time and again, the difference between their scrupulous observation of the law and their sometimes less than scrupulous observation of simple justice.

This also explains why, despite his apparent anti-Pharisee rhetoric, Jesus and the Pharisees are frequently found together. They were basically on the same side. So we have many instances where Pharisees come and listen to him, even if one detects a kind of horrified fascination on their behalf. Luke records three instances where Pharisees invite Jesus to dine with them (Luke 7:36; 11:37; 14:1). And some Pharisees warned Jesus when Antipas wanted to kill him (Luke 13:31). They came to visit him and ask him questions.

Nicodemus is described as 'a leader of the Jews', indicating that he had a place on the Sanhedrin, the Jewish ruling council. The Pharisees had some influence, politically, but they were very much an opposition party. But Nicodemus' inclusion shows that the council must have included moderate elements.[62] There is even a possible identification outside the Gospel. At the time of Jerusalem's destruction there was a wealthy resident called Nakdimon ben Gorion. It is possible that this is the same character who, as a young man, met with Jesus. But the name is a common one and there was probably more than one wealthy Nicodemus in Jerusalem. The fact that Nicodemus visits during the night could merely reflect the fact that the night-time was a time of study and discussion. Perhaps John is hinting at a level of secrecy on the part of Nicodemus. But more than that he is using darkness symbolically. For the moment, Nicodemus is both figuratively and literally in the dark.

The real point lies, though, in Jesus' demand that he needs to be born again – born from above (3:7). As we have seen, birth and kinship was the defining social characteristic of the ancient world, defining status, tribe and race, and, of course, whether you were Jew or Gentile. But it was possible for Gentiles to become Jews, and they did this by being 'born again'.

Proselytes to Judaism – Gentile converts – were 'like a newborn child'. They would be reborn – into Judaism. This new birth was seen as so complete by some Jewish commentators that they suggested it meant that a proselyte could, technically, marry his own mother. She was, after all, only his mother in a former life, and that life was gone.[63]

Part of this proselyte conversion process, as we have seen, was immersion in water. The convert was baptised and circumcised (normally done, remember, to eight-day-old Jewish boys). They were new creations. So just as John's baptism was the sign of an intentional new start, Jesus is, essentially, suggesting to this Pharisee, this leader, this orthodox Jew, that he should convert to Judaism! He is offering Nicodemus an alternative route to the kingdom. Not a physical thing, but a 'spiritual proselyte baptism'.[64]

For an orthodox Jew like Nicodemus this would have been an outrageous, even offensive, suggestion. Nicodemus may miss Jesus' point through a misunderstanding, or he may be so outraged by the suggestion that he become like a Gentile convert that he chooses to misunderstand. Jesus is saying that all people – even the most orthodox – need to start again. It is not enough to coin the Baptiser's term: to be born a child of Abraham, you have to choose it.

If you are going to do this thing, you have to do it properly. And that goes for everyone.

'Into the Judean countryside'

> After this Jesus and his disciples went into the Judean countryside, and he spent some time there with them and baptised. John also was baptising at Aenon near Salim because water was abundant there; and people kept coming and were being baptised – John, of course, had not yet been thrown into prison. (John 3:22–24)

Jesus left Jerusalem, but did not return to Galilee. Instead he went to 'the Judean countryside' where he began baptising people like John. He was not with John, however, because according to John's

Gospel the Baptiser had gone north, to Aenon near Salim.

Aenon – like all the locations associated with John the Baptist – is a bit of a riddle. Salim we know: its name is preserved in the village of Salim, near to the site of the ancient city of Shechem. There are the ruins of a village called Ainun about seven miles north-east of Salim, so perhaps that was Aenon. But there are problems with this identification, not least the fact that there are no springs at Ainun.[65] In fact, 'aenon' need not mean the village. The word simply means 'springs', so John was baptising at the springs near Salim. While there are no springs near Ainun, there are springs near Salim: five of them, close together, which would have provided plentiful water for the Baptiser's work.

So there you go. The springs near Salim. Case solved. Except for one tiny detail. The springs are on the eastern slope of Mount Gerizim, and that puts us smack bang in Samaritan territory.[66]

The enmity between Jew and Samaritan was centuries old. Nearly five hundred years earlier, when Nehemiah returned to Jerusalem after the exile in Babylon, he considered Sanballat the Samaritan to be a Gentile and refused any contact with him. When Sanballat's daughter married Joida the high priest, Nehemiah banished the pair immediately (Neh. 13:8). During the Maccabean era, John Hyrcanus burned the Samaritan temple on Mount Gerizim to the ground and utterly destroyed the town of Shechem – the ruins were still visible during Jesus' day, near the town of Sychar. Hyrcanus had destroyed the temple because it was seen as an abomination by the Jews. There was only one true temple and it was in Jerusalem, not on Mount Gerizim. To Jews this proved an insurmountable problem. 'When shall we take them back?' asks a later rabbi about the Samaritans. 'When they renounce Mount Gerizim and confess Jerusalem and the resurrection of the Dead.'[67] Unsurprisingly, the Samaritans concluded that there could never be any reconciliation between the two sides: they were a separate people, and they would always be separate.

Politically both Samaritan and Jew were under the same master: Rome. When Pompey captured Palestine he gave control of the city of Samaria and the surrounding region to the province of Syria.[68] It returned to Jewish control during the reign of Herod, who, in a typically shrewd diplomatic move, invested heavily in the infrastructure of the city of Samaria. He renamed it Sebaste, the Greek version of the name Augustus, built a temple dedicated to the emperor and settled the city with his veteran soldiers and neighbouring peoples. According to Josephus, some six thousand colonists were settled in Sebaste. One of Herod's wives, Malthrace, may have been Samaritan; at any rate she came from the area, and was a Gentile.[69]

There were still sectarian outrages and attacks. Josephus records that during the early years of Roman rule some Samaritans infiltrated the temple and put dead bodies in the courts, an act which rendered the entire building unclean.[70] To Jerusalem Jews, Samaritans were renegades, unclean, impure mutant Jews who spread false teaching about the temple and engaged in underhand, dirty tricks. Probably Galilean Jews had a slightly better relationship with Samaritans – they might have to travel through the territory to reach the temple. Even so, there was hatred, deep hatred, and nothing would ever change that.

Some scholars reject the identification of Aenon near Salim precisely because it was in Samaritan territory. They assume that such a historical background makes the identification impossible. But the Salim identification is pretty strong, and it is hard to think of a reason why John would have invented this episode: he was writing largely for a Gentile Greek audience who would not be too bothered about Jew v. Samaritan. The inference is that John put it in because he knew it to be true.

We have already seen that, if it was offered to soldiers, John's baptism must have been available to Gentiles. That is shocking enough. But this is the truly startling fact about John the Baptist: he baptised Samaritans.

This explains a detail in the story which follows, the episode of Jesus passing through Samaria and meeting the woman at Jacob's Well. When Jesus gets there, he says to his disciples: 'For here the saying holds true, "One sows and another reaps." I sent you to reap that for which you did not labour. Others have laboured, and you have entered into their labour' (John 4:37–38). Why is it 'here', in Samaria, that the saying holds true? Because the event took place at Jacob's Well. *Bir Yakub.* Just two and a half miles west of Salim. Jesus was reaping what John had previously sown.

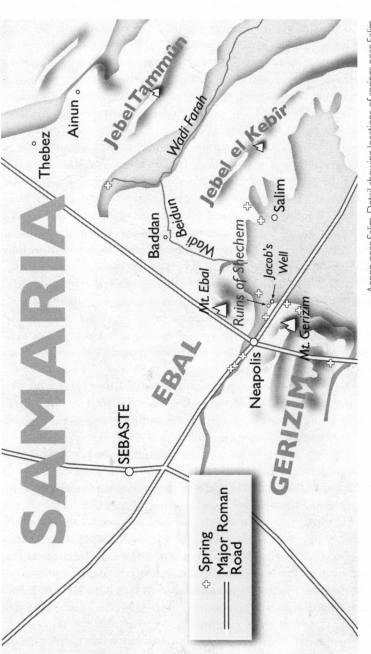

Aenon near Salim. Detail showing locations of springs near Salim.

We are given a wrong impression of John the Baptist. We think of him as just the herald, a man who went into voluntary decline the moment Jesus appeared. But he carried on for some time and his work was only curtailed by his arrest. He did not carry on, as one commentary puts it, to continue 'his ministry of baptism so as to have further opportunity to bear witness to Jesus as the Christ'.[71] He did it because it was still valid in its own right. And dismissing him as the messenger boy ignores the startlingly radical nature of his work. He was reaching out to all kinds of excluded people, using the symbolic action of ritual bathing to bring a whole load of impure, alienated, even heretical people to repentance.

What is more, Jesus joined him. How long Jesus remained part of John's 'team' we don't know, but allowing for a hiatus due to the summer heat, John's chronology indicates that Jesus and John the Baptist were back at work the following autumn – the autumn of AD 30. The Baptiser was in Samaria, near Salim, while Jesus and his disciples were in the Judean countryside, further south. John's account indicates that there was some level of coordination between the two. John has decided to take on a yet more difficult task: a mission to Samaria, while Jesus continues the work down south.

The information we are given in John's Gospel indicates that Jesus was to remain closely linked with the Baptist throughout AD 30 and even into early 31. If his baptism was in autumn AD 29, that means Jesus spent over a year working alongside John the Baptist, gathering his own disciples, doing his own work, but closely linked to the mission and methods of his relative.

Christians do not, perhaps, find it comfortable to think of Jesus as a disciple himself. But Jesus' teaching clearly owed a significant debt to that of his relative. He saw how John was willing to welcome all into a state of repentance. He saw how he subverted the ritual of the temple. He would come to differ with John, to take an even more radical approach, one which led the Baptiser himself to question whether his judgement of Jesus had been correct. But in these months in AD 30, Jesus was John's right-hand man. His agent in Judea. He was Jesus the Baptist.[72]

There were, clearly, tensions between the two. In John's Gospel, an unnamed Jew has a discussion with some of John's disciples about – guess what? – purification. With a slight touch of jealousy, John's disciples go to him and say, 'Rabbi, the one who was with you across the Jordan, to whom you testified, here he is baptizing, and all are going to him' (John 3:26). Jesus was proving more popular, although given that John was working in Samaria, that is hardly surprising. The difference was really in approach. The Gospels imply that the Baptiser's disciples were stricter in adherence to the laws (Matt. 9:14) while, as we shall see, Jesus was notoriously lax.[73] This is the split which is recognised by the disciples of John. 'We thought he was one of us, but he's not doing it right and loads of people are going to him.' The Baptist refuses to rise to the bait. He recognises, perhaps, that his star is on the wane: 'He must increase, but I must decrease' (John 3:30).

His star was soon to fade even more strongly. Sometime in the beginning of AD 31, John the Baptist was arrested.

'For Herod had arrested John'

Now after John was arrested, Jesus came to Galilee, proclaiming the good news of God, and saying, 'The time is fulfilled, and the kingdom of God has come near; repent, and believe in the good news.' (Mark 1:14–15)

The Synoptic Gospels date Jesus' Galilean campaign from one event – the arrest of John the Baptist. Matthew makes the link even clearer: 'Now when Jesus heard that John had been arrested, he withdrew to Galilee' (Matt. 4:12–13).

John had been sailing close to the wind for some time. He was not only outspoken in his opposition to the Jewish aristocracy in Judea, he was directly critical of Herod Antipas.

We do not know where the arrest took place. He could not have been arrested while he was in Samaria. Samaria was controlled by Pilate.[74] It is most likely that he had returned south and gone to the Perea, on the east side of the Jordan, where he had been baptising previously. This would explain why he was taken to the Machaerus fortress, a hill-top palace-fortress in south-eastern Perea. The latter detail comes from Josephus's account, which tells us that Herod 'feared lest the great influence John had over the people might put it into his power and inclination to raise a rebellion (for they seemed ready to do anything he should advise)'.[75]

We can only guess when this happened. There are hints in John's Gospel that it was in the winter of AD 30–31, but we cannot be sure. We do, however, know *why* he was arrested. Two reasons are suggested: Josephus suggests that Antipas was worried John might incite a rebellion, while Mark 6 suggests that the reason was John's criticism of Herod's marital relationship:

> For Herod himself had sent men who arrested John, bound him, and put him in prison on account of Herodias, his brother Philip's wife, because Herod had married her. For John had been telling Herod, 'It is not lawful for you to have your brother's wife.' And Herodias had a grudge against him, and wanted to kill him. But she could not, for Herod feared John, knowing that he was a righteous and holy man, and he protected him. (Mark 6:17–20)

Antipas had initially made a strategic marriage, to the daughter of Aretas IV, king of Nabatea. Nabatea was a kingdom (famous now for the city of Petra) which bordered the Perea. Aretas IV (9 BC–AD 40) was the greatest of their kings, known as 'the lover of his people' who expanded and developed his realm, building, among other things, the Nabatean capital at Petra. Marrying into his family, then, was a good move: this was not a man you wanted to antagonise.

Then, while on a visit to Rome, Antipas fell in love with a woman called Herodias. As the name indicates, she was a member of his own family; indeed, she was his sister-in-law, married to a half-brother (also, confusingly, called Herod).[76] Antipas was besotted with Herodias, who agreed to elope with him, on condition that he divorce his wife, the princess of Nabatea. The princess, meanwhile, got wind of what was happening and did not wait for the divorce: she fled to her own country. Her father, Aretas, promised revenge.[77]

Antipas's marriage to Herodias did not just anger Aretas; it outraged some of his own people as well. Jewish religious customs prohibit anyone from marrying the wife of their brother (Lev. 18:16). Antipas – a ruler of a kingdom the major part of whose subjects were Jews – had through his actions made himself ritually impure (Lev. 20:21).[78]

John had, by now, gained a considerable following. And if he had moved south again, back to the southern end of the Jordan, then John would have been active only twenty kilometres from the border with Nabatea.[79]Any unrest or even hint of unrest in this dangerous border area would be enough to force Antipas's hand. So Antipas arrested John, and incarcerated him in the Machaerus.

John's Gospel records that Jesus left Judea as a direct result of the information he received about the Pharisees: 'Now when Jesus learned that the Pharisees had heard, "Jesus is making and baptising more disciples than John" – although it was not Jesus himself but his disciples who baptised – he left Judea and started back to Galilee. But he had to go through Samaria' (John 4:1–4). I doubt it was the Pharisees who were the real danger. It may be that it was the temple elite who were more inclined to act, ready to crush the Baptist's movement while they could.

It was not really to escape – after all, Antipas was ruler of Galilee as well – but it may have been a case of a wise precaution. Carry on the work, but do it elsewhere. Or, more likely, take this as the moment, the pointer that the next stage of the work is to begin.

John's work is over. Time to step up, move up a gear.

And, for safety's sake, take the quickest route north. Through Samaria.

4. Capernaum, AD 31

They were meeting, as they always did, without him. The people of the town, his family, his friends, making their way to the assembly, celebrating the day, walking through the sunlight, while he was trapped in the dark.

And in the dark the voices spoke to him. Telling him how filthy he was, how impure, how unclean. How those who went to sit and pray and talk and discuss Torah would never include him.

Well, this day he would show them. This day he would come in from outside. This day he would shatter their little world. If he was filthy, he would make everyone else filthy as well. If he was impure, he would contaminate all of them.

And so he walked. Careful now. Don't let them see. Keep to the shadows, the margins, the dark places. Streets are quiet. No work today. Inland, towards the centre of the town, where the centurion had built their simple meeting place. Black stone. The black stone of this black place.

He knew they were there, for they were always there on the Sabbath.

At the door he paused. The voice was loud now. It sounded nervous. There was something new here. He could hear a voice speaking. Announcements of some kind. A new rabbi in town.

Well, he would show them. He would show them all.

'He came to a Samaritan city'

Jesus took the quickest route back to Galilee from the Jordan: north-west through Samaria. Despite the hatred between Jew and Samaritan, he felt confident of a safe passage because he knew that John had been there only a few months before. He may have been a Jew, but he was one of the good guys – an associate of the Baptist. 'So he came to a Samaritan city called Sychar, near the plot of ground that Jacob had given to his son Joseph. Jacob's well was there, and Jesus, tired out by his journey, was sitting by the well. It was about noon' (John 4:5–6).

Jacob's Well has been identified with some certainty as *Bir Yakub*, at the entrance to a ravine which separates Mount Ebal from Mount Gerizim. The narrative supports this identification, with a clear reference to Mount Gerizim (John 4:20). Given that the authenticity of the site is supported by Jewish, Samaritan, Christian and Muslim traditions, it is one of the best-attested sites in the Holy Land.

The details in the narrative fit as well: 'Sir, you have no bucket, and the well is deep,' the Samaritan woman tells Jesus (John 4:11). The well itself is around a hundred feet deep and is fed by underground sources as well as surface rainfall.[1] The literal Greek says Jesus sat 'on the well', which also makes perfect sense, since many wells had a stone cover, with just a hole in the middle through which to lower a bucket. The current Jacob's Well has a capstone in place.[2]

There is also a clue as to the time of year this took place. In a discussion with the disciples, Jesus says, 'Four months more, then comes the harvest' (John 4:35). Since reaping takes place in May or April, this suggests that John's arrest, and Jesus' journey to Galilee, took place in January.

The details, then, provide a good corroboration of the historicity of the event. But what a surprising and even shocking event it is. For a start, Jesus is talking to a woman. A single woman. A single *Samaritan* woman. For any male Jew, talking to a woman alone was taboo. And a Samaritan woman was even worse: 'Samaritan women are deemed menstruants from their cradle,' said the Mishnah, rather spitefully.[3] Menstruant women were, of course, ritually impure, which meant that a Samaritan woman was in a state of permanent impurity. Yet Jesus asks her for a drink from her bucket, a vessel which, by association, would be unclean and impure. 'Jews do not share things in common with Samaritans,' says John's Gospel, in a considerable understatement (John 4:9).

It has been suggested that this woman was not exactly of an unblemished reputation. Women carried water from the well early in the morning or just before sundown – the coolest parts of the day. But this woman is there alone and at midday. Was she avoiding other people? Was it the gossip and abuse which made her choose this time?

The taboo-busting conversation between the two follows an intriguing path. Dimly aware that the conversation is getting out of hand, she tries to divert it into theological backwaters: she talks about *our* well, *our* father Jacob – phrases which would ordinarily happily derail a devout Jew into outraged argument. But Jesus keeps bringing her back to *her* life, *her* response. When he reveals that he knows that she is living with a man and that she has had five husbands previous to him, she tries her last theological gamble: the issue of Gerizim: 'Sir, I see that you are a prophet. Our ancestors worshipped on this mountain, but you say that the place where people must worship is in Jerusalem' (John 4:19–21). It is the 'stop' button of Jewish–Samaritan discussion. But once again Jesus refuses to rise to the bait. Indeed, in Kenneth Bailey's telling phrase, he 'de-Zionises the tradition'.[4] Jerusalem and Gerizim are obsolete: 'Woman, believe me, the hour is coming when you will worship the Father neither on this mountain nor in Jerusalem' (John 4:21). He ends with a deliberately provocative statement. He claims to be the Messiah.

Seen in its social context, then, this is a startling story. Jesus breaks the taboo, crossing the line which forbids men to talk to women and Jews to drink with Samaritans. In its wider context, however, it is merely the continuation of the approach of John the Baptist. Through John's work, Jesus had seen that no one is excluded from the kingdom of God. Not tax-collectors, not soldiers, not Samaritans, not even women.

It also illuminates something which we also see at work in Galilee: the issue of Jesus' relationship with women. This issue – and that of the status of women within the church – has been a bone of contention for centuries. Jesus did not have women disciples, it is stated, as if this offers justification for the 'leadership is male' school. But in the social context of his time, Jesus' relationships with women were quite extraordinary. Given the patriarchal society in which he worked, it is astonishing that Jesus had any contact with women at all. (Anyway, as we shall see, he did, in fact, have women 'disciples'.)

When the woman ran into the town and told the townsfolk what had happened, their response was equally shocking: 'Many Samaritans from that city [Sychar] believed in him because of the woman's testimony' (John 4:39). For two days Jesus stayed in the city before heading north again into Galilee.

'Down to Capernaum'

In John's Gospel Jesus enters Galilee and returns to Cana (John 4:46–54), perhaps a year since he had been here for the wedding. His reputation was such that there was a man waiting for him, a royal officer, a man who had come to Cana, presumably, because he had heard what Jesus had done in that town.

Who was he? An officer of Antipas, an official based at Capernaum. One of the class in that town whom Mark terms 'Herodians'. Since we know Antipas had Gentile officials it's possible he wasn't a Jew.[5] He has come to urge Jesus to go to his son, but Jesus simply issues the order – long-distance miracles were seen as special proof of divinity. So the man begins the long trek down from Cana to Capernaum, by the lake. Again the details fit. Jesus spoke his command at 1 pm. (John 4:52–53). The journey, some fifteen miles, meant an overnight stop. If the official started at one o'clock and stayed overnight on the way, he would arrive at Capernaum in the morning of the next day. There, he finds his son healed.

Sometime in the days that followed, Jesus made the same journey. Down towards Galilee, skirting Tiberias, and round to Capernaum. This time, however, he was not there just for the winter. He was there to make the town his home.

Luke describes Capernaum as a 'city in Galilee', which is a bit of an overstatement. In many ways Capernaum was an insignificant place. Josephus only mentions the place twice, and one of those is just because it was where he fell off his horse.[6] It was a

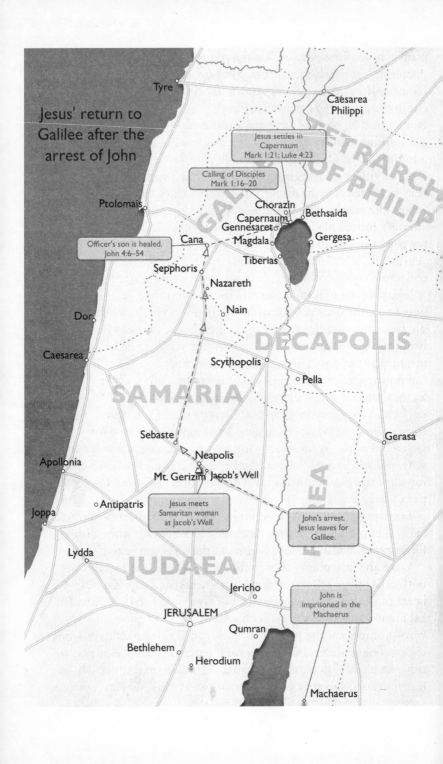

Jesus' return to Galilee after the arrest of John

Tyre

Caesarea Philippi

TETRARCHY OF PHILIP

Jesus settles in Capernaum
Mark 1:21; Luke 4:23

Calling of Disciples
Mark 1:16–20

GALILEE

Ptolomais

Chorazin

Capernaum
Bethsaida

Gennesaret

Gergesa

Officer's son is healed.
John 4:6–54

Cana

Magdala

Tiberias

Sepphoris

Nazareth

Nain

Dor

DECAPOLIS

Caesarea

Scythopolis

SAMARIA

Pella

Sebaste

Neapolis

Gerasa

Apollonia

Mt. Gerizim

Jacob's Well

PEREA

Joppa

Antipatris

Jesus meets Samaritan woman at Jacob's Well.

John's arrest. Jesus leaves for Galilee.

Lydda

JUDAEA

Jericho

John is imprisoned in the Machaerus

JERUSALEM

Qumran

Bethlehem

Herodium

Machaerus

proper town, however, with a population of around a thousand people in New Testament times. Situated on the northern shore of Lake Galilee, on the *via Maris*, the road which ran from Damascus in the east to Caesarea Maritime on the Mediterranean coast. It was also on the border between the territory of Herod Antipas and his brother Philip, and home, therefore, to a number of administrative officials such as toll- and tax-collectors. Nearby was the village of Arbel, a place of myth and legend: the reputed resting place of Seth, son of Adam, and Dinah, the daughter of Jacob, the nearby cliff face was dotted with caves which provided a handy hiding place for bandits and rebels.[7] This might explain the presence of a detachment of soldiers under the command of a centurion (Luke 7:1ff.). They were there to make sure that the tax-collectors could collect the duty on goods crossing the border.

We have seen Rabbi Gamaliel's disdain for the tolls, bath buildings, theatres and taxes of the empire.[8] Toll fees were simple fees for using the roads or bridges. Goods crossing rivers or bridges or from one district to another were taxed, much like import duty today. The rate varied from 2 to 5 per cent depending on the nature of the goods. One of the names for these collectors was *penekostologos* – 'collector of one-fiftieth', i.e. 2 per cent. No toll rates from Galilee survive, but one from Egypt shows the kind of thing: 1 *obol* for a camel, 4 *drachmas* for a covered wagon. At one port a sailor entering had to pay 5 *drachmas*, while a sailor's woman had to pay 20 *drachmas*. The cost for importing salted fish into Palmyra in AD 137 was 10 *denarii* per camel load.

But the tax- and toll-collectors did not just collect duties and taxes. They made money for the authorities in other ways. Fishing, for instance. Because Capernaum, of course, was a fishing town.

Luke and Josephus – men who had sailed the Mediterranean – both call Galilee a *limne*, a lake, but to the locals it was 'the Sea', the heart of the region and the source of local trade and wealth. The fishing industry was the economic basis for this region, providing work not just for the fishermen, but for various linked industries such as boat builders, sail makers and repairers, salt producers and fish preservers. Josephus remarked that the lake contained fish 'different in taste and appearance from those found elsewhere'.[9] It was not just fresh fish, either. Galilean fish were salted and preserved and sent far and wide. Magdala, on the western shore of Galilee, was famous for its salted fish. Indeed, the Greek name for Magdala, Tarichaeae, has been translated as 'Processed-Fishville'.[10]

Fishing was not free. It was a state regulated exercise, with access to the lake controlled by the tax-collectors, who sold fishing rights to fishermen. If you wished to fish the Sea of Galilee, you would first have to pay a local tax-collector for a licence. He might also lend you money to buy the equipment: the boat and nets.[11]

So fishermen were more like franchise holders and the cost of gaining access meant that they would form cooperatives – *koinonoi* – joining together to bid for fishing rights and then pooling their workforce. Luke tells us that Zebedee and Jonah were part of a fishing cooperative:

> So they signalled their partners [*metachoi*] in the other boat to come and help them. And they came and filled both boats, so that they began to sink. But when Simon Peter saw it, he fell down at Jesus' knees, saying, 'Go away from me, Lord, for I am a sinful man!' For he and all who were with him were amazed at the catch of fish that they had taken; and so also were James and John, sons of Zebedee, who were partners [*koinonos*] with Simon. Then Jesus said to Simon, 'Do not be afraid; from now on you will be catching people.' (Luke 5:7–10)

The implication is that Zebedee, the father of John and James, worked in partnership with Jonah, the father of Simon and Andrew. This was a two-family syndicate. Each family owned or leased a boat, and Zebedee's family employed hired workers (Mark 3:19–20). It is among these people, fishermen and tax-collectors alike, that Jesus cast his net and gathered in his catch of disciples.

According to Mark, Jesus arrives at Capernaum to find Simon and Andrew fishing. This implies that they had not been with him in Samaria, nor made the hurried journey out of the Perea. They had, presumably, stayed in Capernaum when Jesus and family were there in the winter of AD 29. Jesus calls them from their nets to become his disciples. He promises that from now on they will catch people, rather than fish.

There are different accounts of the calling of the disciples. As we have seen, John has Jesus meet them first in Judea, while with John the Baptist. Luke has a miracle story in which Jesus gives

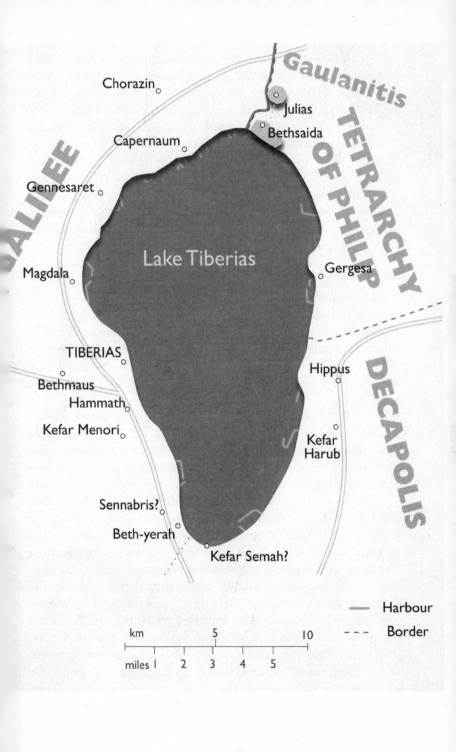

Chorazin

GALILEE

Gaulanitis

Julias

Bethsaida

TETRARCHY OF PHILIP

Capernaum

Gennesaret

Lake Tiberias

Magdala

Gergesa

TIBERIAS

Hippus

DECAPOLIS

Bethmaus

Hammath

Kefar Menori

Kefar Harub

Sennabris?

Beth-yerah

Kefar Semah?

		Harbour
		Border

km   5   10

miles 1   2   3   4   5

Simon and the fishing cooperative a huge catch of fish, a catch so large that they have to call for their partners to help before the nets break (Luke 5:1–11). Mark and Matthew have Jesus arriving in Capernaum and walking along the shoreline. He sees them working in the boats and simply calls on Simon and Andrew, James and John to follow him (Mark 1:16–20; Matt. 4:18–22). None of these stories is incompatible with the others. Mark's story certainly fits with Jesus' arrival in Capernaum. It is not a first encounter, but a reunion. Jesus has come to Galilee and he makes his way to the people he already knows, people who became his followers in Judea. They respond to him. They follow him. And, on a more practical level, they give him somewhere to live.

'He was at home'

'Foxes have holes, and birds of the air have nests, but the Son of Man has nowhere to lay his head,' said Jesus (Matt. 8:20). And from that, we conjure up the image of a man permanently on the move, sleeping rough. But Jesus had places to stay. He stayed in Bethany. He lived for several months at a time in the wilderness near the Jordan. And for around eighteen months he had a house – or a room in a house – in Capernaum.

Most likely, he set up home with Simon. It was there that Jesus healed Simon's mother-in-law, and there that the crowds gathered at sundown. When he later returned to Capernaum after a few days away, 'it was reported that he was at home' (Mark 2:1). And we might even know where that was.

Archaeologists have identified, within ancient Capernaum, what they call 'clan-dwellings'.[12] These consist of a central courtyard, around which were lots of small rooms or houses made of blocks of dense black basalt stone. The floors were made of blocks of stone, with pebbles packed in between, sometimes covered with a layer of yellow-coloured earth. (Easy to lose a coin down the cracks.[13])

A gate from the street led into the first of the courtyards and from there one could gain access into the other rooms or houses. The main family life would have taken place in the courtyard, where there would have been fires for cooking, millstones for grinding corn and hand presses for olives. Stairs within the courtyards allowed access to the roofs, which were made of beams, covered with layers of packed mud. (Easy to break through and lower someone down.[14])

In 1968, archaeologists in Capernaum discovered one of these clan dwellings. It lay beneath two later buildings, the remains of a splendid, octagonal church dating from Byzantine times (c. fifth century AD) and an earlier church with Christian symbols and graffiti, inscriptions to Jesus and Peter. The house, which dated back to the first century AD (and possibly beyond), was part of a complex with two courtyards. At some time this house had been converted into a church: the largest room in the house had been strengthened with an arch, so that its roof could be raised to form a kind of central hall, and the floor, walls and ceiling of the main room were plastered. It is the only house in Capernaum with plastered walls; in Roman times the only rooms which were plastered were rooms used as gathering or meeting places.

So, we have a building that had once been a house. People began to meet there. Soon more people gathered there, so that a wall was knocked down to create more space. Then, much later, a splendid church was built on the original site.[15]

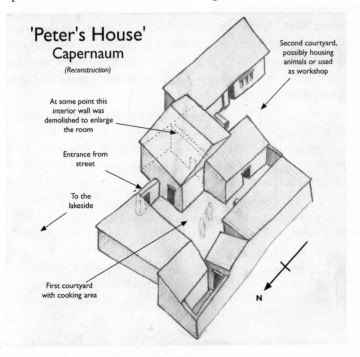

'Peter's House'
Capernaum
(Reconstruction)

Second courtyard, possibly housing animals or used as workshop

At some point this interior wall was demolished to enlarge the room

Entrance from street

To the lakeside

First courtyard with cooking area

N

What we have here, therefore, is a pretty good candidate for Simon Peter's house in Capernaum and for one of the earliest churches in the world. A fourth-century pilgrim called Egeria wrote that in Capernaum 'the house of the chief of the apostles has been turned into a church'.[16] If the house belonged to Peter – chief of the apostles – then it is probably the place where, during his residence in the village, Jesus ate, drank and, most likely, called home.

It was here that people knew where to find him. And very soon, crowds were flocking to the house. Because Jesus had started healing people. In Judea he was Jesus the Baptiser; in Jerusalem he was Jesus the rabbi and rabble-rouser; but in Galilee he was a miracle worker.

'When the Sabbath came he entered the synagogue'

Mark gives us a snapshot of Jesus' life in Capernaum. 'A day in the life of your average Messiah.' An examination of this section of Mark will tell us a lot about Jesus' world: demons and disease, Sabbaths, synagogues and scribes, teaching and talking, and the unremitting pressure on the man of the moment, Jesus of Nazareth.

His description covers some thirty-six hours. He gives us three time references: 'when the Sabbath came' (Mark 1:21), 'that evening, at sunset' (Mark 1:32) and 'in the morning, while it was still very dark' (Mark 1:35). (He also talks about Simon's mother-in-law serving them, which obviously indicates a meal.) We can reconstruct Mark's 'Sabbath day' as follows:

▷ Friday sunset: Sabbath begins. 'When the sabbath came' (Mark 1:21).

▷ Saturday morning: Jesus goes to the synagogue and teaches with authority (Mark 1:21–22, 27). Exorcises a demon (Mark 1:23–28).

▷ Saturday midday: Jesus returns to Simon and Andrew's house. Simon's mother-in-law is healed. The midday meal is served (Mark 1:29–32).

▷ Saturday sunset: Sabbath ends and next day begins. People crowd to the house bringing the sick and possessed (Mark 1:32–34).

▷ Sunday early hours: Jesus escapes the crowd for solitude and prayer (Mark 1:35).

▷ Sunday morning: Simon and the others find Jesus (Mark 1:36–37). Jesus decides to leave to tour the rest of Galilee (Mark 1:38–39).

The opening scene in this narrative starts with Jesus going to the synagogue and astounding people with his teaching 'for he taught them as one having authority, and not as the scribes' (Mark 1:22). As the name implies, scribes were people who wrote things down. In the Greco-Roman world, you could have scribes attached to local councils (Acts 19:35), but in Palestine they were a kind of religious bureaucrat, experts on how things were done. Or they might be attached to the temple, copyists and recorders, a sort of temple civil servant. Although the Gospels tend to lump them all together, they were not a single, unified group. Matthew and Luke tend to depict what we might call Pharisaical scribes, guardians of local traditions and community leaders, active in preserving and protecting Judaism but also in interpreting it and applying it to local life and circumstances. But there were many temple scribes, who would probably have been closer to the Sadducees in outlook.

What the different groups of scribes had in common was an emphasis on precedent and, most importantly, scriptural authority. But, rather than pile up precedent, Jesus just seems to say things – and they seem to his listeners to have a power of their own. His wisdom, his authority, springs from his own convictions and insight, his independence. Unlike the scribes, Jesus does not appeal to authority or precedent, or even, often, to the Torah. His sayings come with 'their own self-evidencing power'.[17]

There was more to Jesus' authority, however, than just the power of his words or the manner of their delivery. His authority was backed up by the things he did. In Capernaum this was demonstrated by the act of exorcism.

'A man with an unclean spirit'

Just then there was in their synagogue a man with an unclean spirit, and he cried out, 'What have you to do with us, Jesus of Nazareth? Have you come to destroy us? I know who you are, the Holy One of

God.' But Jesus rebuked him, saying, 'Be silent, and come out of him!' And the unclean spirit, throwing him into convulsions and crying with a loud voice, came out of him. They were all amazed, and they kept on asking one another, 'What is this? A new teaching – with authority! He commands even the unclean spirits, and they obey him.' At once his fame began to spread throughout the surrounding region of Galilee. (Mark 1:23–28)

The ruins of Capernaum contain an impressive and striking synagogue building. It is not the building from Jesus' time, which was probably a lot simpler and more basic, but it may well mark the spot where, according to Mark, Jesus healed a demon-possessed man and set all Galilee talking.

In ancient cultures, the idea that evil powers – demons – could invade people and take them over was taken for granted. The widespread belief seems to have developed in the period between the Old and New Testaments. There are very few stories of demon possession in pre-Christian literature. Even in the first century, accounts of Jewish exorcisms are rare outside those in the New Testament. But Jesus was not the only contemporary exorcist by any means. Josephus recounts the tale of Eleazar the Jew performing an exorcism in the presence of Vespasian. (He used a special ring and invoked the name and incantations of Solomon. Jewish legends portrayed King Solomon as a master exorcist.)[18] The Qumran community knew about exorcism, although whether they performed any is unknown.

Few events in the Gospel stories seem as alien, baffling and disturbing as the idea of demon possession. Horror images fill our minds: from the movies, or, worse, from real life: tragically misguided – or even evil – exorcists, evangelists and witch doctors. It conjures up a voodoo world and one which, despite still being evident in many parts of the world, we are reluctant to enter. Yet the casting out of demons was a major part of Jesus' work. Indeed, such miracles make up the single biggest category of healing in the Synoptic Gospels.[19]

Today, the most popular 'explanation' for demon possession is that it was the ancient world's version of mental illness, or epilepsy. Certainly there are similarities: convulsions, instances of self-harming, an almost Tourettes kind of shouting out of names,

The synagogue ruins in Capernaum. Although these ruins date from the fourth century AD, they may well be on the site of the first-century synagogue.

perhaps even instances of multiple personalities. Our reluctance to associate such things with demons is partly because we – quite rightly – do not want to 'demonise' mental illness. Yet in the Gospel accounts there is an evil about these things, a destructive, darker, more dangerous power lurking behind these manifestations. Indeed, Jesus' exorcisms are battles against demonic possession. Possession clearly brings about a different persona. People are violent, immensely strong, agitated. They have gatecrashed. Moved in and redecorated. Made the place their own.[20]

Whatever we think about the practice, whether we ascribe the phenomenon to mental illness or to real, demonic powers, we cannot ignore it. It was something which set Jesus apart from John the Baptist, who never did it, as far as we can tell. For Jesus, the defeat of these powers was a sign of the kingdom of God. 'If it is by the finger of God that I cast out the demons, then the kingdom of God has come to you,' he said (Luke 11:20). The exorcisms were proof of the invasion: bridgeheads of the kingdom in the territory of man.

From a Jewish point of view, someone who was demon possessed was spiritually and physically ostracised. Demons defiled
a person, which is why they are sometimes termed 'unclean spirits'. Since, like all impurity, it could be passed on by contact, they
were exiled from the community. No chance to participate in the
synagogue meeting; no chance, indeed, to participate in ordinary
village life. Physical uncleanness was a question of washing; spiritual impurity was much harder to deal with. It was inbuilt, mysterious, ineradicable.

That is why it is odd that this man is even in the synagogue;
normally the very presence of an unclean spirit would mean him
being disbarred from the community.[21] Perhaps this is the first
manifestation of the unclean spirit, or, more likely, he has simply
burst in. 'Just then…' Mark begins the story; just as the man himself has been occupied by the demon, the safe, pure world of the
synagogue is gatecrashed by a disturbing, unclean presence.

The form of words used in this episode conforms precisely to
ancient understandings of magic. The spirit seems almost aggrieved
by Jesus' presence: 'What have you to do with us?' or, in one translation, 'Why are you interfering with us?'[22] Crucially, the spirit starts
out by trying to 'name' Jesus, to identify him, concluding, 'I know
who you are, the Holy One of God.' In the ancient understanding
of magic, this attempt to say Jesus' real name is actually an attack.
To 'know' someone, to know their real identity, was seen as a way
of controlling them, overpowering them.[23] A papyrus of the fourth
or fifth century runs, 'I know your name which was received in heav-
en, I know your forms … I know your foreign name and your true
name.'[24] Another ancient magical text runs, 'I adjure thee, every
daemonic spirit, say whatsoever thou art.'[25] In the most spectacular
of Jesus' exorcisms – the case of the Gerasene demonic – the spirit
names Jesus and then tries to command him using the self-same
formula: 'I adjure you by God, do not torment me' (Mark 5:8).

According to a first-century understanding of magic, then, this
is a pre-emptive strike. In this reading, the spirit's question, 'Have
you come to destroy us?', might be seen as a challenge rather than
a premonition. Jesus meets the challenge head on.

Although the world in which Jesus operated took demonic
powers for granted, their way of dealing with these powers dif-

fered greatly. They would seek to treat the problems with incantations or herbal remedies, or by seeking to invoke a higher power
to overcome a lesser one.[26] Jesus does not use elaborate rituals or
special rings; he does not invoke the name of Solomon or any other Old Testament character; he does not even pray to God, as was
the usual practice. He just rebukes the demons, commands them,
orders them to leave. The Greek word often used is *ekballo*, from
ballo, 'to throw'. Jesus literally chucks them out. Here he is just
as abrupt. He tells the spirit, '*phimotheti*', 'shut up'.[27] Before the
spirit can say any more, before any further defensive manoeuvres
can begin, Jesus begins the process of eviction. 'Come out!' he
commands, and with convulsions and loud cries, the man is free.

The result is that the man is brought back into kinship, into the
worshipping community. Exorcism for Jesus, like other healings,
is never just about curing the problem. It is about restoring people to wholeness. Allowing them to engage in worship. Bringing
them, in short, into the kingdom of God.

This miracle – the exorcising of the demon-possessed man in
the synagogue at Capernaum – is a kind of signature miracle. It
is this miracle, with the town gathered at their community meeting, that really sets the whole region talking. It was not done for
effect, but it has a massive effect. This is a brick chucked through
the window of the powers of darkness. The Greek words used
to describe the synagogue crowd – meaning 'astounded' and
'amazed' – imply a slight nervousness.[28] The demon recognises
what the crowd nervously sense: the normal order has been dis-
rupted. Something has changed.

'They entered the house of Simon and Andrew'

The new kingdom of God is not something restricted to synagogue
meetings or the temple. It is part of the domestic world. From the
synagogue meeting, Jesus returns to his new home at the house
of Simon and Andrew. There he heals Simon's mother-in-law, sick
with a fever (Mark 1:29–31). We have seen Jesus' healing power
already, in the long-distance command – the word spoken at Cana
that landed in Capernaum. This is a simpler, much more domestic,
almost matter-of-fact event. Jesus simply goes to her bed, takes
her hand and lifts her out of bed. The setting, of course, reminds

us that Simon had a home, a family, a job. It was probably not a well-paid job. The fact that his mother-in-law serves them the meal indicates that they did not have servants to do it for them.[29]

The first challenge is simply to define what we are dealing with in these stories. People are 'paralysed'; they have a 'withered hand'; there is blindness, leprosy – which is not what we call leprosy, but encompassed a wide range of skin afflictions. There is no attempt at a detailed pathology of these illnesses, not least because the ancient world was unable to think in those terms.

But even assuming we can identify the disease, what about the cure? What actually happens? The answer is: people get better. At least that's what the Gospels claim. Without medical records and doctor's certificates all we have are the stories and the testimony. But whether we believe in the miraculous, or treat it as some mass delusion, the historical fact is that Jesus both claimed to perform and was believed to perform miracles. For the people of his time he was a healer and an exorcist. Whatever the nature of the individual stories, there are too many of these tales to conclude that all of them were inventions.

Perhaps, as with the exorcisms, we would be better looking at what the miracles signify. Because there is a message behind the miracles. They are acts of compassion, but also, sometimes, of aggression. Many of the healing miracles, for example, take place on the Sabbath in direct contravention of Jewish convention. Strictly speaking, healing was one of the thirty-nine categories of prohibited work in the rabbinical teachings on the Sabbath (although exorcism is not mentioned).[30] But here Jesus escapes censure, either because he is too new, or because the setting is entirely domestic and private. Later on he will deliberately, even provocatively, heal people.

Healing also brought restoration. In a world without medical insurance a peasant with an injury, a deformity or a disease was economically crippled. They were reduced to begging. So Jesus' healings frequently bring someone back to 'wholeness', restoring the ability to feed themselves and others. And some diseases also brought impurity. Lepers and permanently bleeding women were rendered impure by their condition, and, as with those with an impure spirit, excluded from the worshipping community. These people are restored, therefore, in ways which go beyond mere physical health.

The healing of Simon's mother-in-law is the first of the hands-on miracles of Jesus, as it were. But it was swiftly followed by many others. Mark tells us that at sundown – which technically marks the day after the Sabbath – people brought their sick and possessed to Jesus for healing and exorcism (Mark 1:32–34). There are so many healings and there are exorcisms that Jesus is overwhelmed. The pressure on Jesus is already intense and he escapes for a while. In the early hours of the morning, while it is still dark, he leaves the house to find a lonely place, his own precious wilderness.

Apparently he did not go far enough. Simon and his companions track Jesus down. The Greek word used for their pursuit is a very strong verb, the implication being that Simon and the others 'hunted' Jesus down. Like a celebrity caught by the paparazzi, Jesus can only rarely escape the long lenses of his followers.

Already the pressure is intense. The rumours are spreading fast and the desperate, the diseased, the demon possessed are flooding to Capernaum. 'Everyone is searching for you,' says Simon (Mark 1:37). So Jesus leaves.

'He went throughout Galilee'

And he went throughout Galilee, proclaiming the message in their synagogues and casting out demons. (Mark 1:39)

Where did he go? Mark has him in the synagogues in Galilee, while Luke has him preaching in the synagogues of Judea (Luke 4:44).[31] Matthew's account is the most far-reaching: Jesus goes to the synagogues of Galilee, preaching and healing every kind of disease (Matt. 4:23), and his fame spreads throughout Syria, so that soon he is followed by crowds from 'the Decapolis, Jerusalem, Judea, and from beyond the Jordan' (Matt. 4:25).

Jesus tells his disciples that he wants to go to the 'neighbouring towns'; the word used is *komopoleis* (Mark 1:38), and it indicates not the cities, but the smaller centres, something more akin to our market towns.[32] Smaller places even than Capernaum (which was a *polis*). He wants to go to ordinary people, in ordinary places.

Other than that, Mark does not tell us much about this tour. He relates, in fact, only one incident, one which is characteristic of

Jesus – the healing of lepers. What the Gospels call leprosy is not 'modern' leprosy, Hansen's disease. Leprosy in ancient times was a generic, catch-all term for anyone with a scaly skin disease, skin rashes, blemishes or other kinds of disfigurements.[33]

Like possession, leprosy brought impurity with it. Even being under the same roof as a leper made you impure; lying down or eating within the house would necessitate a complete change of clothes (Lev. 14:33–47). According to the Mishnah, even if you stick part of your body in, you will be unclean: 'If a man that was clean put his head and the greater part of his body inside a house that was unclean, he becomes unclean; and if a man that was unclean put his head and the greater part of his body inside a house that was clean, he renders it unclean.'[34]

The only houses which cannot be made unclean through contact with lepers are those owned by Gentiles – who were unclean anyway.[35] In Job, leprosy is described as 'death's firstborn'. Leprosy made you into the walking dead.[36] No pious Jew wanted to touch the dead. To do so made you – guess what? – impure.

For this reason, lepers were kept in a state of almost permanent quarantine. All forms of Judaism presuppose the exclusion of lepers from towns and communities. Anyone with an active or incurable form of leprosy was banned from the city of Jerusalem, let alone the temple. Only those who had recovered could enter, and even then there was a special place in the temple for them – the House of Lepers – where they could undergo the various purification rituals. Like the demoniacs, they were dwellers on the margins, shadowy exiles. The lepers Jesus encounters on the edge of a village in Samaria shout at him from a distance (Luke 17:12).

Significantly, Jesus touches the leper before he is cured (Matt. 8:3; Mark 1:41; Luke 5:13). This makes Jesus ritually impure, but there is no indication that he does anything about this. Jesus seems unafraid of contracting impurity himself; his only interest is making the other person whole. The impure is made pure. The exiles are brought home. The 'dead' are brought back to life.

There is a little bit more to it than that, however. The words Jesus uses seem to indicate that he declares the leper clean – and that was something which only the priests in Jerusalem could do officially. And while most Bible translations have Jesus moved with pity or compassion, some early versions of Mark record that Jesus was 'angry' (Mark 1:41). He seems to send the leper back to the priests in order to prove a point (Mark 1:44). The phrase 'as a testimony to them' is used elsewhere in Mark's Gospel for testimony given before hostile audiences.[37] So this is a challenge to the system. Jesus here is attacking a system which keeps these people at arm's length. He touches the man without fear because he knows that you have to touch these people in order to heal them. And he sends him out as a message – not to everyone, for he orders the leper not to say anything in public – but to the priests. Jesus is indignant. Angry. And it is going to get him into trouble.

'He went up a mountain'

It is at this point in the narrative that Matthew includes perhaps his most famous passage: the so-called Sermon on the Mount. I say 'so-called' because it was not a sermon, and the mount was less a mountain and more what you might call a hill. The title, in fact, comes from much later, from Augustine writing in the fourth century. Calling this a 'sermon' is like calling synagogue 'church'. Jesus sits down and discusses things with his disciples. It is not a sermon on the mount: it is a discussion up the hill.

Or discussions. What Matthew does here is to gather together a core collection of *logia,* or sayings, of Jesus.[38] This material includes some of Jesus' most distinctive and well-known teaching: the beatitudes, with their upside-down kingdom where the poor, the mournful and the merciful are happy; the requirement to be salt of the earth – preserving, purifying, adding flavour; the injunction to give no thought for personal security, but to ask merely for daily bread and to strive for the kingdom of God.

A lot of this material has parallels in other Jewish teachings of the time. Variants of the 'golden rule' of Matthew 7:12, for example, can be found in other Jewish writings. 'What you hate, do not do to anyone,' says the book of Tobit; 'Judge your neighbour's feelings by your own,' says the book of Sirach.[39] In the Mishnah, Rabbi Eliezer said, 'Let the respect owing to your fellow be as precious to you as the respect owing to you yourself. And don't be easy to anger. And repent one day before you die.'[40]

Similarly, Jesus' metaphor of the smooth and easy path relies on Jewish ideas of the 'two ways'. In the Dead Sea Scrolls it says, 'He has placed before you two ways, one which is good and one which is evil.'[41] Jesus' followers were to use the same image in the *Didache* – a kind of discipleship manual for the early church – which opens, 'There are two ways, one of life and one of death and there is a great difference between these two ways.'[42] One of the most famous rabbis, Rabbi Yohanan ben Zakkai, asked his disciples to describe 'the straight path to which someone should stick' and 'the bad road, which someone should avoid'.[43]

While Jesus may be drawing on current thinking, however, he stretches these ideas, tests them to their limits. This is demanding stuff. Up until this moment Jesus has been a welcoming figure: tax-collectors and prostitutes, Gentile soldiers, even Samaritans are welcome. Lepers can be touched, demons chucked out. This is a thoroughly inclusive kingdom where, in story after story, event after event, the poor and the outcast get the best seats in the house. And you start to think: maybe Jesus does want to throw everything out, clear all the Judaisms of their obsession with the Torah.

Then you get this:

> Do not think that I have come to abolish the law or the prophets; I have come not to abolish but to fulfil … For I tell you, unless your righteousness exceeds that of the scribes and Pharisees, you will never enter the kingdom of heaven. (Matt. 5:17, 20)

He does not intend to abolish the Law and the Prophets – he is going to supercharge them. We see this in what are called the *antitheses*: the 'you have heard this, but I say this' formula. You have heard it said, 'Don't commit murder, don't commit adultery, don't swear falsely, an eye for an eye, a tooth for a tooth, love your neighbour …' But I say, 'Don't even be angry, don't even look with lust, don't swear at all, don't take revenge, love your enemies.' It is not that outward purity is wrong, but you have to go way beyond it. It has to be much more than skin deep. External purity is not what matters; the desires of the heart are just as important.

The kingdom is, indeed, open to anyone who wants to find it, but just because anyone can join, it does not mean there is not a price to be paid.

Over the years much of the impact of this incendiary teaching has been softened. The church has tended to spiritualise the teaching, or file it away as an unreachable goal, a counsel of perfection, its only purpose being to show us how inadequate we are in comparison. But this is not how the early church viewed it, nor how it was viewed at the time. It is an uncomfortable fact that Jesus *meant* this stuff.

He was dealing with real problems of his time. Problems of debt, of anger, of oppression. One of the key elements of this teaching is Jesus' support for the underdog. The poor, the persecuted, the mourners, the hungry, those who have been treated unjustly – all these are the blessed, the happy, the fortunate ones. Jesus begins with words of comfort for the poor and the marginalised, but he never says that their poverty or their marginalisation will be taken away. These are arguably the least comforting words of comfort ever.

By calling it 'the Sermon on the Mount' we turn it into a timeless, abstract piece of speculative theology, but that was not what Jesus was doing up this hill. He was discussing with his disciples how they were to live. Jesus' teaching on divorce, for example, has been seen as a blanket injunction for all times. It is wrong. Full stop. But divorce today is very different from Jesus' day. Jesus' teaching on divorce (Matt. 5:31–32) has to be seen first and foremost in the context of protecting the weak and the powerless.

In first-century Judea a woman could be divorced for virtually any reason. Deuteronomy allowed for a man to divorce his wife if he found 'something objectionable about her' (Deut. 24:1) and by first-century AD this catch-all phrase meant that a man could issue a bill of divorce for virtually any reason. Different rabbinical schools argued that it permitted a man to divorce his wife if she burned the dinner (Rabbi Hillel), or even if she were less attractive than another woman (Rabbi Akiba). Women, on the other hand, could only initiate divorce if their husband was impure in some way.[44]

We can observe this in action. Josephus divorced his wife because he was 'not pleased with her behaviour', even though she was the mother of his three children. He subsequently went up in the world and married a Cretan Jew 'of eminent parents'.[45]

So Jesus' injunction – that divorce is only permissible in the case of adultery – not only protects women, but goes way beyond the restrictions of rabbinical Judaism.

In reading the teaching of Jesus we should always pay attention to what it meant for those first listeners. His teaching had – and has – an immediate social impact. Nothing illustrates that better than the one truly ground-breaking and original idea in the teaching: non-violence.

'An eye for an eye and a tooth for a tooth'

In church you do not hear a great deal about Jesus' advocacy of non-violence. On a personal level, I have been a Christian for over thirty years and I cannot recall hearing a single sermon on the topic. Pacifism is something which is restricted to the fringe. Monks, perhaps. Anabaptists and Quakers. Strange people with beards and sandals. We know he said these things, but we do not like to talk about it. Whisper it quietly, but maybe he was a bit misguided on this one.

From a purely historical point of view, Jesus' espousal of non-violent resistance is absolutely fundamental to his message and to the events of his life. Jesus, to put it bluntly, was killed because he refused to fight. We cannot understand the historical Jesus, and certainly not what happened to him, without grasping the principle of non-retaliation and non-violent resistance. Jesus' entire approach to changing society – changing the world – was based on the idea of non-violent resistance.

The root of his teaching lay in his ideas about who constituted our neighbour, and what our attitude to that neighbour should be. 'You shall love your neighbour as yourself,' he tells people (Matt. 19:19; 22:39; Mark 12:31; Luke 10:27). But when asked to define who this neighbour is, he tells the story of the good Samaritan, completely overturning the conventional wisdom. Neighbours were not those in your street or those in your clan or your tribe or your nationality: your enemy was, in fact, your neighbour. Your neighbours were everywhere. And they should be loved. This was a truly, astonishingly radical idea. 'There is a sweeping universality in the love Jesus demands which has no parallel in Jewish literature.'[46] Take one of the most famous passages:

You have heard that it was said, 'An eye for an eye and a tooth for a tooth.' But I say to you, Do not resist an evildoer. But if anyone strikes you on the right cheek, turn the other also; and if anyone wants to sue you and take your coat, give your cloak as well; and if anyone forces you to go one mile, go also the second mile. Give to everyone who begs from you, and do not refuse anyone who wants to borrow from you. (Matt. 5:38–42)

'Eye for eye, tooth for tooth' is in the Torah (Exod. 21:24). It is a way of limiting the extent of revenge, of avoiding an escalating blood feud. But Jesus goes way beyond the Torah, rejecting the use of any violence at all. He goes on to illustrate how this might work in a number of very specific first-century circumstances.

'Turn the other cheek,' he says. But why the right cheek, for example? Why is that one specified? Because for most people, that would be the cheek that was struck with the back of the hand. Most people are right handed. Striking someone's cheek with the palm of the hand would mean hitting their left cheek, but the right cheek was the one that would be struck with a dismissive, back-of-the-hand swipe. It is the kind of gesture associated with those in power – soldiers, interrogators. In the social context it is a serious, even demeaning personal insult.[47]

Then there is that odd phrase, 'if anyone wants to sue you'. This is not about charity. This is not about someone simply in need of a coat who asks for a loan of yours. The Greek word translated 'coat' implies something nearer to what we would call a shirt, something worn next to the skin. It was the undergarment, while the cloak was worn on top. This, then, is a lawsuit where the creditor is demanding the shirt off your back, and then takes your jacket as well.[48] Who, in Jesus' society, would do that? Those who were suing for the repayment of a debt. The image recalls a passage in Deuteronomy:

When you make your neighbour a loan of any kind, you shall not go into the house to take the pledge. You shall wait outside, while the person to whom you are making the loan brings the pledge out to you. If the person is poor, you shall not sleep in the garment given you as the pledge. You shall give the pledge back by sunset, so that your neighbour may sleep in the cloak and bless you; and it will be to your credit before the LORD your God. (Deut. 24:10–13)

This picture shows a debt pledged by the only thing a poor person has to guarantee security: his garment. Deuteronomy says to give it back by sunset because, for many poor people, their outer garment served as their bedding as well. For the peasant followers of Jesus, encumbered by debt, owing taxes and tithes, this message would be shocking. Unfair, even. In this context, a prayer like the Lord's Prayer (Matt. 6:9–13) has to be read somewhat differently. 'Forgive us our debts,' it runs, 'as we also have forgiven our debtors.' The Greek word is *opheilema*, which refers to a monetary debt.[49]

To think of it as sins – or the archaic 'trespasses' – is not wrong, in the wider context of Jesus' teaching, but it misses the very real application for his first-century listeners who were owed money. The forgiveness from God was conditional on how they treated those who were in hock to them.

Then there is the 'second mile'. Who forces you to go a mile? Soldiers. This is a specifically military issue; an imperial issue, indeed. 'Forces you to go' (*angareuo*) is a technical term for the Roman soldier's practice of commandeering civilian labour in an occupied country. The same word is used when Simon of Cyrene is compelled to carry Jesus' crossbeam (Matt. 27:32). Imperial soldiers could simply order a peasant to act as a porter and the peasant had to comply. Jesus suggests that his disciples should go beyond the *milion* – which is a Latin word for the Roman military mile of 1,000 paces. So this is an unmistakably imperial, military situation, a situation born out of occupation.[50]

Then the final illustration: give to beggars and do not refuse those who want to borrow from you. The beggars clause is self-explanatory, but why would someone in Jesus' time refuse to lend someone money? Probably because they thought they would not get it back. There were two reasons for that: either the loanee was too poor to repay, or the loan itself would become null and void. We are back on debts again, such a huge issue for Jesus' audience.

Torah law had specific clauses designed to protect people from falling into long-term debt. Every seventh year – the Sabbath year – debts were cancelled. No more money needed to be paid. The intention was good, but the effect was to make credit harder to gain, since no one was going to lend money near the Sabbath year.

Rabbi Hillel found a way round it, by inventing a loan secured by a *prozbul*, a declaration that the loan would not be remitted in the seventh year.[51] But that too backfired, because the effect was to bypass the Sabbath legislation entirely and so introduce permanent debt.[52]

So one implication of Jesus' message here is that the creditor should not refuse to lend money because it is near a Sabbath year. Just loan it anyway. It is a strong message to creditors, which included not just the wealthy citizens, but the temple as well. The temple was the richest institution in Jewish Palestine. Its wealth was invested in the land through loans to needy peasants, and when the loans were defaulted on, the land passed into temple ownership.[53]

We can see from this examination that the illustrations Jesus gives are specifically grounded in his time and society. He is talking to poor peasants being sued by their creditors, to oppressed citizens being struck by soldiers and forced to act as porters, to those at the bottom of the social scale, brutally dismissed with a back-of-the-hand slap. He is talking to people with real enemies. He is telling them to show astonishing, utterly subversive generosity in the face of aggression.

Ironically, it was this kind of radical submission, this unblinking repudiation of violence and revenge, which made Jesus the most dangerous, most potent threat to the authorities. It was precisely because he refused to fight in any conventional way that the authorities did not know how to combat his ideas.

Jesus' teaching on non-violent resistance owes nothing to any previous teacher. It always has been dangerous, radical. Kurlansky has pointed out that non-violence is such a radical concept that there is no positive word for it. It can only be defined by what it is not.[54]

It remains radical because the underlying issue is common to all times and all societies. 'Most political orders are established by violence and certainly use violence to maintain themselves.'[55] That was certainly true in Jesus' day and it must have been very hard, for Jesus' Jewish audience, to grasp the idea that those who oppressed them – the enemies of Israel – should not be struck down.

For Jesus, violence was an option. Jesus had power and used power. The devil assumes that he has the power to command the angels, James and John assume he has enough power to lend some to them so they can zap a Samaritan village. But Jesus understood that, in the words of Mark Kurlansky, 'violence is a virus that infects and takes over'.[56] The same is true of hatred and lust and all the negatives which Jesus fought so hard against. This is why drastic action had to be taken. Jesus talked about stopping these thoughts in terms of amputation. Cut the hand off, pluck the eye out. And ultimately, he was proved right. The only way to take a stand about the violence was through violence itself: not through inflicting it, but through evicting it. Amputating violence. Conquering it.

His followers in the early church took Jesus' teachings and ran with them. The early church is the first known group to reject militarism. They lived among some of the most militaristic societies on earth, but they refused to fight and the hallmark of their communities was peace. In the earliest of the Christian writings, the letters of Paul, we can clearly see this teaching. Paul's injunction to bless our enemies shows clearly that Jesus' words were already circulating in the church. 'Do not be overcome by evil,' he says, 'but overcome evil with good' (Rom. 12:21). As Richard Hays has written, 'There is not a syllable in the Pauline letters that can be cited in support of Christians employing violence.'[57]

Thirty years after Paul, that most revolutionary of tracts, Revelation, depicts the followers of the Beast as violent and the followers of the Lamb as peaceful.[58] Later still, writers like Ignatius and Origen actively promoted non-violence. 'We Christians do not become fellow soldiers with the Emperor, even if he presses for this,' wrote Origen. They did not condemn the military, they sought converts within the army, but they would not sign up. Tertullian wanted to convert soldiers so that they would not fight.[59] The fact is that 'for the first three hundred years of its life the church was almost universally pacifist'.[60] The victory over evil had already been won, by Jesus through his sacrificial death, and in so far as they had to fight at all, they had to fight it with the same 'weapons' as Jesus: humility, mercy, self-sacrifice to the point of martyrdom.

Later, of course, when Christianity became the religion of empire, it somehow had to accommodate violence within its theology. And so began the gradual diminution of this teaching, its expulsion to the margins or its recategorisation as 'spiritual' more than practical. For the best part of two thousand years the church has been disarming Jesus, the preacher whose most potent weapon was peace.

'He returned to Capernaum'

Mark does not tell us how long Jesus toured Galilee. He just uses the stock phrase 'after some days' (Mark 2:1). However long it was, it was not long enough to dampen the fevered interest in him. When it is reported that he is 'at home', the crowds once again flock to his door, so much so that at one point the flat roof of (presumably Simon's) house is opened up and a paralysed man let down in order to be healed. The word used to describe the stretcher on which the man was carried is a Latinism, a *krabatton*, which describes the mattress of a poor man, or the simple bedroll of a soldier.[61]

Jesus heals the man and, for the first time, a frisson of unease goes through those attending – because Jesus not only heals the man, but says, 'Son, your sins are forgiven' (Mark 2:5). The scribes, their antennae tuned to any hint of blasphemy, immediately respond, 'It is blasphemy! Who can forgive sins but God alone?' (Mark 2:7). Jesus answers them by commanding the man to rise up and walk, which he does.

Further questions are raised by Jesus' choice of friends. Levi, son of Alphaeus, is sitting at his tollbooth when Jesus calls him. Levi is a toll-collector, rather than one of the so-called 'tax-farmers'. Levi's job was to collect the duties owed on goods travelling to and from the territory of Herod Philip. Toll-collectors were usually Jews, and were under the authority of the local ruler – in this case, Levi is a low-level official working for Antipas. Toll-collectors, like border guards and customs officers in many parts of the world today, had great opportunities for bribes and kick-backs. They were renowned for their dishonesty and they were widely shunned by other Jews.[62] Not only does Jesus call Levi to be a disciple, he eats with him and with other 'tax-collectors and sinners' (Mark 2:15).[63] Mark leaves no room for doubt about the intimacy of the occasion: Jesus reclines at table with the tax-collectors. He is not distant or aloof. No wonder the scribes are outraged. (There are hints, too, of other splits, other divisions. Jesus is doing things differently from the Baptiser's disciples [Mark 2:18–22]. And reports, presumably, reach the ears of John, far away in his prison.)

'One Sabbath he was going through the cornfields'

Then there is the Sabbath. Few things were so characteristic of the Jews – or so odd, from the Gentile point of view – as their observance of the Sabbath. The Sabbath was a day set apart for God, a sign, a token of their devotion. It was more than just a quaint ritual, more even than making clear that there were some things in life more important than work. It was a way of imitating God: for six days he worked, and then he took a rest.

The rules governing Sabbath observation were complex. The Bible said that no work should be done – but what, exactly, was work? The tractate Sabbath in the Mishnah contains thirty-nine kinds of forbidden activity, everything from sowing seed to carrying an object, tying or untying knots, even writing two letters of the alphabet. Not only that, but any work which could not be finished on the day before – such as putting cloth in dye, or setting traps for birds, should not be begun.[64] A Jew was only permitted to travel 1,000 cubits on the day and, according to the book of Jubilees, all sex was prohibited, although whether this was deemed 'work' it does not say.[65]

To other nations the practice appeared baffling. The Romans believed that the Jews were simply lazing about and eating cold food. Seneca mocked the Jews for losing 'in idleness almost a seventh of their life'.[66] On the Sabbath, Jewish soldiers were only allowed to fight in self-defence. In fact they had previously not been allowed to fight at all, but, according to the book of Maccabees, the Syrians launched an attack on the Sabbath and a thousand Jews were massacred because they would not take up arms. After this the Jews decided that they must at least be permitted to defend themselves.[67]

For all this, it would be wrong to see the Sabbath as a dour, joyless day. For black, gloomy Sabbatarianism we have to look to Calvin much more than the Torah. For Jews it was a day of feasting and thanksgiving. The beginning of the Sabbath was marked by a prayer of dedication over the glass of wine, the end of the Sabbath by a prayer of thanksgiving.

According to rabbinical records, Sabbath was actually deemed to have begun when three stars appeared in the sky. The first two stars served as warnings. When the first star appeared, the *hazzan* would go onto the roof of the highest building in the neighbourhood, taking with him a 'trumpet of the Sabbath' which he would use to alert the workers in the fields to leave their tasks. When the second star appeared he blew again, to warn the merchants to stop trading, and when the third blast was heard the Sabbath lamp was lit and the Sabbath proper had begun. As soon as the lamp was lit, Sabbath had begun and the family would sit down to their meal. Following this meal, however, no food was eaten until after the synagogue service on Saturday morning. This explains the hunger of the disciples when they were walking through a field of wheat on the Sabbath (Matt. 12:1–8; Mark 2:23–28; Luke 6:1–5).[68]

Sabbath observance was *complicated*. It needed careful preparation. During the day on the Friday the house would be prepared and carefully cleaned and the food for the Sabbath prepared in advance, since any cooking on the day itself was forbidden. The lamp would need to be filled with oil. Some people would wash – particularly those in unclean trades like tanners. Various ways were found to get round Sabbath legislation. It was forbidden, for example, to carry a tool or utensil or food, or anything really, from one home to another. But if the homes were joined in some way – for example, if they shared a common courtyard – they were regarded as a common dwelling and the food could be placed in the middle of the courtyard and shared. And what if you were living day to day, hand to mouth? How could you set aside enough food to observe the Sabbath?

It was not just the day, either. There was the whole business with the Sabbath year. Every seven years the land was supposed to lie fallow. The earth was to have a kind of Sabbath-day rest. It is a great idea in principle – the earliest recorded instance of crop rotation – but what did this mean for the hard-pressed peasant? It is hard to imagine that they would ever have been able to do that.

In the Gospels there is a definite feeling that something had gone wrong with Sabbath observance. Something which should have brought people closer to God was pushing them further away. It is perhaps for this reason that, from Capernaum onwards, Jesus deliberately and provocatively sets about undermining the practices surrounding the Sabbath. For Jesus, what you can and cannot do on the Sabbath becomes a crucial issue. 'The sabbath was made for humankind,' he said, 'and not humankind for the sabbath' (Mark 2:27).

In a passage that Matthew places just before the incident in the wheatfield, Jesus even likened himself to the Sabbath: 'Come to me, all you that are weary and are carrying heavy burdens, and I will give you rest. Take my yoke upon you, and learn from me; for I am gentle and humble in heart, and you will find rest for your souls. For my yoke is easy, and my burden is light' (Matt. 11:28–30).

In this section of Mark, Jesus is accused of two irregularities. First, his disciples pluck heads of grain and eat them – a process which could be seen as gathering food. When he is accused of breaking Sabbath law, he refers to the story of David's men plucking grain to eat when they were fleeing for their lives. It is hardly, to be honest, a fair comparison, but Jesus seems intent on making a point. He is not just picking grain, he is picking a fight.

That is then underlined in the synagogue when he heals a man with a withered hand. 'Is it lawful to do good or to do harm on the sabbath,' Jesus asks, 'to save life or to kill?' (Mark 3:4). It is a deliberately inflammatory gesture. There was nothing life-threatening about the disease, nothing that could not have waited until either the Sabbath was over or until Jesus was in private. In fact, there is no indication that the man actually wanted healing: Jesus has to call him forward (Mark 3:3). It is political theatre, a deliberate act, as are all Jesus' acts on the Sabbath and in the synagogue. He is not some naive good man, innocently doing good and surprised at the consequences. He knows precisely what he is doing.[69] And although he wins, according to Mark the result is that the Pharisees and the Herodians start to plot against him.

It is a curious combination of foes. The name implies that these were supporters of the Herodian regime, which was undoubtedly the case, since what Mark is probably referring to is Herodian employees: officials appointed by Antipas to provide local government. They would have had little worry about Jesus' attitude towards the Sabbath, but they might have been worried about Jesus' increasing popularity. There may also have been a more pointed reason for their dislike of Jesus' healing: they may have been responsible for some of the people's afflictions.

'They came to him in great numbers'

According to Mark, Jesus sets out for the 'sea' where he is joined not just by Galileans, but by people 'from Judea, Jerusalem, Idumea, beyond the Jordan, and the region around Tyre and Sidon' (Mark 3:8). They are coming from all directions: north, south, east and west. 'He told his disciples to have a boat ready for him because of the crowd, so that they would not crush him; for he had cured many, so that all who had diseases pressed upon him to touch him' (Mark 3:9–11).

This brief passage (Mark 3:7–12) is full of the vocabulary of pressure. Not just one unclean spirit, but many call out, naming Jesus in the futile hope that they will escape exorcism. The crowd press in on him – the Greek word *epipipto* can mean 'to embrace', but it also means 'to press', 'to fall on', 'to cause damage by falling on'. Screaming fans. Jesusmania.

Those who are doing this are described as 'all who had diseases', but the word which is translated as 'disease' is *mastis*, which is the Greek word meaning 'to whip' or 'scourge'. The text literally says that 'all those who were scourged pressed on him to touch him'.

Now Mark does use it elsewhere in the sense of suffering and bodily affliction, but only in one specific case, the woman who was bleeding for twelve years (Mark 5:29). The woman in Mark is afflicted, tormented, 'scourged' by her disease. Luke also uses it – there it is translated as 'plagues': 'Jesus had just then cured many people of diseases, plagues [*mastigon*], and evil spirits' (Luke 7:21).[70]

It can be used as a metaphor for afflictions, but it always has the connotation of being lashed, whipped, beaten. Elsewhere in the Gospels, *mastis* is used when someone is interrogated by scourging. The same word is used when Jesus is beaten by soldiers (Matt. 20:19; Mark 10:34; Luke 18:33; John 19:1) and by Jesus himself, to predict that his followers will be beaten in the syna-gogue (Matt. 10:17; 23:34). It is the same word used when Paul is to be 'examined by flogging' (Acts 22:24).

Why does Mark choose this word? In 1:34 he describes a vir-tually identical scene, and uses the normal Greek word for dis-eases – *nosos*. Treating this word metaphorically certainly makes it consistent with Mark 1:34, but that is the point, surely? Mark was not being consistent. He was using a different word.

What if this *was not* a metaphor? What if the word meant what it said: beatings, lashes? What if Jesus cured people of dis-eases, whippings and evil spirits? Then we have a very different picture. We have people coming to Jesus who had been beaten by the authorities; by the Herodians, the soldiers, the administrators and magistrates who were working for Antipas.[71]

There is a hugely political aspect to Mark just under the sur-face. The idea that Jesus was somehow separate from the political realities of his day is simply not true. He engaged with them in a different way – in the wrong way, according to some people. His was not the way of violence, but of peace. His answer to beat-ing was not revenge, but healing. Jesus' engagement with political issues was also evident in the next incident recorded by Mark: the selection of the twelve apostles.

'He appointed the twelve'

Jesus had many followers. There were Jerusalem-based disciples such as Nicodemus and, possibly, the Beloved Disciple; there were Lazarus and Simon the Leper at Bethany and Nathanael in Cana. We know that Joseph Barsabbas and Matthias were also well-known disciples, as they were nominated to replace Judas (Acts 1:23). Others, such as Zacchaeus and Bartimaeus, would join in Jericho. There are, as well, the seventy or seventy-two disciples whom, according to Luke, Jesus sent ahead of him as he was making his way towards Jerusalem. Not to mention the women who supported his cause.

Out of all these, the twelve disciples selected in Galilee are the core group, the inner circle. Mark terms them the 'apostles', a word which means someone sent out, an envoy or representative sent with a message.

So it comes as some surprise to find that the lists in the Gospels (Mark 3:13–19; Matt. 10:1–4; Luke 6:12–16) are not all the same. And John does not give us a list at all.

Mark and Matthew have Thaddaeus, while Luke has 'Judas son of James'. Matthew is called 'the tax-collector' in the Gospel which bears his name, where we also have more or less the story of Levi, but with 'Matthew' as the main character. So is it the same person? It seems to me more likely that the writer of Matthew's Gospel, knowing that Matthew was a tax-collector, assumed the story of Levi was about him. But Mark, where Levi has just featured, makes no mention of him in the list, nor does he indicate that Matthew is the same person.

Clearly Jesus' closest associates are Simon, James and John. These three also accompany Jesus to the transfiguration, which may indicate that they were the inner inner circle. They are also the only people he renames.

Simon becomes 'Peter' (Mark 3:16). It has become such a widely accepted name that we forget that *petros* is just the Greek version of the Aramaic word *cephas*, which means 'stone' rather than 'rock'. Until Jesus invented it, *petros* was a noun, not a person's name. It is not used as a name anywhere in Greek literature before the Christian era. *Cephas* was, possibly, used as a name – apparently it appears as an Aramaic name in a fifth-century BC text – but if that is the only other appearance, it is hardly a common one. So we could imagine this as saying 'Simon, to whom he gave the name Stony'. The Rock. Rocky.[72]

The same problem is true of the Sons of Thunder (Mark 3:17). *Boanerges* is a word entirely without any other parallels. The real problem is that no one is sure of the derivation of *Boanerges*. It has been suggested that it refers to a 'commotion' or 'excitement', the 'rumbling of the sea' or even an earthquake. All we can take from this is the impression of excitement, or a sudden turmoil likely to burst from beneath the surface.[73]

Then there are others whom we have met with John the Baptist in Judea: Andrew, Simon's brother, Philip from Bethsaida.

Beyond the three closest disciples, there are new and comparatively little-known characters. Philip and Andrew are Greek names, Bartholomew is actually a surname: Bar Talmai, son of

Talmai. Matthew is a shortened version of the Hebrew name Mattathias; if he is the same as Levi it is hard to see how one name leads to the other. Thomas is an Aramaic name meaning 'twin' – hence his Greek translation *Didymus*. James the son of Alphaeus may be the same as the younger James mentioned in Mark 15:40 whose mother was called Mary and brother Joses. We should note that Levi was also a son of Alphaeus (Mark 2:14). Were these all part of the same family? Did Levi's call result in his brothers James and Joses following Jesus and his mother being there at the cross?

Mark and Matthew have Thaddaeus (Matt. 10:3), but Luke has Judas the son of James (6:16; Acts 1:13). It is possible that these are the same person, and that Luke was preserving his original name, Judas – a name which rather fell out of favour after the events of Jesus' death.

We can see, therefore, that the people who accompanied Jesus came from a variety of backgrounds. At least four were fishermen. Matthew was a tax-collector. And one, at least, was a former political extremist.

Simon the Zealot in Luke is Simon the Cananaean in Mark and Matthew. 'Cananaean' here does not refer to a place name, however, but is a Greek version of his nickname: the Greek word *kananion* is a transliteration of the Aramaic *qanana*, meaning 'zeal'. Simon is a political activist.

The Zealots were the left-wing radicals. The Provisional wing of the Pharisees. They advocated guerilla action against Rome and the withholding of all taxes and financial support. They were violently anti-high priest. When the Zealots gained control of Jerusalem during the first war of independence, they murdered the high priests Ananus and Gamaliel.[74] However, that was over three decades away from Jesus' time. Mark's and Matthew's use of 'Cananaean' probably records an earlier name, for the Zealots as any kind of organised political force really only arise in the decades immediately before the Jewish revolt. It seems likely, however, that there was a continual undercurrent of insurgency against Roman rule. Josephus talks about a 'fourth way' which he links with a man called Judas who led a revolt against a Roman census in AD 6. 'These men agree in all other things with the Pharisaic notions,' he writes, 'but they have an inviolable attachment to liberty.'[75] There may have been other proto-Zealots among the apostles as well. Some ancient manuscripts of Matthew 10:3 have the name Judas Zelotes instead of Thaddaeus.[76]

The presence of a Zealot in Jesus' disciples has led to speculation that Jesus himself was a political revolutionary of that sort.[77] But you might as well argue that Matthew's inclusion meant that Jesus was a tax-collector – and to anyone advocating an armed struggle against Rome, 'loving your enemies' would have been a betrayal. It would, in fact, have put Jesus on the side of their enemies. The presence of both a former revolutionary and a former state functionary – a tax-collector – in Jesus' core disciples simply demonstrates how dramatically an encounter with Jesus could change one's life.

Then there is Judas Iscariot. The surname is opaque, like the character of the man. The most widely accepted meaning is 'man from Kerioth', a town near Hebron mentioned in Joshua 15:25. There are parallels in Josephus to this type of naming, but there are doubts that the town existed at the time of Jesus. So perhaps there are other explanations. The Aramaic term *sakar* means 'liar' or 'fraud', but that seems too little a word for what he did. Another suggestion is that it refers to *sicarius* – a Latin word meaning 'assassin'. The *Sicarii* were a group of radical revolutionaries, like the Zealots. However, this is an anachronism – the Sicarii were not active until much later, during the revolution. So it seems likeliest that Judas came from Kerioth. A small, almost forgotten town. Not unlike Nazareth.[78]

And it was to the region around Nazareth that Jesus went next.

5. Galilee, AD 31

Evening.

Once it was certain that he was going to die, they had prepared his body for the burial, wrapped it in cloth. He looked dead already. When the moment came the women started the usual wailing and tore their garments, but she wasn't sure if she had the strength left even to do that.

They anointed the body and laid it on the plank of wood.

Then they started the walk, down through the streets and out of the town. Two flute players led the way. One woman, wailing. Professionals. And slowly, the son born on the shoulders of four men, they made their way towards the burial ground, to the cave that had swallowed up her husband and would now devour her son.

She had thought herself too tired to weep, but here the tears came. She cried for her son, of course, and for her husband. And for herself, for who would look after her now? Where would she go for help? She had been a widow, now she was a childless one.

Through her tears she could see a crowd coming towards her. Many people. Coming to the funeral? No. Of course not. Her misery and tragedy were just a speck on their horizon.

For the first time, she felt truly alone.

'Then he went home'

Mark's location is imprecise: 'Then he went home,' he writes. And the crowd, that confused *ochlos*, arrive in such numbers that even ordinary eating is impossible (Mark 3:19b–20).

The implication is that this was Jesus' home in Capernaum. Certainly Luke has Jesus returning to Capernaum, where he heals the slave of a centurion (Luke 7:1–10). The centurion is a 'God-fearer', a proselyte, a Jewish convert who has built a place for the synagogue to meet in Capernaum. Jesus issues the word and the man is healed; it may be that this is a version of the healing that John reports in Cana.

But then Luke whisks Jesus away to a town called Nain, about twenty-five miles from Capernaum, across the lake and on the southern border of Galilee, just before you enter Samaria. Jesus is heading south, it seems – and this is really the scene for the next act in the drama.

Luke records that Jesus entered Nain accompanied by a large crowd. As he enters the city he meets a funeral cortège, carrying the body of a man on a bier. If usual Jewish custom was followed, then, once death was certain, the body would have been prepared for burial, wound in a cloth. When death came, the body was anointed and then placed on a plank of wood. That evening – the same day on which the man had died – he would have been carried out of the town, accompanied by flute players and professional wailing mourners.[1] The deceased is described as a 'man'; his mother was a widow, a position which left her incredibly vulnerable in society.

Jesus touches the bier to halt the procession – ignoring the ritual uncleanness of the dead body.[2] He calls on the man to rise, and 'the dead man sat up and began to speak, and Jesus gave him to his mother' (Luke 7:15). His mother has her son back, but more, she has her life back, her security.

This is the first of several stories in Luke which describe Jesus' relationships with women, but more impressively, it's the first of the several tales of Jesus bringing the dead back to life. At Capernaum there had been healings of the sick, but this is another level altogether. What are we to make of this? It's certainly not a 'one-off': every Gospel has stories of Jesus bringing the dead back to life, although not necessarily the same story.

▷ Widow's son at Nain (Luke 7:11–15): 'Young man, I say to you, rise!'

▷ Jairus's daughter (Mark 5:21–43; Matt. 9:18–26; Luke 8:40–56): 'Little girl, get up!'

▷ Lazarus (John 11:1–44): 'Lazarus, come out!'

Once again we are rather beyond the limits of history. The idea that these miracles were all inventions runs against the fact that in one case, at least, Jesus gives a simple command in Aramaic: he says to Jairus' daughter: *talitha cum*. Hard to imagine a later Greek writer making that up. All we can really say is that every Gospel reports such activities on the part of Jesus – although they are scarcer than the healings and exorcisms – and that these, naturally enough, added to the furore over Jesus in the district. Luke reports that this event spreads 'throughout Judea and all the surrounding country', which is shorthand for the whole of Jewish Palestine.[3]

Two groups in particular have heard stories about Jesus, two of his 'kin', if you like. First, his relatives hear what is happening, and second, still imprisoned in the mountain fastness of the Machaerus, John hears. Neither set of relatives is at all convinced.

Which brings us back again to Mark's 'home'. Maybe the 'home' Mark was talking about was not Capernaum, but Jesus' family home – his home territory. Nain is only six miles from Nazareth, and the next incident that Mark describes is all about Jesus' family.

'A family divided against itself cannot stand'

You do not hear this fact in churches very much, but Jesus' family thought he was mad, and they tried to stop him: 'When his family heard it, they went out to restrain him, for people were saying, "He has gone out of his mind"' (Mark 3:21).

This is another tick to the credibility of the Gospels: such a fact would have been very embarrassing to the early church, and yet they kept it in, so we are undoubtedly dealing with a true story here. It is easy to understand the family's point of view. Jesus was attracting the attention of both the religious and the Herodian civil authorities. He was a hero to the poor and the marginalised;

but a disruptive and disturbing figure to those in religious and secular power. Politically, things were volatile. John had been arrested by Antipas, and now here was Jesus, in an area of Galilee just a few miles from Tiberias and Sepphoris, gathering bigger crowds than John ever did, and performing startling and deliberately provocative miracles.

Whether or not his family agreed with the accusations of madness, they certainly agreed that he needed to be restrained. The word Mark uses here, *krateo*, is the word for taking control of someone, by force if necessary. It is the same word used elsewhere by Mark to describe those who want to arrest Jesus.[4] It's a family arrest.

Others said his problem was worse than madness. Mark puts here an accusation which appears in all the Gospels: that Jesus was in league with demonic powers. 'He has Beelzebul … the ruler of the demons,' said his opponents (Mark 3:22).[5] Beelzebul is an obscure name, but it is a synonym for Satan, the prince of demons.[6] This is the classic smear tactic of religious and political campaigning: demonise your opponent – literally, in this case. They did it to John the Baptist (Luke 7:33), and now they are doing it to Jesus, claiming that he is working for the very forces he claims to oppose.

Jesus destroys their logic. If Beelzebul is fighting his own demons, then that means civil war, and a civil war means that the kingdom is doomed. He illustrates his point by a parable: 'No one can enter a strong man's house and plunder his property without first tying up the strong man; then indeed the house can be plundered' (Mark 3:27). The image is reflected as well in one of the earliest images of Jesus shared by the early church: the thief in the night (1 Thess. 5:2, 4; 2 Pet. 3:10). He is going to break into the strongholds of evil and steal people away.

Then Jesus issues his sternest rebuke. Whoever sins against the Holy Spirit can never be forgiven. This is a verse which has engendered masses of comment and interpretation over the years, by people trying to define what the unforgivable sin is. (Often it turns out to be the sin that they themselves wish to condemn the most.) In context, however, it seems that Jesus is talking about the kind of thing that has just happened: the accusation that he is evil. Those who look at what he is doing and categorise it as demonic cannot be forgiven. For, having dismissed their Saviour, who are they going to ask?

The arrival of his family indicates that Jesus is still in the south-west part of Galilee, perhaps at Nain or Magdala. Close to Naza-reth, anyway, and the family have an opportunity to take charge of him. But they have two difficulties. The first is the sheer weight of numbers. They cannot get to him because of the crowd (Luke 8:19). The second is that he refuses to let them in anyway.

> Then his mother and his brothers came; and standing outside, they sent to him and called him. A crowd was sitting around him; and they said to him, 'Your mother and your brothers and sisters are outside, asking for you.' And he replied, 'Who are my mother and my broth-ers?' And looking at those who sat around him, he said, 'Here are my mother and my brothers! Whoever does the will of God is my brother and sister and mother.' (Mark 3:31–35)

For Jesus' first audiences, it is one of those sharp-intake-of-breath moments. To treat your family this way was outrageous. Jesus' family – his mother, especially – should have been accorded an honoured passage through the crowd. They should have been VIPs. At the top of the guest list. Instead Jesus makes them wait outside, and he uses them to make a point. He gestures at his dis-ciples – and clearly they are male and female – and says 'You are my family, my sisters and brothers.'

The language of family conflict is found several times in Jesus' teaching. He tells his followers, 'Truly I tell you, there is no one who has left house or wife or brothers or parents or children, for the sake of the kingdom of God, who will not get back very much more in this age, and in the age to come eternal life' (Luke 18:29–30). Again, 'Whoever comes to me and does not hate father and mother, wife and children, brothers and sisters, yes, and even life itself, cannot be my disciple' (Luke 14:26).

'Hate' is hyperbole. The point is that Jesus was aware of how the family or clan was a tie that bound people – for good and bad. He was not anti-family. His followers clearly had families. He lived with them and helped them. But in a society where *every-thing* was defined by the kinship structure, Jesus was suggesting a radical break with tradition.

The fact is that, throughout his campaigns, Jesus' family did not really understand what he was doing. His mother is with Jesus at the cross, but his brothers clearly are not (and we shall soon see them in conflict again).

'Are you the one who is to come?'

It is not just his close family who have doubts about Jesus. Far away in his mountain-top prison, John the Baptist has heard something of what Jesus has been doing and he is worried, confused. He sends a delegation, two of his disciples, to check Jesus out. His concern is so great that he is unsure whether Jesus really is 'the one who is to come' (Luke 7:19). But why? It has been suggested that John was concerned by the level of hostility which Jesus was arousing, but that can't be right – John himself was not exactly polite to his opponents, and anyway he was in prison at the time, which indicates an ability to live with a certain level of hostility. Also, Jesus uses words for his opponents which he learned from John (Matt. 3:7; 12:34; 23:33; Luke 3:7). It cannot have been the fact that he was welcoming the wrong people into the kingdom, for in that, too, what Jesus says reflects what we have heard from John. Nor can it be the miracles that Jesus is performing, because those are exactly what Jesus chooses as examples to send back to John to reassure him (Luke 7:21).

It can only be one thing which continually drove a wedge between the two groups: Torah observance. 'John's disciples ... fast and pray, but your disciples eat and drink' (Luke 5:33). That was the difference between them. There were specific occasions when you fasted: notably the Day of Atonement, which was a national fast, and also the four days which recalled the fall of Jerusalem. Add to that the normal Jewish practice of personal fasting and abstinence, with particularly zealous Jews fasting twice a week.[7] Jesus seems to have gone the other way. It is Jesus' reputation as a glutton, as someone who is always eating and drinking, which causes John problems. His lack of respect for Torah observance.

You can understand it, on a human level. Here is Jesus, gaining a reputation as a man who loves a banquet, while John festers in prison. Perhaps John was even expecting rescue. But Jesus came declaring the marriage feast not the religious fast. Time enough for that later on, he said.

Whatever the case, Jesus does not dismiss his concerns. He does not swat John away as he did the Pharisees or the scribes, or even his family. Instead he reassures the messengers, tells them what he is doing. And far from criticising John, Jesus launches a passionate defence of his erstwhile mentor. Whatever doubts John had about Jesus, Jesus had no doubts about John.

> 'I tell you, among those born of women no one is greater than John; yet the least in the kingdom of God is greater than he.' (And all the people who heard this, including the tax-collectors, acknowledged the justice of God, because they had been baptised with John's baptism. But by refusing to be baptised by him, the Pharisees and the lawyers rejected God's purpose for themselves.) (Luke 7:28–30)

No one was greater than John – and yet everyone is. The first shall be last, leaders shall be slaves. It is an upside-down world that Jesus is creating here. But it is a world which is welcomed by Jesus' followers. Allowing for a bit of anti-Pharisee editorialising by Luke, it is clear that Jesus' followers included a great many people who had been baptised by John the Baptist. John had taken the functions of the temple out to the outsiders and the dispossessed. Now Jesus was not only including them in the kingdom, he was making out that they were all on an equal footing. Their leaders complain, like little children, that no one is joining in their games or paying any attention to their tantrums (Luke 7:32–35).

While in Nain, Jesus is invited to the house of a Pharisee called Simon. As he is eating, a woman enters – a 'sinner', in Luke's euphemistic description. A prostitute, most likely. The woman washes Jesus' feet with her tears and dries them with her hair. Then she breaks open a bottle of perfume and anoints Jesus' feet with it. This is one of two tales of Jesus' feet being anointed. It is possible that they are the same story in different guises, but this one has a different feel and some different characteristics.

Jesus is reclining at the table, his sandals removed, his feet pointing away from the table. Foot-washing was an act which was restricted to certain groups of people: wives, children or slaves. It was also to become a crucial image in the formation of the church after Jesus' death. Perhaps it is here that Jesus gets the idea for what he will later do in the Upper Room. Certainly it fits, following his statement about the status of John the Baptist and others in the kingdom.

In this context, it is hard to understate the scandalous nature of this act. For an unmarried woman – especially one of dubious moral standing – to anoint a single man was shocking. Women were dangerous, threatening. They provoked lust in a man and brought him into danger of committing a sin. The later rabbis were emphatic about the danger of even looking at a woman.[8] Even in death a woman could be a temptation, which is why men were hanged naked, but women clothed.

And this woman uses her hair! A woman's hair was considered sexually provocative, much in the same way as her breasts might be considered in Western society today. Going out with your head uncovered was like showing a lot of cleavage: pious women covered their heads in public (and the ultra-pious even kept their hair covered in the home).[9] In the list of offences for which a man may divorce his wife without any financial settlement, the Mishnah includes, 'If she goes out with her hair unbound, or spins [in the sense of spinning yarn] in the street, or speaks with any man.'[10] In the Babylonian Talmud, Rabbi Meir teaches that it is the religious duty of a man to divorce a woman who does this.[11]

This explains the shocked response of Simon the Pharisee to what happens in his house. There is a carnality to her actions. Not only is this woman a notorious sinner, but she does something that for married women was grounds for divorce.[12] Heaven knows what John the Baptist would have made of it.

Jesus, however, does not disapprove or rebuke. He understands that in the world of this woman, this is all she can do to show love and thankfulness. In her vocabulary she has only physical acts as words to offer. It is the only language she knows.

Jesus seems to understand the nature of this woman's world. And his empathy with women is reflected by the number of them who accompany him on his journey. When Jesus leaves Nain and goes on a tour of the region (Luke 8:1) he is accompanied not only by his male disciples, but also by a number of women. Luke mentions three in particular: Susanna; Joanna, the wife of Herod Antipas's steward Chuza; and Mary Magdalene. All three are among women who 'had been cured of evil spirits and infirmities', particularly Mary, 'from whom seven demons had gone out' (Luke 8:3). Nothing is known of Susanna, who does not appear anywhere else in the New Testament. Joanna is more intriguing. Her husband was an *epitropos* – an administrative official – in Antipas's court. It is possible that he was the manager of Herod's estate. He could have been based either in Sepphoris or in Tiberias, both of which are in the region where this action takes place. Tiberias is more likely, as that was Antipas's Galilean headquarters after around AD 20. Joanna was evidently wealthy enough to support Jesus, a risky venture given her husband's employer. Or perhaps her husband had died and she was a wealthy widow.

We know as well that such women received teaching while they were with Jesus. After seeing the empty tomb, they 'remembered Jesus' words' (Luke 24:8), so clearly he had given them the same kind of warnings he gave to his disciples. One intriguing possibility is that Joanna is to be identified with the Junia of Romans 16:7 who became a notable apostle in the early church. (Junia is the Latin version of Joanna.) Junia was Jewish (a kinswoman of Paul) and converted before him, which makes it likely she was a follower of Jesus when he was alive. Although her husband is called Andronicus, it was possibly a Latin nickname and Andronicus could simply mean 'conqueror of men'.[13] Or, more likely, she could have remarried. Whatever the case, Joanna was one of the women who saw Jesus after his resurrection (Luke 24:10).

And then there is Mary. Another woman who saw the risen Jesus: Miriam from Magdala, or Tarichaeae as it was sometimes known. Mary Magdalene.

She has become a creature of myth and legend, has Mary, the poster girl for the Gnostic-lovers and the conspiracy theorists. She has been elevated to Jesus' wife, or to the leader of the church after his death. All clap-trap. In fact we know hardly anything about her. We know she came from Magdala/Tarichaeae, the fish-processing town on the west bank of Lake Galilee. The only other detail we have about her is that she had been exorcised: seven demons had gone out from her. Freed by Jesus, she followed him to the end. Beyond the end, in fact: she was standing at the cross when he died and met him in the graveyard after his resurrection, when she thought he was the gardener.

Magdala was a city with a dodgy reputation. The presence of a hippodrome indicates that there was a significant Gentile population and later the rabbis attributed its decline to its loose morals.[14] (Perhaps that is why this poor girl gets identified as the 'sinful woman' we have just met in Nain. Luke certainly does not imply this: if he had known it was her, he would have said so.)

From the second century onwards, Gnostic writings start to focus on Mary. She features in the *Gospel of Thomas* and then in her very own *Gospel of Mary* where she has secret revelations about Jesus. In the late third century a more romantic note creeps in, and in works like the *Gospel of Philip*, Mary is portrayed as someone whom Jesus frequently kisses and whose close relationship with Jesus leads to envy among the disciples.[15] Mary is a blank canvas, a figure on whom people can project a picture of feminism or romanticism, or even an aristocratic yearning for a divine royal family. You want a wife for Jesus? Or children? You want a female apostle with secret knowledge? She is your girl.

It is all nonsense. There is not a shred of credible historical evidence. What we see in the Gospels are women who were faithful disciples of Jesus, who were healed by him, who followed him and believed in him every bit as much as the men. As we shall see, it is these women who remain with Jesus, right to the bitter end – and even beyond.

'A sower went out to sow'

The mission to take charge of Jesus, to save him from himself, fails. He heads down to the 'Sea'. And he tells some stories on the way. 'He did not speak to them except in parables,' Mark writes (Mark 4:34). Stories all the time, then. Given how accessible the parables were, it makes the verse in Mark rather confusing:

> When he was alone, those who were around him along with the twelve asked him about the parables. And he said to them, 'To you has been given the secret of the kingdom of God, but for those outside, everything comes in parables; in order that "they may indeed look, but not perceive, and may indeed listen, but not understand; so that they may not turn again and be forgiven"'. (Mark 4:10–12)

It is a curious comment, but it implies that the parables form part of the dividing line between insider and outsider. The outsiders listen but just do not get it. In that sense, the parable of the sower, which Mark puts here, is almost a parable about parables. Those who listen to Jesus and get the point are fertile ground for the gospel.

There is not space in this book to go into Jesus' parables in detail, but we can note a few things about them in general. They were a characteristically Jewish way of teaching. (Some teachers specialised. Rabbi Meir was renowned for having a collection of 300 fox parables, only a few of which have survived.[16]) They are one of Jesus' favourite methods of communication, making up about a third of his teaching. They were very much a contemporary method of teaching. Only five parables appear in the whole of the Jewish Scriptures compared with over thirty in the New Testament.[17] Interestingly, while a staple of the Synoptics, John's Gospel includes no real parables.

Parables do not just contain stories. The category includes riddles ('How can Satan cast out Satan?') or similes ('like sheep without a shepherd'). They can be interrogative ('To what shall I liken this generation?'). They can be deliberately 'open', forcing the listener to make a judgement ('Which of these showed mercy?'). In this they were related to the Hebrew *mashal*, which could include stories, but also riddles, proverbs and 'any dark saying intended to stimulate thought'.[18]

They are comparative stories. The Greek word *parabole* is derived from the word *paraballo*, which means 'to set beside or parallel with'. 'The kingdom of heaven is like ...' But they always have a point. Sometimes a very sharp point indeed.

Above all, though, they root abstract concepts in the world around the listeners. Jesus' stories take place in the real, physical world of his time. They are full of peasant farmers worrying about their crops, corrupt judges, absentee landlords, indebted peasantry, widows so poor that the loss of one coin drives them into a frantic search. In this world the landless labourer, the lowest of the low, really did go to the marketplace to wait for harvest work; the road to Jericho from Jerusalem really was dangerous for lone travellers; and, as we have seen, noblemen like Archelaus and Antipas really did go to a distant country to get royal power for themselves (Luke 19:12).

The parable of the sower, for example, reflects the agricultural practice of the time. It begins with a farmer scattering seeds. In Palestine seeds were sown and then ploughed in. The ground was not cleared first: thorns and weeds were ploughed into the soil. Most of the seed would not bear fruit. As all peasants grimly recognised, hopes of a good harvest were not always fulfilled. But, Jesus says, sometimes the tiny seed is triumphant. For people for whom a tenfold yield would be a bumper year, Jesus' predictions of a thirty-, sixty- and hundredfold return are pictures of an unimaginable abundance.[19]

In that sense, all parables are risks. Jesus' parables might sow seeds of repentance in some people, but in others they lead to anger and resentment and a desire for revenge. These are not children's stories. These are incendiary narratives.

'The country of the Gerasenes'

Jesus' presence in western Galilee explains why Mark describes the next location – the country of the Gerasenes – as being 'on the other side' of the lake. Jesus is finished on the western side of the lake and decides to cross the sea. Even this does not avoid the crowds, as a small flotilla of boats set sail from the Tiberias region.

Suddenly a squall comes up, the waves beating the boat and threatening to swamp it. Terrified, the disciples wake Jesus, who stills it with a word, a miracle which more than ever causes the disciples to wonder who this man really is. The literal Greek sums up their feelings: 'they feared with a great fear' (Mark 4:41). Obviously there are all kinds of difficulties with this historically, but we should note first that sudden squalls are common on Lake Galilee. The lake is surrounded by hills, with narrow valleys running down to the lakeside. The wind funnels down these valleys, smacking into the lake surface and whipping up a storm. (During a visit to Galilee I was amazed to find that the lakeside terrace where I was standing was windless and calm, but that high, powerful waves were smashing against the jetty. Clearly they were being whipped up by the wind in another part of the lake entirely.) We should also note the detail in the story. Jesus is precisely located – in the stern of the boat – and he has even got some kind of cushion with him.

Whatever we think of this miracle, it comes in a precisely detailed and well-observed package.

Corroborative details, however, are a bit more of a problem with the story which follows. 'They came to the other side of the lake, to the country of the Gerasenes. And when he had stepped out of the boat, immediately a man out of the tombs with an unclean spirit met him' (Mark 5:1–2). According to Mark, when they come to the other side of the sea, they reach 'the country of the Gerasenes'. Since Gerasa was thirty miles inland, we can only assume that they had built up quite a head of speed.

Clearly Gerasa cannot be the precise location for this miracle, which sees a bunch of pigs plummet off a cliff into the lake (unless we believe that the pigs took a long run-up). Other ancient manuscripts read Gergasenes or Gadarenes. Probably Mark is just intending to convey the area, rather than a specific locale. We know that it took place in the Decapolis, a loose federation of ten cities and their dependent territories (Mark 5:20). This was a Gentile area (hence the pigs). It was the eastern frontier of the Roman Empire. Beyond this the empire ran out, on the steppes of the Arabian desert. Beyond here were the Parthians, the Eastern empires. This, as far as a Roman was concerned, was the last outpost of civilisation.

This is the most dramatic of all the exorcisms. There is the urgency of the situation: Jesus is confronted the minute he steps out of the boat. There is the violence of the symptoms: the man is unnaturally strong, he lives among the dead, he self-harms with sharp stones. In exorcism terms, this is the 'perfect storm'.

The Gentile setting colours the entire incident. We have pigs, for a start, unclean animals found nowhere on Jewish territory. (Today archaeologists can identify areas of Jewish settlement by the absence of pork bones.) Then there are the names. The name the demon tries to use against Jesus is a Hellenistic phrase, 'Son of the Most High God' (Mark 5:7). This would have been tautological (not to mention blasphemous) to a Jew: you cannot have the most high God when there is only one God. But in the Gentile culture, with their pantheon of numerous gods and goddesses, it makes sense.

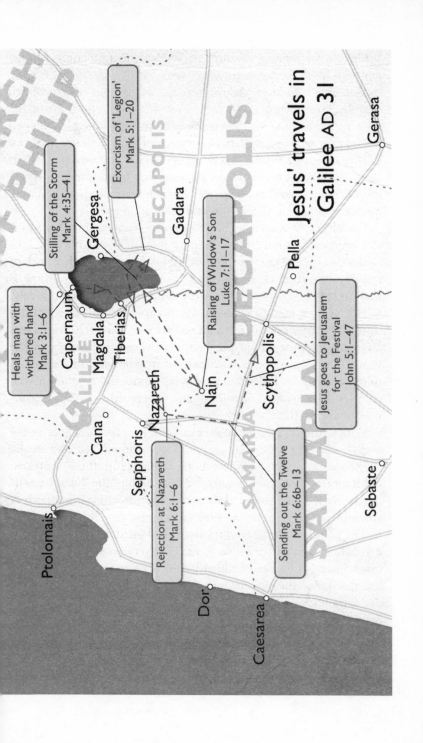

Jesus' travels in
Galilee AD 31

Heals man with
withered hand
Mark 3:1–6

Stilling of the Storm
Mark 4:35–41

Exorcism of 'Legion'
Mark 5:1–20

Raising of Widow's Son
Luke 7:11–17

Jesus goes to Jerusalem
for the Festival
John 5:1–47

Rejection at Nazareth
Mark 6:1–6

Sending out the Twelve
Mark 6:6b–13

TETRARCHY OF PHILIP

GALILEE

DECAPOLIS

SAMARIA

Ptolomais
Cana
Sepphoris
Nazareth
Capernaum
Magdala
Tiberias
Gergesa
Gadara
Pella
Gerasa
Nain
Scythopolis
Dor
Caesarea
Sebaste

The actual events follow the pattern already identified. The demon tries to gain control over Jesus, but is thwarted. Instead, Jesus demands to know the demon's name. And it is many. It is, in fact, Legion. He throws out the demon(s), who flee into a herd of pigs. Maddened, the pigs charge into the sea and drown. At which, however, the grateful populace beg Jesus to leave (Mark 5:1–20).

There are many questions here. Why does the demon use that name? Why are these demons so scared of leaving their territory? And why do the residents of the area want Jesus to go? The answer is that this is an exorcism with a political and military undercurrent. It has dangerous implications, this exorcism, and not just for the pigs.

The demon's name first: Legion. The usual explanation is that it is simply testimony to the multiple personalities plaguing this poor soul, enough to inhabit two thousand pigs. But it is a very specific term. It is not the Greek for 'many', it is the Latin technical term for a group of six thousand soldiers. And the word used for those pigs is 'herd' which, since pigs do not travel in herds, is unusual. But the word (*agele*) was also used to refer to a band of military recruits.[20] Jesus dismisses them with a military command and they charge, like rampaging soldiers, into the lake. Enemy soldiers being swallowed by the waters. There is a Moses reference here, a picture of the Egyptians who enslaved the Israelites being swallowed by the waters around the Sea of Reeds (Exod. 15:4).

The reason why the demons enter the pigs is that they beg not to be sent out of their country (Mark 5:10). Why? They are a Legion. It is *their* country, *their* empire; the last piece of land before the barbarians begin. Like any troops, they do not want to desert their posts. And the emblem of the Roman legion which was stationed in Syria – the *Legio X Freitensis* – was a wild boar.[21]

So this event is drenched with anti-Roman imagery. Was the demonic possession of the man a result of Roman occupation? Had the fact that they were in his land driven him mad?[22] Was Jesus threatening violent revolution? Of course not. Was he sending out a signal to the Romans that their legions would one day be washed away and their power destroyed?

It is certainly capable of interpretation this way. The presence of Legion causes immense suffering to the man, causes him to live among the tombs, with the dead. It defiles him. Their destruction brings liberation and freedom. It's hard to ignore the political meaning in there, intentional or not.

Whether or not this really was an anti-imperialist message – and theologians have played down these aspects for years – you can see why it might have made people a bit twitchy. This was a border area. A highly sensitive political zone. Indeed, much later, during the Jewish revolt, the Romans came to Gerasa and destroyed the town, butchering a thousand men and burning and looting their houses.[23] That event took place decades later, but it hints at why the residents were so scared. Stories like this had a habit of making their way back to the authorities.

This, I believe, is also why this exorcism takes centre stage in Mark's Gospel, why it is described in so much detail. We should remember that Mark is writing in the AD 60s, a time when persecution against the church is beginning to emanate from Rome. In AD 64 the Neronian persecution of Christians began: Christians painted with pitch and used as human torches, or dressed in animal skins and thrown to the wild beasts in the amphitheatre.

There was always something demonic about the Roman Empire, as there is about every empire. They were a police state which dealt with the countries they conquered in a brutal and devastating fashion. They butchered humans for sport. They burned cities to the ground. They were capable of majestic acts, certainly, of art and literature and architecture. But for many of the people who encountered them during their time of power, that is not what struck them.

To them the Romans were pigs, their snouts in the trough.

'He strictly ordered them that no one should know'

There is another significant thing about the Gerasene-or-wherever-it-was demoniac: Jesus did not try to stop him telling other people about it.

The miracles on the other side of the lake, or further north in Jewish territory, are usually accompanied by instructions from Jesus not to tell anyone. He instructed the leper at Capernaum to 'say nothing to anyone' (Mark 1:44). In the event that immediately follows the incident with Legion, Jesus raises a little girl from the dead and then tells the people not to say anything about it (Mark 5:43).

It happens throughout the Gospels. Jesus keeps doing stuff that gets people talking, and then tells them to keep quiet. It is known as the 'messianic secret', and it has been used as a stick to beat the Gospels with for a long time. The argument is simple: Jesus did not want anyone to know he was the Messiah. Why? Because he did not think he was the Messiah.

Except that in the case of the demoniac in the Decapolis, Jesus gives precisely the opposite instruction. The demoniac wants to come with Jesus, but Jesus commands him to go back and tell everyone what has happened.

Why the difference? Why keep quiet on one side of the lake and not on the other? The answer must lie in the location. In the Decapolis – the site of the Legion incident – we are in a Gentile culture. Here there are no competing Judaisms with their different blueprints for what the Messiah should be like.

On the other side of the border, however, in Jewish Galilee, messianic expectation was more strident and more complex. In Jewish territory, Jesus played down expectations, not because he was not the Messiah, but because he was not *their* kind of Messiah. Throughout his campaign, Jesus refused to be categorised. In particular, he rejected any ideologies of popular kingship. Anytime anyone starts talking to him about political power, he runs a mile. He leaves the scene of the feeding of the five thousand – a classic messianic deed if ever there was one – because they start trying to make him king (John 6:15). Views differed about what, exactly, a messianic kingship might be like – some saw it as a restoration of the House of David, others as a return to political independence as had been enjoyed under the Maccabees. To the peasant masses it must have symbolised a rule of justice and equality. But all of these differing views assumed that it meant kicking out the Romans.[24] This, surely, is why he did not want the Decapolis demoniac to accompany him to Galilee. A man who had just thrown a demon called Legion into a bunch of suicidal pigs? What message would that send out to the eager Galileans?

'Secret' is the wrong word, anyway. If Jesus had wanted to keep himself secret, then running around Galilee performing miracles is a funny way to go about it. What he was suppressing was the terminology. He knew that their conception of what the Messiah was, and the way in which he would have had to act to fulfil that conception was wrong.

He was the Wrong Messiah, and he had no intention of letting anyone make him into the right one.

'If I but touch his clothes, I will be made well'

So Jesus refuses to take the lad with him. Instead, he gets back in the boat and crosses once again to the other side where – surprise, surprise – a large crowd gathers. We do not know where he was, but it was a town big enough to have a synagogue with a well-known synagogue leader. His name was Jairus, and his daughter was dying.

This is a town of two miracles. On his way to Jairus's house, a woman touches Jesus, a woman who has been bleeding for twelve years. The disease had caused her enormous suffering – Mark's phrase 'she had endured much under many physicians' tells you all you need to know about the state of medical care in first-century Galilee. It had also cost her financially, perhaps in the form of money offered to the gods of healing. Apart from any physical issues, there was a reason why she was so desperate to get rid of the disease: it left her in a state of permanent impurity. The bleeding was probably some kind of menstrual irregularity, something which meant that her period came frequently, or lasted longer than normal. This meant that she was always ritually unclean. Menstrual women were treated as if they had leprosy-lite: they were not allowed to enter the temple or be a part of the worshipping community (Lev. 12:1–8; 15:19–30). Normally after their period there would have been a time of purification, but this would have been impossible for this woman; there was simply no respite from her impurity.

She reaches out and touches Jesus – and she is healed. Once again, the healing brings with it restoration to the community. The chance to worship, to be a part of the society around her. The healing of this 'daughter', as Jesus calls her, is echoed by the healing of Jairus's daughter, the little girl who is brought back from the dead. Both events are a kind of resurrection. The girl is brought back to life from death, the woman is brought into the community from a kind of living death.

The event is also a reminder of the Jewishness of Jesus. The woman touches the 'fringe of his clothes' (Luke 8:44) indicating that he was wearing *tzazit*, or fringes. The Torah enjoined all Israelite men to wear fringes on their garments as a reminder to 'remember all the commandments of the LORD and do them, and not follow the lust of your own heart and your own eyes.' (Num. 15:39). Later, when Jesus returns to Gennesaret, the crowd beg to touch 'even the fringe of his cloak' (Mark 6:56). Jesus was, in modern terms, wearing a prayer shawl. His criticism of the Pharisees – that 'they make their fringes long' (Matt. 23:5) – implies that the fringes on his cloak were short, however.[25]

That this event took place in western Galilee – over on the western side of the lake – is underscored by the fact that from this unnamed town, Jesus goes on to his home town: he returns to Nazareth.

'A prophet has no honour'

> When he came to Nazareth, where he had been brought up, he went to the synagogue on the sabbath day, as was his custom. He stood up to read, and the scroll of the prophet Isaiah was given to him. He unrolled the scroll and found the place where it was written: 'The Spirit of the Lord is upon me, because he has anointed me to bring good news to the poor. He has sent me to proclaim release to the captives and recovery of sight to the blind, to let the oppressed go free, to proclaim the year of the Lord's favour.' (Luke 4:16–19)

Luke places this event at the beginning of his account of Jesus' Galilean mission. But since the story indicates that Jesus had already been active at Capernaum (Luke 4:23) and that news of Jesus has already spread through 'all the surrounding country' (Luke 4:14–15) it makes more sense later in Jesus' campaign.

As we have already seen, it was Jesus' habit to go to the synagogue on the Sabbath.[26] He was not going just to participate, but to teach, to demonstrate his message. In that sense, Jesus went to the synagogue because that was where the people were. If you wanted to reach a crowd, you went to the synagogue. Later on, Paul would use the same technique.[27]

Synagogues were not necessarily buildings. The term '*synagogue*' comes from the Greek word meaning 'assembly' or 'congregation'. (The word *ekklesia* used by the early church is a similar term.) No first-century synagogue buildings have ever been found in Palestine and the earliest actual synagogue buildings date from the third century AD.[28] Probably, for many smaller towns and villages, the synagogue was just the open meeting place. In the Mishnah there is a rule that those who sell 'their open space' must use the proceeds to buy a synagogue. This deals with the principle that 'what is holy must be raised in honour and not brought down'.[29] In other words, if the synagogue had met in an open space and that place was sold, a synagogue building was the only replacement.

The Gospels indicate that there were some synagogue buildings. In Capernaum, according to Luke, the centurion had sponsored a building, and the Gospels and Acts are full of references to synagogues, some of which must have occupied a public building of some sort. In the bigger cities there were synagogues for particular classes of people, such as the 'synagogue of the Freedmen' (i.e. Jews who had been freed from slavery) mentioned in Acts (Acts 6:9). In a tiny village like Nazareth, however, the primary meaning is not the building, but the assembly of the people, a village gathering.[30] Synagogue was when the people of the village got together, where they discussed not only the Scriptures, but the issues which affected their life together. (Anyway, the distinction between 'life' and 'the Scriptures' is meaningless, since the Torah was the basis of their legal code.)

The synagogue met several times a week. Early rabbinic sources indicate that it assembled on Monday and Thursday to discuss village issues. It was basically a sort of village council: supervising public works, overseeing local law and order, educating the children and providing for the religious occasions.[31]

The synagogue had a leader, who may have been elected, or simply chosen, or even inherited the post.[32] There were also probably local treasurers who oversaw the collection and distribution of goods for the poor. And there was a *hazzan,* or synagogue attendant, who looked after the day-to-day running of the synagogue. (The attendant mentioned in Luke 4:20 was probably this person.) In the bigger towns, as is the case with Jairus, the post of leader carried a high status and in some places these leaders and other noted scribes sat in places of honour – a habit which Jesus treated with typical disdain: 'As he taught, he said, "Beware of the scribes, who like to walk around in long robes, and to be greeted with respect in the marketplaces, and to have the best seats in the synagogues and places of honour at banquets!"' (Mark 12:38–39).

Women and children went to the synagogue as well, although they did not take an active part in the services.[33] It is important to note that the rabbis and the Pharisees were not part of this structure. The rabbinic teachers had their own groups of disciples and their own 'academies'. Synagogues were not, it seems, a part of their Judaism until later. Rabbinic writings show a certain contempt for village affairs and for the peasantry in general: 'R. Dosa b. Harkinas says, "(1) Sleeping late in the morning, (2) drinking wine at noon, (3) chatting with children, and (4) attending the synagogues of the ignorant drive a man out of the world."'[34]

Nor was the synagogue a place of worship as such – that was the temple: it had no altar for sacrifice. It was a place for discussion, for prayer, for reading and discussing Torah.

And, apparently, for having a stand-up row. At least when Jesus visited.

The scene described by Luke in the Nazareth synagogue is the earliest extant account of a synagogue service. If it followed the pattern of later accounts in the Mishnah, there would be six readings from the Torah – the Law – and then a reading from the Prophets. The *hazzan* would take the scroll from its place, unwrap it and hand it to the first of seven readers, each of whom would say a blessing before and after his reading.[35] It was important for accuracy that the words of the Torah were *read* from the scroll. They were not to be recited from memory, in case people misremembered them.[36]

So Jesus may have been the last of seven 'preachers' that day and he chose a passage from Isaiah about the year of the Lord's favour: the Jubilee. At the end, he says, 'Today this scripture has been fulfilled in your hearing' (Luke 4:21). The Jubilee was part of the Sabbath year legislation. Every seven years there was supposed to be a Sabbath year, when the soil would be left fallow, all debts would be written off and all Jewish slaves would be freed. Additionally, in the Jubilee year, the fiftieth year, all family property would be returned to the individual. It was like pressing the reset button on society. Everything goes back to the beginning. Back to the factory settings.

Leviticus, in which these prescriptions are found, sees it as a way of relying on God. He will provide (Lev. 25:20–21). There is little evidence that the Jubilee legislation was ever enacted. It was too radical, too extreme. But the idea of Jubilee is critical to Jesus' teaching, and here he was declaring that it had happened. Right in their midst.

You would have thought that the listeners would have been pleased. They were not. They were furious. The text is usually translated so as to imply that the synagogue congregation were initially approving and then changed their minds. But the first part literally means 'they witnessed him'. There is no indication of whether it was a good thing they witnessed or a bad. Jeremias has suggested that the text could be translated as 'And all witnessed against him and were amazed at the words of mercy that came out of his mouth, and they said "Is this not Joseph's son?"'[37] So they might have been irritated from the start.

Why were they so angry? The answer lies in Jesus' use of Scripture. His text is Isaiah 61:1–2, but when we look at the original passage, we can see that Jesus' use of Scripture is 'relaxed' to say the least. He omits one phrase entirely, compresses another part about providing liberty to the captives, and then introduces a phrase from an entirely different part of Isaiah – Isaiah 58:6 ('to let the oppressed go free').

It seems as if Luke has made a mistake, but his account fits perfectly with what we know of synagogue practice. Unlike when reading the Torah, where accuracy was paramount, the Nebi'im or Prophets could be adapted. 'They may leave out verses in the Prophets but not in the law,' says the Mishnah. 'How much may they leave out? Only so much that he leaves no time for the interpreter to make a pause.'[38]

The interpreter was the person who translated the reading from Hebrew to Aramaic, since not everyone understood Hebrew. So the person reading could skip verses, or select other verses, while the translator was translating the verse before! It is a scriptural mash-up. Jesus re-edits the Scripture, mixing up a version that enrages his listeners.

And it is not what he says which enrages his audience, but what he leaves out. The original passage in Isaiah concludes with a condemnation of Israel's enemies: 'to proclaim the year of the Lord's favour, *and the day of vengeance of our God*' (Isa. 61:2, my italics). Jesus leaves out vengeance. He edits the text, adds in a bit from somewhere else, cuts off the crowd-pleasing ending, then sits down and says that it all refers to him anyway. Then he goes on to refer to two other biblical episodes – Elijah in Zarephath and Elisha's healing of Naaman the Syrian, both of which indicate that it is foreigners, rather than the people of his home town, who are going to get the blessing.

Whatever the opposite of crowd-pleasing is, this is it. The crowd rush him to a nearby precipice in order to throw him off. They were, in fact, going to stone him. Stoning was the most common method of execution in the Bible. It was the punishment for apostasy, sorcery, serious Sabbath violation and, in this case, blasphemy.[39] Jewish practice required that the victim of stoning should first be thrown down from a place twice the height of a human person. One of the witnesses would throw down the victim in such a way that they fell on their back. If the person died as a result of the fall, the execution came to an end. If not, then a second person would drop a heavy stone on the victim, over the heart. Only if that failed would the crowd finish the job with a volley of smaller rocks.[40]

For the first time in the Gospels, Jesus is threatened with real physical violence. His message in the village meeting at Nazareth is a tough homecoming. Like his family – and in such a small place Jesus would have had many relatives among the crowd – the people of Nazareth cannot accept that Jesus knows what he is doing. But it has gone beyond restraining him. Now they want to kill him.

He escaped. Slipped away, according to Luke. But he did not leave the region. According to Mark, he went through the villages, teaching.

It is in this region – to the west of Lake Galilee – that Jesus decides to send the twelve apostles out on their own tour, in pairs. Up until now Jesus has been teaching and performing the miracles, while the disciples look on. Now it is time for them to have a go. He insists that they model the lives of those among whom they are campaigning: no money, no security, no food, not even an extra tunic.[41] Their way of life must correspond to that of the poor. They proceed through the countryside as men without possessions, dependent on the help and protection of others, proclaiming the need for repentance and freeing people from sickness and oppression (Mark 6:8–13).

He will not accompany them. Instead he takes the opportunity to go south. To Jerusalem.

'There was a festival of the Jews'

In John's Gospel, Jesus makes four visits to Jerusalem, before his final visit at Passover AD 33.

▷ Passover, spring AD 30. Temple cleansing, visit from Nicodemus (John 2:13–3:21).
▷ 'A festival of the Jews', autumn/winter? AD 31. Healing in Pool of Bethesda (John 5:1–47).
▷ Festival of Booths, autumn AD 32. Controversy. Light of the world teaching. Healing of man born blind (John 7:10–10:21).
▷ Festival of Dedication, winter AD 32. Teaching in Solomon's Portico (John 10:22–39).

These trips are helpful in establishing an overall chronology of Jesus' life, but they are not easily coordinated with the Galilean campaign described in the other Gospels. The first one is simple enough: that takes place before Jesus' Galilean campaign begins. But this second visit is tricky. It takes place at an unnamed festival. It has been suggested that it was the festival of Booths or Tabernacles, but perhaps a better candidate is the feast of Dedication or Sukkoth, which was a winter festival. This would make sense of Jesus' likening of John the Baptist to 'a burning and shining lamp' (John 5:35), since one of the highlights of the feast was the lighting of lamps.[42] Josephus called it the Festival of

Lights because 'such a freedom shone upon us'.[43] Hannukah is also closer to Passover, which marks the next Galilean episode in John (John 6:4).

It therefore makes sense to place the event around autumn/winter of AD 31. Especially since Jesus is free from 'looking after the kids', as it were. (In John's account, the disciples are not with Jesus in Jerusalem.) And Jesus has just come from Nazareth, which would make it relatively easy for him to reach Jerusalem in a few days. So we can imagine that in autumn AD 31, with his disciples off in pairs, Jesus takes the opportunity to go down to Jerusalem for the festival of Booths. And to cause, as he so often does, a little havoc.

If John is a little hazy on chronology, he is pretty detailed on topography. 'Now in Jerusalem by the Sheep Gate there is a pool, called in Hebrew Bethzatha, which has five porticoes. In these lay many invalids – blind, lame, and paralysed' (John 5:2–4) – all of them hoping against hope for some kind of miracle cure.

The Sheep Pool lies just north of the Temple Mount (in the grounds of the current-day Monastery of St Anne) and north of the Pool of Israel. It was really two pools, divided by a walkway, and together about the size of a football pitch. The five porticoes probably ran along the four sides and across the gap between the two pools.[44]

The pools were commissioned around 200 BC by Simon the high priest to supply water to the temple. Although Herod replaced them with a new pool – the Pool of Israel, just to the south – they continued to be used both as a place of healing and, as the name implies, as a place to wash livestock being taken to the temple for sacrifice. Although most maps of the temple omit it, there was a north entrance to the Temple Mount – the Tadi Gate – which, according to the Mishnah, 'was not used at all'.[45] This probably means that it was not a public entrance, but it would have served to bring animals in, since it was the only temple gate that did not have steps. A vast amount of sheep and other animals were needed for the temple sacrifices: the north entrance was the only place where you could enter the temple on level ground.

The name Bethzatha or Bethesda is an Aramaic phrase meaning 'House of Mercy', which probably refers to the porticoed building, not the pool itself.[46] Surrounding it were new houses – Bezetha, or 'the new city' – built outside the existing walls to cater for Jerusalem's expanding popula- tion. Jesus was in the suburbs.[47]

The ancient world held strong beliefs about the healing properties of waters; Herod visited the warm baths at Jeri- cho, but there were other healing springs at places like Tiberias and Emmaus-Nicop- olis.[48] After the Jews

The Pool of Bethesda in Jerusalem.

were banned from Jerusalem in AD 135, the Romans carried on using these baths for healing and built a temple dedicated to Sera- pis/Asclepius, the god of medicine and healing.[49]

It is not clear from the text why there was such competition to get in, or how the waters actually moved (John 5:4, which explains that an angel stirred up the waters, is a later addition and is not in most modern Bibles). It is possible that it was caused by move- ment of water between one pool and the other. Clearly, though, some people got left behind. This is why the lame man misun- derstands Jesus. He thinks that Jesus is merely going to help him get into the pool. But instead Jesus tells him, 'Stand up, take your mat and walk' (John 5:8). (His mat would have been the simplest possible floor-covering. For the poor, typically, it would have been woven out of palm leaves.[50])

Jesus is attacking two systems in this miracle. The first is the quasi-pagan idea that healing came about through mystical waters and springs. 'You want a *real* god of healing? Take a look

165

at this.' But, second, this is another attack on the Sabbath, the Jerusalem version of his provocative Sabbath healing in Capernaum. This time Jesus takes it further: he incites the lame man to Sabbath-breaking as well. Carrying a mat was considered 'work' under the tortuous Sabbath laws. Shockingly, Jesus justifies his actions by equating himself with God (John 5:17). Although Genesis describes God resting on the Sabbath, Jewish tradition understood the impossibility of God actually stopping all activity. Jesus says that he too is at work.

John says that, when they heard it was Jesus doing these things, 'the Jews started persecuting Jesus' (John 5:16) – an unfortunate phrase, given the history of Jewish–Christian relations. John does use this term to describe the Jewish people in general (e.g. John 4:22; 11:19), but in the majority of instances – especially in Jerusalem – it is a shorthand to describe the Jewish authorities and leadership, analogous to the Synoptics' use of 'the scribes and the Pharisees' to describe general Jewish leadership. John is certainly not talking about an ethnic identification – 'Jews' in general – not least because he himself was almost certainly Jewish.[51] What we have here is the first sign of the Jewish temple elite's animosity to Jesus. Jesus' claims about himself and his disregard for Sabbath laws mean that the religious leadership start 'seeking to kill Jesus'.

In the discourse that follows the healing, Jesus, once again, praises his former mentor, John the Baptist: 'He was a burning and shining lamp,' he says, 'and you were willing to rejoice for a while in his light' (John 5:35).

But it was around this time – possibly even while Jesus was in Jerusalem – that the lamp was extinguished.

6. Tyre, Sidon, Caesarea Philippi, spring/summer AD 32

From the ramparts he could see for miles. To the west lay his domains. But in the opposite direction, to the south-east ... Aretas was out there with his army. At some point the storm would break, he knew. At some point there would be a price to pay for Herodias. There was *always* a price to pay for Herodias.

They call this place the hanging mount. Not a scrap of vegetation on the hills. They had climbed up the narrow path, which wound round the mountain like a vine, clinging to the side of the hill. The slaves carrying the litter had stumbled at times. Couldn't blame them really, given the terrain. Still, they would be punished.

Every time he came here he could see why his father had rebuilt it. The viaduct from the spur of the mount to the south-east was the only way in. Even the water had to come across that viaduct, flooding in during the rainy season to be imprisoned in the huge cisterns below where he stood.

But inside the walls, beyond the towers, a tiny miracle: a palace. Sophisticated. Civilised. Marble corridors. The colonnaded courtyard with its greenery, where he would walk in the cool of the evening. A bathhouse to wash away the dirt of the journey. And the dining room, for tonight's banquet.

But one look outside and you knew how artificial this was; this was a fortress more than a palace. Strong, secure. A good place to defend the border. And to keep prisoners.

Should he go and speak with him? Listen to his words? No. Best not. Not tonight. Tonight was for the banquet.

Time enough for that tomorrow.

'The head of John the Baptiser'

Mark tells us the story in graphic detail. For a long time, perhaps over a year, the Baptiser has been languishing in a dungeon in the Machaerus. Although Herodias, Herod's wife, wanted him dead, the tetrarch was stalling. Perhaps he feared the people. More likely, given what we know of his character, he actually had a grudging respect for John, an interest in what he represented and the things he had to say.

All that came to an end on the night of Antipas's birthday.

> Herod on his birthday gave a banquet for his courtiers and officers and for the leaders of Galilee. When his daughter Herodias came in and danced, she pleased Herod and his guests; and the king said to the girl, 'Ask me for whatever you wish, and I will give it.' And he solemnly swore to her, 'Whatever you ask me, I will give you, even half of my kingdom.' She went out and said to her mother, 'What should I ask for?' She replied, 'The head of John the baptiser.' (Mark 6:21–24)

The death of John the Baptist is a macabre story, a vivid, visceral mix of sex and horror which has spawned thousands of paintings, films, operas, plays and novels. Salome's dance before Herod is portrayed as a striptease – the dance of the seven veils. But the Bible does not say anything about what type of dance it was, nor does it mention the girl's name with any clarity, as we shall see. Far from being a stripper, the real picture might show a mere girl, only twelve years of age, uncertain, unsure, used as a pawn in a power game between husband and wife.

The banquet is attended by Antipas's inner circle, including the leaders from Galilee. Some take this to imply that the event had to be in Galilee, in Tiberias, whereas Josephus places John in the Machaerus – but it is not impossible that Galileans would have made a special journey south for such an occasion, especially if it coincided with a festival at Jerusalem.

The Machaerus was one of Herod's palace-fortresses, set atop a hill commanding a view of the country around. It was a remote place, but the palace itself was lavish. Josephus tells us that Herodias had a daughter called Salome from her first marriage,[1] and since this is the only daughter we know of from Herodias's first marriage the identification seems pretty secure. Some manuscripts of Mark, however, name her Herodias, which may be an alternative name, or may indicate another daughter – possibly even the daughter of Antipas and Herodias. Mark uses a specific word to describe her: *korasion*. It appears to be a diminutive of the Greek word for 'girl' or 'maiden': a girl who is not quite of marriageable age. The same word is used of Jairus's daughter, who is twelve years old (Mark 5:42). Roman law set the minimum age of marriage as twelve, but the law seems to have been frequently flouted and younger girls got married.[2] Salome was old enough to marry Philip before he died in AD 34. Assuming she was fourteen then, if John was beheaded in late AD 31/early AD 32, Salome would have been around eleven or twelve.[3]

This puts a different perspective on things. It does not have to be an erotic event. Salome could have entertained the guests without any loss of dignity – or clothing. Antipas might have been out of his head, but Herodias knew exactly what she was doing. When Herod made his drunken offer, Salome ran off to get further instructions from Mummy. This is the real grubbiness of the tale. It is not a nubile stripper at a Herodian stag night. It is a scheming mother using her own daughter as a lure. What Herodias wants, she gets. And what she wants here is the head of John the Baptist. On a plate.

The Machaerus: site of the execution of John the Baptist.

So John was executed. His followers retrieved his body and buried it – probably near the Machaerus, since it was the usual custom in the Middle East to bury the body on the same day. Then they went off to tell Jesus.

Herod, it seems, never really recovered from the crime. Hearing reports about Jesus bring all his guilt and fear rushing back to the surface: 'John, whom I beheaded, has been raised' (Mark 6:16).

Mark calls Antipas 'King' (6:14) – a satirical, ironic comment, perhaps, because he was never a king. In fact it was Herodias's scheming and manipulation to get him the title that was to cause his downfall. Salome married Antipas's brother, Philip, and when he died in AD 34, perhaps Antipas and Herodias hoped to get his territory. It did not happen: Tiberius simply took all Philip's lands under direct Roman rule. More disappointment was to follow. Sometime around autumn AD 36, Antipas's forces were disastrously defeated in a battle with Aretas, his former father-in-law, who had never forgotten Antipas's treatment of his daughter. Then, when Tiberius died, the new emperor, Gaius Caligula, gave Antipas's nephew Agrippa the territory of his late uncle Philip, and also the title of king. Outraged, Herodias persuaded Antipas to go to Rome to petition the emperor to be made king as well. Against his will, Antipas agreed.

It was a disaster. Agrippa sent a secret letter to Caligula, accusing Antipas of planning a secret alliance with the Parthians. Instead of rewarding him, therefore, the emperor confiscated all his lands and his money, and banished Herod Antipas and his wife Herodias to Lugdunum Convenarum, now Saint-Bernard-de-Comminges in France. They ended their days in poverty and obscurity on the other side of the empire, thousands of miles away from home. As Josephus puts it, 'And thus did God punish Herodias for her envy at her brother, and Herod also for giving ear to the vain discourses of a woman.'[4]

In Mark, the story of John's death comes between the sending out of the Twelve and their return. It is a sober reminder, perhaps, of the real fate awaiting them. When they rejoin Jesus – probably back in Capernaum – they are on a high, buzzing with their success (Mark 6:30).[5] But their true fate, hints Mark, may not lie in the towns and villages of Galilee, but in the dungeons of the

Roman Empire and its many petty, drunk, corrupt client-kings.

When Jesus hears of John's death he retreats to a deserted place (Matt. 14:13). As so often in times of pressure or emotional turmoil, the wilderness is his only comfort.

Yet even here the crowds find him. And they are hungry.

'All ate and were filled'

The feeding of the five thousand is one of the few events which is recorded in all four Gospels (Matt. 14:13–21; Mark 6:30–44; Luke 9:10–17; John 6:1–13). It is, according to John, near to Passover, which would make it the spring of AD 32 – a fact confirmed by the lush grass in the area (John 6:10) – some months after Jesus' Jerusalem visit.

The traditional title underestimates the real amount: there were five thousand *men* there, according to the Gospel accounts: add in women and children and the number was greater. Locating the spot is, again, tricky. Jesus arrived there by boat, but it was actually quicker to get there by foot – which is how the crowds preceded them (Mark 6:32–33). Mark places it in a 'deserted place', where there is a mountain on which Jesus can pray. He also places it on the 'other side' of the lake to Bethsaida (Mark 6:45), which would put it more around Tiberias. Luke, however, starts the story in Bethsaida; but then, without any notice, we are suddenly in a deserted place. John says that the day after the event, boats from Tiberias came near the spot and took people to Capernaum 'on the other side of the lake' (John 6:23–25). So he seems to back up Mark. Matthew removes all the location markers altogether. (Probably the best approach, on balance.)

The crowd have nothing to eat. Jesus suggests that the disciples feed them, but they point out that this would cost 200 denarii – eight months' wages for a labourer who made a denarius a day (Matt. 20:2). So, using only the five barley loaves and two fishes, Jesus has the people recline on the grass in groups of hundreds and fifties. He organises a series of banquets.

The event not only links him theologically with Moses and the manna in the wilderness, it links Jesus politically with other messianic movements. Isaiah 25:6–9 talks of the Messiah feasting with his people in the wilderness.

No wonder that the crowd finally decide to take action. John articulates a fact which the Synoptic writers either did not know or chose to omit: the crowd tried to force Jesus to be their king (John 6:15). He had fed them in the wilderness. He had revealed his true hand. They knew who he was: no use denying it.

But Jesus refused the prize. They offered him the kingdom and he walked away. Instead, he sends the disciples off on their boat, across the sea, and goes up a mountain alone. The wilderness, again. Temptations, again. 'Make these stones into bread,' Satan had said before offering him all the kingdoms. That was a dress rehearsal for this moment. Once again Jesus passes the test.

Meanwhile, out on the lake, the disciples are in trouble. A storm blows up and their boat is blown off course. Then they see Jesus walking across the water towards them, a nature miracle akin to the stilling of the storm. John's account has Jesus walk right past the boat, Mark has Jesus get into the boat, and Matthew has Peter walk on the water to join Jesus, until his fear drags him under. This confusion is not made any easier by their destinations: the Synoptics have the boat arrive at Gennesaret on the east shore of Galilee, while John has a complicated section about the people noticing that Jesus did not leave with the disciples and then discovering him in Capernaum.

In John's account, after the crowd find him at Capernaum, Jesus gives a speech during which he states, 'I am the bread of life' (John 6:35–40) and the range of response is illuminating. Most of his listeners are simply baffled: 'How can this man give us his flesh to eat?' (John 6:52). Even his disciples were perplexed. 'This teaching is too hard,' they complain. Then John drops in a little bombshell: 'Because of this many of his disciples turned back and no longer went about with him' (John 6:66).

Things have changed. While the Synoptic Gospels do not state this as overtly, there are unmistakable signs of discontent. Mark records that the disciples 'did not understand about the loaves, but their hearts were hardened' (Mark 6:52). They have almost become like Jesus' enemies: Mark uses the same phrase to describe the Pharisees (Mark 3:5; 10:5) and Jesus repeats the accusation in frustration at the disciples' lack of understanding (Mark 8:17). Why would their hearts be hardened? (The implication is that this goes beyond simple misunderstanding into an almost wilful incomprehension.) Perhaps it was because their hopes, too, were being confounded. Jesus had clearly and definitively rejected the kingship pressed on him by the crowds. But the disciples, too, had bought into the idea of the Right Messiah. Now they were beginning to question when exactly Jesus was going to fall into line. He had all that power – when was he going to use it?

Then a delegation from Jerusalem comes to see Jesus and an argument breaks out – again – over the issue of washing (Mark 7:1–5). The meeting concludes with Jesus calling the crowd together and saying 'Listen to me, all of you, and understand: there is nothing outside a person that by going in can defile, but the things that come out are what defile' (Mark 7:14–15).[6]

The statement is the culmination of Jesus' teaching. He had spent over a year demonstrating the practices of the new kingdom: eating with tax-collectors, talking to Samaritan women, touching lepers and dead people, healing on the Sabbath. He had waged an all-out war on the obsession with external purity, and they were still blathering on about washing. So, indoors with his disciples, he states it simply and clearly: anything you eat just goes into your stomach and then into the *aphedron* – the Greek word meaning 'toilet' or 'latrine' (Mark 6:19). (Most Bible translations, showing a delicacy which Jesus never did, translate it as 'sewer', while some omit the noun entirely. After all, we cannot have Jesus using the word 'toilet', can we?[7] What defiles a man is personal sin: sleeping around, stealing, murder, avarice, wickedness, deceit, lying … the list goes on.

One item is intriguing: *ophthalmos poneros*, the 'evil eye', which is usually translated as 'envy'. A common Jewish superstition held that certain beings – people, demons, gods or even animals – had the power of the evil eye: they could cast a spell simply by looking at you. Behind this belief is the idea that the eye was a window to the soul and could therefore transmit the evil intentions of the heart. It was a form of sorcery.[8] Apparently, even how you looked at people could make you impure. The list is not just a list of thoughts: these are things you do as well. What they have in common is that they involve personal sin. It is that which defiles a man; it is what he does and thinks which defiles him.[9]

What was the reaction to this statement? Well, if Mark is right in where he places this event, it is possible that the crowd, as John implies, were not entirely on Jesus' side. And their animosity may explain why he leaves Palestine altogether. He goes north to Tyre and Sidon. He goes into hiding.

'He could not escape'

Only Matthew and Mark contain the account of this trip. Luke includes elements of it – Peter's confession of faith, for instance – but most of it, in what has been punned the 'Great Omission', he ignores completely.[10] It is not an easy trip to outline, because the geographical details are a bit confusing. Six locations are mentioned in Mark 7–8:

▷ Jesus goes to Tyre and meets a Syrophoenician woman.

▷ He returns to the Sea of Galilee 'by way of Sidon'.

▷ He goes to the Decapolis and heals a deaf man.

▷ He feeds four thousand people and then goes to the district of Dalmanutha.

▷ He cures a blind man at Bethsaida.

▷ He goes to the district of Caesarea Philippi.

There are some problems here, not least that going to Galilee from Tyre via Sidon is actually heading in the wrong direction. However, Mark is actually describing a tour, so it is not impossible for Jesus to head up the coast towards Sidon, before returning.

Then there is the mysterious Dalmanutha. In Matthew, 'Dalmanutha' is replaced by Magadan, which might help if we actually ly knew where Magadan was. It seems safest to put it on the west side of the lake, possibly near Magdala. This would necessitate a boat ride across the lake from the Decapolis – a ride which Jesus has already made several times.[11]

Possibly the order of events was slightly different to that in Mark – that it was more of a 'round trip', because the journey back to the Decapolis would take Jesus right by Caesarea Philippi, the location of Peter's declaration about Jesus. So it seems more likely that the declaration about Jesus and the transfiguration took place before Jesus returned south to the shores of Galilee, before the feeding of the four thousand and the crossing to Dalmanutha.

First, though, Jesus crosses a significant boundary: he leaves Jewish territory completely and enters the city of Tyre. Why do this? Perhaps because he thought – wrongly as it transpired – that it would bring him seclusion. He is clearly in hiding: Mark tells us that Jesus 'entered a house and did not want anyone to know he was there' (Mark 7:24). Fat chance. Jesus was already known there. People from Tyre had come to Galilee to hear him teach (Mark 3:8; Luke 6:17). But it was a Gentile city and well beyond the reach of the authorities in Galilee and Jerusalem.

Tyre was one of the main ports and trade centres of the eastern Mediterranean. It housed a mint, making the silver coins which were the only approved currency for the temple tax. It was a centre of the slave trade, shipping slaves to and from Palestine, and its proximity to the sea supplied it with the murex snail shell, crucial in the dyeing of purple cloth. (The trade was so closely associated with Tyre that some of the coins feature the snail shell on the reverse.) It was one of the many cities which had received gifts from Herod the Great: he donated halls, porticoes, temples and a marketplace to the city.

There follows one of the strangest encounters in the Gospels. A 'Syrophoenician woman' comes and bows at his feet, and begs him to exorcise her daughter. Jesus refuses, citing some kind of proverb: you do not take the children's bread and throw it to the pups. It is really rather shocking. The woman, undaunted, offers a witty reply: even the dogs get to have some of the children's crumbs. With that, Jesus admits defeat and sends her home. Her daughter is made whole.

This is Jesus beyond the borders. This woman is 100 per cent Gentile, a pagan. A foreigner. An idol worshipper – Matthew describes her as 'Canaanite', which describes not her ethnicity, but her religious beliefs. There may even be another layer to this story. In Rome, where Mark was probably writing his Gospel, a 'Syrophoenician woman' also meant a woman from the seamier side of town. Juvenal, in one of his Satires, writes about a gentleman who 'decides to go to some tavern that never closes, on his way he is met by a perfumed Syrophoenician, coming up at a run to hail him as Lord and master'.[12]

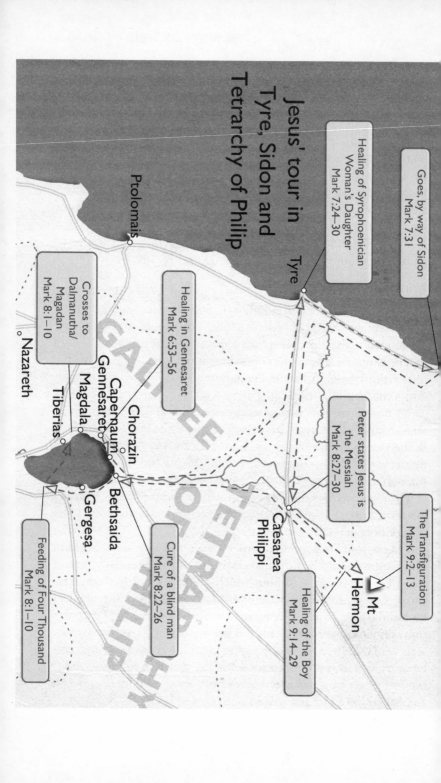

Jesus' tour in Tyre, Sidon and Tetrarchy of Philip

Goes, by way of Sidon
Mark 7:31

Healing of Syrophoenician Woman's Daughter
Mark 7:24-30

Ptolomais

Tyre

Crosses to Dalmanutha/ Magadan
Mark 8:1-10

Healing in Gennesaret
Mark 6:53-56

Nazareth

Magdala

Chorazin

Capernaum
Gennesaret

Tiberias

Bethsaida

Gergesa

Peter states Jesus is the Messiah
Mark 8:27-30

The Transfiguration
Mark 9:2-13

Caesarea Philippi

Cure of a blind man
Mark 8:22-26

Feeding of Four Thousand
Mark 8:1-10

Healing of the Boy
Mark 9:14-29

Mt Hermon

GALILEE

TETRARCHY OF PHILIP

The incident shocks us for two reasons. First, Jesus appears so thoroughly rude. For that reason it is hard to believe that this event is an invention of Mark's. By the time he was writing, Christianity was well established among Gentile congregations: indeed, there were 'disciples' there in the time of Paul (Acts 21:3–5). Second, Jesus is outwitted by this woman. Of course, one problem with the Gospels is that it is hard to catch the tone of voice. Is Jesus tired here? Is it a test? Or is he playful? Is the whole thing a bit of banter? Certainly the woman seems to join in with some kind of game. And she wins this encounter.

She is a woman; a Gentile; a pagan. Maybe a sinner. Yet Jesus grants her request.

'You are the Messiah'

After his time in Tyre and Sidon, Jesus heads back towards Galilee. In this section of Mark, we have a series of miracles: another feeding miracle – this time with four thousand men – and the healing of a deaf man with a speech impediment in Gentile Decapolis; the restoration of sight to a blind man in Jewish Bethsaida; in Dalmanutha the Pharisees demand a sign; out on the lake again the disciples have difficulty making sense of the signs they have already seen (Mark 7:31–8:26). Two distinct trajectories can be discerned in the stories from now on: along with the increasing conviction that Jesus is the Messiah, there is an increasing realisation that it is all going to end messily.

The high point – literally as well as metaphorically – comes during Jesus' trip into the Decapolis, with Peter's declaration that Jesus is the Christ and the transfiguration on the mountain. Either on the way back from Syria, or on another journey, Jesus and his disciples are at Caesarea Philippi. (Luke rejoins us at this point.) We are in quasi-Gentile country. Although Herod Philip was Jewish, his territory was predominantly Gentile. Close to Galilee, in cities like Bethsaida-Julias, there were many Jews, but to the west the population was almost entirely Gentile. The youngest of those of Herod's sons who inherited power, he was in many ways the most able and he oversaw a long and peaceful reign. He stayed at home, married the former dancing girl Salome, refused to meddle in things which did not concern him, and died childless in AD 33/34.

He had only a mild dose of 'his father's building craze'.[13] He embellished and improved the city of Paneas (named in honour of Pan, the Greek god) where Herod had built a temple to Roma and Augustus. He renamed it Caesarea Philippi to honour, of course, the emperor. It was a place where there were many shrines, to many gods – not least the Roman emperors. (It had also been a place where Baal was worshipped.) Later it would change again, morphing into Neronia, in honour of the Emperor Nero. This city was a barometer of the 'real' powers in the universe: the Roman gods, the Roman emperors. It was here that Titus celebrated victory when Jerusalem fell and the temple was destroyed.[14]

So it is a deliberately ironic setting for the truth about Jesus to come out. In a place dedicated to the powers of the Roman empire, Jesus is 'crowned' by his disciples. Jesus has been called many things before this point. The people call him a prophet; his followers call him teacher or master; the Jewish religious leaders call him a blasphemer; the demons call him 'the Son of God'; Antipas thought for one hungover moment that he was John the Baptist back from the dead. But this is the crunch moment: 'You,' Jesus asks his disciples, 'what do *you* say?' Peter takes a leap: 'You are the Messiah' (Mark 8:29).

It is a pivotal point in the story. For the disciples it should have been the moment when the odds paid off, when everything they had guessed or thought or deduced or intuited turned out to be correct. He was the Messiah, and they were his closest friends. What, for a pious Jew, could be better than that?

Yet there is an immediate sense of anticlimax. No sooner has Peter identified Jesus, than Jesus sternly warns them not to tell anyone. They have won first prize in the Jewish lottery, but they can't tell anyone about it. Then Jesus starts telling them what else is going to happen:

> Then he began to teach them that the Son of Man must undergo great suffering, and be rejected by the elders, the chief priests, and the scribes, and be killed, and after three days rise again. He said all this quite openly. And Peter took him aside and began to rebuke him. But turning and looking at his disciples, he rebuked Peter and said, 'Get behind me, Satan! For you are setting your mind not on divine things but on human things.' (Mark 8:31–33)

When Peter tries to correct Jesus – a 'rebuke' is how Mark terms it – he is peremptorily, almost savagely, dismissed. Why? Because Peter is the tempter, the one who is trying to get Jesus to change the ending. It's that old temptation: save yourself. Fly away. In response, Jesus calls 'the crowd' – the group following him contained not only his disciples but also the women and others – and offers them a paradox: if you wish to save your life, you will lose it; if you want to follow Jesus, take up your cross.

For centuries the idea of 'taking up your cross' has been taken to mean 'endure suffering' or 'struggle on through illness'. It's equated with a kind of stoic piety, like going without chocolate for Lent. But it could not have been understood that way by Jesus' listeners. There was only one kind of person who took up their cross: it was the condemned slave or criminal, who was carrying his crossbeam to a point of crucifixion. Plutarch wrote, 'Every criminal who is executed carries his own cross.'[15] Nobody took up their cross unless they were going to die. This is no metaphor. Jesus was preparing his followers to be ridiculed, spat on, beaten, publicly shamed, killed: the common thread is the stain of criminality. Any follower of Jesus was going to be a criminal, in the eyes of the Greco-Roman world and the Jewish temple aristocracy, from now on.

Certainly when the early church took up this image they understood it in a concrete way. Sharing in the suffering of Christ meant actual suffering. Paul talks of how believers will suffer like Christ (Phil. 1:29). When Peter talks to slaves who are being harshly treated by their masters, he points to the example of Christ (1 Pet. 2:18–22). The bearing of a cross is not just the patient coping with affliction, pain, suffering. It involves ostracism, ridicule and death.[16] And today, despite the watering-down of the term in Western Christianity, many Christians around the world understand exactly what it means. Those who have been imprisoned, or tortured, know exactly the temptation to 'save oneself'. And those who face death for following Jesus know precisely what Jesus meant by taking up the cross.

Despite the downbeat, gloomy images, Jesus was not preaching defeat here. This is the first of three predictions of his death, but all three end with Jesus rising again (8:31; 9:31; 10:33–34). But from here on in, their journey will take them through a world of suffering, pain, uncertainty, fear and darkness. There is a light at the end, but it is a long, bloody tunnel.

They were right about him being the Messiah. It was just the rest of it they got wrong.

'He was transfigured before them'

One more mountain-top experience before the long descent into the dark. The transfiguration is an event which is wreathed in mystery. It places Jesus alongside Elijah and Moses, the two great figures of Israel's past, one the great prophet, the other the great law giver. But it is a mysterious, cosmic event.

Which mountain is unknown. Given that it happened near Caesarea Philippi, either Mount Hermon or another mountain in that range is the obvious choice. These are the biggest mountains in the region and far bigger than anything in Lower Galilee (especially the one traditionally associated with the event, Mount Tabor).[17] The only direction we have is the distance from Caesarea Philippi, although even that differs between the Synoptics: in Mark and Matthew it takes six days to get there, in Luke it takes eight (Matt. 17:1; Mark 9:2; Luke 9:28).

Jesus appears in bright white garments. His clothes are described as being whiter than any fuller (i.e. a first-century launderer) could bleach them. To the early church this imagery drew on the 'Ancient One' in the apocalyptic vision of Daniel whose 'clothing was white as snow, and the hair of his head like pure wool' (Dan. 7:9). It is further reflected in Revelation where Jesus appears with head and hair 'white as white wool, white as snow' (Rev. 1:14). But it has also been pointed out that the other people who wear white robes in Revelation are martyrs.[18]

Peter suggests that the event be celebrated: three 'booths' or shelters should be made. Why? Well, Luke tells us that they were 'speaking of his departure, which he was about to accomplish at Jerusalem' (Luke 9:31–32), and the word for 'departure', the Greek word, is *exodon*. They were discussing Jesus' exodus. The exodus was the Jewish rescue story, the great Torah example of salvation, and this time around – Jesus' personal reliving of the rescue story – it is going to happen in Jerusalem. So this vision has 'exodus' written all over it: up a mountain, a cloud comes down, Jesus' clothes shine like Moses', the man himself also puts in an appearance, and they discuss a future *exodon*.

No wonder Peter turns to an 'exodus' celebration. Peter's suggestion of booths draws on the feast of Tabernacles. This was one of the major festivals. Men, and boys old enough not to need their mothers, would construct booths and then live in them for the week.[19] The booths or shelters were made of intertwined branches and were intended to remind Jews of their time in tents in the wilderness. But the event is not to be commemorated. Not even to be talked about. Jesus again uses the event to underline the hard road ahead. Elijah has returned 'and they did to him whatever they pleased'. The Son of Man must suffer 'and be treated with contempt' (Mark 9:12–13). They have been to the mountain top, but it is all downhill from here.

'I believe; help my unbelief!'

At the base of the mountain there is a village, and in the village there is an argument going on. The disciples are squabbling with some scribes over their failure to cast a spirit out of the boy. Matthew identifies the disease as epilepsy (Matt. 17:15). Certainly the symptoms fit: foaming at the mouth, grinding teeth, convulsing, an inability to speak (Mark 9:17–18). From childhood the boy has been shut up in this hell, unable to speak or hear.

When the crowd see Jesus, they are 'overcome with awe' (Mark 9:15) at Jesus' appearance. The Greek term indicates an awe 'so extreme as to cause emotional distress, bodily tremors and psychological bewilderment'.[20] It seems that something of the events of the night before are still clinging to him.

This episode has a confrontational feel to it. It is crowded, confused. Jesus seems angry here, frustrated, not so much with the disciples, more with the crowd, the faithless generation, whose lack of faith has prevented the healing from happening. And with the father of the boy, perhaps: Jesus seems to take the father's request to heal his son – 'if you are able' – as a kind of challenge. And Jesus performs the exorcism, according to Mark, when he sees 'a crowd [come] running together' (Mark 9:25). This does not sound like a crowd milling around Jesus: this sounds more like a mob.

The crucial point, however, is the father's statement – a statement which every Christian has echoed at some time or other: 'I believe; help my unbelief!' (Mark 9:24). The spirit's departure leaves the boy like a corpse, but Jesus lifts him up. He is free.

And this sense of confrontation increases. When Jesus goes through Galilee back towards Capernaum Mark makes it clear that this journey is made in secret. There is a growing sense of threat here. It is almost as if it is no longer safe for Jesus in Galilee, as if the tide has suddenly turned against him.

Along the way Jesus again talks of dark days ahead; but the disciples seem unable or unwilling to confront this reality. Instead they start arguing about who is the greatest. (Easy to see how this could come about. One can imagine the three disciples who had been up the mountain looking condescendingly at those who had failed at the mountain's base.) Jesus responds to this in a formal, rabbinic style: he sits down and calls them to him (Mark 9:35). It is a seminar, a class about leadership. And, like everything else in the kingdom, it is upside down. The bottom is the top, the first is the last. The visual aid is a child. It is a striking image, because no one in the first-century Jewish world would see a child as a religious role model. Jesus is talking about service here. Whoever welcomes – i.e. 'serves' – these children is serving him; but in the household of his time the women, children and slaves did the welcoming, brought you food, washed your feet. In Aramaic the word for 'child' and the word for 'servant' are the same – *talya*.[21]

The disciples are behaving childishly, but they need to behave like children. Jesus' teaching on leadership is informed all the time by a subversion of the models he sees around him. Leadership, for Jesus, is all bound up with service. We shall see this in its fullness in the Upper Room, the night before his execution. His description of how honour and status work in the kingdom he is establishing is all about role reversal. It is an upside-down world, where the last is first, where the landless day labourer who works for one hour gets the same rate as those who worked all day, where those who expect the seats of honour will get put at the other end of the table.

It seems to me that Christianity has spent the better part of its history ignoring these principles. Take, for example, Jesus' impatience with titles and honorifics.

> But you are not to be called rabbi, for you have one teacher, and you
> are all students. And call no one your father on earth, for you have
> one Father – the one in heaven. Nor are you to be called instructors,
> for you have one instructor, the Messiah. The greatest among you will
> be your servant. All who exalt themselves will be humbled, and all
> who humble themselves will be exalted. (Matt. 23:8–12)

I'm not sure how all the Fathers and the Reverends and the Can-
ons and the Rectors and the Monsignors and the Senior Apostles
and the Most Reverends have got around that one.

No status. No titles. No thrones or seats of honour. Slavery,
servanthood, a childlike welcome to all. This may be why Mark
also inserts here the story of the unauthorised exorcist. Someone
has been casting out demons in Jesus' name without seeking prior
approval or filling in the forms. The church has a long history
of dismissing those doing good because they were not working
through official channels, or because they were unorthodox, but
Jesus puts it into perspective. 'Whoever is not against us is for us.'
Don't knock them: they are on our side.

'The collectors of the temple tax'

By now Jesus and his disciples are back at Capernaum for the last
time. The travels to the north are over. But before they head south,
there is a tiny event involving a fish and some money.

> When they reached Capernaum, the collectors of the temple tax
> came to Peter and said, 'Does your teacher not pay the temple tax
> [lit. didrachma]?' He said, 'Yes, he does.' And when he came home,
> Jesus spoke of it first, asking, 'What do you think, Simon? From whom
> do kings of the earth take toll or tribute? From their children or from
> others?' When Peter said, 'From others', Jesus said to him, 'Then the
> children are free. However, so that we do not give offence to them,
> go to the lake and cast a hook; take the first fish that comes up; and
> when you open its mouth, you will find a coin [lit. stater]; take that
> and give it to them for you and me.' (Matt. 17:24–27)

Despite the fairy-tale nature of the story, it must be taken seriously as an early testimony, because it concerns the payment of the
temple tax – an issue which was not something that later Christians
would bother inventing a story about, and which was certainly not

an issue after AD 70, when the temple was in ruins.

The temple tax was a half-shekel, paid annually by every Jewish man over twenty years old towards the upkeep of the temple. According to the Mishnah, the temple tax was collected from 15 Adar onwards – around the beginning of March.[22] Hence it seems likely that this event took place earlier in the year.

The temple authorities may have claimed a precedent from Exodus 30:13ff., where a half-shekel is demanded on occasions when a census takes place, but otherwise there is no precedent in the Torah.[23] In Jesus' day it was probably still viewed as a recent innovation, which is why it was controversial. People argued over whether it was an annual payment, or a one-off tax. There was also a sense of grievance over the fact that priests were exempt.[24]

The tax was not compulsory, but it was expected. When the money was taken to the temple, it had to be processed by the money changers. The Mishnah records that it had previously been paid in a variety of coinage, including Persian *darics*, and even Roman *denarii*.[25] By Jesus' day, however, you could pay in only one, official, currency: the Tyrian shekel.[26]

This was nothing to do with friendship – the Tyrians always hated the Jews.[27] Nor was it because the Tyrian shekel did not have an offensive graven 'image' on it (it did not have a picture of the emperor, but it did have the god Melkart [Heracles] on it – hardly an improvement).[28] The real reason why the Tyrian shekel was chosen is that it contained more silver than the other kinds. Silver coins from Antioch contained only 80 per cent silver on average; Tyrian shekels averaged 90 per cent, and their silver content was tightly regulated.[29] This was a commercial demand wrapped up as a religious choice.[30]

The Tyrian shekel came in two denominations – a *didrachma* (double-drachma) equivalent to a half-shekel, and a *tetradrachma* (quadruple-drachma) or one shekel. The temple authorities preferred the latter coin, as it was bigger and therefore contained more silver. But there was a problem: the set rate of temple tax for one man was half a shekel. So what they did was to put a surcharge of 8 per cent on every individual half-shekel payment. The idea was to get people to club together, so that two men paying the tax would use the *tetradrachma* – the more valuable coin.[31] In other words, if you went to the temple and paid what you were supposed to pay, you were charged extra.[32] Imagine it this way: every year you have to pay half a pound/dollar/euro to support the church. If two of you club together, you can pay one pound/dollar/euro between you. But if you make just a single payment, they are going to charge you 54 pence/cents. It was the temple's version of a credit card surcharge. Or maybe an encouragement to pay by direct debit.

This is exactly what happens in this passage. Literally, the collectors ask Peter, 'Does your master pay the *didrachma*, i.e. the single man's tax?' And the 'coin' that they find in the fish is actually a *stater* – equivalent to the *tetradrachma* coin and payment for both Jesus' and Peter's tax. Without the surcharge.

So despite the fishy business, the historical details are accurate and precise. And the political, historical inference is equally clear: if the kings of the world exempt their own family from paying tax, how much more should the priestly aristocracy do so?[33] Jesus is saying that Jews should not be taxed by the leaders of their own faith. The 'children' should be free of these obligations. In the end he does pay, but just to keep people quiet. (And he pays by a miracle, rather than out of his own pocket.)

This is not a ringing endorsement of the temple tax. He paid, for now. But, later, he will make his displeasure known.

There is a kind of darkness and oppression about this section of the narrative. The crowds – the mob – whom Jesus castigated at the foot of the mountain, the secrecy with which he makes his way back to Capernaum, the statement by Jesus that 'whoever is not for us is against us' – all imply that things had turned sour in this part of Galilee.

This may be why Jesus later denounces Chorazin, Bethsaida and Capernaum. They had their chance – they saw who Jesus was and what he could do – but they did not take it. In the end they rejected him.

So he leaves, shaking the dust from his sandals as he goes. He is going to head south. To Samaria, Judea, the Jordan.

And to Jerusalem.

7. Galilee, Samaria, autumn/winter AD 32

The news from Rome was terrible. Sejanus fallen, his family slaughtered. Little Junilla raped and murdered. The mob on a rampage. The body of his friend and patron torn to pieces on the Gemonian stairs.

For months he had waited for the recall to Rome, but it never came. Perhaps he had successfully convinced Tiberius of his loyalty. Or perhaps the emperor was just waiting for him to slip up.

Up the coast, Pomponius Flaccus had arrived. A new governor. Jew-friendly; or that was the rumour, anyway. The emperor's new policy, to 'speak comfortably to them'. Comfortably! Did he know what life was like out here? Did he have any idea of how difficult these people were?

Of course not. Every festival – *every festival!* – someone got it into their heads to do something stupid. Do anything to their holy city and there were protests. Put a shield up and you'd have a delegation visit you. You couldn't even build an aqueduct without a protest of some sort. Negotiations got you nowhere. Force was the only language they understood. That was the way with the Jews.

And they knew when you were weak. He thought the shields would be OK this time. No pictures on them, just some words. After all, Herod, that old monster, had put the imperial eagle up in his day. But it was the same thing again. Protests and arguments and this time four of Herod's whelps coming and registering their protests. Self-important little pups.

All right. He'd survived worse. Been in more dangerous battles. He could ride this one out. All it required was to play the dice carefully. The temple hadn't worked. The shields hadn't worked. Just keep your head down, keep quiet and keep the money flowing back to Rome.

Diplomacy. That was what was needed. Smile, treat these little people and their complaints seriously. But make sure they know that you are always ready to spill some blood.

'One town and village after another'

Mark proceeds rapidly, galloping from Galilee to Jesus' triumphal entry to Jerusalem in a mere fifty-two verses. In Luke the journey takes much longer: Jesus leaves Galilee and enters Samaria at the end of chapter 9, but does not arrive near Jericho until nine chapters later. What Luke seems to indicate is that Jesus spent a great deal longer in the north – around the Galilee/Jericho border – before heading south. A few geographical pointers give us clues.

▷ Jesus is rejected (Luke 9:51–56) – Samaria.
▷ Jesus visits Martha and Mary (Luke 10:38–42) – Bethany.
▷ Jesus goes through 'one town and village after another' (Luke 13:22) – making his way to Jerusalem.
▷ Jesus is warned to 'get away from here, for Herod wants to kill you' (Luke 13:31) – Galilee or the Perea.
▷ Jesus heals lepers (Luke 17:11) – region between Samaria and Galilee.
▷ Jesus approaches and enters Jericho (Luke 18:35, 19:1) – er … Jericho.

It's a difficult itinerary, but one thing it does show is that Jesus spent a long time around the border between Galilee and Samaria. Herod's threat only makes sense if Jesus is in his territory: either Galilee or the Perea. But if we follow Luke, he cannot have been in the Perea, because four chapters later he is still in the Samaria/Galilee region. He probably does not spend long in Samaria, because he keeps having dinner with Pharisees – none of whom would have a house there. And the constant crowds imply Jews, not Samaritans.

We also know from John's account that Jesus made two visits to Jerusalem before the final week: for the feast of Tabernacles in autumn AD 32, and the feast of Dedication in winter AD 32.

So Jesus does not set out from Capernaum and progress in a slow but steady manner to Jerusalem. What he does is leave Capernaum, travel to the southern edge of Galilee, and stop. Or, at least, move around within that region.[1] He spends around three months in what Luke describes as 'the region between Samaria and Galilee', the southern fringes of Galilee. From there he launched the mission of the seventy to preach the good news – some of whom were sent, guerilla-like, into Samaritan towns. Meanwhile the mention of Mary and Martha indicates that Jesus also went on a mission himself, albeit a clandestine one, and further south. He then went from Galilee to Judea, wintering in a place called Ephraim, until the time came to go to Jerusalem for the Passover.

'The Lord appointed seventy others'

Was it harvest time? Jesus' use of the imagery of an abundant harvest with only a handful of labourers to gather it in may indicate that he was looking at the crops around them as they moved to their new base of operations (Luke 10:2). That would fit with the timing: late summer, early autumn, the fruit growing heavy on the vine – soon there will be labourers waiting in the market squares, looking for work.

Luke tells us that Jesus 'sent messengers ahead of him' (9:52). They would visit a number of towns. Jesus presumably wanted to make the most of the few days in each place, by preparing the way. But at the first Samaritan village they come to, it is made clear that Jesus is not welcome. Whereas before, just after the Baptist's arrest, Jesus received a warm welcome, this time the people would not welcome him at all. James and John – still stuck in their old view of the Messiah – suggest raining down fire from heaven on the village. Jesus rebukes them.

He uses the occasion to underline again the conflict and difficulty of following him (Luke 9:51–56). You cannot look back. Even sacred duties like burying one's parents are unimportant given the urgency of the task (Luke 9:59–62). Although the dead burying their own dead has been interpreted spiritually – 'leave that sort of thing to the spiritually dead' – Jesus is probably making a joke. Jewish burial practice was in two stages: the first stage where the corpse was enwrapped and interred in the tomb, and then a

GALILEE, SAMARIA, AD 32

year later, when the flesh had decomposed, the second stage – the bones were collected and put into an ossuary or 'bone box'.[2] The man is not asking Jesus, 'At least let me go to my father's funeral.' It is more like, 'Let me wait for a year until I can finish the whole process.' But Jesus says, let the other corpses in the tomb do the job. He is not asking someone to go entirely against the injunction to honour their parents with a decent burial, he is saying do not use it as an excuse. There is a harvest to gather in.

Next Jesus very consciously widens his circle. He has trained – as much as their understanding will let him – twelve missionary disciples. Now he appoints seventy more with the same instructions: go out into the villages, in twos, no money, no luggage, not even any footwear. Dress like the poor, and take only the good news with you.

When might this have taken place? Back to those Samaritans for a moment. The reason Luke gives for their antagonism towards Jesus is that 'his face was set towards Jerusalem' (Luke 9:53). The Samaritans clearly consider Jesus and his followers to be a pilgrimage party going up to Jerusalem for the festival, and all the old enmities swing into play.

Why, though, would they consider his group a pilgrimage party? The only explanation is that they *were* a pilgrimage group – some of them, at least.

'Show yourself to the world'

John gives us another story of dissension among Jesus' family, a story which must have taken place just before Jesus left Galilee for Samaria. The incident took place in the autumn of AD 32. We know that Jesus' brothers were not among his disciples; they certainly were not present at the crucifixion. But they may have been with him at this time, on the first stage of his tour in south Galilee/Samaria, because they were going up to Jerusalem for the festival. The natural route from Capernaum to Samaria would take Jesus towards Sepphoris and past Nazareth where his family lived. Naturally then, Jesus' brothers would join his group, as their route lay in the same direction. They were all going south. This may be why the Samaritans reacted so strongly. Jesus' party contained pilgrims. It contained, specifically, his brothers.

189

> Now the Jewish festival of Booths was near. So his brothers said to him, 'Leave here and go to Judea so that your disciples also may see the works you are doing; for no one who wants to be widely known acts in secret. If you do these things, show yourself to the world.' (For not even his brothers believed in him.) (John 7:2–5)

It is the old temptation. Show what you can do. Only they do not really believe that he will. And Jesus refuses. He tells them to 'go themselves' if they want to. 'My time has not yet fully come' (John 7:8). So his brothers set off without him.

Then Jesus abruptly changes his mind: 'After his brothers had gone to the festival, then [Jesus] also went, not publicly but as it were in secret' (John 7:10).

Once again, none of the disciples feature in the episode as recounted in John's Gospel. The implication is that, just as he had at the festival in winter AD 31, Jesus takes the opportunity to go to Jerusalem, while they are off evangelising.

John's picture of Jerusalem is of a city abuzz with rumour. The crowd is alive with argument and speculation about Jesus. Some say he is a good man, others that he is 'deceiving the crowd'. There is, however, no open discussion of Jesus, 'for fear of the Jews' (John 7:13). It is a scene out of a modern dictatorship. The streets of Burma or Iran. Is the people's champion going to show his face? And is he really their champion, or just another failed wannabe king? Or worse, a government stooge?

Worryingly, the Jewish authorities are already expecting Jesus. They are on the lookout, saying, 'Where is he?' How did they know he was coming? It has been nine months, perhaps a year, since he last showed his face in Jerusalem. Most of that time he has spent up north, some of it even outside Galilee. Two major festivals – Passover and Pentecost – have passed without him appearing. The crowd's fervour may have been stoked by stories of the feeding of the five thousand. But the worrying suspicion is that somehow this is linked with Jesus' brothers urging him to go to Jerusalem. Had they told the authorities that Jesus would be there? After all, considering that they did not believe in him, they were very keen for him to act in a very public way. This might sound like sacrilege – especially since at least one of his brothers was a leader of the Jerusalem church – but even if we accept that Jesus' brother Jude authored the letter which bears his name, that still leaves two brothers unaccounted for, two brothers who, for all we know, never followed Jesus, never believed their brother was anything other than a madman. It is a disturbing thought, perhaps, but maybe Judas was not the only mole in the camp.

Jesus, of course, does arrive – in 'the middle of the festival' (John 7:14). With his usual tact and sensitivity, he marches straight into the temple and starts arguing with the crowd. An arrest squad is even sent out.

This would not have been Roman soldiers – of which there were only a handful in Jerusalem – but the temple police who provided the security force for Jerusalem, under the control of the high priest and the Sanhedrin. The force was several thousand strong: during the first Jewish revolt, 8,500 temple guards were killed.[3] Drawn, like the priests, from the Levite tribe, the temple police maintained order in the temple, served as gatekeepers at the entry to the sanctuary, patrolled the temple courts, and stood guard on the rampart around the Court of the Gentiles.[4]

Nothing happens. No arrest is made and when the guards return empty handed, the authorities mock them. When Nicodemus tries to argue that Jesus at least deserves a fair hearing, he is ridiculed: 'You're not from Galilee too, are you?'

The words of the Jerusalem elite are revealing: 'Has any one of the authorities or of the Pharisees believed in him?' (John 7:48). (Notice: the authorities are different from the Pharisees.) What the temple elite are saying is, 'No one with any education, any sophistication, has been taken in by this man. *He comes from Galilee.*'

Galileans. Uncultured, uneducated northerners. For the urban elite in Jerusalem, Galilee was a remote, uncivilised place. It was poor, rural, cut off from the 'home' of Judaism by the hated Samaria and ringed by Gentile cities – home, indeed, to many more Gentiles than were in Judea. It was not as if it had always been a part of their country. Galilee had effectively been a separate region under the Hasmoneans, and it was only annexed into the Hasmonean kingdom at the end of the second century BC. The view of Galilee, then, was not unlike a Londoner's view of Scotland right after the Act of Union in 1707.

For the sophisticated Jerusalemite, the difference was summed up in their accents: Galileans did not speak 'proper'. There is a story about a man from Galilee in a Jerusalem market trying to buy something that sounded like *amar*; the market traders mock him because they do not know if he wants a donkey to ride on (*hamâr*), a drink of wine (*hamar*), a dress ('*amar*, meaning 'wool') or a lamb for sacrifice (*immar*).[5] (This is how, later, Peter was identified as one of Jesus' followers so easily: he spoke in the ridiculous, yokel, uneducated accent of the north.)

This prejudice is reflected in the crowd. Some argue that he cannot be the Messiah, because he comes from Galilee and everyone knows that the Messiah must come from Bethlehem (John 7:40–4). Others disagree, arguing that 'when the Messiah comes, no one will know where he is from' (John 7:27). One group even claims that Jesus comes from Samaria: 'Are we not right in saying that you are a Samaritan and have a demon?' (John 8:48). The demon accusation is familiar and surfaces three times in this visit: the first time to explain Jesus' paranoid belief that the crowd is trying to kill him (John 7:20), the second and third times in response to his teaching (8:48, 52; 10:19–21). But the Samaritan accusation is a new one. Perhaps it reflects a garbled version of the truth: he had come here from Samaria. Or maybe they are just trying as hard as they can to smear Jesus. Make out that he's possessed. Dismiss him as an ignorant northerner. No, better still, let's call him a Samaritan!

Interestingly, Jesus denies the accusation of demonic possession, but says nothing about being a Samaritan. In fact, it was probably around this point that he told one of his most famous stories, a story that really only makes sense if told in Jerusalem.

'A man was going down from Jerusalem to Jericho'

Although Luke implies that Jesus told this story in Galilee, for various reasons it makes better sense in a Jerusalem setting. It breaks rather abruptly into the narrative, for one thing, and as a story it relies on its audience knowing the local landmark: the road from Jericho to Jerusalem. Those in Jerusalem would have been only too aware of how dangerous the road was. From 2,500 feet above sea level to 800 feet below, the road is a long descent through rocky terrain. For any pilgrims in the crowd the route would also have been familiar: if you took that route to Galilee, through the Perea, you could avoid Samaria. Given the import of the story, the idea that the road is a Samaria-avoidance route for pilgrims adds an extra layer of irony.

The main reason, however, why the parable would be better located in Jerusalem is that the whole thing is an anti-temple story.

It begins with an argument over who is meant by the 'neighbour' in Leviticus 19:18, 'You shall love your neighbour as yourself.' Traditionally, this was taken to mean fellow Israelites, though it would include resident aliens who are living in the land (Lev. 19:33–34). But once again, Jesus takes the Torah text and stretches it almost to breaking point.

He tells the story of an unidentified everyman, who is attacked, robbed and left for dead. As he lies there, two people come by: a priest and a Levite. The important thing is that both characters were thoroughly and completely associated with the temple. Both priests and Levites served in the temple. The story indicates that they are going down the road, away from Jerusalem: the implication is that, like Jesus' relative Zechariah, they have done their turn on the rota in the temple. There is no rush. They have done their duty. They are going home.

It is the temple, then, that is represented by these people. It is the 'temple' which does nothing to help this wounded man. The 'temple' does nothing for its neighbours. But a Samaritan does. Priests and Levites arrived at their position because of genetics, because of their ancestry: holiness was woven into their DNA, just as the Samaritans had impurity woven into theirs. Yet it is the Samaritan who helps the man, who takes him to the inn and gives two days' wages to the innkeeper to pay for his care.

One of the strangest features of the story is that a Samaritan should be anywhere near Jerusalem in the first place. And why he is going north-east, towards Jericho and not north, which would lead to Samaria?

There were Samaritans in Jerusalem, though. They were in the Antonia fortress. They were in the army.

When we talk about the Roman army, that word 'Roman' can be misleading. We imagine Latin-speaking Italians, far from home, pining for the vineyards. But there were hardly any actual Italian 'Romans' in Palestine. Those who were there were probably officers, centurions and officials in Pilate's small entourage. The rest were locals.

Judea was not garrisoned with Roman legionaries, but with five cohorts of auxiliaries. Auxiliary troops were local recruits – not Jews, who were exempt from military service, but local provincials, non-Jewish residents of Samaria and Caesarea.[6] Josephus gives us the name of one of these cohorts: the *Sebastii* – named after *Sebaste*, the Greek word for Augustus. And Sebaste was the Greek name for the city of Samaria. These were Samaritan recruits.[7] Samaritans were not exempt from military service as Jews were.[8]

So it is possible that the Samaritan in this story was a soldier. Admittedly, Jesus does not say as much, but it does make sense. As one scholar puts it, 'Would a Jew normally regard a Samaritan as a model of kindness, picture him travelling in Judea, or think that a Judean innkeeper would trust him?'[9] Not an ordinary Samaritan, no. But one class of Samaritans must have travelled in Judea and, if they are like their counterparts anywhere else in the world, must have used the inns: soldiers. This Samaritan has a horse. He has provisions: oil and wine. He has his pay.

There is another military connotation as well. The word for 'robbers' used by Luke here is *lestai* – bandits (Luke 10:30). *Lestai*, as we have seen, were those guerilla bandits who attacked official convoys and imperial treasuries, rebels, terrorists. Two *lestai* will be crucified alongside Jesus.

So. Put the telling of this parable in Jerusalem. Have Jesus near the temple. Look up: beyond the temple, overlooking it, there is the Antonia fortress, full of Greek and Samaritan soldiers. The point of the story does not change, really: your neighbour is anyone. But the heroes and villains of this story take on a different dimension. The priest and the Levite were representatives not of Judaism, not even of legalism, but of the temple that lay at the heart of their Judaism.

And the temple was, in Jesus' eyes, symbolic of a limited religion, a religion which walked on by, ignoring people in need.

'Rabbi, who sinned?'

Talking of people in need …

John includes a story here about the healing of a blind man at the Pool of Siloam. It follows a familiar pattern: Jesus deliberately heals the man on the Sabbath. Not only that, he does the healing in a deliberately provocative way: he spits into the mud and kneads it into a paste to smear on the man's eyes (John 9:6). Kneading is work, of course, and the Pharisees, as usual, rise to the bait.

The Pool of Siloam was at the southern end of the Tyropaean valley – the valley which ran north–south through Jerusalem. There was a tower nearby which collapsed at some point, killing a number of people (Luke 13:4). Jesus' order that the man wash in the pool may be related to the festival; according to later Jewish writing, at the feast of Tabernacles a golden vessel containing water from the Pool of Siloam was carried in a procession up to the temple and the altar.[10] Similarly, Jesus' teaching about being the light of the world (8:12) fits with the practice of lighting great lamps during the Tabernacles feast.

Like the troubled end to the Galilean campaign in Mark, these Jerusalem chapters of John are full of conflict. There are multiple attempts to arrest Jesus (John 7:30, 32, 44; 8:20) and one to stone him (John 8:59). John puts the failure to arrest Jesus down to divine intervention, to the fact that Jesus' hour 'had not yet come'. Jesus' escape from stoning was more prosaic: he hid himself and went out of the temple (John 8:20, 59).

In the febrile, heady religious atmosphere, Jesus was not the only person under threat of stoning. In most Bibles you will find a story at this point about a woman caught in adultery. It is not in the earliest manuscripts of John's Gospel and is written in a different style. It is possible that it comes from a now-lost gospel, the *Gospel of the Hebrews*. The few fragments we have from this lost gospel include a slightly different version of the Lord's Prayer and an account of Jesus' resurrection appearance to his brother James.[11] Papias, writing around AD 130, wrote, according to Eusebius, of 'a story about a woman accused falsely of many sins before the lord, which the Gospel of [the] Hebrews contains'.[12] So this story may well originate from a different Gospel.

195

It certainly fits into the general atmosphere of the city at the time. Technically only the Romans had the right to execute people, but one doubts the Romans would worry about a Jewish woman being stoned by a mob. In the end, Jesus completely undermines their self-righteous fury and they slink away. But the woman, the sinner, is told to go and 'sin no more'.

The visit to Jerusalem is not mentioned in Luke, but he does relate an event which must have taken place during this visit, or a similar time. Because it takes place at a house just two miles from Jerusalem, in the village of Bethany.

'The better part'

Mary, Martha and Lazarus lived in Bethany, a village on the eastern slopes of the Mount of Olives. Far enough outside the city to escape the crowds and the attention, it was Jesus' preferred place to stay when he came to Jerusalem.

We do not know how they met. If this was indeed the Bethany we hear of earlier in John's Gospel, it may have been back in the time when Jesus was with John the Baptist. What we do know is that this family were to play a significant role in Jesus' life. I will examine their rather unusual household in more detail a little later on. For now, though, let us look at the two sisters, two disciples of Jesus.

This story is all about discipleship. While Martha rushes around serving the guests – i.e. the men – Mary sits at the feet of Jesus and listens to his teaching. Martha complains, with some justification perhaps, that Mary has left her to do all the work. 'Tell her to help me,' she says to Jesus. But Jesus gently reproves Martha for being worried and distracted by too many things, while Mary has 'chosen the better part' (Luke 10:42).

The traditional interpretation of this story has centred around a conflict between the active and the contemplative life. Martha is the active one, Mary is the contemplative, faith-focused sister who sits and listens. Actually it is not about that at all. If there is a conflict at all, it is between a sister who knew her place, and one who did not.

Mary is behaving in a way unbecoming to her gender. Instead of serving the men, she is sitting and learning. She wants to be part of the conversation. She sits at the feet of her rabbi, her teacher, adopting the traditional pose of a disciple. And disciples had to be male.

In rabbinical thinking, it was a fundamental belief that God simply did not talk to women. 'In the name of R. Eliezer b. R. Shimeon: we have not found that the Almighty spoke to a woman except Sarah,' runs one source.[13] In the same way, rabbinic teaching largely excluded women from the study of the Torah. Rabbi Eliezer said that 'anyone who teaches his daughter Torah, it is as though he has taught her lechery'.[14] Women did attend various religious assemblies, but they were there to listen, not to debate. Eleazar ben Azariah interpreted the command, 'Assemble the people – men, women and children' (Deut. 31:12), to mean that the men should come to study, the women to listen and the little ones 'to receive the reward for those who bring them'.[15] Martha's complaint against Mary is not that she is a contemplative, but that she is a rebel. This is why Martha is so concerned to get her back to work. She wants her back within the acceptable boundaries.

This, then, is an attempt by Mary to play a fuller part in the kingdom of God. She wants to be a disciple of Jesus in the fullest possible sense. She wants to listen and to learn. She wants to follow Jesus like the others do. She wants what the men have. Mary, in sitting at Jesus' feet, is actually getting above herself. And Jesus, far from dismissing her, commends her for it.

It should be clear by now that Jesus did have women disciples. They are never called that in the Gospels: under the culture of the day that was impossible – the very word itself was masculine. But they could act like his disciples, even if doing so meant that they had to step outside the cultural norms of their society.

'A cloud rising in the west'

Neither John nor Luke indicate exactly where Jesus went next. John's Gospel moves rather seamlessly from the feast of Booths to the feast of Dedication three months later, but I think we would be correct in assuming that Jesus returned to the Galilee/Samaria border to meet up with his seventy disciples. In Luke, well after the events in Bethany he is still going 'through the region between Samaria and Galilee' (Luke 17:11).

And the weather is changing. For those who could read the signs, there was a storm brewing. Peasants, through necessity, grew expert at reading the weather. Jesus talks about their ability to look at the clouds and see the rain coming; they can feel the sirocco wind from the south, from the desert, and know that it brings a scorching heat to burn up their crops (Luke 12:54–56). But what Jesus is talking about here is the political climate. It is changing, and they cannot see it.

Luke includes a detail which tells us something about the tinderbox atmosphere of the time.

> At that very time there were some present who told him about the Galileans whose blood Pilate had mingled with their sacrifices. He asked them, 'Do you think that because these Galileans suffered in this way they were worse sinners than all other Galileans? No, I tell you; but unless you repent, you will all perish as they did. Or those eighteen who were killed when the tower of Siloam fell on them – do you think that they were worse offenders than all the others living in Jerusalem? No, I tell you; but unless you repent, you will all perish just as they did.' (Luke 13:1–5)

Jesus uses these incidents, these news stories, to talk about the nature of judgement. But who were these Galileans? And what tower are we talking about? Did the tower fall during the time he was in Jerusalem? Frustratingly, we do not know. But the story introduces one of the major players in events to come: Pontius Pilate, prefect of Judea. And the incident with the Galileans may be indicative of a wider, more troubled political picture, because by the winter of AD 32, Pilate was in trouble.[16]

The only physical evidence we have for the rule of Pontius Pilate is a dedication inscription to a Tiberieum, a temple or shrine built in honour of Tiberius, the emperor of Rome. It was discovered in Caesarea in 1961 and it reads, 'Pontius Pilate, the Prefect of Judea, has dedicated to the people of Caesarea a temple in honour of Tiberius.'[17] It is not much to go on, but it gives us two pieces of valuable information: first, that Pilate's proper title was *Praefectus Iudaeae* – 'Prefect of Judea'; and second, that he was keen to please the emperor.

Pilate had risen through the ranks to become prefect. He came from the second layer of the Roman class system: the equestrians.[18]

Most equestrians were part of a local elite: such power as they had lay in the provinces or cities. Back home in Rome it was the senators – the upper class of aristocracy – who had real clout.

Roman names have three parts: *nomen*, *praenomen* and *cognomen*. *Nomen* signified your tribe, *cognomen* your family, and *praenomen* your personal name. We do not know Pilate's *praenomen*, his personal name. Although later traditions record it as Lucius, that is just a myth. His tribe – his *nomen* – were the Pontii. They were originally Samnites, a tough, warlike people from the south-central Apennines in Italy. In the distant past, the Samnites had almost brought Rome's rise to power to a halt. In 82 BC the Roman dictator Lucius Cornelius Sulla defeated the forces of another Pontius: Pontius Telesinus. Sulla inflicted such a wave of slaughter and destruction that the Samnites were never again to have any real power. 'No Roman', said Sulla, 'would ever know peace as long as they had the Samnites to deal with.' The towns and cities of Samnium were reduced to villages 'and some have even vanished altogether'.[19]

Pilate, then, had something in common with the Galilean Jesus. His people had also experienced Rome's brutal, crushing power. Only he had joined the fight, become one of them. His *cognomen*, or family name, was Pilatii, from *pilatus* or 'spear'. Perhaps they were always a warlike, fighting family. If that was the case, Pilate carried on this tradition. As an equestrian prefect, he was a career soldier, serving in battle, gaining promotion, until finally he was given command of Judea.

His job was simple: to collect taxes and keep law and order. He was responsible for the administration of justice, but only the most important cases would have been brought before Pilate. Life and death cases, in fact, for the prefect, only, had that power. Josephus tells us that the first procurator, Coponius (also from the equestrian ranks), was granted extensive powers. 'And now Archelaus's part of Judea was reduced into a province, and Coponius, one of the equestrian order among the Romans, was sent as a procurator, having the power of [life and] death put into his hands by Caesar.'[20]

Pilate was appointed prefect of Judea in AD 26. He was not appointed by the emperor, though, but by a man called L. Aelius

A copy of the inscription found in 1961, commemorating the building of a Tiberieum by 'Pontius Pilatus'.

Sejanus, who at that time was the *de facto* ruler of Rome. The Emperor Tiberius had almost retired from public life, spending his days in his villas in Campania and Capri and leaving the government of the empire largely in the hands of his trusted lieutenant.[21]

While Sejanus remained in power, therefore, Pilate could do pretty much as he liked. We can see this reflected in coins. For the first three years of his rule Pilate was careful not to mint coins with images that might offend the Jews. But on coins minted from AD 29 to 31, the images change. For the first time in Judea, they depict Roman objects and images of power, such as the *simpulum* (a ladle used for pouring wine on sacrificial animals) and the *lituus* (a wand used in augury).[22] Even if these coins caused disquiet among the Jews, what could they do? Tiberius did not care, and it would be no good complaining to Sejanus – he was a notorious anti-Semite. Philo accused him of wishing to 'do away with the nation' and so inventing false slanders against the Jews. In AD 19 he forced the Jews in Rome to burn their religious vestments and expelled them from the city. No Jew would get justice from him.

By AD 31, Sejanus was at the peak of his power: golden statues of the general were being put up in Rome, the Senate had voted his birthday a public holiday, public prayers were offered on behalf of Tiberius and Sejanus and, in AD 31, he was named as consul with Tiberius. Then it all fell to pieces.

Tiberius had realised that Sejanus was too powerful. Secretly, he transferred command of the Praetorian Guard to another officer and Sejanus, the most powerful man in Rome, was tricked into attending the Senate, where he was denounced, arrested and, that evening, condemned to death. He was strangled, and his body cast onto the Gemonian stairs, where the crowd tore it to pieces.[23]

Tiberius took the opportunity to purge Rome, not just of Sejanus and his family, but of all his supporters and associates. Mobs took revenge on anyone even suspected of being associated with Sejanus. His statues were pulled down. His children were all executed and his wife Livilla – Tiberius's own daughter – committed suicide. Sejanus's daughter Junilla was a virgin at the time of her death. According to ancient sources she was raped while the noose was actually around her neck. That's civilised Rome for you.

In Judea, Pilate must have been badly shaken. He was Sejanus's appointee. Were his friends and family under suspicion? Would he be purged, like so many others?

Worse news was to follow. A new governor of Syria turned up. L. Pomponius Flaccus was the first governor of Syria actually to come to the territory in eight years. He arrived in Antioch in AD 32.[24] Even attitudes to the Jews were changing. Philo records that Tiberius 'charged his procurators in every place to which they were appointed to speak comfortably to the members of our nation in the different cities' assuring them of fair trials and calling them a 'naturally peaceable' people.[25]

In the space of a few months, Pilate had lost his supporter at the top, he had a new boss in Antioch and there had been a change of policy regarding the very people of whom he was in charge.

It is these changed circumstances which may have led to that inscription. Roman emperors were routinely deified after their death, but Pilate is the only known official who built a temple to a living emperor. Given the political situation, the *Tiberieum* may have been the first move in Pilate's PR offensive to prove his loyalty to the emperor.[26]

The desire to honour the emperor may also have been behind some other incidents as well. Images of the emperor (as on coins) were considered blasphemous by the Jews, a transgression of the scriptural command to 'make no graven image'. Early in his career Pilate made an attempt to introduce votive shields into Jerusalem – sheilds which bore the image of the emperor. He was only stopped by a non-violent protest from the Jews, who gathered in his head-quarters at Caesarea and, according to Josephus, 'laid their necks bare, and said they would take their death very willingly, rather than the wisdom of their laws should be transgressed'.[27]

But with Tiberius back in power and Pilate's position rocky, he decided to have another go:

> [Pilate] not more with the object of doing honour to Tiberius than with that of vexing the multitude, dedicated some gilt shields in the palace of Herod, in the holy city; which had no form nor any other forbidden thing represented on them except some necessary inscription, which mentioned these two facts, the name of the person who had placed them there, and the person in whose honour they were so placed there.

This time there is clearly a measure of compromise. The shields contain no image, but just an inscription. And they are in the Palace of Herod, the prefect's HQ in Jerusalem, well out of the way. Despite this, rumours about them escape, 'the multitude' hear that the shields are back and all of a sudden there are complaints. Even the Herodian royal family got involved:

> But when the multitude heard what had been done, and when the circumstance became notorious, then the people, putting forward the four sons of the king … and those magistrates who were among them at the time, entreated him to alter and to rectify the innovation which he had committed in respect of the shields.

Although Pilate refused their petition, the leaders threatened to complain to Tiberius. According to Philo, Pilate feared that if an embassy was sent to the emperor, other facts would emerge, such as 'his corruption, and his acts of insolence, and his rapine, and his habit of insulting people, and his cruelty, and his continual murders of people untried and uncondemned, and his never ending, and gratuitous, and most grievous inhumanity'.

In the end, the leaders did write to Tiberius, who replied immediately, ordering Pilate to remove the shields to Caesarea. Philo dates this event late in the period of Pilate's office.[28] Certainly it must have taken place after the fall of Sejanus. And the involvement of the Herodian princes – the 'four sons of the king' – indicates that this was probably at the time of a festival. We do not know who they were, but we can guess at Antipas and Philip at least. Antipas, certainly, was no orthodox Jew. He would have cared little about some shields. This was a chance for them to curry favour with their own people and to show Pilate that the balance of power was shifting.

One can imagine how Pilate felt. Philo describes him as 'a man of a very inflexible disposition, and very merciless as well as very obstinate'. He would not take kindly to being forced to back down, again. If so, we can infer that the argument between the Herodian princes and Pilate occurred before the trial of Jesus and after the fall of Sejanus, which leads us to a festival somewhere in AD 32.[29]

The story shows a man walking a political tightrope, trying at once to please the emperor and placate the Jews. Significantly, perhaps, no coin in Palestine after AD 30/31 shows the pagan *lituus* or *simpulum* symbol. He had learned his lesson.[30]

It is in this context that we have to set the incident with the Galileans. The context – the blood mingled with the sacrifices – suggests that it was during Passover.[31] Perhaps it was tied up with the opposition to the shields. It is not reported by Josephus, indicating that the numbers involved were probably small. Local resentment in Galilee, then, but not registering much elsewhere. But it is clearly a recent event. Sometime at a major festival in AD 32, Pilate had quelled a protest by force, and blood had been spilt. And, remember, they were Galileans and Antipas, not Pilate, was in charge in Galilee. Perhaps this and the shield protest were some of the reasons why Antipas and Pilate were not on friendly terms until after the trial and execution of Jesus.

What it shows is that Pilate needed to keep the peace in Judea. Even if it meant doing deals with the Jewish aristocracy, and spilling a little peasant blood.

'That fox'

It was not just Pilate who was a danger. A little after this incident, Jesus is warned suddenly to flee the district: 'Get away from here, for Herod wants to kill you' (Luke 13:31).

Jesus must still be in Galilee at this point. Close to Herod's main city of Tiberias. It is interesting that the Pharisees bring the message and urge Jesus to escape. Clearly some were on his side.

Why Herod wanted to kill Jesus at this particular moment is a matter of speculation. Certainly the crowds are still following Jesus. Perhaps he got wind of the sending out of the seventy disciples. Whatever the case, Herod is dismissed as 'that fox' (Luke 13:32). It is almost a lighthearted remark, but such remarks could easily prove fatal. Herod may not have had the title of king, but he had many of the powers. He had his own troops. And he could certainly execute people if he wished.

It may have been this threat – a reminder, perhaps of the arrest of John the Baptist – which caused Jesus to leave the area, and move south. 'Large crowds', says Luke, 'were travelling with him' (Luke 14:25). Luke gives us pictures of crowds gathering by their thousands, trampling one another to hear Jesus (Luke 12:1). Luke's account is full of people asking Jesus questions or promising to follow him. He is clearly still picking up followers.

For Luke, this is overwhelmingly a time for teaching, for preparing the disciples – the larger band, including the women – for what lies ahead, and we get a glimpse of what awaits his followers. The kind of fate, in fact, that Luke himself was to write up in the second part of his history. To follow Jesus means giving up everything. There will be a cost, he says. Work out the cost of the building before you start to build, he says. And, perhaps with Antipas in mind, nervously contemplating war with his erstwhile father-in-law in Nabatea, if you do not have enough troops to win, do not start the war (Luke 14:31–33).

At one point, in the region between Galilee and Samaria, Jesus heals ten lepers, only one of whom – a Samaritan – returns to thank him (Luke 17:11–19). Luke precedes this story with the phrase 'On the way to Jerusalem', so perhaps we should infer that, after the time spent in southern Galilee, the journey south has commenced.

Jesus points out time and again the perils and costs of discipleship. The literal cost, in fact. A rich young 'ruler' comes to Jesus and asks what he has to do to live for ever. One senses Jesus' excitement at this question and at the young man's willingness to follow him, an excitement only matched by his disappointment when the man cannot sign up to the last, most difficult request: 'sell everything you have and give to the poor' (Luke 18:22 NIV).

Who was he? A 'ruler'. Sometimes translated as 'magistrate', the Greek word is *archon*. He is not a synagogue leader. And just because he claims to have kept the commandments, it does not mean that he need be a religious leader. His wealth is the key issue here. Wealth born of status and privilege. An aristocrat of some sort, then. An Herodian, perhaps, come down from Tiberias to listen to Jesus for the day. There is, in fact, a candidate for the post: in Acts, Luke mentions a man called Manaen, a prophet and teacher in the young church at Antioch (Acts 13:1). Manaen is described as a *syntrophos* of Herod the tetrarch, i.e. Antipas. *Syntrophos* means 'brought up together with', 'foster brother', or 'companion from youth'.[32] We are not sure of the exact relationship, but it was clearly very close. Manaen was probably one of Luke's main sources of information about Antipas. So perhaps he was this rich young Herodian who at the time went away saddened, but later became a disciple.

Whoever he was, Jesus' reply indicates the difficulty of the rich getting into the kingdom, like trying to fit a camel through a needle. Many attempts have been made to defuse this remark, including the entirely fictitious explanation that 'The Eye of the Needle' was a narrow gate in Jerusalem through which a fully laden camel would have had trouble fitting. Sadly for the young man, Jesus meant what he said.

At this point, Luke has once again joined up with Mark. Mark places this story, along with Jesus' blessing of little children, after Jesus has gone to the 'region of Judea and beyond the Jordan'. It is clear they are getting closer to Jerusalem. In Luke's account, immediately after this Jesus takes his disciples aside for a third prediction of his death: 'See, we are going up to Jerusalem ...' (Luke 18:31). Before that final visit, however, he was to make one more solo trip to the city. He went there quietly, almost secretly, to a place he had been before: the pinnacle of the temple.

'It was winter'

In the winter of AD 32 Jesus made an unannounced visit to Jerusalem. John tells us he was there for the festival of Dedication, celebrated in early December. We find him, according to John, walking under Solomon's Portico. He is both literally and figuratively under cover.

There are no obvious pointers here to show how this visit might link in with the Synoptic accounts. Presumably he slipped away from the entourage either while they were making their way south, or from the place where they had based themselves.

From Mark we know that he was beyond the Jordan (Mark 10:1). John confirms this, because after this final visit to Jerusalem Jesus goes to 'the place where John had been baptizing earlier' (John 10:40). So we can make a sensible reconstruction. After the time spent in the borders of Galilee and Samaria, Jesus makes his way south with his followers and they base themselves across the Jordan, in the place where Jesus had been baptised. This was where it had all begun.

And talking of beginnings ... The festival of Dedication celebrated the liberation of Israel from pagan influence. The story comes from the book of Maccabees. Antiochus IV Epiphanes, the Hasmonean king, had tried to establish throughout his empire the worship of Zeus. The climax of this policy was the attempt to set up an altar of Zeus – probably with his human likeness – in the temple at Jerusalem. In December 167 BC a sacrifice was offered on this altar. Following that, the Jews revolted and their army, under Judas Maccabeus, drove the enemy forces from Jerusalem. The temple was cleansed and, exactly a year to the day after this 'abomination of desolation', as it became known (Dan. 9:27), the temple was rededicated. It was decreed that the event should be celebrated every year after that, with an eight-day festival, beginning on 25 Kislev (1 Macc. 4:36–59). As we have seen, it was called the Festival of Lights – an appropriate setting, therefore, for Jesus' speech about the light of the world.

Everything about this meeting is clandestine. There are no Galilean disciples present. Although Jesus is discovered and – typically – enrages people so much that they want to stone him, his antagonists do not seem to be the priests or the scribes or the Pharisees, just 'the Jews', John's catch-all term for members of the temple elite. 'If you are the Messiah,' they say, 'tell us plainly.'

So Jesus does tell them: 'The Father and I are one.' It is a reply which drives them to violence (John 10:30ff.).

Why did he go? What was the purpose of this visit? Not just to stir up the Jews, surely? There was no need to make the pilgrimage; Jews could celebrate this festival in their homes, by lighting eight lamps on a lampstand. He did not intend to make some messianic pronouncement; that was merely a by-product of his presence in the temple.

A couple of reasons, perhaps. First, he had arrangements to make. He needed to meet some people. He needed to make preparations. The following Passover, he was going to come up to Jerusalem for the final battle. And he wanted to make some plans. Plans involving upper rooms. And donkeys.

Second, perhaps, there is a clue in the location. John describes Jesus as being in Solomon's Portico: the large, colonnaded, covered space, which ran along the southern edge of the Temple Mount. At the western end it overlooked the city of Jerusalem; at the eastern end the drop led to the Kidron valley. And that was the pinnacle of the temple.

Two years earlier, after his baptism, Satan had taken him to the same place. He was back: contemplating his fate, perhaps. Facing up to temptation once again. He went there to make plans and, perhaps, to check, once more, whether he was strong enough to do what he had to do. Whether he could resist the temptation to change the ending. And it would explain why the enraged Jews he encounters there are so quick to think of stoning: they had Jesus in exactly the right place (John 10:31). (It did not work. Once again, Jesus was able to slip away.)

'Whoever does not carry the cross cannot be my disciple,' he said. The lights may have been blazing, but the dark nights were closing in.

8. Jericho, spring AD 33

It was a constant balancing act. Balancing the demands of the people against those of the Romans. Balancing the demands of the Torah against the demands of government. Balancing one set of supporters against another.

Delicate adjustments were needed, all the time. Compromises, new agreements. Fifteen years he had been the high priest. Fifteen years since Gratus had appointed him. Fifteen times longer than his brother-in-law Eleazar had lasted and six years longer than the old man had managed. That gave him a certain prestige within the family. He doubted any of the other brothers would do half as well. Too outspoken. Too hot-headed.

He walked carefully down the steps and into the bath, feeling the cool waters slowly covering him, purifying him. A daily ritual.

There were other rituals to be performed today, some in the temple, some elsewhere. It was his fifteenth Passover. Time soon to make his journey to the palace and play the usual game with Pilate. He would request that Pilate return the vestments permanently, a request which Pilate would politely refuse. The prefect would then authorise him to have the vestments for the duration of the festival and no longer. They had had the same conversation now for seven years. It had turned into a ritual, this game, joining all the other rituals in his life.

Then there would be the usual housekeeping. Requests for information, warnings of dire consequences should the festival get out of hand. Then back to the temple, where the vestments would be delivered to his priests by the captain of the guards and then purified so that he could wear them. The day after the festival they would go back into storage, until seven days before Tabernacles, when the whole game would begin again.

He rose up out of the water, the thin white garment clinging to his skin. Another compromise. A small price to pay for keeping the Romans happy. They never understood that, those hot-heads who called for rebellion. Those idiots who called for the cessation of the daily sacrifice. They never understood just how close to the precipice the country was. They talked of the day of judgement and the prophets and the Messiah. They really thought that the Lord would fight their battles for them.

Well, perhaps he would. Who could tell what the Lord would do? But what would they do if they turned against the Romans and the Lord did not step in to bring about the new kingdom?

Do not put the Lord your God to the test, it said in the Torah. Keep the faith. Keep the temple standing. Keep the Romans happy.

Keep on balancing.

'Lazarus of Bethany'

According to John's Gospel, Jesus escaped the threat of violence in Jerusalem and went 'across the Jordan to the place where John had been baptizing earlier'. We do not know where that was, but it was probably down in the Perea, just on the east bank of the Jordan. It would have been a good place to spend the winter. He did not go back to Jerusalem until the climactic events of Passover AD 33.

Sometime in the early spring of AD 33, however, Jesus received a message from Mary and Martha. Their brother Lazarus was ill and they wanted Jesus to come urgently. Jesus was probably not far away: it is only eighteen miles or so from Bethany to the east bank of the Jordan. Two days' walk. One if you hurried.

But he delayed, staying two days longer, and during that time Lazarus died.

Why did Jesus wait? John portrays Jesus as preparing a sign (John 11:4–6), but perhaps he really was anxious about the risks of returning to the vicinity of Jerusalem so soon. The disciples understand this only too well. When Jesus finally decides to go, they argue with him: 'Rabbi, the Jews were just now trying to stone you, and are you going there again?' (John 11:8). But Jesus is adamant and Thomas cheerily sums up the mood: 'Let us also go, that we may die with him' (John 11:16).

Outside Bethany, as Jesus approaches, he meets Martha, and then Mary. No parents. No husbands. No grieving wife. Time to examine this curious household.

Individuals in the New Testament are identified in a number of ways. The relatively limited choice of personal names meant that some other form of identifier was needed. It might be their home town (e.g. Joseph of Arimathea, Mary Magdalene) or a characteristic (e.g. Thomas Didymus – 'Thomas the Twin'; Matthew the Tax-Collector), but by far the commonest practice was to identify them by their family relationships, usually their father (e.g. Simon son of Jonah, James and John the sons of Zebedee, or even Barabbas, Bartimaeus, i.e. son of Abba, son of Timaeus).[1]

Women, reflecting the patriarchal nature of society, were usually identified by their relationship to their husbands or sons (e.g. Mary the mother of James and Joseph, or Mary [the wife] of Clopas).[2] Daughters were normally identified by their father's name.[3] Mary and Martha, however, are only ever identified by their relationship to their brother. The parents are never mentioned. Nor is Lazarus placed in any family context at all. He is merely Lazarus of Bethany (John 11:1).

What is more, there is no hint of a husband for either Mary or Martha. As we have seen with Jesus' mother, it was normal for a Jewish girl to marry between the ages of fourteen and eighteen, and a Jewish man by the time he was twenty-one or so. Rabbinic sources indicate that both men and women were expected to marry younger rather than later.[4] The implication of all this is that the household consisted of Lazarus – the head of the household – and his two sisters. And that all three were young and unmarried, and both parents were dead. This is a family of single people.

In this reconstruction, Lazarus would be the sole provider for the household. They may not have been poor – evidently the house had enough room for Jesus and his followers, not to mention their possessing a large, expensive bottle of perfume. But the girls were in a perilous position. If Lazarus died, the girls were in danger of being disinherited. Torah law about inheritance protected daughters but not sisters: '[If a man dies, and] has no brothers, then you shall give his inheritance to his father's brothers. And if his father has no brothers, then you shall give his inheritance to the nearest kinsman of his clan, and he shall possess it' (Num. 27:8–11).

What wealth they had would have passed to their uncle or to the nearest male relative. So the death of their brother has huge implications for the sisters. No wonder they were so desperate for Jesus to come to them. This catastrophe meant not just the loss of a beloved brother, but the loss of house, money and status. If women were second-class citizens, unmarried women were third class.[5]

So Jesus and his followers went up to Bethany, and there, in the graveyard just outside the village, Jesus did what he had done in Galilee: he raised Lazarus to life. Before that, however, he asks Martha a question. He gives the last of John's famous 'I am' sayings: 'I am the resurrection and the life.' And then he asks Martha a question: 'Do you believe this?' (John 11:25–26).

It is a question we have encountered before, in Caesarea Philippi, surrounded by the temples of the various gods, when he asked his disciples, 'Who do you say I am?' Now Jesus allows Martha to answer the same question. He is, by implication, including her in the disciples. Martha, who complained about Mary acting the part, gets to answer the same question as any other disciple, and she answers the same way: 'I believe that you are the Messiah, the Son of God, the one coming into the world.' She is right up there with Peter, this girl.

Jesus calls Mary and then they go to the tomb. And there, Jesus weeps. Indeed, the whole passage is full of agitation. The Greek implies that Jesus gets progressively more moved. Most translations describe Jesus as 'greatly disturbed in spirit and deeply moved' (John 11:33), but there is more here. The word 'indicates an outburst of anger', writes one expert, 'and any attempt to reinterpret it in terms of an internal emotional upset caused by grief, pain, or sympathy is illegitimate'.[6]

The anger and frustration grows in him until he bursts into tears. It is a stunning moment: one of the few times in the Gospels when we see Jesus distraught. Even in his frustrations with his disciples, his anger with the Pharisees and the scribes, even during the intense pressure brought on by the attention of the crowds, there is nothing like this sense of breakdown, of emotional release.

Why the tears? Not, surely, for Lazarus, although that is how the onlookers perceived it. And not, as many commentators have rather smugly suggested, because of the lack of faith of the women. How on earth were they to know what Jesus was going to do? No, Jesus is angry because the whole situation is appalling. Something is so wrong about this.

Although this is the most extreme example, we see this kind of feeling many times in Jesus' mission. When Jesus sees the harassed, exhausted crowd, when he sees the leper excluded from society, when he is greeted by blind men, when he sees the widow in Nain mourning the loss of her only son, when he drives out the demon at the foot of the mountain, the Gospels use the rather wonderful Greek word *splanchnizomai*.[7] This is translated as 'to have pity, show mercy, feel sympathy'. But the root of it comes from *splanchnon,* which meant the 'inward parts' or 'entrails' of an animal or even a human (when Judas dies, his bowels – his *splagchna* – burst out).[8] The English words do not capture the gut-wrenching nature of Jesus' feelings. He is gutted. He is stomach-wrenchingly moved. Bland English translations fail to capture this about Jesus: he felt things incredibly deeply, viscerally. Here, in Bethany, faced with the grief, the hopelessness, the despair, Jesus weeps. The whole situation stinks.

Unlike Lazarus. For when Jesus comes to the tomb – again 'greatly disturbed' – and the stone is rolled away, there is no stench. Which is why, at that moment, Jesus prays a prayer of thanks: he knows his prayer has been answered. Another command: 'Lazarus, come out!' And Lazarus staggers, shuffles, somehow makes it to the entrance of the tomb.

John describes his appearance in detail: his hands and feet bound with strips of cloth, his face wrapped (John 11:44). Lazarus would have been placed on a long, wide strip of linen, with his feet at one end. The cloth would then have been drawn over his head, wrapping him end to end. The feet would have been bound at the ankles, and the arms secured to the body with linen strips. The jaw was bound to stop it falling away from the face during decomposition. Walking would have been incredibly difficult. But if you are in a tomb and you wake up, I doubt you worry too much about keeping your dignity on the way out.[9]

Wealthier Jews did not cover the face, because they could afford the necessary embalming. Poorer Jews tended to cover the face because the skin would go back and it was thought shameful.[10] Perhaps this indicates that the family were not that rich. Enough money to bury Lazarus properly, but not enough to embalm him. It certainly explains why Martha thinks he might stink. They simply did not have the money to have him anointed with spices and expensively embalmed.

The raising of Lazarus, for all its miraculous nature, had some very down-to-earth consequences. Jesus' disciples had been right to be wary about returning to the Jerusalem region so soon. There were Jews there from nearby Jerusalem – and they went back and reported the incident to the Pharisees who, in turn, took it to the council, the Sanhedrin.

They took it to Caiaphas, the high priest.

'It is better for you to have one man die for the people'

In 1990 archaeologists found twelve ossuaries – bone-boxes – in a cave in the northern Talpiot area of Jerusalem. Six of these were untouched, and one of them even contained a coin from the days of Herod Agrippa (AD 42–3). Two of the ossuaries bore the name of Caiaphas, one of which contained the bones of a sixty-year-old man. We cannot be certain that this was the high priest mentioned in the Gospels, the man running Jerusalem and its environs during the time of Jesus. But it was a fancy tomb, and he was a *very* wealthy man.[11]

When Jesus arrived at Bethany, in the spring of AD 33, Caiaphas had been high priest for around fifteen years. Given the volatile nature of politics in his day, and given the fact that the Romans appointed the high priest, this was quite a remarkable feat of longevity. In all, he was to remain in post for nineteen years. When Pilate was recalled from Judea, it was only a matter of months before Caiaphas went as well. Clearly this is why he stayed in post so long. Pilate trusted him, or, at least, distrusted him less than any of the alternatives.[12]

To attain the position of high priest – and to make a success of it – required a number of things. It required significant personal wealth, for one thing, since the high priest had to pay for certain key sacrifices, such as those on the Day of Atonement, out of his own pocket. But that was OK. Although we do not have any data about the income of the high priest, it must have been significant and it was probably drawn from the temple treasury. The fact that, as high priest, he appointed his own relatives to key posts such as temple treasurer would have given him access to a huge amount of capital.[13]

This is borne out by archaeology. Excavations in Jerusalem have uncovered a weight measure from a home in the Upper City with the name 'Bar Kathros' on it. Kathros, as we saw earlier, was the name of one of the high-priestly families and the remains of other monumental houses nearby indicate that the neighbourhood was a wealthy one. And a religious one. One mansion – the so-called 'Palatial Mansion' – covers 600 square metres and contains a number of *miqvaot* for ritual bathing. This, then, was a house of wealth, but also of scrupulous attention to ritual purification: the kind of house, in fact, that might be owned by a high priest.[14]

So you needed to be wealthy. And you certainly needed to use all the force associated with collaborationist regimes. You also needed a great deal of political nous. In particular, you needed the ability to compromise.

The Romans used a wide variety of imperial propaganda to remind their subjects of the benefits of Roman rule and the perils of resistance. Every coin in the empire carried some kind of imperial message: celebrations of victory, imperial symbols, pictures of the emperor as sun-god. Add to that the regular festivities such as local celebrations, imperial anniversaries and the commemoration of famous victories. Throughout the empire there were plenty of opportunities for orations and speeches in praise of Rome. This was reinforced by the emperor cult, in which the emperor and his forebears were worshipped as gods.

Such a cult could not operate in Jewish Palestine. The Jews, to the continual bafflement of the Romans, were monotheists. There was no God but Yahweh. As we have seen, even a picture of the emperor would cause bloodshed.

Jews were seen as aloof. They did not 'join in' as the Romans expected. While the religions of Egypt, Greece and Rome could accommodate any number of gods, the Jews (and the Christians after them) had room for only one.[15] Unlike wealthy leaders from other nationalities, rich Jews from Judea rarely became citizens and no Jewish senator has ever been recorded. They considered themselves the chosen race, the people of God. They refused to share a table with impure Gentile pagans. They were a 'hostile, prickly people, quick to take offence and unfriendly to aliens'.[16]

Rome was willing to make allowances for the Jews' troubling eccentricities, but they, like every other subject nation in the empire, had to do something to affirm their loyalty. So the Jewish leadership made a compromise: twice every day in the temple, a bull and two lambs were sacrificed for the emperor.[17] *For* the emperor, not *to* the emperor; the sacrifice was for his health, and for the well-being of the Roman people. Better that two bulls and four lambs should die than the whole nation perish.

Although necessary, the sacrifice was extremely unpopular. In AD 66, on the eve of war with Rome, the first act of revolutionary reform was to stop this sacrifice, an act which was opposed by 'many of the high priests and principal men'.[18] They knew with absolute certainty that such acts could only end in disaster.

Nor was this sacrifice the only sign of Roman power: the vestments worn by the high priest at the times of festival were in the keeping of the Romans. They were kept under lock and key in a stone chamber, sealed by the priests and guarded by the captain of the guards. Every day the captain would light a lamp to check, presumably, that the seal was unbroken. Seven days before the festival the captain delivered the vestments back into the keeping of the temple leadership, and the day after the festival Caiaphas delivered them back to the Romans.[19] They were a kind of pledge – holding the people to ransom, if you like. And if those subtle assertions of power did not work, there were always those 30,000 troops up the coast at Antioch. This anxiety is reflected in John's account of the council meeting:

> So the chief priests and the Pharisees called a meeting of the council, and said, 'What are we to do? This man is performing many signs. If we let him go on like this, everyone will believe in him, and the Romans will come and destroy both our holy place and our nation.' But one of them, Caiaphas, who was high priest that year, said to them, 'You know nothing at all! You do not understand that it is better for you to have

one man die for the people than to have the whole nation destroyed.'
(John 11:47–50)

The threat is perceived to be to 'our holy place and our nation'. The two were intrinsically linked: in a way, the temple was the nation. So Caiaphas suggests a compromise.

There will need to be a further sacrifice.

'Some Sadducees came to him, saying that there is no resurrection'

The act of bringing Lazarus back from the dead, then, sealed the fate of Jesus. It also led to a death sentence being passed on Lazarus. John relates that 'the chief priests planned to put Lazarus to death as well, since it was on account of him that many of the Jews were deserting and were believing in Jesus' (John 12:10–11).

Lazarus became a local celebrity. He was evidence of the power of Jesus, but he was also evidence of another sort. Lazarus showed that life after death was possible. And that was a problem for Caiaphas and many of the aristocratic elite, because they were Sadducees, and the Sadducees did not believe in life after death.

The Sadducees do not appear in the Galilean portions of the Gospels.[20] The reason is that they were largely a Jerusalem-based elite. Josephus says that their doctrines were 'received but by a few, yet by those still of the greatest dignity'.[21] The Sadducees, then, had a particular following among the wealthy and politically powerful, unlike the Pharisees who 'had the multitude on their side':

> The Pharisees have delivered to the people a great many observances by succession from their fathers, which are not written in the law of Moses; and for that reason it is that the Sadducees reject them and say that we are to esteem those observances to be obligatory which are in the written word, but are not to observe what are derived from the tradition of our forefathers; and concerning these things it is that great disputes and differences have arisen among them, while the Sadducees are able to persuade none but the rich, and have not the populace obsequious to them, but the Pharisees have the multitude on their side.[22]

The Sadducees were fundamentalists, the *sola scriptura* party. Their practice was based on the Torah and the Torah alone. Not all the priestly class were Sadducees: there were Sadducean priests, Pharisaical priests and some who may not have been aligned at all.[23] The New Testament reflects this: in Acts 4:1, Luke talks about 'the priests, the captain of the temple, and the Sadducees'.

We cannot be sure that Caiaphas was a Sadducee, but we do know that one of his family was: Ananus ben Ananus, who, in AD 62, was responsible for the execution of James, brother of Jesus. Here is Josephus again: 'this younger Ananus, who, as we have told you already, took the High Priesthood, was a bold man in his temper, and very insolent; he was also of the sect of the Sadducees, who are very rigid in judging offenders, above all the rest of the Jews, as we have already observed'.[24]

This 'younger Ananus' was the son of Ananus, or Annas, whom we shall meet later. It is highly likely that the younger Ananus was following in a family tradition: they were all Sadducees. That was their faith, their denomination, their political party. And Caiaphas, remember, had married into this family: he was the younger Ananus's brother-in-law.

That act in Bethany, then, put two people's lives at risk. It was too hot for Jesus to stay there. Before, when he had been involved in disputes in the temple, they were small scuffles, between Jesus and whatever Jews happened to be standing nearby. Or they were with the Pharisees who, though involved in the temple, had no real political power.

This was different. For the first time, it seems, Jesus was on the Sadducean radar and, in particular, the radar of the high priest.

Time to move on – quickly. Escape to the wilderness, and prepare for the final act.

'Do for us whatever we ask of you'

Jesus is a marked man. After the resurrection of Lazarus, he heads to a town called Ephraim in 'the region near the wilderness'. This was probably Aphairema, the modern et-Taiyebeh. It is a village four miles north-east of Bethel and some fifteen miles from Jerusalem. It stands on a high hill, overlooking the plains of Jericho and the Dead Sea.[25] It may be that Jesus did not stay in the village itself, but nearby, where warm, secluded valleys offered good water supplies and shelter from the winter weather.[26]

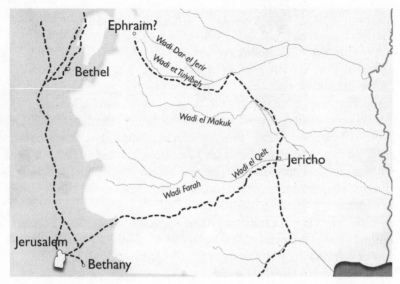

Ephraim, showing routes to Jericho and Jerusalem.

It is here, in the months leading up to Passover, that James and John come to Jesus with a request: they want to sit at his right and left hand in his 'glory' (Mark 10:37). In Matthew's Gospel it is not just the brothers, but their mother too, who make the request (Matt. 20:21), but probably all three were involved in the petition. In Jewish tradition older women were treated with respect, and as we have seen, this may have been Salome, the sister of Mary (Matt. 27:55; Mark 15:40; John 19:25). They are family. But they are asking the impossible. Although they confidently assert that they can drink the cup that Jesus will drink, they have completely misunderstood the nature of status in his kingdom. They think that what is being planned in the ravines of Ephraim is some kind of messianic coup. But in the hours of his 'glory', the only people at Jesus' left and right hand will be convicted criminals.

James and John do not know what they are asking, but, in Myers' words, 'they do know how the ruling class operates'.[27] To sit at the right and left hand of a ruler was to sit in the highest places of honour. At banquets and public events, people jostled for positions of influence and patronage among the nobility. This is why Jesus slaps them down with his condemnation of the leadership among the Gentiles – by which he clearly means the Romans. The statement drips with sarcasm: 'You know that among the Gentiles those whom they recognise as their rulers lord it over them, and their great ones are tyrants over them' (Mark 10:42). You can sense the quote marks here: the 'so-called' rulers, the 'great ones'.

In fact, he goes to the other extreme. Whoever wants to lead in his kingdom will be like a slave in the Gentiles' world. Far from sitting at the top table, the kingdom leader's role is to be a waiter, a nobody. 'For who is greater,' asks Jesus, 'the one who is at the table or the one who serves? Is it not the one at the table? But I am among you as one who serves' (Luke 22:27). Jesus uses two words here: *doulos*, which means 'slave', and *diakonos*, which means 'servant' (Matt. 20:26–28). It is significant that when the early church came to name the officials who looked after their churches, they chose one of the words used here: they became 'deacons'. They became servants.

The images of slavery are also behind Jesus' closing words: 'For the Son of Man came not to be served but to serve, and to give his life a ransom for many' (Mark 10:45). The term 'ransom' (*lutron*) has a very deliberate political connotation, especially in the light of the tyranny mentioned by Jesus before. Only two kinds of people were ransomed: those captured during war and those working as indentured slaves.[28]

Some Judaisms, looking at the day of judgement, saw only gloom ahead for the sinners: 'And now, know ye that ye are prepared for the day of destruction: wherefore do not hope to live, ye sinners, but ye shall depart and die; for ye know no ransom; for ye are prepared for the day of the great judgement, for the day of tribulation and great shame for your spirits.'[29]

In early Christian teaching, however, they recognised that all people were able to be ransomed. An early church piece of liturgy, quoted by Paul, runs: 'For there is one God; there is also one mediator between God and humankind, Christ Jesus, himself human, who gave himself a ransom for all' (1 Tim. 2:5–6).

Jesus came to free people. To liberate them from fear and guilt. But he was not going to do it through military conquest, like the so-called rulers. His cup was not a banqueting cup of triumph, but one of service, suffering and martyrdom.

And James, at least, came to understand this only too well: he was executed some time around AD 44 (Acts 12:2).

'He entered Jericho'

March AD 33. The final push. Leaving base camp in Ephraim, Jesus goes towards Jerusalem, via Jericho. At first sight this does not appear to be the most direct route, but there was a Roman road or track which led from the site of Ephraim down the Wadi et-Taiyebeh, south-east to the Jericho plain.[30] This would allow Jesus and his disciples a relatively secure route, avoiding Judea and emerging from the wilderness north of Jericho, where they could join the crowds of pilgrims travelling from Galilee.

On the way into Jericho, Jesus heals a blind beggar called Bartimaeus (in Luke he is unnamed; in Matthew there are two blind men and the incident occurs on the way out of Jericho). It would be a good place and time for a beggar to sit by the road: the crowds of pilgrims heading into Jerusalem for the Passover would mostly come through Jericho. The incident is significant for the phrase that the beggar uses: 'Jesus, Son of David, have mercy on me!' (Mark 10:47). Mark records that the crowds try to shut the man up, but he persists and his persistence is rewarded. (His faith is such that he throws away his cloak – and the beggar's cloak was not just a piece of clothing, it was what he spread out in order to receive alms, his shopfront. It was his means of livelihood.[31]) This is the first time that Jesus is called Son of David – an explicitly messianic title. Why now? Well, obviously there is the irony in the story: this blind man sees more clearly and accurately than the crowd around him. But David was always associated with Jerusalem, the City of David. It must have been clear then. Even the blind can see where Jesus is heading. It also explains why the crowd try to hush him. They can sense that this is a triumphal procession, but in their Judaism the Messiah is not interested in low-status beggars.

And that goes double for tax-collectors.

Luke follows Bartimaeus's story with that of Zacchaeus. It is an interesting story in that he tells us three things about Zacchaeus: his social status, his wealth and his physical appearance. All three mark him as an outcast. He is an *architelones*, a chief tax-collector, a man in charge of tax-collectors in Jericho, a job which has made him rich (Luke 19:2). Jericho was a prime location for a tax-collector: the city was on several major trade routes, including the route from the lands beyond the Jordan to the east.

More, in the only physical description in his Gospel, Luke describes him as 'short in stature'. The ancient world believed in physiognomics: that the outward appearance reflected the inner reality. Blind? Then either you or your parents have sinned (John 9:2–3). Unnaturally small? There is something wrong inside. A writer known only as 'Pseudo-Aristotle' shows only too well the way in which small people were viewed in the first-century world: 'These are the marks of a small-minded person: he is small-limbed, small and round, dry, with small eyes and a small face, like a Corinthian or a Leucadian.'[32]

To the crowd in Jericho, therefore, Zacchaeus's unclean profession is reflected in his appearance. This is a story about assumptions, about judgement. The people have made up their mind about Zacchaeus, just as they had made up their mind about Bartimaeus. Perhaps it is not just the crowd, either. Based on what we know of tax-collectors, modern readers have probably made up their minds as well. It is a simple equation: tax-collectors = cheats + swindlers = impure. It is a test of our assumptions as well, for there is no indication in Luke's account that Zacchaeus had cheated anyone. 'Half of my possessions I will give away,' he says, 'and *if* I have cheated anyone of anything I'll pay back four times as much.'[33]

Zacchaeus is physically excluded from the inner circle: he cannot see over the crowd. But he climbs a tree, and is spotted by Jesus, who, in a remarkable display of acceptance, insists on staying at Zacchaeus's house. And here is the final ironic flourish to this tale: the name Zacchaeus comes from the Hebrew *Zakay*, meaning 'pure, innocent'.[34]

What this tale is about, therefore, is the overturning of all assumptions. While all the spiritually perfectly proportioned rage and grumble, this small man, this man about whom everyone had made up their minds long since, is welcomed into the kingdom of God. The kingdom of God is not about appearance. It is not based on outward qualities, on the seating plan, on the social status or even the religious purity of its citizens. On the eve of Jesus' entry to Jerusalem we are given a final reminder of the wrongness of this Wrong Messiah. 'He is the guest of a sinner,' grumble the crowd. He does everything in the wrong way.

'A nobleman went to a distant country'

At the banquet for Zacchaeus, Jesus tells a story. It is a story about a king. A king, in fact, whom they all knew. It is a story about Archelaus.

Kings feature in several of Jesus' parables. Matthew has the king with the unforgiving servant (Matt. 18:23–35), the king who throws a wedding banquet (Matt. 22:1–14) and the 'cosmic' king who sorts the sheep from the goats (Matt. 25:31–46). Luke has two kings: one who makes peace because his army is not strong enough (Luke 14:31–32) and the king in this story (Luke 19:11–27). They come with the usual trappings of kings: thrones, armies, executioners and even torture chambers (Matt. 18:34). Like those tyrannical 'great ones', they are capable of acting almost on a whim, forgiving debts and inviting beggars to banquets, but also casting someone into a dungeon because they are improperly dressed. Above all, they are also capable of brutal acts of power, executing summary justice. Opponents are slaughtered in the king's presence (Luke 19:27). Troops are sent to burn cities and kill the inhabitants (Matt. 22:7). The stories reflect real life. This was how kings behaved. Behind each of these stories are the real powers that be: local client-kings and their ruler, the great emperor.

In the parable Jesus relates as they head towards Jerusalem, one can sense him thinking back to the events surrounding his birth.

> ... he went on to tell a parable, because he was near Jerusalem, and because they supposed that the kingdom of God was to appear immediately. So he said, 'A nobleman went to a distant country to get royal power for himself and then return ... But the citizens of his country hated him and sent a delegation after him, saying, 'We do not want this man to rule over us.' (Luke 19:11–12, 14)

When Antipas and Archelaus went to Rome to argue about their father's will, a delegation of Jews followed them and, in an audience with Augustus, issued a long catalogue of the crimes of Herod the Great. Their argument was that Archelaus was merely more of the same and they would rather have the Romans rule them than another 'Herod'. They wanted to be 'delivered from kingly and the like forms of government, and might be added to Syria, and be put under the authority of such presidents [i.e. Roman governors, prefects, etc.] of theirs as should be sent to them …'[35]

Augustus dismissed their arguments and confirmed Archelaus as ethnarch of Judea and Samaria, on condition that he 'governed his part virtuously'. As we know, this did not happen and in AD 6 Archelaus was deposed and the Jewish leaders got their wish: the Romans were in control.

This, then, is a parable with an unmistakably political setting. The slaves are given a *mina*, worth 100 *drachmas*. This was not an insignificant amount. It would buy you a hundred sheep or twenty oxen. Or even twenty-five slaves.[36] Those who do well with their master's money are entrusted with cities to rule (Luke 19:17, 19). But the slave who did nothing with what was entrusted to him has all his power taken away. And he is linked with those enemies of the king, the ones who sent a delegation: 'But as for these enemies of mine who did not want me to be king over them – bring them here and slaughter them in my presence' (Luke 19:27).

Where is Jesus? Approaching Jerusalem. This has a not-so-subtle political implication, then. We have heard Jesus criticise the rulers of the Gentiles. Now he criticises the rulers of the Jews. The Jewish leaders who wanted Archelaus gone got what they wanted. They asked for Roman rule and they got it. And what did they do with it? Nothing. They took what they had been given, and buried it in the ground. Why? Because they feared their political masters. So it will be taken away from them.

Jesus' way of doing things was different. In the new kingdom of God, the style of leadership, the way of valuing people, the resistance to judging by appearance, the lack of submission to the tyrants and great men – everything was different.

Even the processions.

9. Jerusalem,
Saturday 28 March–Friday 3 April AD 33

It had been a long journey from Greece. Wearisome boat journeys along the coast of Asia and then across to Ptolemais. But he had been determined to come: to fulfil his lifetime's ambition of seeing the Holy City and worshipping in the temple.

And here he was, crushed, along with thousands of others, a veritable flood of pilgrims flowing into the city. Ahead of him he could see, above the walls, the huge slab of the Temple mount.

He found himself swept through the gate and up the stepped street. All around him, stall-holders and street-vendors were plying their trade: everything from fruit to fancy glassware, jars of cheap wine, mounds of bread and cloth. And other necessities: 'You want a place to stay?' 'Need animals for the sacrifice?' To his left he could see narrow, steep streets, the Lower City, with the alleyways dark and forbidding. He knew those kinds of areas all right: every city had its slums. But that was not his destination.

He started up the wide set of steps through the arched triple gate and into a tunnel. A crush of people, climbing now, slowly shuffling up through the darkness; a passageway, through the very Temple Mount itself, right under the Royal Portico on the south side. The darkness was disorientating; the crush more oppressive with every step. Then, suddenly, he emerged onto the Temple Mount itself. And everything was light and space and noise ...

Ahead of him the Court of Gentiles was spread out, people milling around, gazing in awe, walking, talking, doing business even, sitting around in groups discussing the finer points of the law. Behind him the Royal Portico was crowded with money changers and animal sellers. He could hear the animal noises, smell that familiar livestock market stench of frightened animals. He went and bought animals to sacrifice. Expensive. More than he'd thought. But he had no choice. The animals had to be perfect, the sacrifice had to be made.

As he headed towards the sanctuary he could hear other noises: the low murmuring of the Levites as they sang and chanted, a blast on the trumpet from the walls, the low murmur of prayers. From beyond the walls he caught the scent of roasting meat from the sacrifices.

He reached the first barrier, a low wall. Guards on duty and a sign in Greek: a warning to all Gentiles not to enter on pain of death. But he could pass. He went on, this time round to the right, towards the main entrance to the Sanctuary itself. The first court was the Court of Women. At each corner of this were chambers, two storing wood and oil for the sacrifices, the other with a line of people outside: these were purification places for those who had taken the special Nazirite vows. And for those recovering from leprosy.

Beyond that there was a small set of steps rising to the Nicanor Gate, its bronze gleaming in the sunlight. More guards there, for this was as far as women could go. From now on, it was for Jewish men only. The priests at the gate checked he had passed the purity rituals. He had washed. He passed inspection. He entered the Court of the Israelites, the goal of his journey.

Ahead was a low barrier, lined with priests taking sacrifices from the worshippers. The noise here was tumultuous: the chanting of the Levites, the prayers of the priests, the screaming of the frightened, panicking animals in their death throes. And the rich, visceral stench of incense and roasting flesh and sweat and urine and dung. It was the smell of sacrifice. It was the smell of worship.

Beyond this was the Court of Priests. There the huge basin containing water for ritual washing. And there the temple sanctuary itself, gleaming white and gold. In the entrance he glimpsed the enormous golden vine. Through there, he knew, was the Holy Place, the golden tables and the candlesticks and the incense smouldering in the dappled darkness. And beyond that the Holy of Holies, the navel of the world, the still, silent centre.

He made his way forward to the wall. The doves were taken from his hands. He had made it. Journey's end. The goal of the pilgrimage. The centre of the world.

'Then he entered Jerusalem'

According to Mark's detailed chronology, Jesus' entry to Jerusalem took place on Sunday 29 March.* According to John, Jesus had spent the night before at the house of Lazarus in Bethany. This was to be his base for the week: during the day he and his disciples went to Jerusalem, at night they retreated to Bethany.[1]

Early on the Sunday, Jesus sent two unnamed disciples to fetch a colt from the village (Mark 11:1–6). There is nothing in the Gospel text to indicate that this was some kind of miraculous provision. In fact it was all part of a prearranged plan, organised either the night before, or in that surreptitious visit to Jerusalem in the winter of AD 32. The disciples even have code words to indicate to its owner who needs the colt.

Once Jesus mounted the colt – probably near the crossroads on the main Jericho–Jerusalem road, where the road to Bethphage goes off to the south – he was ready.[2] Time to make the grand entrance, over the Mount of Olives, cresting the hill and then down into the Kidron valley and a sea of people. It was Passover, and everywhere there were pilgrims sleeping in tents, under makeshift shelters, or wherever they could.[3] No wonder the excitement catches, like a spark to the dry grass: soon there is a mass of followers, cheering, shouting, caught up in the moment, waving branches and joining in the chanting.[4]

Throughout his campaigns in Galilee and Samaria, Jesus avoided making overt statements about his messianic status. Not so now. Nothing Jesus ever says is more of a signal than this donkey ride into Jerusalem. Jesus is using the symbolic vocabulary of Zechariah: 'Rejoice greatly, O daughter Zion! Shout aloud, O daughter Jerusalem! Lo, your king comes to you; triumphant and victorious is he, humble and riding on a donkey, on a colt, the foal of a donkey' (Zech. 9:9).

* AUTHOR'S NOTE

Jesus' last week accounts for a significant percentage of the Gospels. In terms of chapters it takes 37.5 per cent of Mark, 28.5 per cent of Matthew, 23 per cent of Luke and 45 per cent of John. It would take an entire book to do justice to it – which is why I wrote one. If you want more detail on the last week of Jesus' life, my book *The Longest Week* will provide it. In order to preserve my sanity and keep this book down to a manageable level, I am concentrating here on those parts of the story which have a direct relationship to Jesus' messianic claims.

It is his clearest statement yet of his messianic credentials. 'I am the king' is the message, and the people respond. Greeting him according to a custom usually associated with royalty, they throw their cloaks on the ground.[5] But Jesus is giving out other messages as well. Because, as Jesus was entering Jerusalem, another procession was taking place on the other side of the city.

Pilate lived in Caesarea, not in Jerusalem. A week before each major festival he came into Jerusalem, both to authorise the handing over of the ceremonial vestments and to ensure that order was kept. The festivals were, in Josephus's words, 'the usual occasion for sedition to flare up', so it was important for Pilate to be present.[6] Accompanied by his retinue, his family and, of course, extra troops, he would have entered on the other side of the city, along the road from Joppa (past the crucifixion site and burial ground), and towards the former Palace of Herod the Great, the most splendid building in Jerusalem and Pilate's headquarters for his visits.[7]

Two processions, then. One from the east, tumbling down the Mount of Olives, wild with cheering and rich with messianic symbolism. The other coming from the west, but just as symbolic: gleaming armour and burnished leather, cavalrymen on horseback and the imperial eagle leading the way. From the west comes the kingdom of the world; from the east comes the kingdom of God.

Jesus' entry to Jerusalem was not only a statement of his messianic claim. It was also a politically charged act, a two-fingered salute to the empire, the world and the Gentile ways of power.

'A den of robbers'

The next day, on the way into the city, Jesus does a curious thing. He goes to a fig tree to look for fruit and, when he finds none, he curses it (Mark 11:12–14). It seems rather unfair on the tree, as it was not actually the time for the fig harvest. But the key is the location. Jesus is on the Mount of Olives, looking across the Kidron valley. On the other side of the valley is the temple. Like the parable he told on his way in, the fig tree is linked to the temple.

'He who has not seen the Temple in its full construction has never seen a glorious building in his life.'[8] So wrote the later rabbis, and they were not exaggerating. It was one of the wonders of the Greco-Roman world. Herod had transformed the relatively modest temple building of Zerubbabel's time, adding a large entrance porch and a second storey, raising the height of the building to 100 cubits. He also added new wings on each flank of the entrance hall, turning the overall building into a kind of T-shape. He refaced it with white marble inlaid with gold.[9]

Jews were encouraged to donate to the temple. The gates were plated with gold by one Alexander the Alabarch, an Alexandrian Jew.[10] A man from Rhodes called Paris, son of Akestor, helped pay for the pavement.[11] And just inside the doors there was a huge golden vine which hung from vertical columns and to which individuals could donate a golden leaf or a berry.[12]

Surrounding the temple Herod created a huge, raised plaza covering an area of around fourteen hectares – some 12 per cent of the city's area – which was entered by a series of steps, walkways and tunnels.[13] Everything about the temple was luxurious, magnificent. Even the high priest's vestments were fabulously ornate. According to the Mishnah, the clothing cost 10,000 *denarii*, an almost unbelievable amount. We are talking about clothing that on today's scale would cost £400,000. No wonder they hated handing them over to the Romans.[14]

The temple was fabulously rich. It was, in our terms, one of the top-grossing visitor attractions in the ancient world. Every year hundreds of thousands of visitors made their way to Jerusalem. In addition to the temple tax sent from throughout the Roman Empire, it made money through tithes, the surcharge on the temple tax, and by selling animals to all the pilgrims. Because every visitor to the temple had to make a sacrifice.

The Greco-Roman world was big on sacrifice. Virtually all religions sacrificed animals. Temples were religious abattoirs, and any priest was also a skilled butcher, operating with surgical precision on their sacrificial beasts. The temple, especially, relied on it. Through sacrifice, people gave thanks to God and shared in his peace; they celebrated major festivals and asked for forgiveness. Through sacrifice, they were able to be cleansed from impurity.[15]

Every pilgrim who came, therefore, either brought an animal with them or, more often, bought an animal from the stalls in the temple. These did not come cheap. The very basic sacrifice – a pair of doves – cost 1 *denarius*: one day's pay for the average labourer. A lamb cost 4 *denarii*, a ram 8, a calf 20, and an ox anything between 100 and 220 *denarii*.[16] At festivals, supply and demand – those two timeless pagan gods – made things even pricier. A passage in the Mishnah tells us that at one festival in Jerusalem, a pair of doves cost 'a golden denar'. Since there were 25 silver *denarii* to 1 golden *denarius*, the price was clearly extortionate.[17]

The wealth of the temple caused some resentment. And this was further stoked by the fact that it acted as a bank, lending money to those in need – then, when they could not pay, foreclosing on the debt and taking their land. The temple became one of the biggest landowners in Judea. The resentment of this activity can be seen in the fact that after the revolutionaries took control of the temple in AD 66, one of the first things they did was burn the record of debts.[18]

It is these kinds of factors which lie behind Jesus' actions on that Monday morning.

[H]e entered the temple and began to drive out those who were selling and those who were buying in the temple, and he overturned the tables of the money-changers and the seats of those who sold doves; and he would not allow anyone to carry anything through the temple. He was teaching and saying, 'Is it not written, "My house shall be called a house of prayer for all the nations"? But you have made it a den of robbers.' (Mark 11:15–18)

All four Gospels record this incident (although John puts it at the beginning of Jesus' mission). It was clearly not a serious attempt to start a riot or a violent revolution.[19] No guards intervened, no soldiers rushed down from the Antonia Fortress to restore order. Jesus even went back there the next day. Nor was this an attack on the sacrificial system. If Jesus had wanted to do that, he would have gone to the Court of Priests, where the sacrifices took place. More than any other act, Jesus' temple protest, and his statement about the destruction of the temple, were the things which sealed his fate: because he was not attacking the money changers or the traders themselves, he was attacking the system which sanctioned them. He was attacking their bosses: the family of the high priest.

The temple undoubtedly made money from money-changing and from the sale of animals. But it is possible that some of those who directly profited from the trade were the family of the high priest himself. Animals were bought and sold in the temple precincts on the south side near Solomon's Portico. But they were likely sold elsewhere in the city, too, and according to one account, near to the temple were the shops of Hanaun, or Hanan.[20] We must be careful here, because the name is not an uncommon one, but Hanan is a version of the name of the high-priestly family Ananus. So it may well be that the stalls selling animals in the Court of Gentiles were, in the words of Jeremias, 'supported by the powerful high-priestly family of Annas [Ananus]'.[21] The high-priestly family themselves were making their fortune from the selling of animals for sacrifice.

They certainly had stores of grain. A line in some later rabbinic writings says that the storehouses of the 'children of Hanin' were destroyed three years before the rest of Israel 'because they failed to set aside tithes from their produce'. The reference implies that they claimed some kind of exemption from the practice.[22]

This puts a sharper point on the temple protest. This is personal. This was a protest directed at the very top: at Annas, his son-in-law Caiaphas, and all the members of that dynasty who were to run the temple over succeeding years. And it explains some subsequent events. Caiaphas and Annas saw that Jesus was punished, but the grudge went beyond that. According to Luke, after Jesus' resurrection and ascension, Peter and John were arrested in the temple and dragged before a council that included 'Annas [Ananus] the high priest, Caiaphas, John, and Alexander, and all who were of the high-priestly family'.

The John mentioned here is probably Ananus's son Jonathan. Faced with such a 'jury', Peter's statement – 'Jesus Christ of Nazareth, whom *you* crucified, whom God raised from the dead' (Acts 4:10, my italics) – is not an accusation against the Jews in general, or even the Sanhedrin, but against the whole house of Hanan: *you* crucified this man.

And further still, there is the tale of the death of Jesus' brother, executed, according to Josephus, around AD 62 by Ananus, son of Ananus. It was clearly a partial and unfair trial: fair-minded

inhabitants of the city were outraged at this treatment, they complained to King Agrippa and even met the new Roman governor,
Albinus, on his way to the province. Albinus was furious at the
high-handed action and Ananus was hastily removed from office.[23]
Why did Ananus suddenly pick on James? Why did he take this
action? Perhaps because thirty years earlier, James' brother had
called the house of Hanin a bunch of thieves.

The temple protest, like the donkey ride into the city, was both
a critique of those in power and a messianic sign. One of the key
roles of the Messiah was that he would renew the temple. The
belief goes back to the book of Zechariah, which saw a king and
a priest together, rebuilding the temple:

> Here is a man whose name is Branch: for he shall branch out in his
> place, and he shall build the temple of the LORD. It is he that shall build
> the temple of the LORD; he shall bear royal honour, and shall sit and
> rule on his throne. There shall be a priest by his throne, with peaceful
> understanding between the two of them. (Zech. 6:12–13)

Zechariah may have meant the leaders of his day by this – King
Zerubbabel and Joshua the high priest – but later interpreters,
faced with the fact that the second temple was not particularly
glorious and that the restored kingdom proved to be even less
of a success, projected this forward. The belief that the Messiah
would renew the temple is widely reflected in the messianic literature. The Qumran community, who regarded the high-priestly
dynastic families as illegitimate usurpers, believed that their own
community was a divinely approved temporary substitute for the
temple, and that when God returned a new temple would be built.
An apocalyptic work known as 1 Enoch contains a passage known
by the rather Disney-esque name of the 'Animal Apocalypse'. This
reflects a deep dissatisfaction with the temple priesthood and a
belief that the sacrifices were impure. It talks of the destruction of
the 'ancient house', its columns and ornaments taken away. Then a
new 'house' is set up 'greater and loftier than the first one'.[24]

This condemnation of the temple is graphically illustrated the
next morning, when, as Jesus and his followers descend the hill
towards Jerusalem, they see that the fig tree cursed the day before
has 'withered away to its roots' (Mark 11:20). It is a sign. The
temple will be uprooted and destroyed, root and branch.

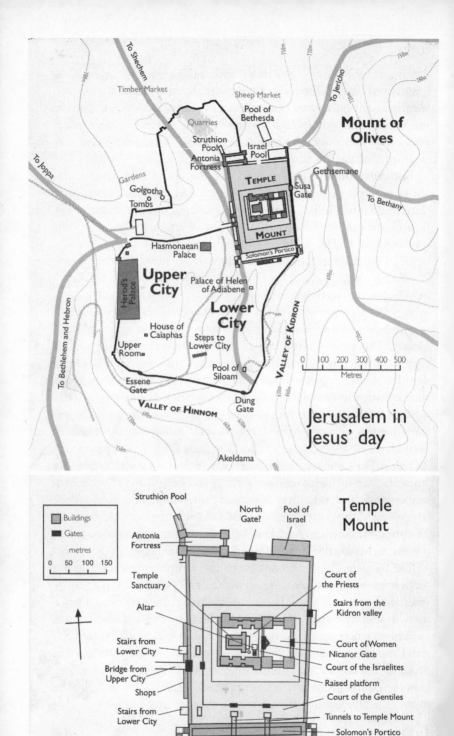

Jerusalem in Jesus' day

To Shechem
Timber Market
Sheep Market
To Jericho
Quarries
Pool of Bethesda
Struthion Pool
Israel Pool
Antonia Fortress
Mount of Olives
Gardens
TEMPLE MOUNT
Susa Gate
To Joppa
Golgotha
Tombs
Gethsemane
To Bethany
Hasmonaean Palace
Solomon's Portico
Herod's Palace
Upper City
Palace of Helen of Adiabene
Lower City
House of Caiaphas
VALLEY OF KIDRON
To Bethlehem and Hebron
Upper Room
Steps to Lower City
Pool of Siloam
Essene Gate
Dung Gate
VALLEY OF HINNOM
0 100 200 300 400 500 Metres
Akeldama

Temple Mount

Buildings
Gates
metres
0 50 100 150

Struthion Pool
North Gate?
Pool of Israel
Antonia Fortress
Temple Sanctuary
Court of the Priests
Altar
Stairs from the Kidron valley
Stairs from Lower City
Court of Women
Nicanor Gate
Court of the Israelites
Bridge from Upper City
Raised platform
Shops
Court of the Gentiles
Stairs from Lower City
Tunnels to Temple Mount
Solomon's Portico
Double Gate
Ritual Bath-house
Triple Gate
Pinnacle of the Temple

'What do you think of the Messiah?'

Given what had happened the day before, it is odd that Jesus went straight back into the temple and started teaching. But he was protected by the presence of the crowd. Unable to arrest him because of this popular support, the temple authorities send out their intellectual crack troops in an attempt to discredit Jesus.

The chief priests, the scribes and the elders ask a question about religious authority: 'By what authority are you doing these things?' (Mark 11:28). The Pharisees and Herodians ask a question about politics: 'Is it lawful to pay taxes to the emperor, or not?' (Mark 12:14). The Sadducees ask a question about theology: 'In the resurrection, whose wife will she be?' (Mark 12:23).

Jesus swats these questions away with a variety of counter-questions and challenges. The first question is easily swatted away with a crowd-pleasing counter-question: 'Did the baptism of John come from heaven, or was it of human origin?' (Mark 11:30). This places Jesus' questioners in an impossible bind. If they say what they actually believe – that John the Baptist was deluded – the crowd will go mad. But if they admit that John the Baptist had heavenly authority, then they not only give credence to John's anti-temple message, they open themselves to the question of why they did not follow him. It is a spectacular own goal.

The second question is trickier. This little grenade is lobbed at Jesus by the Pharisees and Herodians, a combination which we first saw in Mark back in Capernaum after the healing in the synagogue. It revolves around the key political issue of the day: the Roman Empire. 'Is it lawful to pay taxes to the emperor, or not? Should we pay them, or should we not?' (Mark 12:14–15).

The Romans demanded tribute money from all their conquered territories, but some Jews (notably the Zealots) refused to comply with this demand. Jesus is on the back foot here. Answer 'yes', and he will lose the support of all those ardent nationalists in the crowd who oppose Roman rule. Answer 'no', and his enemies will brand him a rebel against Roman authority. Jesus changes the point of the conflict. It is not Rome versus Israel – both of those charge taxes anyway: it is 'Rome' versus God.[25] The issue of giving money to the Romans pales into insignificance compared to the need to give everything to God. Despite his avoidance of the question, something of this attack sticks. Later his accusers will claim that he 'forbade people' to pay taxes to Caesar (Luke 23:2).

The final question is a theological challenge about the resurrection – an idea that they rejected because it was not found in the Torah. This was fine for them, because they had the comfort in this world. As Goodman has written, 'Sadducaism embodied a smug self-congratulation about the status quo that only the rich could accept.'[26] Jesus nukes their argument. He accuses these men – the fundamentalist Scripture-only party – of not having read their Scriptures. God has the power to sort all this out; what makes you think the resurrected life is going to be like things down here?

The final question of the day comes from a scribe. Unlike the rest, this is a genuine enquiry. This scribe wants to know which commandment is the first, the best. And Jesus, in a moment of magisterial wisdom, summarises the Law and the Prophets down into a handful of words. The scribe's response is amazing: 'This is much more important than all whole burnt-offerings and sacrifices' (Mark 12:33b).

Jesus uses the question to launch an attack on the scribes and, particularly, their understanding of the Messiah. How can the scribes call the Messiah 'the son of David', he asks, when David calls the Messiah 'my Lord'? (It is a quote from Psalm 110:1.)

This is one of the few times that Jesus actually mentions the Messiah and the only time that he actually ventures into any kind of discussion about the idea. There are plenty of times when people identify him as the Messiah, for example Peter (Matt. 16:16), Andrew (John 1:41), Martha (John 11:27), Pilate (Matt. 27:17), the high priest (Matt. 26:63), the crowds in Jerusalem (John 7:41), the crowds at the cross (Mark 15:32) and even one of the thieves crucified next to him (Luke 23:39), not to mention all those demons. And Jesus never denies the identification, even if he rarely confirms it. The only times he actually positively states that he is the Messiah are to the high priest during his interrogation (Mark 14:60–62), to the woman at the well in Samaria (John 4:24–26) and during his prayer in the Upper Room (John 17:2–4). The rest of the time he is either silent, or he says things like 'Blessed are you' and 'You say so' and 'I have told you' (Matt. 16:17; Luke 23:3; John 10:25).

The only points where Jesus himself mentions the Messiah are listed below.

▷ 'How can the scribes say that the Messiah is the son of David?' (Mark 12:35; Matt. 22:42).

▷ 'For you have one instructor, the Messiah' (Matt. 23:10). (Both in Jerusalem in the temple, discussing the scribe's theories about the Messiah.)

▷ 'For many will come in my name, saying, "I am the Messiah!" and they will lead many astray' (Matt. 24:5).

▷ 'Then if anyone says to you, "Look! Here is the Messiah!" or "There he is!" – do not believe it' (Matt. 24:23). (Both on the Mount of Olives, talking about the future.)

▷ 'Was it not necessary that the Messiah should suffer these things and then enter into his glory?' (Luke 24:26).

▷ 'Thus it is written, that the Messiah is to suffer and to rise from the dead on the third day, and that repentance and forgiveness of sins is to be proclaimed in his name to all nations, beginning from Jerusalem' (Luke 24:46–47). (Both after his resurrection, one on the way to Emmaus, the other on the shore of Galilee.)

Six times in the entire Gospels, then, Jesus actually uses the word. That is not many. This small incident shows why. Jesus is, in effect, challenging the biblical basis for their use of the phrase 'son of David' to mean a temporal king. This, Jesus claims, is an aristocratic fantasy, a hopelessly misdirected romantic ideal, without any inspired scriptural source.[27]

It is wrong. It will never happen. Jesus hardly mentions the Messiah, not because he was not the Messiah, but because he did not want to talk about it much. He wanted to talk about the kingdom of God that he was establishing. He wanted to talk about money, debt, peace, love and repentance, and all the important things in life. He did not want to get enmeshed in first-century Israel's self-centred, inward-looking dreams of political glory. This is one of the key things about the Wrong Messiah – he was just not that interested in messianic theories.

There were far more important things to discuss.

'All will be thrown down'

> As he came out of the temple, one of his disciples said to him, 'Look, Teacher, what large stones and what large buildings!' Then Jesus asked him, 'Do you see these great buildings? Not one stone will be left here upon another; all will be thrown down'. (Mark 13:1–2)

Imagine, in today's hypersensitive climate of fear, someone standing outside the Houses of Parliament, or the White House, and saying to a group of followers, 'This is all going to be destroyed!' and you get an idea of the impact of Jesus' words. This was a politically dangerous statement. In hindsight we can see it as prophecy, rather than threat, but that is not how it was reported, and not how it would be perceived. Those experts in 'whispering', the house of Hanan, would perhaps have had people in the crowd to 'overhear'. They would have interpreted it as a clear statement of revolutionary messianism.

Over on the other side of the valley, sitting there as the sun goes down behind Jerusalem, the disciples ask for more information: 'When will this be, and what will be the sign?' (Mark 13:3–4). Jesus responds with a tale of death and destruction, of cities besieged, of earth-shattering events and people running to the hills. A tale, in fact, of the apocalypse.

The Greek word *apokalupsis* actually means 'revelation'. An apocalyptic work is something that reveals what will happen. Scholars are divided (as they are on most things) about how to define apocalyptic literature. There is an 'otherness', a strangeness, about apocalyptic literature which marks it out. It is the literature of the marginalised and ignored. The statement of faith of the disbelieved. We see it today on a thousand websites and blogs, warning us of alien invasions and lizard people who walk among us.

But this is actually why it flowered among Jews and Christians during this period. They were the marginalised and oppressed. Apocalyptic literature gave them the vocabulary to express what was going on. And early Christianity produced, in the book of Revelation, perhaps the most influential work of apocalyptic literature that has ever been written.

Like much apocalyptic literature of the time, the apocalyptic passages in the Bible are dense and cryptic, difficult to decode.

In fact, that is the problem: we forget sometimes that they are talking in code, and we take it all a bit literally. Because apocalyptic literature uses earth-shattering language, we conclude that it must be about the actual shattering of the earth. It must, in short, be about the 'apocalypse', a word which has come to mean 'the end of the world'.

That is not always the case. Apocalypse is about transformation, change. It is about new things coming into being.[28] And it is not about the far-distant future, but about the imminent present. Jewish apocalyptic literature is nearly always about what is happening all around, or what is just about to happen. The same is true of the apocalyptic passages in the Bible. Mark 13, Matthew 24 and Revelation are, it is generally agreed, about the 'end times'. But they are also – perhaps mainly – about times near to when they were written. They are explaining what is to come, but also what is starting to happen all around them.

Jesus' message, like that of John the Baptist, was about the 'end times'. It was, to use another complex term, strongly eschatological. This word was coined by theologians in the seventeenth century and describes the 'last things': the end of an empire, or the end of the world, or even the end of the life of an individual.

Eschatological writings were often overtly political – looking ahead to a definitive, eternal political order, usually under the rule of an ideal king. The Romans, for example, had an eschatological view of empire: they considered themselves an empire without end. In Virgil's *Aeneid*, Jupiter concludes: 'For [the Romans] I set neither bounds nor periods. Dominion without end I give to them.'[29] *Imperium sine fine*: an idea which most empires since have embraced at their peak. This is it. The empire on which the sun never sets. The Third (and final) Reich, Marxism, Fascism, liberal democracy have all made eschatological claims for themselves as the ultimate system.[30]

Those who 'feared Rome's peace' saw things rather differently. The Jewish Sibylline Oracles denounce Rome for its greed and arrogance and prophesy that the wealth will be returned to Asia.[31] Revelation is a profoundly anti-Roman tract, in which Rome – Babylon – will be destroyed.

Beyond political constructs, beyond kingdoms and empires,

Christian and Jewish writing does also look at the end of the world itself. Revelation argues that there will be a new heaven and a new earth (Rev. 21:1). Jewish writing, too, looked to a cosmic eschatology. *The Apocalypse of Weeks* in 1 Enoch says that there will be a point when the world will be marked for destruction. The old heaven will be taken away and replaced with a new one. The Qumran community wrote of fiery floods of Belial which will consume the earth. At the end of the first century AD, the apocalypse of 4 Ezra portrays seven days of primeval silence, between the destruction of the old world and the coming of the new creation.[32]

In Jesus' time, some said that this was already happening. What is distinctive about Jesus' eschatology is that it seems already to be here. This has been termed 'realised eschatology'. Jesus seems to indicate that the kingdom of heaven starts now; that life after death can begin a bit early. The classic expression of this idea is found in the Gospel of John, in which Jesus assures his followers that 'anyone who hears my word and believes him who sent me has eternal life, and does not come under judgement, but has passed from death to life' (John 5:24).

A close reading of Mark 13 shows all of these elements at work. Although it contains elements of a cosmic eschatology, it is primarily about real political events, events that were realised within a few decades of Jesus' death. It starts with Jesus answering a question from the disciples with a description of the destruction of the temple. That took place in AD 70.

In AD 66 the revolution finally broke out in Judea. There is not space to rehearse the events here, but although the Jews had initial successes, it ended with 30,000 Roman troops surrounding Jerusalem. The city was a hellhole of sickness, suffering, starvation and internecine brutality. The Jews inside the city spent almost as much time killing each other as they did repelling the Romans. In the end Jerusalem was recaptured, but in the process the temple was burned to the ground. It was a wound from which the Jews as a nation were never to recover.

Because both Mark 13 and Luke 19:42–44 describe these events, they are often cited as proof that the Gospels date from after AD 70 – on the grounds, basically, that prediction is impossible. I have argued elsewhere why that is a false assumption.[33] Even Caiaphas, forty years before, knew that one wrong turn would bring the Jewish way of life and the temple crashing down. Jesus grew up in an area which had seen exactly what the Romans could do. You did not, frankly, have to be the Son of God to see which way the wind was blowing.

For now, what concerns us is that it is another moment where Jesus specifically mentions the Messiah: 'And if anyone says to you at that time, "Look! Here is the Messiah!" or "Look! There he is!" – do not believe it. False messiahs and false prophets will appear and produce signs and omens, to lead astray, if possible, the elect. But be alert; I have already told you everything' (Mark 13:21–23).

The passage ends with a flood of apocalyptic imagery: a darkening of the sun and the moon, falling stars and the Son of Man arriving on clouds. We have to take care with the vocabulary of apocalyptic literature. It is clearly not literal: in what literal sense, for example, can stars 'fall'? In which direction would that be? Instead, Jesus is describing, in a highly stylised language, what happens when the kingdom of God starts to break in.

We still use such imagery today. We talk of institutions being 'rocked to their foundations' when no actual earthquake has occurred. We have been through a period of financial meltdown, but as far as I am aware no banks have actually melted.

Which is not to say that this is not about the 'second coming'. Certainly the early church lived in the belief that Jesus would return. Matthew follows his version of the apocalyptic discourse with a number of parables and strange tales, all of which have a common theme of sudden appearance or disappearance. The sudden arrival of the rain in Noah's time, for example (Matt. 24:38–39); of people being somehow 'whisked away' (Matt. 24:40–41); of the arrival of thieves, masters and bridegrooms (Matt. 24:45–25:13). It is Jesus as the *lestai*, the bandit, coming in the dead of night to bind the strong man once and for all.

The main thrust of all this, however, is to 'keep on keeping on'. Stay awake and be on guard. There are judgement parables, certainly, and the parable of the sheep and goats has been interpreted as indicating what will happen 'at the end'. But, this is not a time for hiding the treasure, but for giving it away. The hungry must be

239

fed, the naked must be clothed and the thirsty must be given water. Bad stuff is going to happen, but there is work to be done.

Matthew ends this section with a warning: 'When Jesus had finished saying all these things, he said to his disciples, "You know that after two days the Passover is coming, and the Son of Man will be handed over to be crucified"' (Matt. 26:1–2).

The end times are coming. The temple is about to be torn down. It is going to take some rebuilding.

'Ointment of nard'

It was two days before the Passover and the festival of Unleavened Bread. The chief priests and the scribes were looking for a way to arrest Jesus by stealth and kill him; for they said, 'Not during the festival, or there may be a riot among the people.' (Mark 14:1–2)

Two days to go.[34] The imminence of Passover meant that Jesus had to be arrested soon. Once the festival was over he would be away, out of their reach. But Jesus still has protection. The crowd are still on his side and any arrest will cause a riot. They need a plan. They need someone on the inside.

Enter Judas.

We do not know much about him. Just his father's name, Simon (John 6:71), and probably the town he came from, Kerioth. (Even that is a bit of a guess. In the Greek, the Gospels spell his identifying name, Iscariot, in ten different forms.[35]) He is a man of mystery, and the greatest mystery of all is, 'Why did he do it?'

We know *what* he did. He did not so much betray Jesus as give away the optimal location for an arrest. Jesus' enemies already had enough to form charges against him. What they needed was a place and time when the arrest could be made.

As to 'why?', there have been many ideas put forward. Perhaps he had grown frustrated at Jesus' rejection of the 'right' way of being the Messiah. So he was trying to force his hand. Jump-start the revolution. Or maybe he was disillusioned. Maybe he had had enough of Jesus' flagrant shattering of social and religious mores. I think, however, that just like most other sordid little betrayals, it was all about money. The disciples, after all, were poor. 'Look, we have left everything and followed you,' said Peter (Mark 10:28). And now they were in the richest city in Judea, and all Jesus was doing was telling stories and arguing and getting into trouble. No revolution. No takeover of the temple and the treasury. No seats of honour. It was clear that, despite Jesus' promises of some kind of reward, nothing was going to happen. He might be the Messiah, the Anointed One, but he was doing it all wrong.

And even when he *was* anointed, he got that wrong as well.

The same evening that Judas agreed to betray him, Jesus and the disciples went to dinner at the house of Simon, the (presumably recovered) leper in Bethany.[36] There are different accounts of what happened at this meal, but here is the basic plot: Jesus is sitting at the table, a woman comes up to him, breaks open a jar of expensive perfumed ointment, and pours it on his head. The people in the room complain, pointing out that the ointment was valuable and could have been sold to feed the poor. Jesus rejects their arguments: the poor will always be there, he says, but this woman has done something that will be remembered for ever.

That is Mark's version (Mark 14:4–9). John places it in the house of Lazarus in Bethany, and it is Mary who anoints Jesus, wiping the ointment away with her hair. The behaviour fits: she had a lot to thank Jesus for, and anointing him with the entire contents of a valuable pot of perfume is exactly the kind of hero-worship you might expect from an impulsive young woman.

Whether it was Mary or someone else, this woman expresses her feelings for Jesus in the only way she was allowed. As we have seen, in the Greco-Roman world generally, and in Judea certainly, women were second-class citizens. Restricted mainly to the home, they would serve the men, wash their feet perhaps, certainly prepare and serve the meal. They were not, as we know, supposed to be disciples. Not for them the right to say what they thought. Seen and not heard, that was the rule.

But this woman *has* to be heard. She knows, in the way that only the marginalised could know, what will happen to Jesus. So she literally creates a stink: breaks open the bottle and fills the house with fragrance. In doing so, she writes the first commentary on Jesus' death, and she has done it without saying a word.[37]

It is also a direct acknowledgement of Jesus as the Messiah: the word means 'anointed one'. In the Old Testament, anointing usually does two things: it sets a person or thing apart as holy and consecrated, and it confers authority on a person who is anointed. It could be done to places, e.g. the temple and its furnishings (Exod. 40:9–10), or even garments (Lev. 8:30), but its usual role was to symbolise the holiness and authority of leaders: priests and kings.

The high priest was anointed with holy oil. Saul, Israel's first king, was anointed by Samuel, who also anointed Saul's replacement, David. Kings were referred to as 'the Lord's anointed'. In the Old Testament, certainly, the very idea of killing the anointed king was viewed with horror.[38] But the person doing the anointing also had to have authority. Usually it was the high priest who anointed the king. Both Nathan the prophet and Zadok the high priest anointed Solomon (1 Kgs 1:34).

Jesus is only anointed twice in the Gospels, and neither time by anyone considered 'important'. He was not anointed by the high priest, nor by any prophet (unless we count his baptism by John). He was anointed by two women: one a prostitute in Nain, the second Mary in Bethany. So Mary's statement works on two levels. It is a statement about what will happen to him, but it is also an affirmation of who Jesus is: Messiah. *Christos*. Anointed one.

And if nobody else is going to anoint him, then she will do it.

'I will keep the Passover at your house'

> On the first day of Unleavened Bread, when the Passover lamb is sacrificed, his disciples said to him, 'Where do you want us to go and make the preparations for you to eat the Passover?' (Mark 14:12)

Passover was the festival at which Jews remembered and celebrated their rescue from slavery in Egypt. In the Jewish calendar it was celebrated on 14 or 15 Nisan (April/May) and was followed by the feast of Unleavened Bread, which ran from 15 to 21 Nisan. These days were usually known as the week of Passover.

There are some problems with the chronology. Mark and Luke describe the Thursday as 'the first day of Unleavened Bread, when the Passover lamb is sacrificed' (Mark 14:12; Luke 22:70; Matthew simply calls it 'the first day of Unleavened Bread' (Matt. 26:17)). In the Synoptic Gospels, therefore, the Last Supper is a Passover meal. John, however, dates the Last Supper a day earlier than the Synoptics, and puts the crucifixion on the day of Preparation (John 13:1;

18:28; 19:14, 31, 42). John never calls it a Passover meal; he says that the day of Jesus' execution was Passover, the day when the lambs were slaughtered.

Although it is often assumed that John changed it so that he could use the symbolism of the Passover lamb, the fact is that John's dating fits a lot better with the way in which Passover operated in first-century Jerusalem.[39] John knows, for example, the distinction between the Passover and the feast of the Unleavened Bread, whereas Mark seems to blur the two. (Technically, the first day of Unleavened Bread was the day after the Passover lamb is sacrificed.[40]) The speed with which the event was processed, the refusal of priests accusing Jesus to enter Gentile territory for fear of being made impure, the convenience of arresting, trying and executing Jesus while everyone else was concerned with preparations for Passover, all fit in with John's timing.[41]

And even though the Synoptics say it was a Passover meal, hardly anything in their account actually looks like Passover. Jewish custom demanded that the night, not just the meal, should be spent in Jerusalem; yet immediately after the meal, Jesus leaves the city for Gethsemane.[42] And in the meal itself, there is no lamb! The one crucial element of the Passover feast is conspicuous by its absence.

Perhaps this was a 'Passover meal' of Jesus' own devising. The Passover meal was a meal with a meaning: every element told a story. It is that element which Jesus appropriates from Passover: the idea of rescue, and the elements of bread and wine which will tell how the rescue took place.[43]

'A man carrying a jar of water will meet you'

In a manner reminiscent of the arrangements for the triumphal entry, Jesus sends 'two of his disciples' to prepare the room. It is all clandestine, cryptic. Jesus' name is never mentioned, only 'the teacher'. No miracles needed here, but this is a secret venue. So secret that even the Twelve do not know. Mark says that they came in later with Jesus from Bethany (Mark 14:17).

> While they were eating, he took a loaf of bread, and after blessing it he broke it, gave it to them, and said, 'Take; this is my body.' Then he took a cup, and after giving thanks he gave it to them, and all of them

drank from it. He said to them, 'This is my blood of the covenant, which is poured out for many. Truly I tell you, I will never again drink of the fruit of the vine until that day when I drink it new in the kingdom of God.' (Mark 14:22–25)

Mark's account of the Last Supper is only eight verses long (Mark 14:17–25); Matthew has nine verses (Matt. 26:17–30); Luke pushes the boat out at twenty-four verses (Luke 22:7–38). John has 155 verses – five chapters (13–17). Even then he could not find room for the eucharistic prayer or the bread and the wine, which the others place at the heart of the feast! But he does include one radical, challenging event which is absent from the Synoptics: the washing of the feet.

Ancient cities were filthy. Walking through the streets was a matter of negotiating the dirt and the dust, the excrement and waste matter, ashes from fires, rotten food … At a basic level, then, washing your feet was simply a matter of hygiene. It was also another piece of purity legislation: anyone entering the temple was expected to wash their feet and hands, at minimum.[44]

The task itself was reserved for second-class citizens. You could ask your wife to wash your feet, or your children. But the only male you could ask to wash your feet was a slave. But here's the crucial thing: you couldn't ask a Jewish slave to do the task. In Judea there were two kinds of slave: Jewish and Gentile. Gentile slaves were mainly Syrians, shipped in from Tyre and auctioned in Jerusalem.[45] Jewish slaves were generally not acquired in the same way. Usually they were convicted thieves who could not afford to pay their allotted compensation, so were sold as slaves instead. Sometimes they were people who had sold themselves into slavery because of extreme debt.[46]

The Torah had other stipulations about Jewish slaves. Their status was protected by the rule in Leviticus which equated a Jewish slave to a 'hired labourer' (Lev. 25:40). That meant they could not be asked to do acts that would make them impure – and one of the things you could not ask a Jewish slave to do was to wash your feet.[47] No such problems for Gentile slaves: they were Gentiles. They had impurity built in.

So, in doing this act, Jesus deliberately aligns himself with the lowest status groups. Jesus has not only taken off his clothing, he has taken off his status. He has removed his maleness, his Jewishness, his very freedom. It was a compelling, shocking, outrageous demonstration of leadership in the new kingdom. He – their Lord and master – was doing the lowest job that was available. He was, in essence, kick-starting the church. And they learned his lesson well. Their leaders went on to claim that 'There is no longer Jew or Greek, there is no longer slave or free, there is no longer male and female; for all of you are one in Christ Jesus' (Gal. 3:28). This is one of the most incendiary, revolutionary things you could possibly say in the ordered world of the Roman Empire. The church celebrated this act in one of their earliest hymns:

> 'Let the same mind be in you that was in Christ Jesus, who, though he was in the form of God, did not regard equality with God as something to be exploited, but emptied himself, taking the form of a slave, being born in human likeness. And being found in human form, he humbled himself and became obedient to the point of death – even death on a cross.' (Phil. 2:5–8)

That night, Jesus did what only a slave would do. And the next day he died like a slave as well.

After that comes the meal. Proper Messiahs would have had a victory banquet. Jesus has bread and wine: the universal foods of the Greco-Roman world. The sound of the mill stones and the smell of baking filled the streets of every city, town and village. Equally, vineyards were everywhere on the hillsides and in the villages; even in the city we may assume that vines were grown, effectively forming roofs along some of the narrower streets. There was nothing exotic about this feast, and certainly no 'Holy Grail' – an object not mentioned anywhere in literature until nearly 1,200 years after this event.[48] Just a cup. Bread and wine. A simple prophecy of what is to come, and a celebration which would spread around the world.

'Across the Kidron valley'

> After Jesus had spoken these words, he went out with his disciples across the Kidron valley to a place where there was a garden, which he and his disciples entered. (John 18:1)

The moon was red that night. Five weeks after Jesus' death, Peter gave a speech where he quoted the prophet Joel: 'The sun shall be turned to darkness and the moon to blood, before the coming of the Lord's great and glorious day' (Acts 2:19–20, quoting Joel 2:30–31).

The Gospels claim that at Jesus' death there was an unnatural darkness, but also, on the evening of Friday 3 April AD 33, there was a partial lunar eclipse, visible in Jerusalem. During a partial lunar eclipse, the moon turns orange or red. It may be that the quote from Joel was seen by the early church as a prophecy of two strange occurrences linked with the death of Jesus: an unusual darkness and a blood-red moon.[49]

Sometime in the early hours Jesus and the disciples made their way across the city and into the Kidron valley then onto the lower slopes of the Mount of Olives. Mark tells us the name of the garden: Gethsemane. The name probably comes from the Aramaic *Gat-semani*, meaning 'oil press'. This was a market garden; a plot of land, enclosed by a wall, with olive trees and an oil press. From the garden they could see the temple itself, silhouetted in the moonlight. The huge walls and, on the south-east corner, the pinnacle.

The old temptation.

He could have changed the ending so easily. Gethsemane lay close to the Jerusalem–Jericho road of the story. Just carry on! Keep walking, brave the robbers and the bandits and head down, down to Antipas's territory: Jericho, the Perea. Freedom. All Jesus had to do was keep going and he could change the ending. But he stopped.

In the garden, at a stone's throw from the disciples, he faces up again to the struggle: 'Abba, Father, for you all things are possible; remove this cup from me; yet, not what I want, but what you want' (Mark 14:36).

'I don't want to do this.' Not, 'I will not do this.' A request, not a refusal. All things are possible, but for Jesus the possibilities were about to run out.

'The Jewish police arrested Jesus and bound him'

It is not certain who arrested Jesus. Probably it was the temple guards.[50] The temple was just across the valley: it would have been simple for a snatch squad to emerge from the eastern entrance to

the temple and cross the Kidron valley to Gethsemane. And Jesus'
statement about their level of force, about arresting him as if he
were a bandit, makes much more sense if the temple police formed
the main part of the arresting party.[51]

Judas identifies Jesus with a kiss. A scuffle breaks out. There is
violence and Jesus heals the victim – a slave called Malchus. Once
the possibility of resistance has been extinguished, the disciples
evaporate.[52] The snatch squad have their man. Jesus is bound and
taken back across the valley and up into the streets of Jerusalem.

He was taken to the Upper City, to the house of the high priest.
But the first interrogation is not with Caiaphas, but with his
father-in-law, Annas: 'So the soldiers, their officer, and the Jewish police arrested Jesus and bound him. First they took him to
Annas [i.e. Ananus], who was the father-in-law of Caiaphas, the
high priest that year' (John 18:12–13).

Ananus was the elder statesman of the house of Hanan, a
political grandee, the founder of a dynasty; exactly the kind of
man to retain influence and power even when his official role is
over. Technically he had no legal jurisdiction – but that assumes
that these trials, hearings and beatings have anything to do with
legality at all. Jesus' lack of respect for Annas is rewarded by a
punch in the face. Jesus' complaint – 'If I have spoken rightly,
why do you strike me?' – tells us that we are in the shadows of
legality here.

After this, there is a series of meetings, the order differing
between the Gospels. But broadly, we can see the following pattern of events.

▷ Jesus is arrested and taken to the high priest's mansion.
▷ He has an initial interrogation with Annas.
▷ He is then interrogated by Caiaphas and his group of advi-
  sors, who charge him with wanting to destroy the temple and
  accuse him of blasphemy.
▷ While this meeting is going on, Peter denies knowing Jesus.
▷ Jesus is taken back through the courtyard, where he sees Peter
  (Luke 22:61).
▷ He is subjected to physical abuse, then held in custody (Luke
  22:63).

▷ At daybreak, Jesus is taken before a second group from the temple, possibly a hastily convened Sanhedrin, including those who were not present at the night-time meeting. There he is accused of blasphemy and it is agreed that they will send him to Pilate.

Much analysis of the trial dismisses the Gospel accounts because they depict legal irregularities, such as a night trial. But the whole idea that the hearing must follow a legal pattern shows a naively optimistic faith in the rule of law. Ancient society was not like a modern democracy. There was no free media, there were no watchdogs overseeing judicial probity, no Geneva Convention or UN Charter on Human Rights. This is the world of twilight politics, of beatings and mockery and humiliation and deals between power brokers. It is, at best, only quasi-legal. And anyway, the decision to kill Jesus had been taken days, even months, ago. This is just going through the paperwork. Applying the rubber stamp. This, just as Jesus always claimed, was how the leaders of Jerusalem treated their prophets.

The main charge against Jesus is the threat to the temple (Mark 14:56–61). He is charged, essentially, with planning a terrorist act. Caiaphas asks about Jesus' messianic pretensions (Matt. 26:63–66; Mark 14:62–64) and this, the only point where Jesus actually answers, condemns him in their eyes: 'But he was silent and did not answer. Again the high priest asked him, "Are you the Messiah, the Son of the Blessed One?" Jesus said, "I am; and 'you will see the Son of Man seated at the right hand of the Power', and 'coming with the clouds of heaven'"' (Mark 14:61–62).

No more denials. It was not the claim to be the Messiah which was blasphemous, since Jews did not view the Messiah as a divine figure. It was the claim to sit at the 'right hand of power'. Jesus was equating himself with God.

'Peter was below in the courtyard'

During this time, while Jesus faces his accusers inside, Peter has managed to make his way into the courtyard of the high priest's house. The story of Peter's denial is a core text of the early church, and another of those episodes that appear in all four Gospels. Never mind the criterion of embarrassment, this is the criterion of shame. If you were inventing the history of Jesus' week, would you invent a story in which the key leader of your new movement actually betrays his master?

Although the story shows Peter failing, we underestimate how much guts it took to go in there in the first place.[53] Once in the courtyard, of course, the full reality of the situation must have hit home to Peter. He is alone, and in the heart of enemy territory. And every time he opens his mouth, his Galilean accent gives him away. There were other factors as well. One of his interrogators is a relative of the man he attacked in the garden (John 18:27). Perhaps this man had been one of the arresting party and had seen Peter escape in the gloom.

Mark records the first and second denials as happening in different places. The first denial happens in the courtyard (*aule*). The second denial happens in the *proaulion*, or forecourt. This was further away; Peter has retreated.[54] Physically and mentally he is beginning to distance himself from his leader.

Then Luke includes a detail that is difficult to fit: he shows Jesus turning and looking at Peter (Luke 22:61). Was this a piece of poetic licence, underlying the depth of Peter's betrayal? Or does it mean that Peter was still in the courtyard, still in the heart of the high priest's house, and that, as Jesus is led out from the hearing to a place of imprisonment, their eyes meet? If so, no wonder Peter went out. No wonder he wept bitterly.

He was not the only one with regrets. Judas, according to the Gospels, gave back the money and went out and committed suicide. There are two accounts of his death and the only thing they have in common is a place: *Akeldama*, or 'the field of blood'. According to Luke, Judas bought the field with the money he had earned for betraying Jesus. In the field he seems to have exploded: 'falling headlong, he burst open in the middle and all his bowels gushed out' (Acts 1:18). Matthew depicts Judas as bitterly regretting what he had done. When he saw Jesus condemned, he threw the money back into the temple and went and hanged himself. It was, in Matthew's account, the chief priests who took the money and bought the field with it, on the grounds that it was now impure, so could not be returned to the temple.

Whatever the case, to ancient readers, Judas's suicide would have been seen as an additional sign of disgrace, rather than being viewed with compassion. Jewish attitudes to suicide were harsher than in our day. For suicides, one did not mourn openly. A suicide's body was not buried – it was exposed until sunset.[55] He had made, it seemed, a terrible mistake. And no one would even mourn for him.

'The chief priests held a consultation'

As daybreak came, Jesus was taken from whatever temporary cell he had been held in and dragged before another meeting of the temple hierarchy.

Mark describes the participants as the 'chief priests', the 'elders and scribes and the whole council'. The word he uses for council is *Sanhedrin* (Mark 15:1). The Mishnah describes the Sanhedrin as a lofty, idealised supreme court, where all the members were Torah scholars and the president of the Sanhedrin was the leading rabbinic sage.[56] This is nonsense. The Sanhedrin was tightly controlled, convened by order of the high priest. At best it was an advisory body; at worst, a bunch of yes-men.[57]

Even assuming this was a 'proper' meeting of the Sanhedrin, they would not have needed all of them to be there. Of the seventy-one members, only twenty-three were needed to pass sentence. It would have been perfectly possible for Caiaphas to convene twenty-two of his supporters, which would explain how someone like Joseph of Arimathea could be part of the council and yet not part of the verdict. Also, Mark's account mentions scribes and elders, but no Pharisees. They were probably not involved in the trial at all.[58] The scribes would be required for the legal ruling; the 'elders' were probably the city's elder statesmen, rich, powerful people who needed to be kept in the loop.

The die is cast and the verdict declared. Jesus must die. But now the process hits a snag. They do not, in fact, have the authority for that. John writes that the Jewish authorities were 'not permitted to put anyone to death' (John 18:31). It was the prefect who had the *ius gladii* – the right of life and death.[59]

At the time of Jesus, then, the Jewish leadership were not allowed to execute people.

For that you needed the Romans.

'Are you the King of the Jews?'

Pilate, as we have seen, was under pressure. The one thing he could not afford was any major trouble. So one imagines that he was not best pleased when, on the morning before Passover, he received a deputation from the temple with a prisoner. And his mood cannot have been lightened when, due to their concerns about Gentile impurity, the priests accompanying the prisoner refused to enter the palace itself for fear of being contaminated (John 18:28).

This explains why Pilate is, initially, reluctant to grant their request. The charge against Jesus was different depending on which body was trying him. For the high priest it was the threat against the temple. For the Sanhedrin it was the claim to be the Messiah. For Pilate, now, it is a straightforward bit of revolution: 'We found this man perverting our nation, forbidding us to pay taxes to the emperor, and saying that he himself is the Messiah, a king' (Luke 23:2).

No blasphemy, nothing about the temple; just a direct challenge to Roman rule. The charge is one to which Pilate has to respond: the refusal to pay taxes and the claim to be the real ruler. By now, though, Jesus hardly looks like a king. Deprived of sleep, beaten, spat upon. Pilate's question, 'Are *you* the King of the Jews?' is clearly sarcastic (Mark 15:2). But his sarcasm is met with Jesus' deadpan response: 'You say so.'

Pilate's immediate response is to reject the request (Luke 23:4). There is a strong sense of irritation in Pilate's words in this first encounter. But the temple authorities persist with their accusations and Pilate hears a word which offers him an easy way out: 'He stirs up the people by teaching throughout all Judea, from Galilee where he began even to this place' (Luke 23:5).

Galilee. Those Galileans again. The ones who caused problems at the last festival. Possibly the delegation mention Galilee because they know Pilate had some Galileans killed last time. But they miscalculate. Pilate has a score to settle with those annoying Herodian princes, who forced him to climb down.

Jesus is from Galilee, so let the ruler of Galilee deal with it. Send the man to Antipas.

'He sent him off to Herod'

From Pilate's point of view, this was a good move. First, he could hand the problem over to someone else. Second, it was a shrewd bit of diplomacy. He was paying Antipas a compliment, keeping him in the loop. And that meant that Antipas could not possibly cause a problem later by complaining about any decision.

The venue for this meeting with Antipas was probably the old palace of the Hasmoneans in the Upper City, just across from the Temple Mount. Josephus records that the palace stood in an elevated position, with excellent views of the city. Antipas, we are told, had anticipated meeting Jesus for some time (Luke 9:9). Perhaps he was hoping for debate and discussion, perhaps he was hoping to assuage the guilt of John the Baptist's death. Certainly he must have believed that he would be treated with respect. But Jesus utterly refuses even to speak to him. Nothing could be more calculated to raise Antipas's wrath. For this man, who felt slighted and disrespected all his life, that must have been intolerable. So the interview ends in mockery and contempt.

Powerless to make Jesus speak, Antipas exerts his power by dressing him up like a doll (Luke 23:8–11). But the clothes are a message. Luke describes how Jesus is dressed in robes, literally in a 'bright or shining garment'.[60] Several suggestions have been made regarding these garments. Some have suggested that they were an elaborate joke: that Antipas dresses Jesus up in the clothes worn by candidates for office, or the soft robes that befit a king. But Antipas, we are told, first dresses Jesus in these clothes and then sends him back to Pilate. When Jesus returns, Pilate takes one look at Jesus and says to the chief priests: 'I have examined him in your presence and have not found this man guilty of any of your charges against him. Neither has Herod, for he sent him back to us. Indeed, he has done nothing to deserve death' (Luke 23:14–15).

How does he know Antipas's verdict on Jesus? Antipas could have sent a message, of course, but it is not mentioned. The robes themselves are the message. For 'bright' clothes, we should understand 'white', the colour of innocence. It is, I suppose, to Antipas's credit that he passes on this message. He is not going to have another John the Baptist on his conscience. Jesus may have been insolent, he may have lacked respect, but Antipas does not

consider him guilty. He dresses Jesus in white, the colour of innocence.[61]

It takes us back again to that mountain, to the clothes of daz-
zling white, whiter than any fuller could make them. It is the colour of martyrs. The innocents who would nonetheless be killed.

'Which of the two do you want me to release for you?'

Luke says that, from that day on, Pilate and Antipas were friends.
Pilate's diplomacy has worked. But the immediate problem is still
there. As far as Jesus' trial by Pilate goes, the broad outline of
events includes the following.

▷ Interrogating Jesus (Matt. 27:11–14; Luke 23:13–16; John
18:29–38a).
▷ Offering Barabbas in exchange (Matt. 27:15–18; Mark 15:6–
14; Luke 23:18–19; John 18:38b–40).
▷ Declaring Jesus innocent (Matt. 27:24–25; Luke 23:20–23;
John 19:6–12).
▷ Having Jesus beaten and crowned with thorns (Matt. 27:27–
31; Mark 15:16–20; John 19:1–5).
▷ Sending Jesus to be crucified (Matt. 27:26; Mark 15:15; Luke
23:24–25; John 19:12–16a).

The idea that Pilate is an innocent party in all this is not one
which is entertained by any of the Gospels. It is actually an idea
which is promulgated by those who would rather that no Western
European could be blamed for Jesus' death. But all the Gospels
agree that Pilate ordered Jesus to be crucified. Pilate was afraid at
points, and he was, to a certain extent, manipulated. But he was
also manipulating others. His overriding concern throughout this
is not that an innocent man would be killed, but that he, Pilate,
would be blamed.

In John's account, Pilate's dialogue with Jesus consists almost
entirely of questions: 'Are you the King of the Jews?' (John 18:33);
'What have you done?' (John 18:35); 'So you are a king?' (John
18:37); 'What is truth?' (John 18:38). The cynical *realpolitik* of
this statement shows us the truth about Pilate's world. This is not
about the truth; it is about what is effective, what is best for Pilate,
for Rome. Pilate does not care about Jesus, whatever his wife may

have dreamed (Matt. 27:19). If he wanted to release Jesus, he could have done. He could have held him in custody until after the festival. He could have ridden out the storm. But what would that have gained him?

The fact is that Pilate wants to use this opportunity to strengthen his position, but he has to find out whether Jesus has any popular support. The way to do that is to give the people in the courtyard a choice. 'Now a man called Barabbas was in prison with the rebels who had committed murder during the insurrection ...' (Mark 15:6–15).

There is no known precedent for this: provincial governors do not seem to have had the right to grant a pardon.[62] However, amnesties are not unknown in the Greco-Roman world. Matthew and Mark suggest that it was a regular custom at Passover, but John implies that it was a Jewish custom.[63] In that case, it may be a custom dating back to Herod's rule – or even before. The strongest argument for the historicity of the event is that it is in all the Gospels and the historical details in the Gospels must, at least, have been credible to their readers and listeners. If prefects *never* released a prisoner on amnesty, then one would have thought that the story would not appear so prominently in all the Gospels. The fact that it is there means that it was not impossible.

We do not know much about Barabbas. All we have is his surname: 'son of Abba or Abbas'. But the tradition in some later manuscripts that he was called Jesus may be original. It is unlikely that later Christians would have chosen the name Jesus for a villain. Mark describes how he is in prison with 'the rebels who had committed murder during the insurrection'. Matthew says he was a 'notorious prisoner' (Matt. 27:16). John says he was a bandit (John 18:40), and Luke says he was in prison for insurrection and murder (Luke 23:25). Clearly, Barabbas was part of a group of bandits, *lestai*. Pilate offers the crowd a choice between two political prisoners: Jesus of Nazareth, a man who has advocated nonpayment of taxes and claims to be king, and Barabbas, a bandit who has been involved in terrorism and who may or may not have committed murder.

This is not a heroic attempt on Pilate's part to release Jesus. He could have done that any time he wanted. It is a way for him to test out Jesus' popularity. It is a focus group, an opinion poll. Pilate knows that the temple aristocracy have handed Jesus over 'out of jealousy' (Mark 15:10). What he does not know is whether doing what the high priest wants is going to cause him trouble.[64] The answer is clear: in this crowd, Jesus has no popular support. This crowd want Barabbas.

Talking about the crowd, we are back to the idea that 'the Jews' wanted to crucify Jesus. The charge is derived mainly from the verse in Matthew: 'Then the people as a whole answered, "His blood be on us and on our children!"' (Matt. 27:25). The word Matthew uses for people is *laos*, which is often used to mean the people as a whole, i.e. the Jewish nation. But Matthew cannot possibly mean 'all the Jews', because we know that there were many Jews who were opposed to this verdict. He cannot even mean 'all the Jews in Jerusalem', since that would go against Matthew 26:5 where the leaders could not arrest Jesus because there would be a riot among the 'people' (and here Matthew uses the same word: *laos*).

No, this is not the general populace, but a carefully controlled mob. The temple elite have not spent a week waiting to catch Jesus only to have an independent crowd ruin everything at the last moment. They have brought along their own supporters. We know they had such groups. During the revolt the household servants of the ex-high priest Ananias used bullying tactics to secure his power, while two other ex-high priests – Jesus ben Damnaeus and Jesus ben Gamalas – fought back with their gangs.[65]

It was not 'the Jews' who bayed for Jesus to be killed. It was the gangs of the chief priests and leading families of Jerusalem. This is why the chief priests were able to stir up the crowd to do what they wanted (Mark 15:11): they were issuing instructions to their gangs.

How far Pilate fully understood the nature of this crowd is open to debate. His track record at understanding the minutiae of Jewish religious politics was never great. Pilate thought that this group would act as an opinion poll. What he did not know was that they had already had their opinions decided for them. That was why they were there.

The different Gospels have different 'decision' points. Matthew

255

implies that Pilate feared a riot was about to start (Matt. 27:24). John shows Pilate still uncertain, and still affected by something about Jesus. Which is when the temple leaders play their trump card: 'If you release this man, you are no friend of the emperor. Everyone who claims to be a king sets himself against the emperor' (John 19:12).

It is the perfect leverage. This is a specific threat. Caesar's Friends – *amici Caesaris* – were an informal grouping whose membership was reserved for high-ranking Romans awarded this status. Loss of the rank *amicus Caesaris* led to political and social ostracism, even suicide.

So Pilate makes a decision. As far as he can see, Jesus is without popular and political support, and the Jewish leaders are threatening to take their complaint to the emperor. Time for action. Or inaction, if you prefer. 'So when Pilate saw that he could do nothing, but rather that a riot was beginning, he took some water and washed his hands before the crowd, saying, "I am innocent of this man's blood; see to it yourselves"' (Matt. 27:24).

Nothing to do with me, guv. My hands are clean. Having given into the crowd, Pilate absolves himself of personal responsibility. He has Jesus brought out and gives them one last chance: 'Shall I crucify your King?' The question is deliberately mocking. That is the point, he is *not* their king. Pilate is winding them up. And it works, for the chief priests answer, 'We have no king but the emperor' (John 19:15).

Brilliant. Back of the net. Despite the precariousness of his position, despite his appearance of being manipulated, Pilate has secured from the chief priests a proclamation of loyalty to Rome and the emperor.

That's Pilate for you. What a cunning, highly attuned political manipulator the man is. Just when you think he is down and out, just when you think the grizzled old soldier is beaten, he pulls this out of the bag. He has mended his relationship with Antipas, secured a declaration of loyalty from the Jewish leadership, maintained order, quelled a potential riot and freed himself of responsibility, even though it will be his troops who carry out the sentence. And all it cost was the death of one Galilean peasant.

Not bad for a Friday morning. And it's not even nine o'clock.

'Hail, King of the Jews!'

> Then the soldiers led him into the courtyard of the palace (that is, the governor's headquarters); and they called together the whole cohort. And they clothed him in a purple cloak; and after twisting some thorns into a crown, they put it on him. And they began saluting him, 'Hail, King of the Jews!' They struck his head with a reed, spat upon him, and knelt down in homage to him. After mocking him, they stripped him of the purple cloak and put his own clothes on him. Then they led him out to crucify him. (Mark 15:16–20)

Jesus is flogged and humiliated, paraded before the crowd. The first steps into hell. The flogging – a punishment the Romans frequently used on lower-class or foreign offenders – was designed to strip the flesh of the victim. It was savage and unrelenting. The victim would lose control of his bodily functions.[66] And it would have been all the more savage for being carried out by non-Jews. The Gospel portrayal is clear that soldiers beat Jesus and crucified him and that there was at least one high-ranking officer present.[67] And the soldiers were auxiliaries: Greeks, or even Samaritans. This is why they take such relish in the beating and the humiliation. 'Hail, King of the Jews!' It is not just humiliating a pathetic peasant; it is mocking the pretensions of the whole Jewish nation.

Jesus, already bleeding and broken, is brought back into the main square, where the entire cohort join in the fun. They dress him in a coloured robe. Although the translation says 'purple', the word can mean a range of colours from blue to red, and it is unlikely that they would have had a true purple robe handy – they were way too expensive to risk getting covered in blood.[68]

Then they weave a crown of thorns and press it into his head. This is usually presented as a ring of thorns, like a Western circlet crown, but images of kings from that time have been found on coins, depicting crowns that radiate out from the head, like the rays of the sun. And with regard to the thorns, it is reasonable to suppose that the soldiers used whatever thorny plants they could find nearby. The most common would have been the date palm, *Phoenix dactylifera*, which has ferociously sharp thorns that stick upwards.[69] One further irony: what was waved during Jesus' entry to Jerusalem? Palms. *Phoenix dactylifera*.

The Wrong Messiah has the wrong kind of crown. Six days

earlier, he had entered Jerusalem in triumph. On Friday morning, in the chillingly plain words of Mark, 'they led him out to crucify him' (Mark 15:20).

The Greco-Roman world did not discuss crucifixion, but it was a fact of life. Everyone knew it went on. There were permanent crucifixion sites in most of the cities. But it was a death reserved for the lowest classes; for slaves or rebels. Not a subject for polite conversation.[70] Crucifixion was a shameful death. That was the point. It was a death designed to humiliate and terrify, to frighten people into obedience. Because crucifixion was 'the slaves' death', it was a way of terrorising slaves into obedience. The slave rebellions of the second century BC culminated in mass crucifixions; the victorious Crassus had six thousand slaves crucified, lining the main road into Rome. But a slave could expect this terrible punishment for all manner of offences.[71] It was, in the words of Borg and Crossan, an act of 'imperial terror'.[72]

After flogging, the victim had the crossbeam of the cross strapped to his arms, across his shoulders. He would then be led out to the place of execution. It was not far away. Pilate was undoubtedly in Herod's Palace, not the Antonia, and the traditional site of Golgotha is just a few hundred metres north.[73]

No, it was not far, but even so, it was too much for Jesus, such was the savagery of the beating that had been meted out to him. So the Romans co-opted someone to help. Someone to go the mile, as we saw way back in Galilee. The Synoptics identify him as 'Simon of Cyrene, the father of Alexander and Rufus' (Mark 15:21). He or his sons probably became followers of Jesus afterwards: Mark mentions his sons, in a manner which suggests that they should have been known to his readers, and there was a 'Rufus' in the church in Rome (Rom. 16:13).

The place of execution was known as Golgotha, or the Place of the Skull. It was just outside the city, as all such sites were. With typical Roman efficiency, it was about the nearest point outside the city to the Herodian palace – a graveyard in an old quarry. Today there is a church on the site, one of the most ancient and famous churches in the world. The Western church calls it the Church of the Holy Sepulchre, but the Eastern church, more optimistically, calls it the *Anastasis* – the Church of the Resurrection.

It has a good claim to be the site. The church does, indeed, stand above a first-century graveyard: graves have been found beneath the building. So, if it was not the place, it was near the place. If the rock within the church is not Golgotha, then it is somewhere very near to it.

It was there, at nine o'clock in the morning, that Jesus of Nazareth, 'King of the Jews' and so-called 'Messiah', was executed.

'They crucified Jesus there with the criminals'

Evidence from a crucifixion victim found near Jerusalem – the only crucifixion victim ever discovered by archaeologists – shows that it did not happen in the way we imagine it. Pictures of Jesus raised way up high on a tall wooden cross are wrong. It happened at eye level. The Christian traditions record that the site of Jesus' crucifixion was on a rocky outcrop – a place that would have meant that lots of people could see it. But the cross itself was not high. Jesus would have been able to look his executioners in the eye.

The victim already had the crossbar tied to him. Either he just remained tied to that, or he was both tied and then nailed through the hands or wrists. The crossbar was set in place on a vertical post, his legs were lifted up and he was mounted on a small peg known as a *sedile*, which stuck out from the upright beam. A single nail was then either driven laterally through his ankles, or his feet were nailed into the side of the main beam.[74] Simple, efficient. Very Roman.

Pilate, in one last jibe at the Jewish leaders' expense, had a sign hung on the cross: 'Jesus of Nazareth, the King of the Jews'. It was written in all the major languages of Jerusalem: Hebrew, Latin and Greek. Despite complaints from the Jewish leadership, Pilate refused to change the wording (John 19:22).

The use of crucifixion as a punishment for rebels lies behind the deaths of the other two prisoners who were crucified alongside Jesus that day. Two bandits, *lestai*, in the same class as Barabbas. Jesus was not crucified between two pickpockets, or housebreakers. He was crucified between two political bandits, two terrorists – at least that was how they looked to the Romans.

One of them seems to recognise that there is something special about this man. 'Remember me', he says to Jesus, 'when you come into your kingdom.' This was a bandit who had fought against the earthly kingdom of the Romans; now he recognises the battered figure next to him as a dying king. Jesus' reply is an extraordinary statement of faith and hope: 'Today you will be with me in Paradise' (Luke 23:42–43). 'Paradise': a word coined from the Persians, a walled garden, trees and shade, coolness and rest.[75] Here, amidst the blood and the dust and the heat, here, in a Roman execution site in a disused quarry, Jesus promises a criminal what he denied himself: a different ending.

The soldiers and the bystanders and the representatives of the temple mocked him with words stolen from the mouth of Satan himself: 'He saved others; he cannot save himself. Let the Messiah, the King of Israel, come down from the cross now, so that we may see and believe' (Mark 15:31–32). It is their final comment on the messianic claims of Jesus.

'It is finished'

At noon it went dark. Unnaturally dark. It can't have been an eclipse, because Passover occurs at a full moon – and you can't have a total eclipse during a full moon. It was just, like a lot of other things which happened that day, weird.[76]

At three in the afternoon the screaming started.

On the other side of the city, they began killing at 3 p.m. The horns blasted and the first of thousands upon thousands of terrified lambs were slaughtered for Passover.[77] The stench of the blood and the plaintive screams of distress from the animals must have filled the city.

At around the same time, according to Mark, Jesus gave a 'loud cry'. The Greek indicates that this was a scream of urgency, a cry for help: a prayer, in fact.[78] Mark says that Jesus screamed out a verse from a psalm in Aramaic: *Eloi, Eloi, lema sabachthani?* – 'My God, my God, why have you forsaken me?' (Mark 15:34). The quotation comes from Psalm 22, and is the only statement uttered by Jesus on the cross that Mark records. It is a cry of utter isolation and alienation, and almost certainly authentic. One cannot imagine a later writer, a follower of a triumphant Christ-figure, making up a cry of such utter despair.

Was it a cry of failure, or a cry of recognition? Traditional

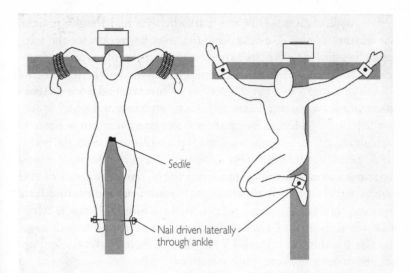

Sedile

Nail driven laterally
through ankle

Evidence from the crucifixion victim found at Giv'at ha-Mivtar near Jerusalem shows
that he had been nailed through the heel bone. Two possible reconstructions have been
put forward, suggesting that he was either crucified straddling the cross (above left) or
in a raised foetal position (above right). Either way he would have been supported by a
sedile – a small peg sticking out from the upright beam.

theology argues that this was the point of abandonment, when
Jesus was suffering for all mankind, but we should remember that
it was a prayer, and prayer always implies the hope that someone,
despite appearances, is listening. And Psalm 22 ends with vindica-
tion and restoration: this is a cry which God hears: 'For he did not
despise or abhor the affliction of the afflicted; he did not hide his
face from me, but heard when I cried to him' (Ps. 22:24).

In Matthew and Mark he gives a loud cry; in John he says, 'It
is finished'; in Luke he says, 'Father, into your hands I commend
my spirit' (Luke 23:46).

And with that, it was finished. Just another death of a failed
revolutionary; another ritual killing on this day of ritual killings;
another daily sacrifice for the well-being of the empire.

He died quickly, that was something. Crucifixion victims could
linger for days – indeed, they were not intended to go quickly.
Crucifixion was expected to keep them in sight, on display, as it
were. The speed of Jesus' death – which came as a surprise to

Pilate – indicates that he was actually badly injured before he even came to the cross. We have seen that he was unable to carry his own crossbeam to the site of execution, despite the distance from Herod's Palace to Golgotha being reasonably short.

He had simply lost too much blood. When the blood loss reaches a certain level, victims enter what is termed hypovolaemic shock, where the blood loss is so great that there is simply not enough to deliver oxygen to the organs. The external bleeding from the whips and the nails, and the internal bleeding from the beating, would have been more than enough. Many people sentenced to crucifixion actually died during the beating.[79] Jesus died on the cross; that is certainly true. But that was not what killed him. He had, essentially, been beaten to death by soldiers that morning.[80]

The bandits on either side of Jesus were dispatched by having their legs broken. This practice – what the Romans called *crurifragium* – did not mean that they could no longer support themselves. They were supported by the small peg on which they sat. What it did was induce more trauma into an already savagely traumatised body. Jesus, however, was already dead.

With Jesus' death, we go further into the twilight world of strangeness that began with the darkness. To be certain of Jesus' death, a soldier stabbed him through the side with a spear and, John tells us, blood and water came out (John 19:31–37). He links it with two Old Testament prophecies; probably it was 'haemorrhagic fluid' in the space between the ribs and the lungs.[81] But it was not normal.

And if that was strange ...

The Synoptic Gospels record that, with Jesus' death, the curtain in the temple was torn from top to bottom (Matt. 27:51; Mark 15:38; Luke 23:45). There were two curtains in the temple: one separating the Holy of Holies from the Holy Place, and one separating the sanctuary from the courtyard. The likelihood is that the writers are referring to the inner curtain, if only for symbolic reasons. In Christian theology, the tearing of the curtain has been taken to mean that Christ's death now allows anyone access to the Holy of Holies, but this is never spelled out in the New Testament. Just as likely is the idea that this was an eschatological event. For Jews such as Josephus and Philo, the temple had a cosmic significance: it was the centre of creation.[82] The curtain, woven from Babylonian cloth and embroidered in blue, scarlet and purple, represented creation, according to Josephus: 'for the fine linen was proper to signify the earth, because the flax grows out of the earth; the purple signified the sea, because that color is dyed by the blood of a sea shell fish; the blue is fit to signify the air; and the scarlet will naturally be an indication of fire'.[83]

Matthew links the curtain with an earthquake: he uses the same verb to describe both the tearing of the curtain and the ripping open of the rocks (Matt. 27:51). So this event is a sign of some kind of massive rupture in the natural order. To Jews who witnessed it, it would have been a sign that something had gone badly wrong with creation. The end, as they say, is nigh.

'Waiting expectantly for the kingdom of God'

There was not much time before sunset and the start of the Sabbath. Joseph of Arimathea made his way to Herod's Palace and persuaded Pilate to let him have the body of Jesus and give it a decent burial.

He is depicted as a wealthy member of the Sanhedrin, although not, perhaps, an influential one. Arimathea, his town of origin, is unknown. It was not in Galilee, since Luke calls Arimathea 'a Jewish town' (Luke 23:51), meaning that it was in Judea.[84] Wherever he had started, he was now permanently domiciled in Jerusalem, which is why he had bought a tomb there. Joseph of Arimathea may also have been a Pharisee. Mark and Luke tell us that he was 'waiting expectantly for the kingdom of God', which would mean that, theologically, he was not a Sadducee (Mark 15:43; Luke 23:50). John says he had kept his interest in Jesus quiet for fear of the Jewish leadership (John 19:38). At this point, however, they were all on the other side of the city, in or around the temple, active in the Passover preparations.

Pilate orders a check on whether Jesus is actually dead. People could recover from crucifixion. In the savage aftermath of the failed Jewish rebellion, when the rebels were being crucified by the Romans, Josephus was given permission to rescue three victims:

> I saw many captives crucified; and remembered three of them as my former acquaintance. I was very sorry at this in my mind, and went

with tears in my eyes to Titus, and told him of them; so he immediately commanded them to be taken down, and to have the greatest care taken of them, in order to their recovery; yet two of them died under the physician's hands, while the third recovered.[85]

Having been assured that Jesus was dead, Joseph was granted permission to take the body and bury it. There was no time for the usual rituals. No time for the complex wrapping of the body, the binding up of the chin as was done in Lazarus's case. Jesus was not even washed – the minimum one would expect, since blood on a corpse was considered unclean.[86] Even in death he did not wash properly.

Jesus was placed in a new tomb, which Joseph had purchased for his family. A disused quarry made an ideal place for a Jewish burial ground, since it would have had plenty of rockface, where a cave could be excavated. Jewish tombs of the period were mainly what are called *loculi* tombs, consisting of a doorway into a central chamber, with *loculi*, or niches, cut into the walls to hold the bodies. The *loculi* were about sixty centimetres wide and tunnelled into the rock to a depth of around two metres.[87] The arrangement is not unlike those drawers in a morgue. Inside the main body of the chamber there would often be a stone ledge or bench on which bodies could be laid. Other types of tomb had shelves or ledges for the bodies rather than *loculi* niches.

Significantly, both types have been found in the area around the traditional location of the burial place: the Church of the Holy Sepulchre in Jerusalem.[88] From very early times this has been identified as the site. Certainly, if one had been inventing the site from scratch, one would not have positioned it there, because by the time Constantine sent builders to search for the place, this site was inside the city walls and hidden under the remains of a huge temple to Aphrodite. Local Christians, though, remembered the place. When Melitto of Sardis came to Jerusalem in the second half of the second century, he was taken by local Christians to the site, which he described as being in the middle of the broad streets of the city.[89]

The tomb was closed by means of a large round stone, which sat in a groove that ran along the front. The stone was rolled across the groove, creating a barrier to any wild animals.

And that was that. Jesus of Nazareth, Yeshu ben Yehosef, was dead. And, as the Passover ovens were lit and the city became filled with celebrating pilgrims, everyone went home.

The adventure was over. They thought he was the one to redeem Israel. They thought he was the Messiah.

Now, they knew they were wrong.

A typical first-century tomb. The stone is set into a grooved channel allowing it to be rolled across the entranceway.

265

Aftermath: the Wrong Messiah

Fifty days after Jesus' death, the leader of his followers – a man who had at one point denied knowing him at all – went out onto the streets of Jerusalem and said that Jesus was the Messiah.

It was the festival of Pentecost, nine o'clock in the morning; the streets, once again, were packed with pilgrims. Peter gave a rousing speech, claiming that God had made Jesus 'both Lord and Messiah' (Acts 2:36). This was something of a puzzle to the onlookers. As far as they knew, Jesus of Nazareth was a Galilean peasant recently executed by the Romans. Never mind Lord and Messiah, failure and fraud would be more appropriate in many people's eyes. No wonder they thought Peter was drunk.

Yet he was not alone. Not just Peter, but all the early followers of Jesus, repeated this assertion. *Kyrios* and *Christos* – Lord and Messiah: those were the words which summed up their beliefs about Jesus Christ.[1] From the very start, the early church was a messianic movement. The belief is woven into their writings. Paul thought Jesus was the Messiah. The Gospel writers thought he was the Messiah. James, John, Jude, the writer of Hebrews and whichever John wrote Revelation thought he was the Messiah. As did the next generation: Ignatius and the authors of the *Didache* and Barnabas.[2] (Even non-Christians like Josephus recognised that Jesus' followers thought he was the Messiah.)

What could explain this? Fundamentally, whatever Judaism you espoused, Jesus failed his messianic exam in every module he took. The Messiah was expected to purge the pagans from the land, but he had been killed by them. The Messiah was supposed to renew the temple, but the temple party had caused his downfall. The Messiah was supposed to bring in the new age, but life was much the same as it had ever been.

He had been beaten and humiliated, spat upon, scourged, bloodied, mocked and finally killed. He had been a great teacher. A miracle worker. A prophet, certainly. But not the Messiah. That was simply delusion. And yet, consistently, determinedly, in the face of ostracism, ridicule and persecution, Jesus' followers claimed that they were right, that Jesus was the Messiah.

Why? Because he had come back from the dead.

'He has been raised; he is not here'

Logically, the historical problem of the resurrection is no greater than when faced with any of the other miracles of Jesus, but there is something even greater in this one. At least with the feeding of the five thousand, or the raising of Lazarus, Jesus was actually alive at the time. He was there to perform the deed. But at the resurrection he was … well, otherwise engaged.

First, we have to acknowledge that the accounts differ in a number of details. For example, Mark and Matthew have one angel, Luke and John have two. Matthew has two women going to the tomb; Mark has three, Luke at least five, and John one. In Mark, Luke and John the stone has been removed; in Matthew an angel appears and rolls it back as the women arrive. John has Mary Magdalene meeting Jesus, Matthew has an earthquake, and Mark is missing the ending.[3] But apart from that …

Perhaps, instead of focusing on the differences, it is simpler to look at what all the Gospels have in common. There is a series of core events, in all the Gospels.

▷ Women go to the tomb. The women are the first witnesses of what happened and they are the ones who tell the news to the disciples and the others.

▷ Mary Magdalene visits the tomb.

▷ There is an empty tomb with the stone rolled back and linen cloths on the floor.

▷ Angels appear.

▷ Further, in three of the Gospels, Peter is featured specifically. In Mark the women are told to 'tell Peter'; in Luke and John he goes to the tomb and investigates.

This at least allows us to reconstruct a possible outline of events, as follows.

A group of women including Mary Magdalene, Mary the mother of James, Joanna and Salome went to the tomb very early. They found it empty, the stone rolled back and the grave clothes on the floor. They then had an encounter with an angel (or group of angels) who told them that Jesus had risen. The women returned to the room where the disciples were – probably the Upper Room, which was only a short walk away. Peter and another disciple went to the tomb to investigate for themselves. They found it as the women said. They were followed by Mary Magdalene, who met Jesus (although at first she thought he was the gardener).

Of course the accounts differ; eyewitness accounts always do differ. But, frankly, people who argue about the differences in the accounts are, to misquote the man who was not there, arguing about gnats while ignoring the camel waiting to be swallowed. Because whatever the differences, all the accounts agree that the tomb was empty. Jesus was no longer there.

You can, if you wish, point to the discrepancies in the accounts as proof of fabrication. But you can also argue the opposite. Fabrication would surely make certain that any differences were edited out. What the differences demonstrate is that the early church carefully preserved traditions, even when those traditions conflicted with each other. Why? Because they were dealing with testimony, with people's stories. And the details were important.[4]

There are many arguments one could make to buttress support for the resurrection accounts: there is the appeal to the women as witnesses, when no self-respecting religion would rely on the testimony of women. There is the complete absence of any counter-claim. The emptiness of the tomb was never, in fact, a subject of controversy. Only the *reason* for its emptiness.[5] There is the sheer weirdness of the event. The Christian belief that resurrection had happened ahead of the end, and that it signalled a general resurrection (as reflected in Matthew's dead people walking about), was very strange.

But this is not 100 per cent proof. For me, a much stronger proof of the resurrection lies in the response of his followers. On the Friday they were in hiding, fearful for their lives and distraught by the shattering of their dreams. But something changed them, something made them leave that room and begin to claim that Jesus had risen from the dead. They claimed to have seen him, in the flesh, not only in Jerusalem, but elsewhere. Early Christianity was, from the start, a resurrection movement. The first Christians believed that Jesus had somehow come out of that tomb, just as he had called Lazarus out. And they simply would not shut up about it.

'He was raised on the third day'

The first datable claims come not from the Gospels, but in Paul's first letter to the Corinthians:

> For I handed on to you as of first importance what I in turn had received: that Christ died for our sins in accordance with the scriptures, and that he was buried, and that he was raised on the third day in accordance with the scriptures, and that he appeared to Cephas [Peter], then to the twelve. Then he appeared to more than five hundred brothers and sisters at one time, most of whom are still alive, though some have died. Then he appeared to James, then to all the apostles. Last of all, as to one untimely born, he appeared also to me. (1 Cor. 15:3–8)

Corinthians was written around AD 54, but Paul is recording something that he had been taught much earlier, when he first became a follower of Jesus only a few months, probably, after Jesus' death.[6] This is clearly a piece of very early church doctrine, an early church formula. It is missing the detail of the Gospel accounts, but it makes an appeal to witnesses who were still alive. Five hundred brothers and sisters saw Jesus, according to Paul. And 'all the apostles' – a group which would most likely have included some missionaries and teachers known to the early church and to the church in Corinth.[7]

Something turned a huddle of frightened peasants into a world-changing phenomenon. Acts depicts the rapid growth of the church – three thousand were baptised on the day of Pentecost alone. Even if we dispute the figures, the sheer fact of history is that Christianity flourished and grew. Despite the frequent persecutions to which it was subjected, it spread rapidly.

Look, for example, at the transformation in Jesus' own family. At the cross, Jesus' male relatives appear to have been absent. But afterwards, according to Luke, the brothers were in Jerusalem:

> When they had entered the city, they went to the room upstairs where they were staying, Peter, and John, and James, and Andrew, Philip and Thomas, Bartholomew and Matthew, James son of Alphaeus, and Simon the Zealot, and Judas son of James. All these were constantly devoting themselves to prayer, together with certain women, including Mary the mother of Jesus, as well as his brothers. (Acts 1:13–14)

His brother James, who initially thought him deluded, ended up leading the first church in Jerusalem. Another of Jesus' brothers, Jude, also became a prominent Christian.[8] So two, at least, of Jesus' sceptical brothers were turned around from disbelief to belief, from scepticism to adherence. How did this happen?

Paul's account shows the early church believed that Jesus appeared to James. A fragment from the now lost *Gospel of Hebrews* tells how James had sworn not to eat until he saw the risen Jesus, then Jesus appears and breaks bread with his brother. The passage suggests that James had already been converted to a follower and that he was present at the Last Supper.[9] It's an apocryphal story, but there is an account in the Gospels of an appearance of Jesus to one of his relatives. Sometime on the Sunday, two disciples – not the Eleven, who were still in Jerusalem – were walking to a village called Emmaus. (Despite strenuous efforts, Emmaus has never been identified. It was probably about seven miles from Jerusalem.)

Along the way they were joined by an unknown man who started talking to them about recent events in Jerusalem. Now these disciples had already heard the rumours. They had been in the room that morning:

> Moreover, some women of our group astounded us. They were at the tomb early this morning, and when they did not find his body there, they came back and told us that they had indeed seen a vision of angels who said that he was alive. Some of those who were with us went to the tomb and found it just as the women had said; but they did not see him. (Luke 24:22–24)

This is interesting, because the phrase 'some of those who were with us went to the tomb' backs up John's account of the event, in which both Peter and the 'Beloved Disciple' went to have a look. Anyway, the stranger proceeds to explain what has happened and they invite him to share their meal in their home. As he breaks the bread, they realise it is Jesus, and he vanishes. Immediately they rush back to Jerusalem to tell the others.

Why does this shed light on other things? Because one of the walkers was probably a member of Jesus' family. Luke identifies him as Cleopas, and a story from the early church tells how the successor to James, as leader of the Jerusalem church, was a relative of Jesus, a man called Symeon son of Clopas: 'He [Symeon] was a cousin – at any rate so it is said – of the Saviour; for indeed Hegesippus relates that Clopas was Joseph's brother.'[10]

Now if we return to John's account of the women round the cross, we find Mary of Clopas, i.e. Mary, wife of Clopas (John 19:25). The probability that Luke's Cleopas and John's Clopas are the same person is extremely high.[11] This would mean that the person whom Jesus meets on the Emmaus road is his own uncle, which fits perfectly with the tradition of Jesus appearing to his relatives, such as James.[12] This would also add to Symeon's qualifications to replace James: he was an apostle, one who had seen the risen Jesus.

By the time Clopas and his companion got back to Jerusalem, others had seen Jesus as well. Luke records that, when the two excited travellers burst into the room, 'they found the eleven and their companions gathered together. They were saying, "The Lord has risen indeed, and he has appeared to Simon!"' (Luke 24:33–35). Which must have rather taken the wind out of their sails. But in Luke, immediately after Clopas and his companion have given their breathless account, Jesus appears, 'standing among them', and demonstrates that he has come back as flesh and bone. He even eats a piece of fish (Luke 24:41–43). John has a version of this story as well and in both accounts Jesus shows them his hands and feet (Luke 24:40; John 20:20). In both accounts Jesus also goes on to talk about the Holy Spirit (Luke 24:49; John 20:22). Over the course of the next few weeks, according to the New Testament sources, many more people were to see Jesus.

Sunday

▷ Mary Magdalene (Matt. 28:9–10; John 20:11–18)
▷ Mary, mother of James and Joseph (Matt. 28:9–10)
▷ Clopas and another disciple (Luke 24:13–35)
▷ Simon Peter (Luke 24:34)
▷ Disciples in the Upper Room (Luke 24:36–49; John 20:19–23)

A week later

▷ Thomas (John 20:24–29)

Up to forty days later

▷ Eleven disciples in Galilee (Matt. 28:16–20)
▷ Seven disciples in Galilee, including Nathanael and the Beloved Disciple (John 21:1–24)
▷ More than five hundred brothers and sisters (1 Cor. 15:6)
▷ James (1 Cor. 15:6)
▷ Paul (1 Cor. 15:6)
▷ Apostles in Jerusalem (Acts 1:6–11)

If we assume that, by 'apostle', Paul and the early church meant one who has seen the risen Lord, then that group would include people like Junia and Andronicus (Rom. 16:7), Apollos (1 Cor. 4:6, 9), Barnabas (Acts 14:14; 1 Cor. 9:5–6), Epaphroditus (Phil. 2:25), Silvanus and Timothy (1 Thess. 1:1; 2:7).

There are, as ever, some difficulties as we consider the endings of the Gospels. Matthew has the women tell the disciples to meet Jesus in Galilee, where they encounter hi m on a mountain (Matt. 28:10, 16–20). John has an extra ending in which Jesus appears by the Sea of Galilee, cooks his disciples breakfast and reinstates Peter (John 21:1–24). Luke, on the other hand, has Jesus insist that his disciples should not leave Jerusalem, but wait there for the Holy Spirit to come (Luke 24:49; Acts 1:4–5). After this Jesus takes them to the Mount of Olives and ascends into heaven (Luke 24:50–53; Acts 1:6–11). The only way of reconciling the accounts is to argue for a split at Luke 24:44: that Luke's 'Then he said to them …' actually happened some time later. After all, Luke uses the same construction ('Then he

AFTERMATH: THE WRONG MESSIAH

led them out as far as Bethany …') to link to the Ascension, and by his own admission he relates that that was forty days later, during which time Jesus had appeared to them numerous times (Acts 1:3). Forty days is plenty of time for them to travel to Galilee and then back. It may have been in Galilee that Jesus appeared to the more than five hundred of 1 Cor. 15:6. This would explain why, in Matthew's account, some worshipped him but some doubted (Matt. 28:17). A crowd of five hundred leaves plenty of room for sceptics.[13]

So, a period of forty days, and appearances to well over five hundred people. Whatever we think of the truth or otherwise of these accounts, what we cannot do is simply dismiss them as one or two people saying, 'I saw him again, honest!' Paul is clear, for example, that most of the people who saw Jesus were still alive at the time he was writing. Nor can we take refuge in the frankly patronising view that the early followers were credulous idiots who did not know a dead body when they saw one. The ancient world was far better acquainted with death than we are. They saw it around them on the streets and in the gutters, in the houses and on the execution sites that studded the Roman Empire. They knew the difference between death and life, between a corpse and a walking, living, fish-eating bloke.

As to that, the point of the hands and the feet and the fish is their physicality. This was not a vision or, worse still, some kind of metaphor. No Gospel writer claims that Jesus went into the tomb as a man and came out as a metaphor.

Whatever we choose to believe about the resurrection itself, the historical facts are that the early church genuinely believed it happened. And in this, they were very different from other messianic movements.

'False Messiahs and false prophets will appear'

We can see this by comparing the response to two other failed Messiahs. The first is a man called Simon bar Giora. Some two years after the revolt against the Romans had erupted, a messianic movement arose among the Judean peasantry, centred around Simon bar Giora. Although Josephus does not use messianic terminology, the activities of Simon have a number of 'Davidic' features.

Simon had been the leader of one of the revolutionary armies. Successful in an attack against the Romans, he was passed over for a command by the priests and the Pharisees who controlled the revolutionary government in Jerusalem. This was a big mistake. Simon subsequently took control of Idumea and southern Judea and led an attack on Jerusalem.

By now he was clearly a king in waiting. Josephus says that his army numbered 40,000 troops.[14] Like David, he was a popular military leader. Like David, he started by taking Hebron before eventually capturing Jerusalem. (The leaders let him in to help them overpower another out-of-control leader, John of Gischala and the Zealots.[15])

Simon, according to Josephus, was regarded with awe and devotion by his followers, so much so that 'at his command they were very ready to kill themselves with their own hands'.[16] He purged Jerusalem of all those who were accused of favouring the Romans. Psalms of Solomon talks of the messianic king 'thrusting out sinners from [the] inheritance' and 'purging Jerusalem and making it holy as of old' (Ps. Sol. 17:26, 36). This, to his followers at least, must have been Simon at his messianic best. He went on to proclaim freedom for the slaves and rewards for faithful followers, and his command of the city lasted nearly two years. Then the Romans arrived in force and, after a siege, took the city and destroyed the temple.

But Simon was not there. Along with a number of his friends and followers who were stonemasons, he had let himself down into a subterranean cavern, along with 'as great a quantity of provisions as would suffice them for a long time'. Their hope was to dig themselves out. The stone proved too tough, however, and when supplies ran low, Simon decided to go out in a blaze of messianic glory. He dressed himself in white robes and a purple cloak, and emerged into the city where, dressed as a king, he stood amidst the rubble of the ruined temple. He voluntarily gave himself up to the Romans and was taken to Rome. Josephus tells us that, after being dragged in triumph 'among the captives' and tormented by those in charge of him, he was executed in the forum.[17]

The second leader rose about sixty years later in the second revolt. This was another Simon, Simon bar Kokhba. In the interim between the two Simons, Jewish hopes of a messianic king to lead them had risen even higher. Bar Kokhba was overtly identified as the Messiah by Rabbi Akiba, who, when he saw him, said, 'This is the king, the Messiah.' Bar Kokhba's revolt, like bar Giora's, spread quickly. They minted coins with the phrase 'Year 1 of the liberation of Israel'. Akiba even applied the star prophecy from Numbers to bar Kokhba. Archaeological discoveries have also confirmed that the revolt emphasised strict religious purity. Again it all ended messily. The Romans sent in a huge force and although bar Kokhba and his rebels held out for a long time, in a kind of guerilla warfare, hiding in caves, they were defeated in the end. The Jews were banned from Jerusalem, which the Romans renamed Aelia Capitolina.[18]

The point about these Messiah figures is that they both, like Jesus, ended their campaigns with apparent failure. Simon bar Giora was beaten, scourged and executed like Jesus. Simon bar Kokhba was called 'the king, the Messiah'. Neither left any lasting movement. When they were defeated, their followers did not suddenly make claims that they were the Messiah after all. Instead they drifted away, looked for other Messiahs, or gave up on the whole idea altogether.

'The stone that the builders rejected'

The followers of Jesus did not give up on the idea. Instead they shouted it from the rooftops. They made it clear that he had been the Right Messiah all along. And not only did they believe he was the Messiah, but by believing that, lives were transformed: 'Now Jesus did many other signs in the presence of his disciples, which are not written in this book. But these are written so that you may come to believe that Jesus is the Messiah, the Son of God, and that through believing you may have life in his name' (John 20:30–31).

They truly believed that the end-time kingdom he spoke about was both still to come and also already arriving. Its full implementation would be in the future, in the new heaven and the new earth, until then it would be found in the revolutionary love of its citizens: the kingdom of heaven arriving in people-shaped instalments.

In the end, Jesus did all the things expected of the Messiah, but he did them all in completely the wrong way. Like Eric Morecambe, he was a Messiah who played the right notes, but not necessarily in the right order. He drove out the enemy, but the enemy proved to be not the Romans, but death. He renewed the temple, but the temple proved to be his body, rebuilt after just three days. He brought in a new kingdom, but it was not a worldly kingdom, it was a kingdom of servanthood, of love, of peace. And it was never to end.

One of the early church's favourite ways of describing Jesus was drawn from the Old Testament. In an image which reminds us of Jesus' career as a builder, they pictured Jesus as the cornerstone of a building, the key foundation point: 'The stone that the builders rejected has become the very head of the corner' (1 Pet. 2:6–7).[19]

They knew that Jesus looked all wrong. He was a misshapen lump of rock to most people, something on which they stubbed their toe, or tripped over. To any right-minded builder he was only good for chucking into the skip. But the amazing thing was that this very stone, this useless lump of rock, became the foundation of a whole new building.

Not a building that looked like anything which had gone before. Not a Roman basilica, not a Herodian palace, not even a Jewish temple. It was an entirely new bit of architecture, this one. A building open to anyone who wanted to come in, a building which offered bread and wine and a welcome to all those who thought that such things were not for them. A building dedicated to peace, not war. A building of worship, friendship, stories and … well, let's just say that all of human life is here.

Of course, over the years things have gone wrong with it. Some of the decoration is a bit old fashioned, some of the floorboards are worn and there are some nasty cracks in the ceiling. It needs a bit of renovation, maybe, this building. Its true purpose has sometimes been forgotten. Each generation needs to take a long, hard look at it, pull some bits down, build other bits up. Restore it to its original use. But that is always the way with old buildings.

It's OK, though, because the foundation is still solid. Still secure. The cornerstone is still in place.

It looks wrong, I know.

But it has proved to be triumphantly, surprisingly, enduringly, eternally right.

NOTES

ABBREVIATIONS

Antiquities Josephus, *Antiquities*

ABD   *The Anchor Bible Dictionary*, ed. David Noel Freedman (New York: Doubleday, 1999)

BDAG   Arndt, William, Frederick W. Danker and Walter Bauer, *A Greek-English Lexicon of the New Testament and Other Early Christian Literature* (3rd ed. Chicago: University of Chicago Press, 2000)

Danby   Danby, Herbert, *The Mishnah, Translated From the Hebrew* (London: Oxford University Press, 1933)

Jeremias Jeremias, Joachim, *Jerusalem in the Time of Jesus: An Investigation Into Economic and Social Conditions During the New Testament Period* (London: SCM, 1974)

NIDNTT *New International Dictionary of New Testament Theology*, ed. Colin Brown (Exeter: Paternoster, 1986)

TLW   Page, Nick, *The Longest Week: What Really Happened During Jesus' Final Days* (London: Hodder & Stoughton, 2009)

War   Josephus, *The Jewish War*

INTRODUCTION

1 *TLW*, 9–12.
2 *Antiquities* 18.3.3.
3 On the authenticity of this passage, see Meier, John P., *A Marginal Jew: Rethinking the Historical Jesus* (New York: Doubleday, 1991), 1: 59–67.
4 *Antiquities* 20.200 in Meier, *A Marginal Jew*, 1: 60.
5 *War* 6.312–315 in Wright, N. T., *The New Testament and the People of God* (London: SPCK, 1992), 312.
6 Frerichs, Ernest S., William Scott Green and Jacob Neusner, *Judaisms and Their Messiahs at the Turn of the Christian Era* (Cambridge: Cambridge University Press, 1987), 3.
7 Ps So. 17.23–24ff. in Charlesworth, James H., *The Old Testament Pseudepigrapha* (London: Darton, Longman & Todd, 1983), 2: 667.
8 For an overview of the different views see Wright, N. T., *Jesus and the Victory of God* (London: SPCK, 1996), 481ff.
9 Wright, *Jesus and the Victory of God*, 658.

1. BETHLEHEM

1 Jerome, Letter 58 to Paulinus, cited in Keener, Craig S., *The Gospel of Matthew: A Socio-Rhetorical Commentary* (Grand Rapids: Eerdmans, 2009), 103.
2 On Gospel stories as testimony, see Bauckham, Richard, *Jesus and the Eyewitnesses: The Gospels as Eyewitness Testimony* (Grand Rapids: Eerdmans, 2006).

3   *Antiquities* 17.167.

4   Irenaeus, *Against Heresies*, 3.21.3; Clement *Stromata*, quoted in Finegan, Jack, *Handbook of Biblical Chronology* (Peabody: Hendrickson, 1998), 276–278.

5   See Ernest L. Martin, 'The Nativity and Herod's Death', in Finegan, Jack, Jerry Vardaman and Edwin M. Yamauchi, *Chronos, Kairos, Christos: Nativity and Chronological Studies Presented to Jack Finegan* (Winona Lake: Eisenbrauns, 1989), 85 ff.; Finegan, *Handbook of Biblical Chronology*, 292ff. On the eclipse see Summers, Ray and Jerry Vardaman, *Chronos, Kairos, Christos II: Chronological, Nativity, and Religious Studies in Memory of Ray Summers* (Macon: Mercer University Press, 1998), 88.

6   Finegan, Vardaman and Yamauchi, *Chronos, Kairos, Christos*, 128; Finegan places the course of Abijah in the week of 17–24 Heshvan (10–17 November). Finegan, *Handbook of Biblical Chronology*, 276–278. See also Roger T. Beckwith, 'St Luke, The Date of Christmas and the Priestly Courses at Qumran', *RQ* 9, 1977, 73–94.

7   These would be lunar, rather than calendar months.

8   Clement suggested that the birth of Christ was dated 194 years, 1 month and 13 days before the death of Commodus. Since Commodus was murdered on 31 December 192, this would make it 18 November 3 BC. The year is probably wrong, but the time of year would be more likely to be remembered.

9   Based on Finegan, Vardaman and Yamauchi, *Chronos, Kairos, Christos*, 124.

10 The word is nothing to do with Nazareth: it is a Hebrew word probably linked to the idea of purity.

11 Nolland, John, *Luke 1–9:20* (Dallas: Word Books, 1989), 65.

12 Crossan, John Dominic, *The Historical Jesus: The Life of a Mediterranean Jewish Peasant* (Edinburgh: T & T Clark, 1993), 124ff. Against this see Shanks, Hershel and Ben Witherington, *The Brother of Jesus: The Dramatic Story & Meaning of the First Archaeological Link to Jesus & His Family* (London: Continuum, 2003), 101; Thiede thinks they were quite well off, but this is unlikely given Joseph's trade; Thiede, Carsten Peter, *The Cosmopolitan World of Jesus: New Findings From Archaeology* (London: SPCK, 2004), 19–20.

13 The regulations are in Leviticus 12:8.

14 m. Ketub. 1:2; m. Yebam. 4:10; 6:4.

15 m. Ketub. 1:2; m. Yebam. 2:6.

16 m. Ketub. 5:2; m. Ned. 10:5; Safrai, Shemuel and M. Stern, *The Jewish People in the First Century: Historical Geography, Political History, Social, Cultural and Religious Life and Institutions* (Crint: Van Gorcum, 1974), 757.

17 Hanson, K.C., *Palestine in the Time of Jesus: Social Structures and Social Conflicts* (Minneapolis: Augsburg Fortress, 2002), 31–32.

18 Bernheim, Pierre-Antoine, *James, Brother of Jesus* (London: SCM, 1997), 33–34.

19 Malina, Bruce J., *The Social World of Jesus and the Gospels* (London: Routledge, 1996), 97.

20 Vermes, Geza, *The Changing Faces of Jesus* (London: Penguin, 2000), 151–152; Crossan, *The Historical Jesus: The Life of a Mediterranean Jewish Peasant*, 4.

21 Keener, *The Gospel of Matthew: A Socio-Rhetorical Commentary*, 93–94.

22 Finegan, *Handbook of Biblical Chronology*, 302–303.

23 Summers and Vardaman, *Chronos, Kairos, Christos II*, 65.

24 *Antiquities* 18.3–4.

25 *Antiquities* 17.42.

26 Barnett, Paul W., 'ἀπογραφή and ἀπογραφεσθαι in Luke 2 1–5', *Expository Times* 85(12), 1974, 378.

27 Brown, Raymond E., *The Birth of the Messiah: A Commentary on the Infancy Narratives in Matthew and Luke* (New York: Doubleday, 1993), 549.

28 Sherwin-White, A. N., *Roman Society and Roman Law in the New Testament* (Oxford: Clarendon Press, 1963), 163.

29 Bailey, Kenneth E., *Jesus Through Middle Eastern Eyes: Cultural Studies in the Gospels* (London: SPCK, 2008), 31ff.

30 m. Qidd 4.14.

31 b. Sanh. 25b, in *Jeremias*, 304.

32 B.K. 94b Bar., quoted in *Jeremias*, 311.

33 Babylonian Talmud: Sanh. 25b.

34 *Jeremias*, 306.

35 Nolland, *Luke 1–9:20*, 79.

36 Meier, *A Marginal Jew*, 1:205.

37 Yeshu and Yeshua remained common names among Jews until around the second century, when they revived the use of Joshua. One reason may well be that the Christians had made the use of Yeshua unattractive.

38 Based on Bauckham, *Jesus and the Eyewitnesses*, 85–89. The list was compiled from data collected by Tal Ilan.

39 http://www.statistics.gov.uk/specials/babiesnames_boys.asp. The top ten are Jack, Oliver, Thomas, Harry, Joshua, Alfie, Charlie, Daniel, James, William.

40 See Genesis 17:11–12; 21:4; Leviticus 12:3.

41 Some studies deny that it was the custom to take the firstborn to the temple for a dedication, but Nehemiah 10:35–36 implies just such an activity.

42 Nolland, *Luke 1–9:20*, 117–118.

43 For a detailed study of Anna, see Bauckham, Richard, *Gospel Women: Studies of the Named Women in the Gospels* (Edinburgh: T & T Clark, 2002), 77ff.

44 Bauckham, *Gospel Women*, 90.

45 On magi, see Keener, *The Gospel of Matthew: A Socio-Rhetorical Commentary*, 99. According to Roman belief, a star guided Aeneas to the place where Rome was to be founded.

46 'ἀπό ἀνατολων' and 'εν τη ἀνατολη' (Matthew 2:1–3).

47 Finegan, Vardaman and Yamauchi, *Chronos, Kairos, Christos*, 41.

48 Finegan, Vardaman and Yamauchi, *Chronos, Kairos, Christos*, 45–46.

49 Keener, *The Gospel of Matthew: A Socio-Rhetorical Commentary*, 101.

50 Keener, *The Gospel of Matthew: A Socio-Rhetorical Commentary*, 104.

51 *War* 1.656. The version in the *Antiquities* (c. AD 94) is even more disgusting than that in the *War* (c. AD 75). See Ladouceur, David J., 'The Death of Herod the Great', *Classical Philology* 76(1), 1981, 30. For more on Herod's death, see Litchfield, W. Reid, 'The Bittersweet Demise of Herod the Great', *Journal of the Royal Society of Medicine* 91, 1998; Sandison, A.T., 'The Last Illness of Herod the Great, King of Judaea', *Medical History* 11(4), 1967.

52 Herodotus, *Herodotus: The Histories* (London: Penguin, 1972), 339; 2 Maccabees 9:9; Acts 12:23. See Ashrafian, H., 'Herod the Great and His Worms', *Journal of Infectious Diseases* 51(1), 2005.

53 Although we know him now as Herod the Great, there is no evidence he was called that in his lifetime. His grandson Agrippa called himself 'the great king' on some of his coins, and probably the title transferred itself to his grandfather. See Richardson, Peter, *Herod: King of the Jews and Friend of the*

Romans (Edinburgh: T & T Clark, 1999), 12–14.

54 Richardson, *Herod: King of the Jews and Friend of the Romans*, 178.

55 Richardson, *Herod: King of the Jews and Friend of the Romans*, 185.

56 Bammel, Ernst and C. F. D. Moule, *Jesus and the Politics of His Day* (Cambridge: Cambridge University Press, 1984), 278.

57 *Antiquities*, 14.403–404.

58 Richardson, *Herod: King of the Jews and Friend of the Romans*, 186–187.

59 *Antiquities*, 15.240–246.

60 Richardson, *Herod: King of the Jews and Friend of the Romans*, 224.

61 On Herod, see 'Herod the Great (Person)', *ABD*, 4:161–169.

62 *Testament of Moses*, 6:2–6, quoted in Richardson, *Herod: King of the Jews and Friend of the Romans*, 298.

63 *Antiquities*, 16.393–394.

64 *Antiquities*, 17.44.

65 Richardson, *Herod: King of the Jews and Friend of the Romans*, 15. The eagle itself was probably a low relief stone sculpture, which had been covered with gold leaf.

66 France, Richard T., 'Herod and the Children of Bethlehem', *Novum Testamentum* 21(2), 1979, 114.

67 Richardson, *Herod: King of the Jews and Friend of the Romans*, 36.

68 Josephus, Flavius, G. A. Williamson and E. Mary Smallwood, *The Jewish War* (Harmondsworth: Penguin, 1981), 121.

2. NAZARETH

1 On the seven different wills of Herod, see Richardson, *Herod: King of the Jews and Friend of the Romans*, 33–36.

2 *War*, 2.50, in Josephus, Williamson and Smallwood, *The Jewish War*, 125.

3 *Antiquities*, 17.269.

4 *War*, 2.60.

5 *Antiquities*, 17.271–272. He was not the only robber-chief trying to seize power. According to Josephus, 'he attacked other aspirants to power', *War*, 2.56.

6 *Antiquities*, 17.288–289.

7 *War*, 2.74–76, in Josephus, Williamson and Smallwood, *The Jewish War*, 128.

8 *War*, 2.293–314.

9 Plutarch, *Precepts of Statecraft* X, quoted in Lewis, Naphtali, and Meyer Reinhold, *Roman Civilization: Selected Readings* (New York: Columbia University Press, 1990), 231.

10 Babylonian Talmud Sabbath 33b. Translation by M. Hadas, *Philological Quarterly* 8, 1929, 373.

11 Josephus, *Life*, 235.

12 Horsley, Richard A., *Galilee: History, Politics, People* (Pennsylvania: Trinity Press, 1995), 110.

13 Hanson, *Palestine in the Time of Jesus*, 58.

14 Based on Bauckham, *Jesus and the Eyewitnesses*, 89–91.

15 It was Jerome, writing in the fourth century, who came up with the idea that Jesus' brothers were actually his cousins. By this time the doctrine of the perpetual virginity of Mary had been joined by the perpetual virginity of Joseph – each of them doomed to a gloomily unfulfilled marriage.

16 Meier, *A Marginal Jew*, 1:318–332 has a detailed discussion.

17 For the different views of Jesus' brothers, see Shanks and Witherington, *The Brother of Jesus*, 94–95; Brown, *The Birth of the Messiah*, 132; P. Bernheim, *James, Brother of Jesus* (London: SCM, 1997), 1–29; Witherington, *The Gospel of Mark: Socio-Rhetorical Commentary*, 192–195.

18 See Meier, *A Marginal Jew*, 1:276–278.

19 Jeremias, Joachim, *New Testament Theology* (New York: Scribner, 1971), 5–6; references Mark 9:43, 45, 47; Matthew 23:7; 5:22; 6:24.

20 Meier, *A Marginal Jew*, 1:258.

21 At Qumran, for example, the literature of the community was produced mostly in 'post-biblical' Hebrew, e.g. The Manual of Discipline, The Thanksgiving Hymns, The Pesher on Habakkuk, The War Scroll, etc. Meier, *A Marginal Jew*, 1:256, 263. Hebrew was a religious language and eventually it developed into the type of Hebrew used for the Mishnah.

22 T. Kiddushin 1.11; Sifre Deut. 46 in Safrai and Stern, *The Jewish People in the First Century*, 947.

23 Safrai and Stern, *The Jewish People in the First Century*, 951.

24 P.T. Sotah III, 19a in Safrai and Stern, *The Jewish People in the First Century*, 955.

25 m. Hagig 1:1.

26 m. Hagig 1:1–4 in Danby, Herbert, *The Mishnah, Translated From the Hebrew* (London: Oxford University Press, 1933), 211, n. 10. This was the school of Shammai's ruling. The school of Hillel had it the other way round.

27 Quoted in *TLW*, 102.

28 On Jerusalem as a temple economy see *TLW*, 82ff.

29 Long, David E., *The Hajj Today: A Survey of the Contemporary Makkah Pilgrimage* (Albany: State University of New York Press, 1979), 27.

30 Philo, *Spec. Laws.* 1.74, 156.

31 Flusser, David and R. Steven Notley, *The Sage From Galilee: Rediscovering Jesus' Genius* (Grand Rapids: Eerdmans, 2007), 11.

32 Sipre Num §22; b Ber 24a; b Yom. 82a, cited Nolland, *Luke 1–9:20*, 127.

33 Bock, Darrell L., *Luke* (Grand Rapids: Baker Books, 1994), 267.

34 See Marshall, I. Howard, *The Gospel of Luke: A Commentary on the Greek Text* (Exeter: Paternoster, 1978), 128.

35 Brown, *The Birth of the Messiah*, 475.

36 Fillon, Mike, 'The Real Face of Jesus', *Popular Mechanics*, 2002. Fillon claims 5'1" but gives no source for the statistics. The male skeletons of the fifteen ossuaries found near Jerusalem were an average of 167 centimetres, or 5 feet 5 inches. See Haas, N., 'Anthropological Observations on the Skeletal Remains from Gi'vat ha-Mivtar', *Israel Exploration Journal* 20, 1970, 38–59. However, these were reasonably well-off people (as they had a family grave). Poorer people would have been shorter because of their diet.

37 Beasley-Murray, George R., *John* (Waco: Word Books, 1987), 347.

38 Hanson, *Palestine in the Time of Jesus*, 20–21.

39 Balz, Horst and Gerhard Schneider, *Exegetical Dictionary of the New Testament* (Grand Rapids: Eerdmans, 1990), 3:342.

40 See Matthew 7:24–27; 21:42; Luke 6:41–42, 48–49; 14:28; 23:31. Guelich, Robert A., *Mark 1–8:26* (Dallas: Word Books, 1989), 310. Gundry, Robert H., *Mark: A Commentary on His Apology for the Cross* (Grand Rapids: Eerdmans, 1993), 290, 296. Thiede, *The Cosmopolitan World of Jesus*, 15.

41 *Antiquities*, 18.27. The University of Florida expedition found many buildings with bedrock foundations, indicating that they were new or rebuilds. This

would support Josephus' account and indicate that buildings such as the theatre were built during the reign of Herod Antipas. Horsley, Richard A., *Archaeology, History, and Society in Galilee: The Social Context of Jesus and the Rabbis* (Valley Forge: Trinity Press International, 1996), 50.

42 Hoehner, Harold W., *Herod Antipas* (Cambridge: Cambridge University Press, 1972), 84–87.

43 Batey, Richard A., 'Is This Not the Carpenter?', *New Testament Studies* 30, 1984, 250.

44 Josephus describes Japha as 'the largest village of all Galilee, and encompassed with very strong walls, and had a great number of inhabitants in it'. *Life*, 1.230; Horsley, *Archaeology, History, and Society in Galilee*, 101.

45 Freyne, Seán, *Galilee, From Alexander the Great to Hadrian, 323 B.C.E. to 135 C.E.: A Study of Second Temple Judaism* (Edinburgh: T & T Clark, 1998), 124; Roller, Duane W., *The Building Program of Herod the Great* (Berkeley: University of California Press, 1998), 243.

46 See Stanton, Graham, *The Gospels and Jesus* (Oxford: Oxford University Press, 1989), 147.

47 It is unlikely that it was a full-on Roman city, though: no evidence of things like a gymnasium or a hippodrome have so far been found.

48 Josephus, *Life*, 33–36.

49 *Antiquities*, 18.36, cited in Richardson, *Herod: King of the Jews and Friend of the Romans*, 306.

50 m. Avot 2.1–2.

51 m. Avot 1.10 in Neusner, Jacob, *The Mishnah: A New Translation* (New Haven: Yale University Press: Accordance electronic edition, 1988).

52 Thomas Carney, quoted in Myers, Ched, *Binding the Strong Man: A Political Reading of Mark's Story of Jesus* (Maryknoll: Orbis, 2008), 51.

53 Horsley and Hanson, *Bandits, Prophets, and Messiahs*, 53.

54 *Antiquities*, 17.318.

55 Carter, Warren, *Pontius Pilate* (Collegeville, Liturgical Press, 2003), 35.

56 The Romans also made money through the selling of monopolies. They owned certain trades and industries and sold licences and contracts to run them. These were often in luxury goods: aromatic balsam, purple dye, cedar from Lebanon, or the vital salt trade. Hanson, K. C., 'The Galilean Fishing Economy and the Jesus Tradition', *Biblical Theology Bulletin* 27, 1997.

57 Myers, *Binding the Strong Man*, 52.

58 Rabbi Gamaliel, quoted in MacMullen, Ramsay, *Enemies of the Roman Order: Treason, Unrest, and Alienation in the Empire* (Cambridge: Harvard University Press, 1966), 148.

3. WILDERNESS

1 Some have suggested that Luke was using the alternative calendar in use in Syria, which began the regnal year on 1 October, but Luke was writing for a Roman audience, so it is unlikely that he used an Eastern system of dating. Or that he used the Jewish system of dating, which began each regnal year on 1 Nisan, i.e. mid-March; Ogg, George, *The Chronology of the Public Ministry of Jesus* (Cambridge: Cambridge University Press, 1940), 200. Supporters of an earlier date for Jesus' ministry suggest that the dating starts from a shared regency with Augustus, dating from c. AD 11–12, but there is little evidence for this.

2 *Antiquities*, 19.275; cf. *War*, 2.215. See Nolland, *Luke 1–9:20*, 140.

3   Funk, Robert W., 'The Wilderness', *Journal of Biblical Literature* 78(3), 1959, 209; Notley, R. Steven and Anson F. Rainey, *Carta's New Century Handbook and Atlas of the Bible* (Jerusalem: Carta, 2007), 18.

4   See also *Antiquities*, 20.167; *War*, 2.622.

5   1QS 8.13b–14, García, Martínez, Florentino and Eibert J. C. Tigchelaar, *The Dead Sea Scrolls Study Edition* (Leiden: Brill, 1997), 89.

6   On other candidates for the Qumran Community see Dapaah, Daniel S., *The Relationship Between John the Baptist and Jesus of Nazareth: A Critical Study* (Lanham: University Press of America, 2005), 38–39.

7   It has been suggested that John was raised at Qumran, sent there by his parents, or after his parents had died – they were, after all, elderly (Luke 1:7). See Dapaah, *The Relationship Between John the Baptist and Jesus of Nazareth*, 41–42.

8   Keener, Craig S., *The Historical Jesus of the Gospels* (Grand Rapids: Eerdmans, 2009), 171.

9   *War*, 1.480.

10 *Antiquities,* 18.116–118.

11 1 Tosephta to m.Shabbat 13b. Quoted in Magen, Yitzhak, 'Ancient Israel's Stone Age: Purity in Second Temple times', *Biblical Archaeology Review* 24(5), Sept/Oct 1998. Of the many ritual baths which have been discovered, almost all of them date from the second temple period.

12 Keener, Craig S., *The Gospel of John: A Commentary* (Peabody: Hendrickson, 2003), 443–444.

13 CD-A 10.11, García and Tigchelaar, *The Dead Sea Scrolls Study Edition*, 567.

14 1Qs V in Vermes, Geza, *The Complete Dead Sea Scrolls in English* (London: Penguin, 2004), 104. See also 1QS III in Vermes, *The Complete Dead Sea Scrolls in English*, 100.

15 See 1QS 3.2–3; 6.17, 25; 7.3, 16, 19. They had to be properly dressed as well. Garments were required to be spotlessly clean or rubbed with incense to purify them, CD 11.3–4; 10.12.

16 'Herod the Great (Person)', in *ABD*, 3:164.

17 Keener, *The Gospel of John: A Commentary*, 445.

18 It's an Aramaic pun: the word for 'children' (*benayya*) is almost identical to that for stones (*abnayya*). Hagner, Donald A., *Matthew 1–13* (Dallas: Word Books, 1993), 50.

19 *Antiquities*, 17.314.

20 *Antiquities*, 17.339–341; *War*, 2.111.

21 Goodman, *The Ruling Class of Judaea*, 40–41.

22 Notley and Rainey, *Carta's New Century Handbook and Atlas of the Bible*, 235.

23 Goodman, *The Ruling Class of Judaea*, 111.

24 Millar, *The Roman Near East, 31 BC–AD 337*, 362. It is possible that Elihoeni, high priest from AD 43–45, was Caiaphas' son and Ananus' grandson; *TLW*, 173.

25 *Antiquities*, 20.8.8, Kraeling, *John the Baptist*, 25.

26 Funk, 'The Wilderness', 210–211.

27 Dapaah, *The Relationship Between John the Baptist and Jesus of Nazareth*, 46.

28 *Antiquities*, 18.4.1.

29 *Antiquities*, 20.5.1.

30 *Antiquities*, 18.118.

31 Matthew 3:11 and Luke 3:16 say 'the Holy Spirit and fire'.

32 Keener, *The Historical Jesus of the Gospels*, 169.

33 Finegan, *Handbook of Biblical Chronology*, 342.

34 'Day of Atonement', *ABD*, 3:73.

35 Tsafrir, Yoram, 'The Maps Used by Theodosius: On the Pilgrim Maps of the Holy Land and Jerusalem in the Sixth Century C.E.', *Dumbarton Oaks Papers* 40, 1986, 133.

36 Matthew has: 'This is my Son, the Beloved, with whom I am well pleased' (Matthew 3:17).

37 The version of Matthew 3:3 in the *Gospel of the Hebrews* runs, 'The mother of the Lord and his brothers said to him, "John the Baptist baptises for the forgiveness of sins; let us go and be baptised by him." But he said to them, "In what way have I sinned that I should go and be baptised by him? Unless, perhaps, what I have just said is a sin of ignorance."' Quoted in Jerome, *Against Pelagius* 3:2. Version found in Throckmorton, Burton Hamilton, *Gospel Parallels: A Synopsis of the First Three Gospels With Alternative Readings From the Manuscripts and Noncanonical Parallels* (Nashville: Nelson, 1979), 10.

38 Dunn, James D. G., *Jesus and the Spirit: A Study of the Religious and Charismatic Experience of Jesus and the First Christians as Reflected in the New Testament* (Philadelphia: Westminster Press, 1980), 63.

39 Dunn, *Jesus and the Spirit*, 62–65.

40 Yoder, John Howard, *The Politics of Jesus: Vicit Agnus Noster* (Grand Rapids: Eerdmans, 1972), 31.

41 Hauerwas, Stanley, *The Peaceable Kingdom: A Primer in Christian Ethics* (London: SCM, 2003), 79.

42 *Antiquities*, 15.412.

43 See Nolland, *Luke 1–9:20*, 181. Nolland is mistaken, however, to say that it only comes from Hegesippus. Eusebius clearly quotes Clement first.

44 Eusebius, *The Ecclesiastical History and the Martyrs of Palestine*, trans. Hugh Jackson Lawlor and John Ernest Leonard Oulton (London: SPCK, 1927), 1:57.

45 Eusebius, *Ecclesiastical History*, 2.22.3 in Eusebius, *The Ecclesiastical History and the Martyrs of Palestine*, 1:56.

46 His authorship has been questioned. Since we only have excerpts from the work, it is a moot point. Harnack believed the work to be the product of a young, unorthodox Clement and that later he changed his mind about some of the statements. If that were true, it would date the work to c. AD 180. See 'The Place of the Hypotyposeis in the Clementine Corpus: An Apology for "The Other Clement of Alexandria"', *Journal of Early Christian Studies* 17(3), 2009, 313–335.

47 *War*, 4.343.

48 Roland, Victor 'The Mosaic Map of Madeba', *The Biblical Archaeologist* 21(3), 1958, 61–62.

49 Beasley-Murray, *John* (Waco: Word Books, 1987), 20–21.

50 Notley and Rainey, *Carta's New Century Handbook and Atlas of the Bible*, 226.

51 For more on this theory see Parker, Pierson, 'Bethany beyond Jordan', *Journal of Biblical Literature* 74(4), 1955. Admittedly it does not work with the timetable. You would be hard pressed to walk the seventy or so miles from Bethany near Jerusalem to Cana in Galilee in two or three days. But that assumes that

John's timetable is a real week and not a literary arrangement. The same argument counts against a location in the southern Jordan valley as well.

52 See Bauckham, *Jesus and the Eyewitnesses*, 391–393.

53 Matthew's version takes place at Caesarea Philippi (Matthew 16:18).

54 Richardson, *Herod: King of the Jews and Friend of the Romans*, 302.

55 Beasley-Murray, *John*, 27; Keener, *The Gospel of John: A Commentary*, 482.

56 Parker, 'Bethany beyond Jordan', 261.

57 Beasley-Murray, *John*, 34.

58 See Derrett, *Law in the New Testament*, 228–238.

59 Finegan, *Handbook of Biblical Chronology*, 348–349.

60 Goodman, Martin, *The Ruling Class of Judaea: The Origins of the Jewish Revolt Against Rome, A.D. 66–70* (Cambridge: Cambridge University Press, 1987), 74.

61 See Martin Hengel, quoted in Bammel and Moule, *Jesus and the Politics of His Day*, 142.

62 Köstenberger, Andreas J., *John* (Grand Rapids: Baker Academic, 2004), 119–120.

63 Keener, *The Gospel of John: A Commentary*, 1:543.

64 Keener, *The Gospel of John: A Commentary*, 1:551.

65 Nor is there any direct route between the two places, making it unlikely that one would be identified by its relationship to the other. Murphy-O'Connor, Jerome, 'John the Baptist and Jesus: History and Hypotheses', *New Testament Studies* 36, 1990, 365. The mosaic map found at Madeba and dating from c. AD 560 shows two Aenon sites; one following Eusebius, and the other marked 'Aenon now Sapsaphas' located east of the Jordan and just north of the Dead Sea; Notley and Rainey, *Carta's New Century Handbook and Atlas of the Bible*, 226.

66 For Robinson's identification see Stevens, Wm. Arnold, 'Ænon near to Salim', *Journal of the Society of Biblical Literature and Exegesis* 3(2), 1883, 133–136. For a modern identification see Murphy-O'Connor, 'John the Baptist and Jesus: History and Hypotheses', 364–365. Others state that both sites were in Samaria: Köstenberger, *John*, 135; Lindars, Barnabas, *The Gospel of John: Based on the Revised Standard Version* (Grand Rapids: Eerdmans, 1981), 165.

67 Tractate Kutim 28.

68 Crown, Alan David, *The Samaritans* (Tübingen: J.C.B. Mohr (Paul Siebeck), 1989), 35.

69 Crown, *The Samaritans*, 35–36.

70 *Antiquities*, 18.29–30.

71 Köstenberger, *John*, 135.

72 It has been suggested that Apollos (Acts 18:24–19:7), who only knew the baptism of John, was actually baptised by Jesus during this period. 'It is neither said or suggested anywhere in the text that Apollos and others were disciples of John. They had received the baptism of John, and the real question is: who administered it?', Murphy-O'Connor, 'John the Baptist and Jesus: History and Hypotheses', 367. This is an intriguing suggestion, which I shall try to take up in the next book in this series!

73 Lindars, *The Gospel of John*, 137.

74 Murphy-O'Connor, 'John the Baptist and Jesus: History and Hypotheses', 369. O'Connor argues that he was arrested in Galilee. This seems unlikely to me, given that he was taken to the Machaerus prison, way down south.

75 *Antiquities*, 18.118–119.

76 Herodias was a relative, the granddaughter of Herod I. See Connolly, Peter, *Living in the Time of Jesus of Nazareth* (Oxford: Oxford University Press, 1983), 39. The Herodian family tree is extremely confusing. There is a huge chart in Richardson, *Herod: King of the Jews and Friend of the Romans*, 46–51.

77 After John's death, Aretas did avenge the insult to his daughter by soundly defeating Antipas' army. See *Antiquities*, 18.109–115. Scobie, Charles Hugh Hope, *John the Baptist* (London: SCM, 1964), 180.

78 Webb, Robert L., *John the Baptizer and Prophet: A Socio-Historical Study* (Sheffield: JSOT Press, 1991), 366–367.

79 Webb, *John the Baptizer and Prophet*, 368.

4. CAPERNAUM

1 *ABD*, 4:608–609.

2 Bailey, *Jesus Through Middle Eastern Eyes*, 201.

3 m.Nid 4.1.

4 Bailey, *Jesus Through Middle Eastern Eyes*, 210.

5 Keener, *The Gospel of John: A Commentary*, 631.

6 Theissen, Gerd and Annette Merz, *The Historical Jesus: A Comprehensive Guide* (London: SCM, 1998), 166–167.

7 Horsley, *Galilee: History, Politics, People*, 194–195.

8 See p. 65.

9 *War*, 3.509.

10 Hanson, 'The Galilean Fishing Economy and the Jesus Tradition'. The name means 'fish-salting tower'.

11 Hanson, 'The Galilean Fishing Economy and the Jesus Tradition'.

12 *ABD*, 1:866–869.

13 Luke 15:8–10.

14 Mark 2:3–4.

15 For a full account of this see Strange, James F. and Shanks, Hershel, 'Has the House Where Jesus Stayed in Capernaum Been Found?', *Biblical Archaeology Review* 8(6), Nov/Dec 1982; Theissen and Merz, *The Historical Jesus: A Comprehensive Guide*, 167; Thiede, Carsten Peter, *Simon Peter, From Galilee to Rome* (Exeter: Paternoster, 1986), 25.

16 Rousseau, John J. and Rami Arav, *Jesus and His World: An Archaeological and Cultural Dictionary* (Minneapolis: Fortress Press, 1995), 40.

17 Woolf, Bertram Lee, *The Authority of Jesus and Its Foundation: A Study in the Four Gospels and the Acts* (London: Allen & Unwin, 1929), 84–85.

18 Meier, *A Marginal Jew*, 2:405.

19 Meier, *A Marginal Jew*, 2:406.

20 Eve, E. C. S., *The Jewish Context of Jesus' Miracles* (Sheffield: Sheffield Academic Press, 2002), 326–327.

21 Hooker, Morna Dorothy, *A Commentary on the Gospel According to St Mark* (London: A & C Black, 1991), 64.

22 Gundry, *Mark: A Commentary on His Apology for the Cross*, 74.

23 Hooker, *A Commentary on the Gospel According to St Mark*, 65; Lane, William L., *The Gospel According to Mark; the English Text With Introduction, Exposition, and Notes* (Grand Rapids: Eerdmans, 1974), 73–74.

24 Quoted in Lane, *The Gospel According to Mark*, 74, n. 118.

25 Deissmann, Adolf and Lionel Richard Mortimer Strachan, *Light From the*

Ancient East: The New Testament Illustrated by Recently Discovered Texts of the Graeco-Roman World (London: Hodder & Stoughton, 1910), 257.

26 Keener, *The Gospel of Matthew: A Socio-Rhetorical Commentary*, 272.

27 See Gundry, *Mark: A Commentary on His Apology for the Cross*, 77.

28 The words are *ekplesso* and *thambeomai*.

29 Corley, Kathleen E., *Private Women, Public Meals: Social Conflict in the Synoptic Tradition* (Peabody: Hendrickson, 1993), 87.

30 Yang, Yong-Eui, *Jesus and the Sabbath in Matthew's Gospel* (Sheffield: Sheffield Academic Press, 1997), 246.

31 Many manuscripts of Luke read 'Galilee'; Bock, *Luke*, 445.

32 'κωμόπλις', BDAG, 580.

33 Kazen, Thomas, *Jesus and Purity Halakhah: Was Jesus Indifferent to Impurity* (Stockholm: Almqvist & Wiksell, 2002), 98.

34 m.Neg 13.8, Danby, *The Mishnah, Translated From the Hebrew*, 694.

35 m.Neg 12.1.

36 Kazen, *Jesus and Purity Halakhah: Was Jesus Indifferent to Impurity*, 109.

37 Mark 6:11; 13:9. See Myers, *Binding the Strong Man*, 153.

38 Material which is brought together in Matthew is liberally distributed throughout Luke. They obviously used the same source, but arranged things differently. Luke even has the opposite terrain: he has Jesus teaching on a 'level place' (Luke 6:17) while his core talk is simpler, more direct (Luke 6:20–49), and probably formed the core of the considerably expanded version in Matthew.

39 Tob. 4:14–16; Sir. 31:14–16.

40 m.Avot 2.10 in Neusner, *The Mishnah: A New Translation*.

41 DSS, The Two Ways, 4Q473, in Vermes, *The Complete Dead Sea Scrolls in English*, 443.

42 Did. 1:1, in Holmes, Michael W., *The Apostolic Fathers: Greek Texts and English Translations* (Grand Rapids: Baker Academic, 2007), 345.

43 m.Avot 2.8–9, in Neusner, *The Mishnah: A New Translation*.

44 m. Gitin 9.10. See Attridge, Harold W., Wayne A. Meeks and Jouette M. Bassler, *HarperCollins Study Bible NRSV* (San Francisco: HarperOne, 2006), 1676, n. 5.32.

45 Josephus, *Life*, 1.426–427.

46 Banks, quoted in France, R. T., *The Gospel According to Matthew: An Introduction and Commentary* (Leicester: IVP, 1985), 128.

47 Donald A. Hagner, *Matthew 1–13*, 130–131.

48 See 'χιτών,' BDAG, 1085 'ἱμάτιον,' BDAG, 475. 'The situation is that of a lawsuit, in which the defendant is advised to give up not only the indispensable χιτον demanded by the opponent, but the ἱμάτιον as well.' In Luke the image is more of highway robbery, with the sequence reversed.

49 Yoder, *The Politics of Jesus*, 66–67.

50 France, *The Gospel According to Matthew*, 127.

51 m.Shebiith 10.3–4 in Danby, *The Mishnah, Translated From the Hebrew*, 51.

52 Horsley, Richard A. and John S. Hanson, *Bandits, Prophets, and Messiahs: Popular Movements in the Time of Jesus* (San Francisco: Harper & Row, 1988), 60.

53 Horsley and Hanson, *Bandits, Prophets, and Messiahs*, 61.

54 Kurlansky, Mark, *Nonviolence: The History of a Dangerous Idea* (London: Jonathan Cape, 2006), 5–7.

55 Enda McDonagh, quoted in Hauerwas, *The Peaceable Kingdom*, 114.

56 Kurlansky, *Nonviolence: The History of a Dangerous Idea*, 184.

57 Hays, Richard B., *The Moral Vision of the New Testament: Community, Cross, New Creation: A Contemporary Introduction to New Testament Ethics* (Edinburgh: T & T Clark, 1997), 321. He goes on, 'Paul's occasional use of military imagery … actually [has] the opposite effect: the warfare imagery is drafted into the service of the gospel rather than the reverse.'

58 Rev. 13:10. See Stassen, Glen Harold and David P. Gushee, *Kingdom Ethics: Following Jesus in Contemporary Context* (Downers Grove: IVP, 2003), 152.

59 Kurlansky, *Nonviolence: The History of a Dangerous Idea*, 21–23.

60 Stassen and Gushee, *Kingdom Ethics: Following Jesus in Contemporary Context*, 165.

61 Witherington, Ben, *The Gospel of Mark: Socio-Rhetorical Commentary*, 114.

62 Myers, *Binding the Strong Man*, 157.

63 It is possible that Jesus invited Levi and the others to *his* house: Mark's Greek is imprecise, although Luke's version claims it was a great banquet in Levi's home (Luke 5:29).

64 Yang, *Jesus and the Sabbath in Matthew's Gospel*, 87.

65 Jubilees 50:6–13. Carson, D. A., *From Sabbath to Lord's Day: A Biblical, Historical, and Theological Investigation* (Grand Rapids: Zondervan, 1982), 45.

66 Seneca, *De Superstitione*, quoted in Yang, *Jesus and the Sabbath in Matthew's Gospel*, 81.

67 Carson, *From Sabbath to Lord's Day*, 45.

68 Daniel-Rops, Henri and Patrick O'Brian, *Daily Life in Palestine at the Time of Christ* (London: Weidenfeld and Nicolson, 1962), 347–349.

69 See Myers, *Binding the Strong Man,* 141.

70 See 'μάστιξ', *BDAG*, 620–621; 'Beat, Chastise, Scourge', *NIDNTT*.

71 Witherington, *The Gospel of Mark: Socio-Rhetorical Commentary*, 143. Hooker sees it as a reminder that disease was originally seen as a 'chastisement for sin', Hooker, *A Commentary on the Gospel According to St Mark*, 110; Cranfield says that the word was used in classical Greek 'as well as the New Testament', Cranfield, C. E. B., *The Gospel According to Saint Mark: An Introduction and Commentary* (Cambridge: Cambridge University Press, 1972), 125. But this is a circular argument. It is only used that way in the New Testament because that is the way it is translated!

72 Guelich, *Mark 1–8:26*, 161.

73 Guelich, *Mark 1–8:26*, 162.

74 *War*, 4.316–317.

75 *Antiquities*, 18.23–24. Judas' descendants seem to have followed his ideas. His sons James and Simon were crucified by Tiberius Alexander, Roman prefect from AD 46 to 48. Manahem, his grandson, was active in the Great Revolt in AD 66 (*War*, 2.444). Another relative was Eleazar, a commander of the Sicarii at Masada. We have a revolutionary dynasty.

76 Bammel, Ernst and C. F. D. Moule, *Jesus and the Politics of His Day*, 115–116.

77 See, for example, Brandon, S. G. F., *Jesus and the Zealots: A Study of the Political Factor in Primitive Christianity* (Manchester: Manchester University Press, 1967). For a refutation of Brandon's theory see Sweet, J. P. M., 'The Zealots and Jesus' in Bammel and Moule, *Jesus and the Politics of His Day*, 1–9.

78 Guelich, *Mark 1–8:26*, 162–164.

5. GALILEE

1 Bock, *Luke*, 649.
2 Nolland, *Luke 1–9.20*, 323.
3 Nolland, *Luke 1–9.20*, 323–324.
4 See Mark 12:12; 14:1, 44, 46, 49. 'κρατέω', *BDAG*, 564.
5 The accusation of being in league with Beelzebul appears in the Synoptics (Matthew 10:25; 12:24, 27; Mark 3:22; Luke 11:18–20). In John, Jesus is accused of having a demon (John 7:20; 8:49, 52; 10:21), but Beelzebul is not specified.
6 Some think the name means 'lord of flies', from Baalzebub, and derives from a fly-god associated with the Philistine city of Ekron. Another suggestion is that it has to do with a Hebrew word meaning '(exalted) abode'. A high power, then. See 'Beelzebul', in *ABD*, 2:638–639.
7 Bock, *Luke*, 515–516.
8 Ilan, Tal, *Jewish Women in Greco-Roman Palestine: An Inquiry Into Image and Status* (Tübingen: J.C.B. Mohr (Paul Siebeck), 1995), 127.
9 Richer Jews got around this by wearing wigs. However, wigs were a luxury which only relatively well-off women could afford, another example of a purity exemption which only the upper classes could attain.
10 Danby, *The Mishnah, Translated From the Hebrew*, 794; Bailey, *Jesus Through Middle Eastern Eyes*, 248.
11 Bailey, *Jesus Through Middle Eastern Eyes*, 248.
12 Bock, *Luke*, 696, n. 10.
13 Bauckham, *Gospel Women: Studies of the Named Women in the Gospels*, 165ff. Witherington, Ben, *What Have They Done With Jesus?: Beyond Strange Theories and Bad History – Why We Can Trust the Bible* (San Francisco: HarperCollins, 2006), 18.
14 Midr. Lam. 2.2 cited in *ABD*, 5:578.
15 See for example Gos. Phil. 63–64.
16 Young, Brad, *Jesus and His Jewish Parables: Rediscovering the Roots of Jesus' Teaching* (New York: Paulist Press, 1989), 2–3.
17 2 Samuel 12:1–4; 14:6–8; 1 Kings 20:39–40; Isaiah 5:1–6; 28:24–28. Estimates vary of the number in the New Testament, depending on whether you include proverbial expressions.
18 Snodgrass, Klyne, *Stories With Intent: A Comprehensive Guide to the Parables of Jesus* (Grand Rapids: Eerdmans, 2008), 10.
19 Jeremias, cited in Myers, *Binding the Strong Man*, 176–177.
20 Myers, *Binding the Strong Man*, 191.
21 Witherington, *The Gospel of Mark: Socio-Rhetorical Commentary*. He is mistaken to say they were stationed in Palestine. There were no legions in Palestine itself, just auxiliaries. The Xth legion were involved in the assault on Jerusalem in the Jewish revolt. It's probable that before that they were stationed up the coast at Syria. No doubt some of their troops came south frequently.
22 Suggested in Myers, *Binding the Strong Man*, 193–194.
23 *War*, 4.488–490.
24 Horsley and Hanson, *Bandits, Prophets, and Messiahs*, 91 ff.; Myers, *Binding the Strong Man*, 64.
25 Levine, Amy-Jill, *The Misunderstood Jew* (New York: HarperOne, 2007), 23–24.
26 Matthew 9:35; Mark 1:21; 6:2; Luke 4:31; 6:6; 4:44, etc.

27 Yang, *Jesus and the Sabbath in Matthew's Gospel*, 244–245.

28 In inscriptions and in Jewish literature in Greek the word *synagogue* is not used of a building until the second half of the first century. There are first-century references to synagogue buildings elsewhere; Josephus uses the term to refer to buildings in cities outside Judea: Dora, Caesarea and Antioch; and an inscription in Cyrenaica from AD 56 talks about 'the synagogue of the Jews in Berenice' resolving that those who 'donated to the repairs of the synagogue' would be properly commemorated. Luke's depictions of synagogues as buildings may, therefore, reflect his own experience of Diaspora Jews in the Greco-Roman world. See Horsley, *Archaeology, History, and Society in Galilee*, 146.

29 m.Meg 3.1 in Danby, *The Mishnah, Translated From the Hebrew*, 204, n. 26.

30 Horsley, *Archaeology, History, and Society in Galilee*, 131–132.

31 Horsley, *Archaeology, History, and Society in Galilee*, 148–149.

32 *ABD*, 5:841–842.

33 Safrai and Stern, *The Jewish People in the First Century*, 2:935.

34 m.Avot 3.10 in Neusner, *The Mishnah: A New Translation*.

35 m.Meg 4.2 Danby, *The Mishnah, Translated From the Hebrew*, 206.

36 m.Meg 2.1 Danby, *The Mishnah, Translated From the Hebrew*, 203.

37 Bailey, *Jesus Through Middle Eastern Eyes*, 151.

38 m.Megillah 4.4 in Danby, *The Mishnah, Translated From the Hebrew*, 206.

39 Apostasy: Leviticus 20:2; Deuteronomy 13:11; 17:5. Sorcery: Leviticus 20:27. Sabbath violation: Numbers 15:35–36. Blasphemy: Leviticus 24:14, 16, 23; 1 Samuel 21:10. 'Punishments and Crimes (OT and ANE)', *ABD*, 6:555.

40 See 'Stephen (Person)', *ABD*, 6:209.

41 Matthew 10:9–10 and Luke 9:3 have an even tougher account. In their versions, the disciples do not even get to carry a staff or wear sandals.

42 See 'Dedication, Feast of', *ABD*, 3:124–125.

43 *Antiquities*, 12.325.

44 Keener, *The Gospel of John: A Commentary*, 636–637.

45 Page, Nick, *The One-Stop Bible Atlas* (Oxford: Lion Hudson, 2010), 93–95.

46 A suggested reading of this verse is: 'There was above the sheep pool (a house) which was called in the Hebrew Bethesda (or Bethsaida or Bethzatha) having five porches', Masterman, E. W. G., 'The Pool of Bethesda', *The Biblical World* 25(2), 1905, 90; Armstrong, Karen, *A History of Jerusalem: One City, Three Faiths* (London: HarperCollins, 1997), 109.

47 Wilkinson, John, *Jerusalem as Jesus Knew it: Archaeology as Evidence* (London: Thames and Hudson, 1978), 95–97; Armstrong, *A History of Jerusalem*, 129.

48 Not the same Emmaus as in Luke's Gospel. See *War*, 1.657; 2.614; 4.11.

49 Murphy-O'Connor, J., *The Holy Land: An Archaeological Guide from Earliest Times to 1700* (Oxford: Oxford University Press, 1986), 29–30.

50 Keener, *The Gospel of John: A Commentary*, 640.

51 On authorship, see Bauckham, *Jesus and the Eyewitnesses*.

6. TYRE, SIDON AND CAESAREA PHILIPPI

1 Salome was later to marry Philip the tetrarch, and after him Aristobulus. Philip was her uncle and Aristobulus her cousin. See Connolly, *Living in the Time of Jesus of Nazareth*, 39. Busch, Fritz-Otto, *The Five Herods* (London: Robert Hale, 1958), 120.

2 Stark, Rodney, *The Rise of Christianity: How the Obscure, Marginal Jesus*

Movement Became the Dominant Religious Force in the Western World in a *Few Centuries* (San Francisco: HarperSanFrancisco, 1997), 106–107.

3 Hoehner, *Herod Antipas*, 155–156.

4 Hoehner, *Herod Antipas*, 168. Roller, *The Building Program of Herod the Great*, 244. Taylor, Joan E., *John the Baptist Within Second Temple Judaism* (London: SPCK, 1997), 247. *Antiquities*, 18.240–255.

5 Arndt, William, *Luke* (Saint Louis: Concordia, 1986), 253.

6 Mark's editorial voice interrupts twice, first to explain the purity regulations and then to explain the implication of Jesus' statement (Mark 7:3–4, 19).

7 'Sewer' in NRSV, NJB, NET. Omitted entirely in NIV, TNIV, ESV.

8 Witherington, *The Gospel of Mark: Socio-Rhetorical Commentary*, 230.

9 The various interpretations of this statement are summarised in Witherington, *The Gospel of Mark: Socio-Rhetorical Commentary*, 228–230.

10 Arndt, *Luke*, 257.

11 See 'Magadan', AYBD, 5:462.

12 Satire 8, trans. Rolfe Humphries, quoted in Corley, *Private Women, Public Meals*, 98.

13 Richardson, *Herod: King of the Jews and Friend of the Romans*, 302.

14 Evans, Craig A., *Mark 8.27–16.20* (Dallas: Word Books, 1989), 13.

15 Plutarch, *De sera*, 9.554b, quoted in Witherington, *The Gospel of Mark: Socio-Rhetorical Commentary*, 244.

16 Yoder, *The Politics of Jesus*, 97.

17 Arndt, *Luke*, 262.

18 Witherington, *The Gospel of Mark: Socio-Rhetorical Commentary*, 260.

19 Bock, *Luke*, 871.

20 Gundry, *Mark: A Commentary on His Apology for the Cross*, 487.

21 Witherington, *The Gospel of Mark: Socio-Rhetorical Commentary*, 270.

22 m.Shek 1.3; Danby, *The Mishnah*, 152. Argued thus Witherington, *The Gospel of Mark: Socio-Rhetorical Commentary*, 316; William L. Lane, *The Gospel According to Mark; the English Text With Introduction, Exposition, and Notes* (Grand Rapids: Eerdmans, 1974), 405.

23 Bammel and Moule, *Jesus and the Politics of His Day*, 278.

24 On the tax, see *TLW*, 95–99. The Qumran community viewed it as a one-off payment, 4Q159 in Vermes, *The Complete Dead Sea Scrolls in English*, 530.

25 m.Shekel 2.4, in Danby, *The Mishnah*, 154.

26 The Talmud records that all 'the money of which the law speaks is Tyrian money', t.Ketub 12.

27 *War*, 4.105.

28 Richardson, *Building Jewish in the Roman East*, 246.

29 Richardson, *Building Jewish in the Roman East*, 247.

30 *TLW*, 98–99.

31 Catherine M. Murphy, *Wealth in the Dead Sea Scrolls and in the Qumran Community* (Leiden: Brill, 2002), 311–312.

32 See m.Shek 1.7.

33 Bammel and Moule, *Jesus and the Politics of His Day*, 283.

7. SAMARIA

1 Luke uses the Greek word for 'go, move along' frequently at the start of the jour-

ney, when they leave Capernaum (9:51–53, 56–57), but only infrequently after that (10:38; 13:31, 33; 17:11; 19:28). Fitzmyer, Joseph A., *The Gospel According to Luke* (New York; London: Doubleday, 1981), 824–825. And the Greek word for 'road' appears at the beginning (9:57; 10:4) but never again during this section. Jesus started going to Jerusalem. And then he halted.

2 Green, Joel B., *The Gospel of Luke* (Grand Rapids: Eerdmans, 1997), 408–409.

3 Sanders, E. P., *The Historical Figure of Jesus* (London: Penguin, 1995), 23–26.

4 *Jeremias*, 211.

5 b.Erubin 53b in Vermes, Geza, *The Changing Faces of Jesus* (London: Penguin, 2000).

6 Pollard, Nigel, *Soldiers, Cities, and Civilians in Roman Syria* (Ann Arbor: University of Michigan Press, 2000), 120.

7 See Freeman, Philip and D. L. Kennedy, *The Defence of the Roman and Byzantine East: Proceedings of a Colloquium Held At the University of Sheffield in April 1986* (Oxford: B.A.R., 1986), 2:311; Millar, Fergus, *The Roman Near East, 31 BC–AD 337* (Cambridge: Harvard University Press, 1993), 45.

8 Crown, *The Samaritans*, 61.

9 Fitzmyer, *The Gospel According to Luke*, 883.

10 Sukk. 4.9, cited in *ABD*, 6:25.

11 Throckmorton, *Gospel Parallels*, 25, 190.

12 Eusebius, *The Ecclesiastical History and the Martyrs of Palestine*, 2:101.

13 y.Sot. 7.1, 21b cited Ilan, *Jewish Women in Greco-Roman Palestine*, 127.

14 m.Sot 3.4 in Danby, *The Mishnah*, 296.

15 t.Sot 7.9, Ilan, *Jewish Women in Greco-Roman Palestine*, 191.

16 For a fuller version of this section, see *TLW*, 188–197.

17 Bull, Robert J., 'Caesarea Maritima: The Search for Herod's City', *Biblical Archaeology Review* 8(3), 1982.

18 The name comes from the *equites*, those Romans with enough money to serve as cavalry officers in the army (knights, in other words). To qualify for the equestrian rank, you had to have property worth 400,000 *sesterces* or more. In return you were given the title *eques* and you got to wear a toga with a purple border and a special gold ring and sit in the front row at the theatre. Goodman, Martin and Jane Sherwood, *The Roman World, 44 BC – AD 180* (London: Routledge, 1997), 172–173.

19 Strabo 5.4.11.

20 *War*, 2.117–118.

21 See Tacitus, *Annals* iv, 41, 57; Suetonius, *Tiberius*, xli.

22 Goodman, *The Ruling Class of Judaea*, 7.

23 Matyszak, Philip, *The Sons of Caesar: Imperial Rome's First Dynasty* (London: Thames & Hudson, 2006), 151.

24 Carter, *Pontius Pilate*, 3–4.

25 Philo, *De Legatione ad Gaium*, xxiv, 159–161 in Philo, F. H. Colson, Ralph Marcus and G. H. Whitaker, *Philo* (Cambridge: Harvard University Press, 1929), X, 81–83.

26 Notley and Rainey, *Carta's New Century Handbook and Atlas of the Bible*, 236.

27 *Antiquities*, 18.55–59.

28 Doyle, D., 'Pilate's Career and the Date of the Crucifixion', *Journal of Theological Studies* 42, 1941.

29 Philo, *Embassy to Gaius*, 299–305. On the dating of these events see Hoehner,

Herod Antipas, 178–183.

30 Doyle, 'Pilate's Career and the Date of the Crucifixion'.

31 Helen K. Bond, *Pontius Pilate in History and Interpretation* (Cambridge: Cambridge University Press, 1998), 195.

32 *BAGD*, 793.

8. JERICHO

1 Jesus' father is referred to as Joseph, son of David (Matthew 1:20); James son of Zebedee (Matthew 4:21); James son of Alphaeus (Matthew 10:3); Judas son of James (Luke 6:16); Simon son of John (John 1:42; 21:16); Judas son of Simon Iscariot (John 6:71; 13:2). Jesus is identified in both forms: Jesus son of Joseph from Nazareth (John 1:45).

2 Matthew 27:56; John 19:25.

3 Ilan, *Jewish Women in Greco-Roman Palestine*, 55.

4 Ilan, *Jewish Women in Greco-Roman Palestine*, 67. For example, Berenice, daughter of Agrippa I, married her first husband when she was thirteen.

5 Myers, *Binding the Strong Man*, 280.

6 Schnackenburg, quoted in Beasley-Murray, *John*, 193.

7 Matthew 9:36; Mark 6:34; Matthew 14:14; 20:34; Luke 7:13; Mark 9:22.

8 See 'Mercy, Compassion', *NIDNTT*.

9 How he got there has generated a considerable amount of discussion. The church father Basil described it as a 'miracle within a miracle'; Basil, *Corderius-Catena*, 295. But there is no need to think it was impossible for the dead man to move.

10 Beasley-Murray, *John*, 196.

11 Vanderkam, James C., *From Joshua to Caiaphas: High Priests After the Exile* (Minneapolis: Augsburg Fortress Van Gorcum, 2004), 435–436.

12 *Jeremias*, 195, n. 153.

13 *Jeremias*, 97–99.

14 Notley and Rainey, *Carta's New Century Handbook and Atlas of the Bible*, 235.

15 Ball, Warwick, *Rome in the East: The Transformation of an Empire* (London: Routledge, 2000), 59.

16 Goodman, *The Ruling Class of Judaea*, 97.

17 Philo, *Embassy to Gaius* 23.157.

18 *War*, 2.409–410.

19 *Antiquities*, 18.93–94.

20 Matthew 3:7 relates them coming to hear John, who was probably close to Jerusalem anyway. Matthew has them coming and asking for a sign along with the Pharisees in Magadan, but the equivalent passage in Mark does not mention the Sadducees, only the Pharisees (Matthew 16:1–12 = Mark 8:11–21).

21 *Antiquities*, 18.16–17.

22 *Antiquities*, 13.297–298.

23 Goodman, Martin, *Judaism in the Roman World: Collected Essays* (Leiden: Brill, 2007), 128.

24 *Antiquities*, 20.199–200.

25 Funk, 'The Wilderness', 210.

26 'Ephraim (Place)', in *ABD*, 3:556.

27 Myers, *Binding the Strong Man*, 279.

28 See 'λύτρον,' *BDAG*, 605–606.
29 Eth. Enoch 98.10, quoted in 'Redemption, Loose, Ransom, Deliverance, Release, Salvation, Saviour', *NIDNTT*.
30 See the Survey of Palestine, sheets XIV and XV.
31 Myers, *Binding the Strong Man*, 282.
32 Quoted in Parsons, Mikeal C., 'Short in Stature: Luke's Physical Description of Zacchaeus', *New Testament Studies* 47 (01), 2001.
33 Hamm, Dennis, 'Luke 19:8 Once Again: Does Zacchaeus Defend or Resolve?', *Journal of Biblical Literature* 107(3), 1988.
34 A legend from a few hundred years later tells how Zacchaeus was made bishop of Caesarea – much against his will. The story is an obvious fiction, but the reasons Zacchaeus gives for not wanting to be a bishop might strike a chord with many a modern cleric: 'only grant me not to have this name,' he says, 'for it teems with bitter envy and danger' (Pseudo-Clement, *Homilies*, 3.63).
35 *Antiquities*, 17.314.
36 'δραχμὴ,' *BDAG*, 261.

9. JERUSALEM

1 John also places the anointing of Jesus' feet here. I prefer the Marcan tradition, so will treat the event as happening at that time.
2 John Wilkinson, *Jerusalem as Jesus Knew it*, 114–115.
3 Josephus refers to Passover pilgrims staying in 'tents outside the temple'; *Antiquities*, 17.213–217.
4 2 Kings 9:13 shows Jehu being greeted in a similar way. Indeed, the practice of spreading garments before a beloved or celebrated figure was known in the Greco-Roman world. Plutarch depicts troops spreading their clothes at the feet of Cato the Younger when he left the army. There is also a sarcophagus of Adelphia which shows a man laying some kind of garment beneath the hooves of the horse on which Adelphia is riding. See Bammel and Moule, *Jesus and the Politics of His Day*, 319–321.
5 Josephus, Williamson and Smallwood, *The Jewish War*, 40.
6 Peters, F. E., *Jerusalem: The Holy City in the Eyes of Chroniclers, Visitors, Pilgrims, and Prophets From the Days of Abraham to the Beginnings of Modern Times* (Princeton: Princeton University Press, 1985), 89.
7 Gemara, Sukkah 51b, quoted in Richardson, *Herod: King of the Jews and Friend of the Romans*, 248.
8 Middoth 4.7. The appearance of the temple is much debated, because Josephus' descriptions do not match the description in the Mishnah. However, Josephus is probably the more trustworthy: he had actually seen the temple, after all. Where the Mishnah is concerned, the depiction of the temple in Tractate Middoth is a literary reconstruction, not a historical description.
9 *War*, 5.201–206.
10 Roller, *The Building Program of Herod the Great*, 180.
11 Middoth 3.8. The Mishnah implies that it took 300 men to move it, such was the weight. This is probably an exaggeration, but no doubt the weight required some substantial columns in the hall. On the entrance see Chyutin, Michael, *Architecture and Utopia in the Temple Era* (London: T & T Clark, 2006), 161.
12 The walled city of Jerusalem covered an area of around 115 hectares. The temple covered 144,000 square metres – 14.4 hectares. *ABD*, 3:747.
13 b. Yoma 35b in Sperber, Daniel, *Roman Palestine, 200–400: Money and Prices*

(Ramat-Gan: Bar-Ilan University Press, 1991), 103.

14 Wright, *Jesus and the Victory of God*, 408–410.

15 *TLW*, 100–102.

16 m. Ker 1.7 in Danby, *The Mishnah, Translated From the Hebrew*, 564. This price was clearly linked to the festivals, since the passage talks of pilgrims being allowed to 'eat of the animal-offerings'. The festivals such as Passover were the only times when the worshippers would eat their offerings. The same supply-and-demand effect happened at the Hajj, *TLW*, 104–105.

17 *War*, 2.427.

18 Bammel and Moule, *Jesus and the Politics of His Day*, 332.

19 *Jeremias*, 20.

20 *Jeremias*, 49.

21 Sifre; cf. j. Pe'a 1.6 quoted in Notley and Rainey, *Carta's New Century Handbook and Atlas of the Bible*, 235.

22 Vanderkam, *From Joshua to Caiaphas: High Priests After the Exile*, 476–477.

23 Wright, *Jesus and the Victory of God*, 411–412. See 1 Enoch 90:28–29 in Charlesworth, *The Old Testament Pseudepigrapha*, 1:71.

24 Wengst, Klaus and John Stephen Bowden, *Pax Romana and the Peace of Jesus Christ* (London: SCM, 1987), 58–61.

25 Goodman, *The Ruling Class of Judaea*, 79.

26 Gundry, *Mark: A Commentary on His Apology for the Cross*, 718.

27 Webb, Robert L., 'Apocalyptic': Observations on a Slippery Term', *Journal of Near Eastern Studies* 49(2), 1990, 115–116.

28 Virgil, *Aeneid*, 1.278–279, in 'Eschatologies of Late Antiquity', in Evans, Craig A. and Stanley E. Porter, *Dictionary of New Testament Background* (Leicester: IVP, 2000).

29 Can there be a more eschatological title than Francis Fukuyama's *The End of History and the Last Man*?

30 Sibylline Oracle 3.350.

31 1 Enoch 91.15–17; 1QH 11.29–36; 4 Ezra 7.30.

32 *TLW*, 126–132. See also Wright, *Jesus and the Victory of God*, 348–349.

33 The Greek phrase *meta duo hemeras* can mean 'on the second day' (i.e. 'tomorrow') and that may be the sense in which Mark is using it here. But the more usual translation – and the one preferred by the majority of modern English versions – is 'two days away', which fits better with John's chronology.

34 Brown, Raymond Edward, *The Death of the Messiah: From Gethsemane to the Grave: A Commentary on the Passion Narratives in the Four Gospels* (London: Geoffrey Chapman, 1994), 1411.

35 There may well have been leper colonies in the region. The Temple Scroll of the Qumran community may reflect reality when it talks of making areas east of the city – which is where Bethany was – the place for lepers; Vermes, *The Complete Dead Sea Scrolls in English*, 207.

36 *TLW*, 142.

37 See Leviticus 4:3, 5, 16; Numbers 35:25; 1 Samuel 9:9, 16; 16:1–3, 6; 24:6; 2 Samuel 1:16; 19:21; Psalms 2:2; 18:50; 20:6; 28:8. Good overviews in 'Messiah', *ABD*, 5:779; 'Anointing', in Ryken, Leland, Jim Wilhoit, Tremper Longman, Colin Duriez, Douglas Penney and Daniel G. Reid, *Dictionary of Biblical Imagery* (Leicester: IVP, 1998), 33–34.

38 Ogg, *The Chronology of the Public Ministry of Jesus*, 232.

39 Jeremias, Joachim, *The Eucharistic Words of Jesus* (London: SCM, 1966), 17.

40 See *TLW*, 147–151.

41 Brown, *The Death of the Messiah*, 124.

42 See Witherington, *The Gospel of Mark: Socio-Rhetorical Commentary*, 371. There are precedents for religious sects 'doing their own thing'. The most notable is the Qumran community. The documents describing their religious activities do not mention the Passover; Segal, *The Hebrew Passover: From the Earliest Times to AD 70*, 247. The calendar of events at Qumran includes the Passover, but this may be a Sadducean calendar, rather than one of the community.

43 Tos. Kelim B. Q. 1.6.

44 *Jeremias*, 36.

45 *Jeremias*, 313–314.

46 *Jeremias*, 314, n. 56.

47 It features in a poem by Chrétien de Troyes dated sometime between 1180 and 1191.

48 Finegan, *Handbook of Biblical Chronology*, 364. Fotheringham, J., 'Astronomical Evidence for the Date of the Crucifixion', *Journal of Theological Studies* XII, 1910. On the moon see Riesner, Rainer, *Paul's Early Period: Chronology, Mission Strategy, Theology* (Grand Rapids: Eerdmans, 1998), 56–57.

49 For the make-up of the group see *TLW*, 164–165.

50 Matthew 26:55; *Jeremias*, 210.

51 On the young man who left his clothing behind, see *TLW*, 168–169.

52 I have suggested elsewhere that the only way he could have got in was through the influence not of 'the Beloved Disciple', but of Judas. See *TLW*, 180–183.

53 Brown, *The Death of the Messiah*, 601.

54 Brown, *The Death of the Messiah*, 644.

55 Goodman, *The Ruling Class of Judaea*, 113.

56 Goodman, Martin, *Rome and Jerusalem: The Clash of Ancient Civilizations* (London: Penguin, 2008), 327.

57 Mark 15:1. Flusser and Notley, *The Sage From Galilee*, 138–139.

58 Schürer, Millar, Vermes and Goodman, *The History of the Jewish People in the Age of Jesus Christ (175 BC–AD 135)*, 1:370.

59 'ἐσθῆτα λαμππάν' (Luke 23:11).

60 Hoehner, *Herod Antipas*, 241–243.

61 Schürer, Millar, Vermes and Goodman, *The History of the Jewish People in the Age of Jesus Christ (175 BC–AD 135)*, 1:370.

62 Bond, Helen K., *Pontius Pilate in History and Interpretation* (Cambridge: Cambridge University Press, 1998), 199.

63 Carter, *Pontius Pilate*, 69–70.

64 *Antiquities*, 20.214, cited in Goodman, *The Ruling Class of Judaea*, 139.

65 *TLW*, 215.

66 Schürer, Millar, Vermes and Goodman, *The History of the Jewish People in the Age of Jesus Christ (175 BC–AD 135)*, 1:371.

67 Gundry, *Mark: A Commentary on His Apology for the Cross*, 942.

68 See Hart, H. St. J., 'The Crown of Thorns in John 19.2–5', *Journal of Theological Studies* 3, 1952.

69 Carroll, John T. and Joel B. Green, *The Death of Jesus in Early Christianity* (Peabody: Hendrickson, 1995), 167–170.

70 Hengel, Martin, *Crucifixion in the Ancient World and the Folly of the Message of the Cross* (London: SCM, 1977), 59.

71 Borg, Marcus J. and John Dominic Crossan, *The Last Week: What the Gospels Really Teach About Jesus's Final Days in Jerusalem* (San Francisco: HarperSanFrancisco, 2007), 146.

72 The tradition of the *via Dolorosa* is a medieval invention which took as its starting point the Antonia Fortress.

73 See Haas, 'Anthropological Observations on the Skeletal Remains from Gi'vat ha-Mivtar', 49ff. and Zias J. and Sekeles, E., 'The Crucified Man from Giv'at ha-Mivtar: A Reappraisal', *Israel Exploration Journal* 35, 1985, 22–27.

74 Nolland, *Luke*, 1152–1153.

75 Nolland, *Luke*, 1156–1157.

76 It is not certain how many lambs would have been killed: thousands certainly, but not the 256,500 given by Josephus (*War*, 6.423–425). On Passover see *TLW*, 230–232.

77 Brown, *The Death of the Messiah*, 1046.

78 *TLW*, 234–236. Hengel, *Crucifixion in the Ancient World and the Folly of the Message of the Cross*, 29, n. 21.

79 Page, Nick, *What Happened to the Ark of the Covenant?* (Milton Keynes: Authentic Media, 2007), 145–151.

80 *TLW*, 236–237. Beasley-Murray, *John*, 356.

81 Hayward, Robert, *The Jewish Temple: A Non-Biblical Sourcebook* (London: Routledge, 1996), 150.

82 *Antiquities*, 3.183.

83 Hayward, *The Jewish Temple: A Non-Biblical Sourcebook*, 150.

84 Several sites have been proposed. Eusebius, the early church historian, suggested Rempthis or Rentis, north-east of Lydda. See Brown, *The Death of the Messiah*, 1213, n. 17.

85 Josephus, *Life*, 1.420–422.

86 m.Oholot 2.2 in Danby, *The Mishnah, Translated From the Hebrew*, 651.

87 Hachlili, Rachel, *Jewish Funerary Customs, Practices and Rites in the Second Temple Period* (Leiden: Brill, 2005), 56–57.

88 Brown, *The Death of the Messiah*, 1249.

89 Biddle, Martin, *The Tomb of Christ* (Stroud: Sutton, 1999), 60. The 'Garden Tomb', while evocative, is not the site of Jesus' burial. Murphy-O'Connor, *The Holy Land: An Archaeological Guide From Earliest Times to 1700*, 124–125.

AFTERMATH

1 Wright, *The Resurrection of the Son of God*, 553.

2 Wright, *The Resurrection of the Son of God*, 556.

3 For an analysis of the differences see *TLW*, 255–257.

4 See Dunn, James D. G., *The Evidence for Jesus: The Impact of Scholarship on Our Understanding of How Christianity Began* (London: SCM, 1985), 65. As Wright says, 'Stories as earth-shattering as this, stories as community-forming as this, once told, are not easily modified. Too much depends on them' (Wright, *The Resurrection of the Son of God*, 611).

5 Dunn, *The Evidence for Jesus: The Impact of Scholarship on Our Understanding of How Christianity Began*, 67.

6 I shall be arguing this chronology in another book. Give me a moment... At the very most, Paul became a Christian just a few years after Jesus' death.

7 Orr, William F. and James Arthur Walther, *I Corinthians: A New Translation* (Garden City: Doubleday, 1976), 321–322.

8 Even if, as some scholars argue, the letter attributed to him did not come from him, the attribution shows that Jude was a prominent figure in the early church. There would be no point in attributing a letter to someone who had never been a follower.

9 The *Gospel of Thomas* also has a saying where the disciples ask Jesus who is to be their leader, and Jesus nominates James; *Gos. Thomas*, Logion 12. The fragment of the Gospel of Hebrews is preserved in Jerome, *De viris illustribus...* in Bernheim, *James, Brother of Jesus*, 98.

10 Eusebius, *The Ecclesiastical History and the Martyrs of Palestine*, 1:78.

11 See Bauckham, *Gospel Women*, 203–223.

12 Indeed, the early church theologian Origen took this one step further and identified the unnamed disciple walking along the road as Clopas' son Symeon. Origen, *Contra Celsus*, 2.62. See Bauckham, *Jesus and the Eyewitnesses*, 43.

13 Arndt, *Luke*, 498–499.

14 *War*, 4.529–534.

15 *War*, 4.574–578.

16 *War*, 5.309.

17 *War*, 7.153–155. On Simon see Horsley and Hanson, *Bandits, Prophets, and Messiahs*, 119 ff.

18 Horsley and Hanson, *Bandits, Prophets, and Messiahs*, 128–129.

19 See also Matthew 21:42; Mark 12:10; Luke 20:17; Acts 4:11; Ephesians 2:20.

Bibliography

Armstrong, Karen, *A History of Jerusalem: One City, Three Faiths* (London: HarperCollins, 1997)

Arndt, William, *Luke* (Saint Louis: Concordia Pub. House, 1986)

Bailey, Kenneth E., *Jesus Through Middle Eastern Eyes: Cultural Studies in the Gospels* (London: SPCK, 2008)

Ball, Warwick, *Rome in the East: The Transformation of an Empire* (London: Routledge, 2000)

Bammel, Ernst and C. F. D. Moule, *Jesus and the Politics of His Day* (Cambridge: Cambridge University Press, 1984)

Bauckham, Richard, *Gospel Women: Studies of the Named Women in the Gospels* (Edinburgh: T & T Clark, 2002)

Bauckham, Richard, *Jesus and the Eyewitnesses: The Gospels as Eyewitness Testimony* (Grand Rapids: Eerdmans, 2006)

Beasley-Murray, George Raymond, *John* (Waco: Word Books, 1987)

Bernheim, Pierre-Antoine, *James, Brother of Jesus* (London: SCM, 1997)

Biddle, Martin, *The Tomb of Christ* (Stroud: Sutton, 1999)

Bock, Darrell L., *Luke* (Grand Rapids: Baker Books, 1994)

Bond, Helen K., *Pontius Pilate in History and Interpretation* (Cambridge: Cambridge University Press, 1998)

Borg, Marcus J. and John Dominic Crossan, *The Last Week: What the Gospels Really Teach About Jesus's Final Days in Jerusalem (Plus)* (San Francisco: HarperSanFrancisco, 2007)

Brandon, S. G. F., *Jesus and the Zealots: A Study of the Political Factor in Primitive Christianity* (Manchester: Manchester University Press, 1967)

Brown, Raymond E., *The Death of the Messiah: From Gethsemane to the Grave: A Commentary on the Passion Narratives in the Four Gospels* (London: Geoffrey Chapman, 1994)

Brown, Raymond E., *The Birth of the Messiah: A Commentary on the Infancy Narratives in Matthew and Luke* (New York: Doubleday, 1993)

Busch, Fritz-Otto, *The Five Herods*, trans. E.W. Dickes (London: Robert Hale, 1958)

Carroll, John T. and Joel B. Green, *The Death of Jesus in Early Christianity* (Peabody: Hendrickson, 1995)

Carson, D. A., *From Sabbath to Lord's Day: A Biblical, Historical, and Theological Investigation* (Grand Rapids: Zondervan, 1982)

Carter, Warren, *Pontius Pilate* (Collegeville: Liturgical Press, 2003)

Charlesworth, James H., *The Old Testament Pseudepigrapha* (London: Darton, Longman & Todd, 1983)

Chyutin, Michael, *Architecture and Utopia in the Temple Era* (London: T & T Clark, 2006)

Connolly, Peter, *Living in the Time of Jesus of Nazareth* (Oxford: Oxford University Press, 1983)

Corley, Kathleen E., *Private Women, Public Meals: Social Conflict in the Synoptic Tradition* (Peabody: Hendrickson, 1993)

Cranfield, C. E. B., *The Gospel According to Saint Mark: An Introduction and Commentary* (Cambridge: Cambridge University Press, 1972)

Crossan, John Dominic, *The Historical Jesus: The Life of a Mediterranean Jewish Peasant* (Edinburgh: T & T Clark, 1993)

Crown, Alan David, *The Samaritans* (Tübingen: J.C.B. Mohr (Paul Siebeck), 1989)

Danby, Herbert, *The Mishnah, Translated From the Hebrew* (London: Oxford University Press, 1933)

Daniel-Rops, Henri and Patrick O'Brian, *Daily Life in Palestine at the Time of Christ* (London: Weidenfeld and Nicolson, 1962)

Dapaah, Daniel S., *The Relationship Between John the Baptist and Jesus of Nazareth: A Critical Study* (Lanham: University Press of America, 2005)

Deissmann, Adolf and Lionel R. M. Strachan, *Light From the Ancient East: The New Testament Illustrated by Recently Discovered Texts of the Graeco-Roman World* (London: Hodder & Stoughton, 1910)

Doyle, D., 'Pilate's Career and the Date of the Crucifixion', *Journal of Theological Studies* 42. 1941

Dunn, James D. G., *The Evidence for Jesus: The Impact of Scholarship on Our Understanding of How Christianity Began* (London: SCM, 1985)

Dunn, James D. G., *Jesus and the Spirit: A Study of the Religious and Charismatic Experience of Jesus and the First Christians as Reflected in the New Testament* (Philadelphia: Westminster Press, 1980)

Eusebius, *The Ecclesiastical History and the Martyrs of Palestine*, trans. Hugh Jackson Lawlor and John E. L. Oulton (London: SPCK, 1927)

Evans, Craig A. and Stanley E. Porter, *Dictionary of New Testament Background* (Leicester: InterVarsity Press, 2000)

Eve, E. C. S., *The Jewish Context of Jesus' Miracles* (Sheffield: Sheffield Academic Press, 2002)

Fillon, Mike, 'The Real Face of Jesus', *Popular Mechanics*. 2002

Finegan, Jack, *Handbook of Biblical Chronology: Principles of Time Reckoning in the Ancient World and Problems of Chronology in the Bible* (Peabody: Hendrickson, 1998)

Finegan, Jack, Jerry Vardaman and Edwin M. Yamauchi, *Chronos, Kairos, Christos: Nativity and Chronological Studies Presented to Jack Finegan* (Winona Lake: Eisenbrauns, 1989)

Fitzmyer, Joseph A., *The Gospel According to Luke* (New York: Doubleday, 1981)

Flusser, David and R. Steven Notley, *The Sage From Galilee: Rediscovering Jesus' Genius* (Grand Rapids: Eerdmans, 2007)

Fotheringham, J., 'Astronomical Evidence for the Date of the Crucifixion', *Journal of Theological Studies* XII. 1910

France, R. T., *The Gospel According to Matthew: An Introduction and Commentary* (Leicester: Inter-Varsity Press, 1985)

France, R. T., 'Herod and the Children of Bethlehem', *Novum Testamentum* 21(2). 1979

Freedman, David Noel (ed.), *The Anchor Bible Dictionary* (New York: Doubleday, 1999)

Freeman, Philip and D. L. Kennedy, *The Defence of the Roman and Byzantine East: Proceedings of a Colloquium Held at the University of Sheffield in April 1986* (Oxford: B.A.R., 1986)

Frerichs, Ernest S., William Scott Green and Jacob Neusner, *Judaisms and Their Messiahs at the Turn of the Christian Era* (Cambridge: Cambridge University Press, 1987)

Freyne, Seán, *Galilee, From Alexander the Great to Hadrian, 323 B.C.E. To 135 C.E.: A Study of Second Temple Judaism* (Edinburgh: T & T Clark, 1998)

Funk, Robert W., 'The Wilderness', *Journal of Biblical Literature* 78(3). 1959

García, Martínez, Florentino and Eibert J. C. Tigchelaar, *The Dead Sea Scrolls Study Edition* (Leiden: Brill, 1997)

Goodman, Martin, *Judaism in the Roman World: Collected Essays* (Leiden: Brill, 2007)

Goodman, Martin, *Rome and Jerusalem: The Clash of Ancient Civilizations* (London: Penguin, 2008)

Goodman, Martin, *The Ruling Class of Judaea: The Origins of the Jewish Revolt Against Rome, A.D. 66–70* (Cambridge: Cambridge University Press, 1987)

Goodman, Martin and Jane Sherwood, *The Roman World, 44 BC–AD 180* (London: Routledge, 1997)

Green, Joel B., *The Gospel of Luke* (Grand Rapids: Eerdmans, 1997)

Guelich, Robert A., *Mark 1–8:26* (Dallas: Word Books, 1989)

Gundry, Robert Horton, *Mark: A Commentary on His Apology for the Cross* (Grand Rapids: Eerdmans, 1993)

Hachlili, Rachel, *Jewish Funerary Customs, Practices and Rites in the Second Temple Period* (Leiden: Brill, 2005)

Hamm, Dennis 'Luke 19:8 Once Again: Does Zacchaeus Defend or Resolve?', *Journal of Biblical Literature* 107(3). 1988

Hanson, K. C., 'The Galilean Fishing Economy and the Jesus Tradition', *Biblical Theology Bulletin* 27. 1997

Hanson, K.C., *Palestine in the Time of Jesus: Social Structures and Social Conflicts* (Minneapolis: Augsburg Fortress, 2002)

Hart, H. St J., 'The Crown of Thorns in John 19.2–5', *Journal of Theological Studies* 3. 1952

Hauerwas, Stanley, *The Peaceable Kingdom: A Primer in Christian Ethics* (London: SCM, 2003)

Hays, Richard B., *The Moral Vision of the New Testament: Community, Cross, New Creation: A Contemporary Introduction to New Testament Ethics* (Edinburgh: T & T Clark, 1997)

Hayward, Robert, *The Jewish Temple: A Non-Biblical Sourcebook* (London: Routledge, 1996)

Hengel, Martin, *Crucifixion in the Ancient World and the Folly of the Message of the Cross* (London: SCM, 1977)

Herodotus, A. R. Burn and Sélincourt De, Aubrey, *Herodotus: The Histories* (London: Penguin, 1972)

Hoehner, Harold W., *Herod Antipas* (Cambridge: Cambridge University Press, 1972)

Holmes, Michael W, *The Apostolic Fathers: Greek Texts and English Translations* (Grand Rapids: Baker Academic, 2007)

Hooker, Morna Dorothy, *A Commentary on the Gospel According to St Mark* (London: A & C Black, 1991)

Horsley, Richard A., *Archaeology, History, and Society in Galilee: The Social Context of Jesus and the Rabbis* (Valley Forge: Trinity Press International, 1996)

Horsley, Richard A., *Galilee: History, Politics, People* (Pennsylvania: Trinity Press, 1995)

Horsley, Richard A. and John S. Hanson, *Bandits, Prophets, and Messiahs: Popular Movements in the Time of Jesus* (San Francisco: Harper & Row, 1988)

Ilan, Tal, *Jewish Women in Greco-Roman Palestine: An Inquiry Into Image and Status* (Tübingen: J.C.B. Mohr (Paul Siebeck), 1995)

Jeremias, Joachim, *New Testament Theology* (New York: Scribner, 1971)

Jeremias, Joachim, *The Eucharistic Words of Jesus* (London: SCM, 1966)

Jeremias, Joachim, *Jerusalem in the Time of Jesus: An Investigation Into Economic and Social Conditions During the New Testament Period* (London: SCM, 1974)

Josephus, Flavius, *Antiquities*

Josephus, Flavius, *Life*

Josephus, Flavius, G. A. Williamson and E. Mary Smallwood, *The Jewish War* (Harmondsworth: Penguin, 1981)

Kazen, Thomas, *Jesus and Purity Halakhah: Was Jesus Indifferent to Impurity* (Stockholm: Almqvist & Wiksell, 2002)

Keener, Craig S., *The Gospel of John: A Commentary* (Peabody: Hendrickson, 2003)

Keener, Craig S., *The Gospel of Matthew: A Socio-Rhetorical Commentary* (Grand Rapids: Eerdmans, 2009)

Keener, Craig S., *The Historical Jesus of the Gospels* (Grand Rapids: Eerdmans, 2009)

Köstenberger, Andreas J., *John* (Grand Rapids: Baker Academic, 2004)

Kraeling, Carl H., *John the Baptist* (New York: Scribner, 1951)

Kurlansky, Mark, *Nonviolence: The History of a Dangerous Idea* (London: Jonathan Cape, 2006)

Lane, William L., *The Gospel According to Mark; the English Text With Introduction, Exposition, and Notes* (Grand Rapids: Eerdmans, 1974)

Levine, Amy-Jill, *The Misunderstood Jew* (New York: HarperOne, 2007)

Lindars, Barnabas, *The Gospel of John: Based on the Revised Standard Version* (Grand Rapids: Eerdmans Marshall, 1981)

Magen, Yitzhak, 'Ancient Israel's Stone Age: Purity in Second Temple times', *Biblical Archaeology Review* 24(5). Sept/Oct 1998

Malina, Bruce J., *The Social World of Jesus and the Gospels* (London: Routledge, 1996)

Marshall, I. Howard, *The Gospel of Luke: A Commentary on the Greek Text* (Exeter: Paternoster, 1978)

Masterman, E. W. G., 'The Pool of Bethesda', *The Biblical World* 25(2). 1905

Matyszak, Philip, *The Sons of Caesar: Imperial Rome's First Dynasty* (London: Thames & Hudson, 2006)

Meier, John P., *A Marginal Jew: Rethinking the Historical Jesus* (London: Doubleday, 1991)

Millar, Fergus, *The Roman Near East, 31 BC–AD 337* (Cambridge: Harvard University Press, 1993)

Murphy-O'Connor, J., *The Holy Land: An Archaeological Guide From Earliest Times to 1700* (Oxford: Oxford University Press, 1986)

Murphy-O'Connor, J., 'John the Baptist and Jesus: History and Hypotheses', *New Testament Studies* 36. 1990

Myers, Ched, *Binding the Strong Man: A Political Reading of Mark's*

Story of Jesus (Maryknoll: Orbis, 2008)

Neusner, Jacob, *The Mishnah: A New Translation* (New Haven: Yale University Press: Accordance electronic edition, 1988)

Nolland, John, *Luke* (Dallas: Word Books, 1989)

Notley, R. Steven and Anson F. Rainey, *Carta's New Century Handbook and Atlas of the Bible* (Jerusalem: Carta, 2007)

Ogg, George, *The Chronology of the Public Ministry of Jesus* (Cambridge: Cambridge University Press, 1940)

Orr, William F. and James Arthur Walther, *1 Corinthians: A New Translation* (Garden City: Doubleday, 1976)

Page, Nick, *The Longest Week: What Really Happened During Jesus' Final Days* (London: Hodder & Stoughton, 2009)

Page, Nick, *The One-Stop Bible Atlas* (Oxford: Lion Hudson, 2010)

Page, Nick, *What Happened to the Ark of the Covenant* (Milton Keynes: Authentic Media, 2007)

Peters, F. E., *Jerusalem: The Holy City in the Eyes of Chroniclers, Visitors, Pilgrims, and Prophets From the Days of Abraham to the Beginnings of Modern Times* (Princeton: Princeton University Press, 1985)

Philo, F. H. Colson, Ralph Marcus and G. H. Whitaker, *Philo* (London: Heinemann, 1929)

Pollard, Nigel, *Soldiers, Cities, and Civilians in Roman Syria* (Ann Arbor: University of Michigan Press, 2000)

Richardson, Peter, *Herod: King of the Jews and Friend of the Romans* (Edinburgh: T & T Clark, 1999)

Riesner, Rainer, *Paul's Early Period: Chronology, Mission Strategy, Theology* (Grand Rapids: Eerdmans, 1998)

Roland, Victor 'The Mosaic Map of Madeba', *The Biblical Archaeologist*, 21(3). 1958

Roller, Duane W., *The Building Program of Herod the Great* (Berkeley: University of California Press, 1998)

Rousseau, John J. and Rami Arav, *Jesus and His World: An Archaeological and Cultural Dictionary* (Minneapolis: Fortress Press, 1995)

Ryken, Leland, Jim Wilhoit, Tremper Longman, Colin Duriez, Douglas Penney and Daniel G. Reid, *Dictionary of Biblical Imagery* (Leicester: InterVarsity Press, 1998)

Safrai, Shemuel and M. Stern, *The Jewish People in the First Century: Historical Geography, Political History, Social, Cultural and Religious Life and Institutions* (Crint: Van Gorcum, 1974)

Sanders, E. P., *The Historical Figure of Jesus* (London: Penguin, 1995)

Schürer, Emil, Fergus Millar, Geza Vermes and Martin Goodman, *The History of the Jewish People in the Age of Jesus Christ (175 B.C.–A.D. 135)* (Edinburgh: T & T Clark, 1973)

Scobie, Charles Hugh Hope, *John the Baptist* (London: SCM, 1964)

Shanks, Hershel and Ben Witherington, *The Brother of Jesus: The Dramatic Story & Meaning of the First Archaeological Link to Jesus & His Family* (London: Continuum, 2003)

Sherwin-White, A. N., *Roman Society and Roman Law in the New Testament* (Oxford: Clarendon Press, 1963)

Snodgrass, Klyne, *Stories With Intent: A Comprehensive Guide to the Parables of Jesus* (Grand Rapids: Eerdmans, 2008)

Sperber, Daniel, *Roman Palestine, 200–400: Money and Prices* (Ramat-Gan: Bar-Ilan University Press, 1991)

Stanton, Graham, *The Gospels and Jesus* (Oxford: Oxford University Press, 1989)

Stark, Rodney, *The Rise of Christianity: How the Obscure, Marginal Jesus Movement Became the Dominant Religious Force in the Western World in a Few Centuries* (San Francisco: HarperSanFrancisco, 1997)

Stassen, Glen Harold and David P. Gushee, *Kingdom Ethics: Following Jesus in Contemporary Context* (Downers Grove: InterVarsity Press, 2003)

Stevens, Wm. Arnold, 'Ænon near to Salim', *Journal of the Society of Biblical Literature and Exegesis* 3(2). 1883

Strange, James F. and Hershel Shanks, 'Has the House Where Jesus Stayed in Capernaum Been Found?', *Biblical Archaeology Review* 8(6). Nov/Dec 1982

Summers, Ray and Jerry Vardaman, *Chronos, Kairos, Christos II: Chronological, Nativity, and Religious Studies in Memory of Ray Summers* (Macon: Mercer University Press, 1998)

Taylor, Joan E., *John the Baptist Within Second Temple Judaism* (London: SPCK, 1997)

Theissen, Gerd and Annette Merz, *The Historical Jesus: A Comprehensive Guide* (London: SCM, 1998)

Thiede, Carsten Peter, *Simon Peter, From Galilee to Rome* (Exeter: Paternoster Press, 1986)

Thiede, Carsten Peter, *The Cosmopolitan World of Jesus: New Findings From Archaeology* (London: SPCK, 2004)

Throckmorton, Burton H., *Gospel Parallels: A Synopsis of the First Three Gospels* (Nashville: Nelson, 1979)

Vanderkam, James C., *From Joshua to Caiaphas: High Priests After the Exile* (Minneapolis: Augsburg Fortress Van Gorcum, 2004)

Vermes, Geza, *The Changing Faces of Jesus* (London: Penguin, 2000)

Vermes, Geza, *The Complete Dead Sea Scrolls in English* (London: Penguin, 2004)

Webb, Robert L., *John the Baptizer and Prophet: A Socio-Historical Study* (Sheffield: JSOT Press, 1991)

Wengst, Klaus and John Stephen Bowden, *Pax Romana and the Peace of Jesus Christ* (London: SCM, 1987)

Wilkinson, John, *Jerusalem as Jesus Knew it: Archaeology as Evidence* (London: Thames and Hudson, 1978)

Witherington, Ben, *The Gospel of Mark: Socio-Rhetorical Commentary* (Grand Rapids: Eerdmans, 2001)

Witherington, Ben, *What Have They Done With Jesus?: Beyond Strange Theories and Bad History – Why We Can Trust the Bible* (San Francisco: HarperCollins, 2006)

Woolf, Bertram Lee, *The Authority of Jesus and Its Foundation: A Study in the Four Gospels & the Acts* (London: Allen & Unwin, 1929)

Wright, N. T., *Jesus and the Victory of God* (London: SPCK, 1996)

Wright, N. T., *The Resurrection of the Son of God* (London: SPCK, 2003)

Yang, Yong-Eui, *Jesus and the Sabbath in Matthew's Gospel* (Sheffield: Sheffield Academic Press, 1997)

Yoder, John Howard, *The Politics of Jesus: Vicit Agnus Noster* (Grand Rapids: Eerdmans, 1972)

Young, Brad, *Jesus and His Jewish Parables: Rediscovering the Roots of Jesus' Teaching* (New York: Paulist Press, 1989)

INDEX